ECONOMIC HISTORY

THE TRADE WINDS

COLONIAL AND IMPERIAL

THE TRADE WINDS

A study of British overseas trade during the French Wars, 1793–1815

Edited by

C. NORTHCOTE PARKINSON

Routledge
Taylor & Francis Group

LONDON AND NEW YORK

First published in 1948

Published 2010 by Routledge
2 Park Square, Milton Park, Abingdon, Oxfordshire OX14 4RN
711 Third Avenue, New York, NY 10017

First issued in paperback 2015

Routledge is an imprint of the Taylor and Francis Group, an informa business

British Library Cataloguing in Publication Data
A CIP catalogue record for this book
is available from the British Library

The Trade Winds
ISBN 0-415-38191-6 (volume)
ISBN 0-415-38006-5 (subset)
ISBN 0-415-28619-0 (set)

Routledge Library Editions: Economic History

ISBN13: 978-0-415-75928-1 (pbk)
ISBN13: 978-0-415-38191-8 (hbk)

THE TRADE WINDS

By Michael Lewis
Professor of History, Royal Naval College
Greenwich

THE NAVY OF BRITAIN

by C. Ernest Fayle

A SHORT HISTORY OF THE
WORLD'S SHIPPING INDUSTRY

THE TRADE WINDS

A Study of British Overseas Trade during
the French Wars 1793-1815

by

C. Ernest Fayle, C. Northcote Parkinson, A. C. Wardle
C. M. MacInnes, Basil Lubbock, J. A. Nixon
Lucy Frances Horsfall, H. Heaton

EDITED BY
C. NORTHCOTE PARKINSON

Late Fellow of Emmanuel College
Cambridge

INTRODUCTION BY
ADMIRAL SIR WILLIAM M. JAMES
G.C.B.

LONDON

GEORGE ALLEN AND UNWIN LTD

FIRST PUBLISHED IN 1948

To

John Masefield

MASTER MARINER

INTRODUCTION

By *Admiral Sir William M. James, G.C.B.*

THE authors of this book have tried to portray, in outline, the background of trade against which the Navy of Nelson's time had to operate. THE TRADE WINDS is the title they have chosen and the book should serve to remind us of many physical facts which then dominated the strategy both of trade and war—the Trade Winds themselves being not the least of them. There is something in that title which conjures up all the magic and romance of the sea, helping us to picture what dry statistics of tonnage may tend to conceal. But the winds upon which our overseas trade was founded were no English monopoly. They blew for all who had the courage and skill to use them. Portuguese, Spanish and Dutch ships were also at sea ; nor was the spirit of adventure lacking in their crews. Undeterred by lack of charts, meagre supplies and the risk of death from strange disease, they had reached the farthest parts of the Indies. French seamen, too, had dared the hazards of the frost-bound St. Lawrence to plant and maintain their flag upon Canadian soil. It would be hard to show that these were less resourceful, less adventurous than the English who supplanted them. The issue was never decided by commercial enterprise or even by seamanship. It was decided by Sea Power. And if the Navy drew its strength from Trade, the Merchant Service looked to the Navy for protection.

In studying this book, therefore—in studying, in fact, the trading background to a war at sea—the war itself must not be forgotten. Ever since that day, June 13th, 1514, when the Henri-Grace-à-Dieu was hallowed at Erith (at the not unreasonable cost, by one account, of 6s. 8d.) the Royal Navy has had a continuous history. If not the first King's Ship, the Great Harry has some claim to be considered the first man-of-war. Dwarfing her predecessors and recorded by many artists, she was the wonder of the age, and may be taken as the prototype of the ships which have since protected our coasts and trade. Without a fleet to prevent seaborne invasion, the British would long since have become vassals to a continental power. Without a fleet to secure and hold the sea lines of communications, the British Empire could never have been established. Without a fleet to shepherd the convoys safely into port, we could never have survived either the war about which this book is written or the wars of this century through which we have just passed.

All this is axiomatic. But the British people themselves have been less aware of the cause of their success than many of their opponents have been. The banners were hung out, there were great junketings and trumpetings, the King and Parliament were lavish with honours and rewards whenever news of a naval victory was received. But with the signing of "perpetual and universal" peace the fleet was paid off, the seamen dispersed and left to fend for themselves, and the ships stripped "to a gantline," that is, with only the lower masts left standing. First Lords of the Admiralty (often distinguished sailors in the old days—Anson, Hawke, St. Vincent) pleaded in vain for an adequate building programme. They were faced with the age-old question, "Why spend money badly needed for other things on ships that will probably never be wanted?" And so in the long history of the Royal Navy we have only one instance of a declaration of war finding it at its war stations and in a strength proportionate to its expected task. That was true of the First World War. In that struggle we were sorely pressed, admittedly, and as near to disaster as we had ever been ; but that was due to the enemy exploiting a new weapon in defiance of international law. As we were to learn again in the Second World War, a new weapon may do incalculable harm before the antidote is found.

We were ready for the First World War because People and Parliament had been stabbed awake to the import of the German Navy's expansion. Some men in high places were blind to this, but to the majority it was clear that an all-powerful German Navy, a fleet too strong for the British to meet on equal terms, would mean the disappearance of Great Britain as a Power in the World. Almost overnight, and for the first time in history, the citizen became really interested in his Navy. *Jane's Fighting Ships* became a best-seller and schoolboys diverted their attention from railway engines to Dread-noughts. But it was the figures—the number of ships, their tonnage, speed, armament and armour—that aroused interest. The meaning of "seapower," and how seapower had been wielded in the past, remained for the majority of people a closed book.

A closed book, for the majority, it was to remain. But some of those with the advantages of a good education were awakened with a start by the American Captain A. T. Mahan, with his *Influence of Sea Power upon History* and his *Influence of Sea Power upon the French Revolution and Empire*. There had, of course, been naval histories by British writers. But these were in many volumes and entered into great detail ; they were for the student, not for the general reader. And indeed, until then, the general reader had shunned books about maritime war. The ways of a ship at sea were quite beyond him ; the account of a naval battle was so much Greek to anyone who did not know how a ship was rigged and manoeuvred. But Mahan told his story in a way which the landsman could understand, and by the time of the First World War there was a sprinkling of people in the British Isles who were aware of the part played by seapower in our history and aware, therefore, of the part it would play in any future war. Several English authors did their best to sustain this interest. Sir John Laughton, Sir Julian Corbett and Sir Geoffrey Callender were the pioneers of a new endeavour to arouse the British to a sense of their seamen's past achievement. It was Robert Louis Stevenson who had written on this subject, "Their sayings and doings stir English blood like the sound of a trumpet ; and if the Indian Empire, the trade of London, and all the outward and visible ensigns of our greatness should pass away, we should still leave behind us a durable monument of what we were in the sayings and doings of the English Admirals." It was these sayings and doings which the naval historians sought to make known, and they made a deep and lasting impression on many. To most, however, it was the romantic aspect which appealed, not the fascination of the strategic pattern without which the Admirals would have left no monument at all.

That romantic aspect must not be belittled. It was said that a man who talked to Pitt came away from his presence feeling a braver man ; the same can be said of those who read of the great Sea

Captains. If Callender and E. F. Benson had done no more than that, they did well to inculcate a pride in the deeds of our forebears. It was this pride which later helped our seamen to save England from conquest and from vassalage under a ruthless, vengeful overlord.

There is, however, a great difference between a romantic pride and a real understanding. For the majority of British Statesmen, for the majority even of naval officers, seapower remained something of a mystery. It was not until after the First World War that Lord Beatty, with four years of experience of war-time command at sea, founded the Naval Staff College. He had seen what previous genera-tions of flag-officers had failed to see ; that if naval officers were to be competent to command in war, they must study war. Only those who understand how the principles of war have been evolved from past experience can know how to apply those principles, with new weapons, to the problems of the future. This reform came none too soon, as memoirs of the period show. It was during the First World War that Lord Esher wrote :

> Why do we worry about history ? Julian Corbett writes one of the best books in our language upon political and military strategy. All sorts of lessons, some of inestimable value, may be gleaned from it. No one, except perhaps Winston, who matters just now, has ever read it. Obviously, history is written for schoolmasters and armchair strategists. Statesmen and warriors pick their way through the dusk.

If we want evidence of this indictment we need only turn to a passage in a book by Lloyd George, who was Prime Minister at that critical moment when, owing to submarine attack, our fate was in the balance :

> After the Battle of Jutland, Admiral Jellicoe came to the conclusion that it was not safe for his imposing armada of enormous Dreadnoughts to undertake prolonged operations to the south of the Dogger Bank, as the risk of mines and submarines was too formidable. They were not to enter the North Sea unless they were forced to do so by direct challenge from the German High Sea Fleet. Meanwhile, the flagship must be interned in safe creeks, and the flag had to be carried on the small craft, the nimble destroyers and the weather-beaten trawlers. Here is the "Nelson touch" up-to-date. There was an atmos-phere of crouching nervousness.

Was ever such ignorance of maritime war displayed by a responsible statesman ? Pitt knew better than that. He knew that all the operations of trade protection, commerce-raiding and attack on the enemy's coast were possible only because the enemy's main fleets were contained. He knew that the issue finally must depend upon victory in battle—battle brought about through pressure on trade routes becoming unendurable for one or other of the belligerents. Although it was not realised at the time, Jutland was that battle. But if, by Cabinet decision, the Grand Fleet had been shorn of its power—and that demand was strongly pressed—then the German Fleet could have emerged from its harbours and, if victorious, could have swept away the whole structure of British defence. No one disputes that today. As to the "Nelson touch," the Prime Minister can never have read the history of Nelson's operations before and after the Battle of the Nile. Like Jellicoe, he would not take his battleships into narrow or coastal waters, and his letters are full of urgent entreaty for smaller vessels to operate where his ships-of-the-line could not.

One explanation for this ignorance of history, and therefore of the fundamental principles of maritime war—an ignorance which many of Lloyd George's colleagues shared—was that its value had become suspect. Those who quoted history too often confused precedent and principle or used some vague analogy to excuse their blunders. This is Lord Fisher's description of a Cabinet Committee in 1909 :

> Custance went back to Cornwallis and Keith, etc. That damned him ! Why not Noah ? Old Haldane shut his eye and "slept." Custance completely obfuscated himself and the Committee.

A misuse of history is apt indeed to defeat itself. Thus, Mr. Winston Churchill, himself a historian, could feel some sympathy for Sir James Craig, whose negotiations with Mr. de Valera in 1921 he describes as follows :

> His conversations were abortive. At the end of four hours Mr. de Valera's recital of Irish grievances had only reached the iniquities of Poyning's Act in the days of Henry VII. There were by that time various reasonable excuses for terminating not a discussion but a lecture.

It is not surprising if those who attended such a meeting as that came away with a distaste for history. And what excellent ammunition it provides for the man who has, all along, thought history but the dust heap of the ages ! Similarly muddled thinking was shown by a responsible officer at the Admiralty who, when asked (after three of our cruisers had been torpedoed while patrolling the Broad Fourteens) why he presented these easy targets to the enemy, replied that all through our history we had *always* maintained a force in that area !

The fact, however, that a slight knowledge of history can be so strikingly misapplied does not lessen the fact that it is on naval history that our strategic principles are based. To a large extent that naval history has been written and is known. Volumes have been written on the fleet actions and the major campaigns. It is in the principles of commerce protection that our histories are weak, and here our statesmen have good excuse for being ill-informed. The First World War had been waged for two years before the British people were aware of the danger in which they stood. But the rapid enlargement of the "Atlantic Graveyard" became known and people realised, perhaps for the first time, how inextricably their fate was bound up with that of their merchantmen. If the ships survived, they would survive ; if the ships died on the trade routes their own collapse would not be long delayed. This was realised at last ; but a cursory knowledge of history would have prevented it ever being forgotten.

A lack of maritime history, in its broader sense, may well account for the lessons of 1793-1815 being lost by 1914. For their being lost again after 1918 there is very much less excuse. But lost, for a time, they were. A powerful campaign was set afoot to convince the public that navy and army were both obsolescent and that future defence must rest in the air alone. It was a campaign which other Powers watched with amazement ; in some instances, with satisfaction. For British merchantmen, passing the greater part of their voyage beyond the range of any aircraft then designed, would have been lost without naval protection. If unopposed at sea, a few enemy cruisers could have ended any war in a matter of weeks. This was realised, fortunately, in the Cabinet. The result—no thanks to this misguided propaganda —was that the outbreak of war found the Navy reasonably strong. The depredations of enemy commerce raiders were reduced to tolerable proportions, the German and Italian warships seldom ventured far afield. Once again, nevertheless, the British people were shocked into the realisation that their existence depended on the merchant ship, and that without it their aircraft would be grounded and their troops forced to surrender.

Will this second rude awakening leave a permanent scar? Will the British people realise that, if the facts of their maritime history had been better understood—not only by their statesmen but throughout the land—all that their forefathers won for them, all that they themselves stand for in the world, the ideals they uphold of honour, justice and fair-dealing, would not have so often been in peril? Will they again be thrown off their balance by the advent of a new weapon, forgetting that such things have their antidote and that the cargo vessel must still need protection throughout her voyage? And will they still think of maritime history as something beyond their ken?

An elementary knowledge of the sea and its history would be far more profitable than much that is taught in our schools and universities. Nor is it so difficult to acquire. Whoever doubts it should turn over the pages of this book. He will find his attention arrested by much that will surprise him. Facts are there but the element of romance is never far away. Today, thanks to some of our recent authors, a knowledge of history is no longer very difficult to acquire. But unless it is richly flavoured with the salt from the sea and the pungent odour of tar and hemp it will be incomplete, the splendid story will be only half-told and so only half-understood.

EDITORIAL PREFACE

IT cannot but appear strange that, in an island defended, enriched and made famous by its ships and seamen, the study of maritime history should be so ignored. Naval history, for long sustained only by the Admiralty, has now some precarious foothold within the academic pale, but maritime history, in the wider sense, has received no encouragement at all. We have text books in which Manchester is mentioned repeatedly, Liverpool seldom and Bristol never. We still read chapters on the cotton industry in volumes which avoid, as by common consent, all but the most distant reference to the sea. When are we to find a history written in which seaports, docks, cargoes, charter-parties and bills of lading are given something like their proper place? Why should the historians of a seafaring race seem to talk of nothing but turnips, Factory Acts and Constitutional Progress? In the Customs House, meanwhile, in Insurance Offices and in the attics belonging to our older shipping firms, a mass of material lies dusty and untouched.

This book is an essay in maritime history, an attempt to survey one fragment of that vast and unexplored field of research and so disturb the cobwebs on a few of the ledgers and files. It is the belief of the contributors that this field is worth exploring. It is their hope, moreover, that this work, in summarising a little of what has been done, may also serve to show how much is still to do. The task has been attacked jointly by a group of people who resemble each other only in this belief and hope. One had practical experience in sail, another in the export trade, one is a distinguished physician and another an expert in marine insurance. Others are drawn from some four Universities in the Old World and the New. We have sought, between us, to steer a course midway between the text book with its oblivion of the sea and the specialist journal with its oblivion of everything else.

At the outset it must be apparent that the scope of such a book as this is difficult to define. Suppose that a general picture is wanted of British Overseas Trade at a particular period. Ideally, perhaps, the book should be a narrative, progressing from year to year and revealing the complex relationships between trade and trade. It should comprise a diary of sailings and arrivals, with due reference to the Admiralty, to Lloyd's and to the Customs. It would pass lightly from 'Change to Trinity House, from Newcastle-on-Tyne to Buckler's Hard. It would necessarily, of course, be the work of a single author. Such a book might well be as fascinating and as valuable as it would certainly be long. But it is safe to say that no man living could write it. The subject is too vast and life is too short. At the moment, a handful of scholars and enthusiasts, each knowing some portion of the field, a particular trade or port, can produce such a volume as this by their joint endeavour. This method, with its rapidly changing viewpoint, has much to commend it. What it cannot provide, however, is a continuous narrative. The result is a description of conditions, not of events; the description of British Overseas Trade during a period of some twenty years.

So far, then, the limits are defined in two directions. It is the list of chapters, however, that will prove the difficulty. Nothing would be easier than to draw up a list which would cover every aspect of maritime life. There could be chapters on the separate branches of the Coasting Trade and another chapter on the Fisheries. There could be a chapter on the smaller ports, and another on Scotland. Ireland would demand two chapters at least and there should clearly be a chapter on the privateers. In each of these instances, considerations of cost have combined with the fear of excessive length to make the decision for us. Excluded also, but for a different reason, is the trade with South America. For the greater part of the period with which we are concerned, that trade was a form of smuggling. And smuggling has been, with some regret, omitted; not as unimportant but as a subject too specialised. As regards South America, moreover, England was at war with Spain from 1796 to 1802 and from 1804 to 1808, and thus the more effectively excluded from a trade which

Spain in any case monopolised by law. Even after 1808 the Spaniards, although Allies, remained intransigent, and trade (as apart from smuggling) amounted to little even by the end of the war. With Portugal, as from 1808, the English relationship was admittedly more friendly, and led to the signing of a commercial treaty in 1810. By the following year the ships engaged in the trade with Brazil were numerous enough to require a separate naval escort. This was, nevertheless, only the beginning of a trade destined to expand enormously after 1815. Its origins, therefore, before that date have been deemed to belong to a later age.

Granting the necessary limitations in length, it might be asked, at this point, why 1794-1815 should be the period chosen—why, in fact, a period of peace and of normal trade should not be preferred. There is room here for different points of view. But it should perhaps be questioned, at the outset, whether peace was, in fact, a normal state of affairs in eighteenth century England. With allowance made for periods of preparation for war, together with months of colonial and naval warfare continuing after peace had been signed in Europe, it would seem doubtful whether England had as many as fifty years of peace throughout the eighteenth century. On any calculation it is evident that the alternating conditions of peace and war are equally worthy of study. The war years, however, have this additional interest, that work done on them is of use to the naval as well as to the economic historian. It must eventually be realised that the story of warfare at sea is incomplete without its economic background. The sea is more than a battlefield and the study of warfare is not the best introduction even to itself. The naval historian is too apt to discuss commerce protection without having first discovered what commerce there was to protect. Worse still, he is tempted to ignore the trade routes altogether and give us nothing but diagrams of battles and anecdotes about Lord Nelson. Only by close attention to strategy—and therefore to trade—can naval history maintain touch with the general field of scholarship.

If it be admitted that trade under conditions of war is worthy of study, the argument for choosing the Napoleonic Wars is obvious.

For those wars, of all others, must seem most topical to a generation which has somehow survived the War of 1939-45. Again and again, the records of that former struggle against Dictatorship read like a description of the years through which we have ourselves lived. Is it of value to see how far the comparison may go? It was certainly of value during the war itself to reflect on similarities which fore-shadowed final victory. Perhaps it is of value now to see how far we have relived the crisis of a century and a half ago. To what extent can we use the same words to describe, say, 1806 and 1943?

On the one hand, we may say, the tyranny of a single nation, under a ruthless dictatorship, had spread over almost the whole of Europe. As against that we can say, of either year, that the Royal Navy had won an ascendancy in European waters which put most of Europe in a state of virtual blockade. The worst period, when we had almost had to abandon the Mediterranean, was past, and the enemy's two obvious gambits had failed. The threat against the British Isles had come to nothing, the attempt against Egypt had ended for the enemy in nothing but disaster. Of our military position we could say with truth that we had recovered from the initial reverses which our ill-trained and ill-equipped army had suffered at Dunkirk and elsewhere. More than that, we had been able to launch a counter-stroke. Using Malta and Sicily as stepping stones, and covered by the Mediterranean Fleet, we had landed an army in Southern Italy. But this, like the colonial expeditions, and like the raids on the French Coast, was only a diversion; the proof, at most, of our ability to re-enter Europe when and where we should choose. Only after the enemy should have shattered his armies in the invasion of Russia might we join our Allies in the final fight for freedom.

Is this an overstatement of the case? Does the recurrence of the old names—Dunkirk, Antwerp, Toulon, Cairo, Messina and Naples—mean, in reality, nothing? And was there no historical instinct in our promotion of Irish Generals? The comparison is real to this extent at least, that we feel akin to our ancestors. We can picture more readily their Volunteer Movement. We can evaluate Sir John Moore's work at Shorncliffe, and we understand why Jane Austen appeared to

B

ignore Napoleon. Our soldiers have voyaged to India round the Cape and we know what is meant by "Peace without Plenty." We are present, even, in spirit, at that final scene—the absentminded return of Java to the Dutch. But it is in the matter of trade, and of commerce protection, that the comparison becomes relevant to this book.

In the French Wars, as in our own time, the central fact, commercially speaking, was the virtual exclusion from Europe of British trade. The Continent went without coffee, sugar and textiles, and England had to seek markets elsewhere, within the Empire, in the United States and in South America. At the same time, there were opportunities of supplying our Continental Allies (and even our enemies) from time to time as the fortune of war allowed, and opportunities of trading with the enemy colonies which fell into our hands. We could also trade by using neutral, and especially American shipping.

As against this restricted trade, the enemy, from an early stage in the war, had no overseas trade at all. British naval superiority, while never absolute, made the sea unsafe for his merchantmen and left him with nothing but such coastwise vessels as could dodge between the French ports under cover of his coastal batteries. His blockade runners were of little use, if only for lack of colonies with which to trade. In a negative sense, however, the enemy ships had to be reckoned with until the very end of the war. His battle fleet, although defeated, diminished and even harassed (as in 1809) at its anchorage, remained in being. It always remained a potential threat, compelling the detachment of heavy ships on convoy duties and involving a constant effort in reconnaissance and blockade. Of more immediate concern, however, were the enemy light craft and privateers. It was these which intercepted our merchantmen; and, although the danger diminished in some degree after 1811, it did not disappear until peace was made.

Privateers, like the submarines of a later age, used to operate in well-defined areas through which their prey would have to pass. They were rarely encountered in mid-ocean, but were met with more often in the approaches to the Channel or the Irish Sea, off Cuba, off the Coromandel Coast or in the Straits of Malacca. Based on places like St. Malo or Mauritius, they relied for their success on speed, on disguise, and on a knowledge of the trade-routes. There were ships which, armed as "runners," would defy capture in this way. Packets did so as a matter of routine. But other merchantmen, slow, ill-armed and undermanned, were compelled to sail in convoy, under naval escort. While thus herded together, they were relatively safe. It was when the convoy straggled or was dispersed by a gale that the privateer saw his chance.

Convoys had been organised regularly during the War of American Independence, and the system then used was re-adopted without much modification in 1793. The rendezvous and appointed dates for sailing were fixed by the Admiralty in consultation with a Committee of the Shippers concerned. Then, when the convoy assembled, the ships' masters went on board the escorting vessel and received an order of sailing, a further rendezvous and the signal code to be used. Thenceforward, all were under the command of the senior naval officer and so remained until he parted company. The Admiralty was often hard put to it to find all the escort vessels needed. Sometimes the sloops and brigs employed were too weak and too few to be a real protection. Even then, however, the convoy sometimes scattered to safety while the escort was being taken or sunk. It was only very important convoys which had the protection of frigates or ships of the line. In all this there is much that is familiar for us today. We too have heard the demand for more and more escort craft. We too have wondered whether our losses were being replaced. And we too have come to realise that a lack of battles does not necessarily mean a truce from fighting at sea.

Since the compilation of this book was begun, the band of contributors has suffered a grievous loss in the death of C. Ernest Fayle, whose chapters are thus published posthumously. In him we have lost the most meticulous of scholars, the ablest of critics and the most generous of collaborators. Whether as part-author of a standard work on the history of marine insurance, as a lecturer at the College of Imperial Defence, or as the inspirer of such a work as this, he is sorely missed; and missed both as a historian, as a teacher and as a friend.

Fully as grievous is the loss of Mr. Basil Lubbock. More widely known than Mr. C. E. Fayle, he had done more than most men living to interest his fellow-countrymen in the history of the sea. Himself a sailor, his works on the Blackwall Frigates and the China

Clippers will long remain unrivalled in their kind. The privilege of publishing what may perhaps prove his last words to appear in print is an honour too dearly bought. For he wrote of the sailing ship with a personal knowledge claimed now by very few. And there is none, there can be none, to take his place.

It remains for me to thank all who have contributed to this book. Subject to all the difficulties under which authors are now labouring, divided from each other by great distances, and finally asked to accept an extreme economy of space, they have responded helpfully to every appeal. Most generous of all was an author whose work it was finally found impossible to include. To him, no less than to those whose names appear, as also to the most understanding of publishers, my thanks are offered.

C. NORTHCOTE PARKINSON

Royal Naval College,
  Dartmouth

CONTENTS

	Page
INTRODUCTION *by Admiral Sir William M. James, G.C.B.*	7
EDITORIAL PREFACE *by C. Northcote Parkinson*	14

PART ONE

I. Shipowning and Marine Insurance *by C. Ernest Fayle*	25

II. The Seaports
    i. LONDON, *by C. Northcote Parkinson*
    ii. LIVERPOOL, *by A. C. Wardle*
    iii. BRISTOL, *by Professor C. M. MacInnes*
	49

III. The Employment of British Shipping *by C. Ernest Fayle*	72
IV. Ships of the Period and Developments in Rig *by Basil Lubbock*	87
V. Seamen *by Basil Lubbock*	102
VI. Health and Sickness *by Professor J. A. Nixon*	121

PART TWO

VII. The East India Trade *by C. Northcote Parkinson*	141
VIII. The West Indian Trade *by Lucy Frances Horsfall, Ph.D*	157
IX. The American Trade *by Professor H. Heaton*	194
X. The Newfoundland Trade *by A. C. Wardle*	227
XI. The Slave Trade *by Professor C. M. MacInnes* *With Appendix by Professor J. A. Nixon*	251
XII. The Post Office Packets *by A. C. Wardle*	278
GLOSSARY	291
BIBLIOGRAPHY AND LIST OF AUTHORITIES	296
INDEX	314

ILLUSTRATIONS

PLATE   PAGE

    Sir Nathaniel Dance, Commander in the service of the Honourable East India Company. Reproduced from the mezzotint by I. R. Smith in the National Maritime Museum, by permission of the Trustees   *Frontispiece*

1   Section of an 18th century ship. Taken from Vol. 5 of a French Encyclopædia published in Paris in 1787. Reproduced from the copy in the National Maritime Museum, by permission of the Trustees   32

2   The New Docks at Wapping, 1803. Reproduced from a print in the National Maritime Museum, by permission of the Trustees   48

3   Plan of the Docks at London, 1808. Based upon plans engraved and published in that year   53

4   Proposed diversion of the Thames. Based upon the Third Plan submitted by W. Reveley to the Committee of 1796   55

5   Plan of the Docks at Liverpool in 1808. Based upon the *British Atlas*, a complete set of County Maps of England and Wales, published in London in 1810   60-61

6   Map based upon Mathews's new and correct Plan of the City and Suburbs of Bristol, published in 1825   68-69

7   Specimen advertisements taken from the *Liverpool Chronicle* of 1804, and illustrating contemporary means of transport   75

8   Unloading a Collier. Reproduced from the drawing by Atkinson in the National Maritime Museum, by permission of the Trustees   80

9   Shipping with two masts. Taken from Vol. 1 of Steel's *Elements and Practice of Rigging and Seamanship*, 1794. Reproduced from the copy in the National Maritime Museum, by permission of the Trustees   96

10   The Quay. Drawing by Rowlandson. Reproduced from Vol. 1 of *Rowlandson the Caricaturist*, by permission from Messrs. Chatto & Windus   112

11   Heaving the lead. Reproduced from the drawing by Atkinson in the National Maritime Museum, by permission of the Trustees   128

12   Model of an East Indiaman (Scale 1-36) of about 1800, in the National Maritime Museum. Reproduced from a photograph, by permission of the Trustees   144

13   The *Lady Juliana* struck by lightning. One of a set of four views of the Jamaica Convoy homeward bound in September, 1782. Reproduced from the Aquatint after Dodd in the National Maritime Museum, by permission of the Trustees   160

14   A Draught of the Harbours of Port Royal and Kingston, reproduced from Long's *History of Jamaica*, published in 1774   192

15   The Port of Boston, U.S.A. Based upon Vol. II of the *Atlantic Neptune*, published under the direction of the Admiralty in 1779-80, together with *A Plan of Boston* from the Survey of Osgood Carleton, made in 1796   208-9

16   The Banks of Newfoundland. Based upon a New Map of Nova Scotia, Newfoundland, etc. From the latest authorities. By John Cary, engineer. (Contemporary)   240-1

17   The snow *Shaw* of 194 tons, Guineaman, built by Rathbone, Blezard and Haselden at Liverpool in 1801. From an oil painting in private possession, reproduced by kind permission of the owner.   256

18   The Coast from Benin Creek to Cameroons. Based upon a map published in *The Memoirs of the late Captain Hugh Crow of Liverpool*. London, 1830   265

19   A Post Office Packet off Liverpool. Reproduced from an oil painting by Robert Salmon (circa 1814), by kind permission of the Parker Gallery, 2 Albemarle Street, W.1   288

NOTE

In Plate 9, Shipping with two masts, the vessels shown are of the following types : 1, Snow ; 2, Brig ; 3, Schooner ; 4, Lugger ; 5 and 6, Man-of-war Pinnaces ; 7, Bilander ; 8, Ketch ; 9, Cutter ; 10, Hoy, and 11, Sailing Barge

PART ONE

CHAPTER I

Shipowning and Marine Insurance

by C. ERNEST FAYLE

lately Lecturer at the College of Imperial Defence

FROM the point of view with which we are here concerned, the
war which broke out in 1793 was the culmination of a long
struggle for maritime, commercial and colonial supremacy, in which
the principal European Powers had been engaged for at least one
hundred and fifty years. "Ships, Colonies and Commerce"—the
motto with which the illuminations at Lloyd's greeted the Jubilee of
George III—represented an aim pursued by force of arms in the
Anglo-Dutch Wars of the Seventeenth Century, in the Wars of the
League of Augsburg, the Spanish Succession and the Austrian
Succession, in the Seven Years War and the War of American
Independence, and pursued as remorselessly by fiscal and diplomatic
weapons during the intervals of peace.

The outstanding feature of this struggle had been the rise of
Britain as a maritime and colonial power. At its start British shipping
was a very poor second to that of Holland. During the first three-
quarters of the Eighteenth Century it appears, from the recorded
clearances, almost to have trebled in volume ; yet as late as 1776,
Adam Smith affirmed emphatically the great superiority of the Dutch
in the carrying trade. Then came the revolt of the American Colonies
and, after the recognition of the United States in 1781, a wave of
pessimism swept over the country. Some observers saw a ray of light
in the exclusion of the New England shipowners from the protected
trades in which they had begun to be formidable rivals, but, for the
most part, economists, moralists and politicians joined in a wail of
lament over the eclipse of Britain's greatness.

Never were prophecies of evil more completely falsified and
nowhere more surely than in the field of commerce. The effects of
the Industrial Revolution were beginning to be felt in an increased
consumption of raw materials, a greatly increased volume and

variety of goods for export and a corresponding increase in the demand for tonnage. In 1774, just before the War of American Independence, the clearances of British ships at ports in Great Britain amounted to 798,000 tons. In 1792, the year before the renewal of war, the figure was 1,563,744 tons. The target which British trade and shipping exposed to attack during the Revolutionary and Napoleonic Wars was far greater than in any earlier conflict. Its defence, too, was of greatly increased importance, owing to the rapid growth of industry, bringing with it increased dependence on oversea sources of supply and on foreign markets.

Side by side with this great expansion of commerce during the Eighteenth Century went a steady process of development in the organisation of business. Four factors in this development were of special importance in the conduct of overseas trade ; the supplanting of the Chartered Company by the individual merchant, the gradual differentiation of the shipping from the trading interest, the rise of the specialized commercial coffee-house, and the growth of marine insurance.

The Chartered Companies had played a great part in nursing the infancy of British commerce. But when once that commerce had settled into established channels and was assured of adequate naval protection and diplomatic support from the State, the system of corporate trading rapidly declined, except in the peculiar conditions of the trade with India and China, where the Honourable East India Company was still, in 1793, in full enjoyment of its exclusive privileges. Most of the other Companies lost their monopolies so early as 1689 by the Bill of Rights, and although several of them were still in existence at the outbreak of war, very few of them retained anything of their old importance.

The most vigorous, as a trading concern, was the Hudson Bay Company, a joint-stock affair, trading as a corporation and owning its own ships. It had, however, lost its legal monopoly in 1689 and its control of the Canadian Fur Trade was being successfully challenged by the North-West Company of Montreal, an unchartered association formed in 1783.(¹)

(¹) After a long period of bitter rivalry, accompanied by much bloodshed, the two companies were amalgamated, with a new charter, in 1821.

The third great joint-stock company, the Royal African, had been converted, in 1750, into a very loose association for the maintenance of forts on the Guinea Coast and the regulation of the slave trade, membership of which was open to any merchant on payment of £2. The South Sea Company, the one Eighteenth Century addition to the list, had long been moribund.

Of the Regulated Companies, the Eastland, Russia, and Levant or Turkey Companies were on their last legs, although the Russia Company retained some interest in the Archangel trade, and the Levant Company, which was suffering acutely from French competition, was kept alive by Government subsidies. The Company of Merchant Adventurers, the oldest of them all, was now confined to its staple at Hamburg,(1) where it continued to carry on business, especially in the distribution of woollens, until the seizure of all British property in the town by Mortier in 1806.

Apart from the East India Trade, the chartered companies had, in fact, ceased for many years to count for much in the growth of British commerce, and as capital accumulated and trade settled into regular channels, the "adventure" system—the formation of temporary syndicates for particular voyages—also fell into disuse. The great bulk of the trade with Europe, Africa and America was now carried on by private mercantile firms, many of them long established. They were mostly identified with some special branch of commerce, such as the West Indian or the Baltic, and with well-established agents or correspondents in the countries to which they traded. When they combined—as in the Committee of West Indian Merchants—it was for such purposes as promoting or opposing legislation affecting their common interests. So far as actual trading was concerned, British commerce at the end of the Eighteenth Century was stubbornly individualistic and fiercely competitive.

Many merchants were also shipowners but, as the century advanced, the differentiation between the trading and shipping interests became more and more marked. There were still, as there were later, firms whose ships were employed solely in the carriage of their own trade, but they were probably in a small minority.(2) Even when a merchant

---

(1) At this period it was usually referred to as the Hamburg Company.
(2) Where they existed, it was outside London: for example, in Bristol. See Chap. II, pages, 67, 69.

was owner or part-owner of a ship as well as partner in a mercantile
house, his trading and his shipowning were usually separate busi-
nesses, and little or none of the ship's cargo might be provided by
his own firm. Many owners, too, were men not otherwise engaged
in foreign commerce; shipmasters, active or retired, ship's husbands,
or agents, shipbrokers, dealers in marine stores, and others who took
shares in a ship or ships purely for investment purposes. At the
beginning of the Nineteenth Century, the General Shipowners'
Society was able to boast that its membership was confined to shipowners pure and simple, free from the entanglements of trading
interests, and though the society was not fully representative, it is
probable that a large majority of British ships were owned, at this
time, by people whose interest in foreign trade was either wholly or
mainly confined to the earning of freights.

The process of differentiation is very clearly illustrated in the
memoirs of two shipmasters who have left us exceptionally full and
clear accounts of their life at sea: Nathaniel Uring, whose deep-water
career covered the first quarter of the Eighteenth Century, and
Samuel Kelly, whose life afloat was confined to its last quarter.(¹)
The ships commanded by Uring were owned by syndicates (of
which he was sometimes a member) who were equally prepared to
purchase and dispose of a cargo on their own account, or to "let the
ship to freight" for the carriage of other people's goods. Sometimes
both methods were simultaneously employed; part of the cargo-
space being filled with the owner's goods, and the remainder "filled
up upon freight." Uring himself points the distinction by reserving
the term "cargo" strictly for goods loaded on owners' account.
"Having delivered the freight wines and sold our cargo," is a
characteristic phrase.(²)

Kelly's employers, on the other hand, were shipowners in the strict
sense of the term, looking to freights and not to trading for their
profits. On one passage only does he record the purchase of a cargo
(salt from the Mediterranean) as a speculation on the owners' part.

(¹) *The Voyages and Travels of Captain Nathaniel Uring*. Ed. by Capt. A. Dewar, R.N.
London, 1928. *Samuel Kelly, an Eighteenth Century Seaman*. Ed. by Crosbie Garstin,
London, 1925.

(²) Uring, op. cit., 232

On all other occasions it is clear that the ships were filled with goods in which the shipowners had no interest beyond the freight to be received for their carriage under the provisions of the Charter Party or Bill of Lading.

In the collection of cargoes, as in the vast majority of business transactions, personal intercourse was still the predominant factor. If a ship were not chartered for the carriage of a whole cargo, the work of filling her entailed a great number of interviews with prospective shippers, and this work fell largely on the shipmaster. It was now unusual, at any rate in the long-distance trades, for the master to have an interest in his ship; he was simply the salaried servant of the owners. But he was expected, as part of his ordinary duties, to do much of the work which is now done by the branch offices of liner companies and by forwarding agents.

Captain Kelly's memoirs give a lively picture of what this entailed. In 1759 the coasting brig which he then commanded was at Bristol, "laid on the berth to load for Liverpool." The freight markets, however, were slack; few prospective shippers came forward with enquiries and Kelly was reduced, in his own words, "to cruise the city for goods"; that is, to tramp round from office to office, seeking cargo from merchants accustomed to supply the Liverpool market.[1] While so engaged, he received instructions from his owners to take coach for Liverpool, where the *John*, "a constant trader to Philadelphia" was waiting for him to take charge of her. He was, however, to break his journey at Birmingham, in order "to wait on several manufacturers who were in the habit of sending goods to America to solicit their favours for the *John*."[2]

This was a laborious process, but prior to the great development and speeding up of communications during the first half of the Nineteenth Century, it was characteristic of all branches of trade. The only remedy available, in existing conditions, was to multiply centres where those interested in any branch of trade could meet together, and the rise of the commercial coffee-house, dating back to the latter part of the Seventeenth Century, had gone a long way to meet that demand. During the investigation into the state of the

[1] Kelly, op. cit., p. 166.   [2] Ibid., pp. 166-7.

marine insurance market which preceded the grant of charters to the Royal Exchange and London Assurance Companies in 1720, one of the most damaging charges brought against the system of private underwriting was the inconvenience and waste of time involved in the necessity for insurance brokers "to pick up the Insurers here and there as they can,"—"cruising the city for underwriters" as Kelly might have put it. The obvious justice of this complaint was almost certainly the determining factor in the rise of Lloyd's Coffee House— already a well-known rendezvous for merchants, shipowners, ship-brokers and others interested in trade and shipping—to the position of recognised headquarters of the private underwriters.[1]

By 1793, Lloyd's Coffee House, now transferred to rooms in the Royal Exchange, had become by far the greatest centre of marine insurance in the world. The Subscribers' Room was strictly reserved for the business of underwriting, but the Coffee House was still frequented for business purposes by people of all kinds interested in foreign trade. From being the chief, it had gradually become practically the only centre in London for the sale of ships by auction, and the Coffee Room was so favourite a resort of shipmasters that by 1812 it had already begun to be referred to as "The Captains' Room."

Other Coffee Houses which provided facilities for people engaged in foreign trade were "Sam's next the Custom House," the Jerusalem, the Jamaica, and the Virginia and Maryland. Sam's, which had been a rival to Lloyd's, in the earlier part of the century, as a haunt of shipbrokers, was still a place where the Captains of ships about to sail could be advertised as attending to meet prospective shippers or passengers. The Jerusalem Coffee House was the resort of East India merchants and the Jamaica was a rendezvous for merchants and ship-masters in the West India Trade. The Virginia and Maryland Coffee House, as its name implies, was frequented by people interested in trade with the United States. Later, with its name changed to the Baltic, it became associated with the import of bulk cargoes of grain, hemp and tallow, and eventually gave birth to the present Baltic Shipping Exchange.

In the short sea trades it is probable that return cargoes were some-

---

[1] *A History of Lloyd's.* Charles Wright and C. Ernest Fayle. London, 1928.

times fixed in advance. The merchants who chartered a ship to carry coal from Newcastle or Sunderland to a Baltic port might themselves be importers of Baltic products such as timber, iron or tallow, in which event the charter would cover the round voyage. Alternatively, a charter for the return voyage might be secured by the shipowners from other East Coast Importers.

In the long-distance trades this would seldom be possible. The passages, when compared even with those of later sailing vessels, were very lengthy, and by the time a ship arrived at her port of discharge, the political situation and the course of the freight and commodity markets might have completely changed. In these circumstances it was essential for shipowners or charterers to leave the arrangements for the homeward passage to the discretion of a representative on the spot.

The usual course, when a ship was sailing under charter, was for the charterers to appoint a supercargo as their representative. It was his business to supervise delivery of the cargo to the charterers' agents abroad, or to effect a sale of the goods if no consignee had been arranged, and to purchase a return cargo with the proceeds. As representative of the charterers, he was usually empowered to order the vessel to a second port of discharge if it should prove impossible to dispose of the whole of the goods at her original destination, or to a neighbouring port where cargo was likely to be forthcoming if no satisfactory purchase could be made at the port of discharge. The carriage of a supercargo was not, however, universal, as a shipmaster of long experience in a particular trade and in whom the charterers had confidence, would frequently be empowered to act for them, in consultation with their agent abroad or the British Consul at the port of discharge.

When a ship was chartered for the outward passage or was loaded on the berth with parcels received from numerous exporters who were not interested in the import trade, the responsibility for avoiding a ballast passage home rested on the shipmaster. For this purpose it was necessary to entrust him with very wide discretion, as the volume of inwards and outwards traffic varied greatly on many of the routes. In the trade with Philadelphia, for instance, while the demand for goods was steady enough to justify the employment of "constant traders"—that is, ships regularly laid on the berth for that port—it was by no means certain that a return cargo for Great Britain would be procurable. Hence, Samuel Kelly, in his first voyage as commander of the *John*, was given "liberty from my owners to embrace a freight for any port most eligible," and in exercise of this discretion actually accepted a charter for Barcelona.[1]

A lengthy cross-voyage to a European port—Kelly was 67 days from Philadelphia to Barcelona—might bring the master again into touch with his owners, through the system of postal packets which ran regularly to the principal ports abroad. As soon as Kelly had fixed his Barcelona charter he sent off a report to his owners, and on his arrival he found their instructions awaiting him.[2]

In some instances ships sailed, like a modern tramp with a cargo consigned "to orders," without the port of destination being definitely fixed. Uring, for example, when sailing under charter from Venice with a whole cargo of wheat for Cadiz, was instructed to proceed to Lisbon if advised that the market at Cadiz was dull, and did actually carry on for the Tagus when he found the winds un-favourable for beating into Cadiz, apparently with the full subsequent approval of the charterers.[3] The extreme dependence of the old wooden sailing ships on favourable winds for a reasonable passage sometimes made it worth while for cargo owners to leave the master or supercargo a still wider discretion, and we read of a ship leaving a Mediterranean port with salt for either America or Ireland, according to the winds encountered after passing through the Straits.[4]

The technique of shipowning had thus arrived at a point permitting considerable elasticity in the operation of the vessels. This was important for, as will be seen in Chapter III, the volume of inwards and outwards traffic on many of the regular routes showed wide discrepancies, and many passages must have been made in ballast had not British shipping been able to wrest from the Dutch the first place in the general carrying trade.

How far the gradual ousting of the Dutch from their supremacy as general carriers was due to the Cromwellian and Stuart Navigation

---

[1] Kelly, op. cit. 170.   [2] Ibid., 175.   [3] Uring, op. cit., 204, 213.
[4] *William Richardson, a Mariner of England.* Edited by Col. S. Childers, London, 1908, p. 27 ff.

Acts and how far to other causes, is still matter of controversy. Probably there was hardly a British statesman, publicist or shipowner in 1793 who entertained any doubt on the matter. The Acts, at any rate, remained the corner stone of British commercial policy and were regarded by the shipowners as the only true begetter of their prosperity.

The complicated system of restrictions imposed on trade and shipping by the Navigation Acts was directed to three main ends: first, to secure as much of the carrying trade as possible for British shipping; secondly, to secure a monopoly of the colonial markets for British goods; thirdly, to make Great Britain the sole entrepot for the supply of colonial produce to other countries.

To secure the first of these aims it was provided that no goods should be imported into or exported from any British oversea possession except in British ships, and that the most important foreign products should only be imported into Great Britain in British ships, or in ships belonging to the country of origin or usual port of shipment. For the purpose of the Acts, a British ship was defined as a ship built and owned in Great Britain or the British possessions, the Master and at least three-fourths of the crew being British subjects. Foreign-built vessels acquired by purchase or capture could acquire the character of British ships for the European trade only. The commercial objects of the Acts were secured by clauses prohibiting any direct import into the Plantations from foreign countries, or the shipment of the leading colonial products to any but a British port.

However helpful these provisions may have been in the infancy of British trade and shipping, they were already beginning to be felt as a serious clog on commerce and some minor modifications had been introduced, especially for the relief of the West India planters. Above all, it had proved absolutely necessary, after the recognition of American independence, to permit direct trade in American vessels between the West Indies and the United States. No breach, however, had been made in the main fabric of the system.

Nevertheless, it would be out of place here to discuss in detail the provisions and working of the Acts, for in time of war their operation was to a large extent suspended. The needs of the Royal Navy and the transport service, together with the competition of privateers,

c

invariably produced a shortage of seamen. So severely was this felt that an Act of 1794 gave permission to extend the employment of foreigners in British ships even up to seventy-five per cent. of the crew.([1]) The supply of tonnage, too, was reduced by the demands of the fighting services for transports and storeships, and even when British tonnage was available there were routes on which it could not be used because of exceptional risks or the extension of French influence over the ports. In these circumstances not only were additional foreign ships attracted into the trades normally open to them, but licences were freely granted for their employment in traffic from which they were normally excluded. The direct trade of Great Britain with India and the colonies remained a close preserve, but foreign shipping was freely employed in the re-export of colonial goods to European ports.

While the legislature was deeply concerned for the protection of British shipping against foreign competition, it did little to ensure its efficiency. The most important recent addition to the Statute Book was the Act of 1787 which provided for the compulsory registration of shipping throughout the Empire,([2]) an admirable measure in itself, but by no means beneficial in some of its effects. It gave, for the first time, a firm foundation for shipping statistics, and, by requiring the names of owners and masters and any subsequent changes in owner-ship and command to be officially registered, it tightened control over shipping; but its main purpose was to assist in the enforcement of the Navigation Laws, two distinct types of certificate being granted, one of "British Plantation Registry" for ships eligible for the colonial trade, the other of "Foreign Ships Registry, for the European Trade, British Property." This was merely in accordance with established policy; where the Act proved definitely harmful was in prescribing an irrational method of tonnage measurement which continued to hamper progress in hull-design until the middle of the Nineteenth Century.

Apart from the restriction of competition, the chief object of legislation was the protection of the revenue, which inspired a series of laws relating to entrance and clearance formalities, of which the

---

([1]) 33 Geo. III, c. 26.   ([2]) 26 Geo. III, c. 60.

most important was the Manifest Act of 1797,([1]) which made the carriage of a full Manifest of the cargo compulsory for British ships. Objects of wider public interest were attended to in the laws relating to Quarantine and Pilotage, but practically the only provisions for the safety of life and property afloat were contained in a series of Acts, of progressive stringency, for preventing by the threat of heavy penalties, the wilful destruction or casting away of ships. The maintenance of any kind of standard in build and upkeep was left to the influence of the underwriters and the Register Books.

For the welfare of the seamen Parliament cared little; for maintaining the supply of seamen it cared much, as on this depended the manning of the Royal Navy. For this reason a regular scale was laid down for the carrying of apprentices, who were protected from impressment during the first three years currency of their Articles.([2]) As a means of checking the desertion of seamen, the signing of Articles of Agreement was made compulsory in 1729 by an Act which also provided for prompt payment of wages after arrival in Great Britain.([3]) In no Act, however, was any provision made for regulating the food or accommodation provided for the crew. What is perhaps more surprising, no kind of test either of knowledge or of efficiency was laid down for shipmasters and mates.

When such was the attitude of the State, it was hardly to be expected that the shipowners should show themselves farsighted or progressive. Lacking either legislative inducements to efficiency or the stimulus of effective competition, their main concern, as a class, was to run up freights and to keep down costs. The development or lack of development in shipbuilding during this period and the conditions of employment afloat are dealt with in other chapters of this book, but it is proper to remark here that the parsimony of shipowners often brought its own punishment. The high rate of marine casualties was undoubtedly due in part to the bad upkeep and equipment of too

---

([1]) 36 Geo. III, c. 40.

([2]) 2 and 3 Anne, c. 6, lays down a scale of one apprentice for every vessel of from 30 to 50 tons burthen, one more for the next 50 tons and one more for every 100 tons thereafter. 37 Geo. III, c. 73 lays down a scale of one apprentice under 17 years of age for every 100 tons, for ships trading to the West Indies.

([3]) 2 Geo. II, c. 36 ; made perpetual by 2 Geo. III, c. 31 ; extended to coasting trade, 31 Geo. III, c. 39.

many of the ships ([1]) and in part to the unwillingness of owners to offer conditions good enough to attract an adequate supply of efficient shipmasters and mates. Often enough, too low pay led to something worse than inefficiency. Ill-paid men of no strong principle could easily be tempted by the attractions of illegitimate gain, and cases of fraudulent stranding or scuttling take up much space in the contemporary minute book at Lloyd's.

More venial, and much more general, was the acquiescence of ship's officers in the wholesale plunder of tackle and cargoes which went on at the ports. Patrick Colquhoun, who estimated the depredations in London alone, prior to the establishment of the River Police in 1798, at £350,000 a year, of which £45,000 fell directly on the shipowners themselves, was of opinion that about one in seven of the mates engaged in the trade of the port was guilty of participation in these robberies or of accepting bribes to connive at them. The figures may be no more than well-informed guesswork, but his general picture of this evil and his analysis of its causes carry full conviction.([2])

> Holding a certain rank in Society, with emoluments very unequal to the wants of a family, they resort generally to illicit trade, as a means of bettering their condition ... The transition from one offence to the other [from smuggling to robbery of cargo] is easy.

A little later, in recording the neglect of many shipowners and ship's husbands in the West India Trade to place their vessels under the protection of the River Police:

> Such is the mistaken policy of men eager in the pursuit of wealth, that an evident benefit, with respect to the safety of property (often of great magnitude) is sacrificed to save a certain trifling expence.([3])

This comment was capable of a much wider application. There were, no doubt, many owners who ran their ships on liberal lines and with a due sense of their obligations, but it would be idle to pretend that, outside the East India Company's service, the standards of the industry were high.

([1]) It is significant, in this connection, that the Committee of Lloyd's strove hard, though unsuccessfully, to make an inspection of sails, anchors and cables compulsory under the Convoy Acts, p. 206-7, *Hist. Lloyds.*

([2]) *A Treatise on the Commerce and Police of the River Thames.* London, 1800. pp. 154, 163-6, 220-21.

([3]) See, further, Chapter 2, page 52.

Until 1802, when the Society of Shipowners was formed, the industry seems to have been wholly unorganised for co-operation in matters of common interest. The early history of the Shipowners' Society—the parent of the existing Chamber of Shipping of the United Kingdom—is still very obscure, but its membership seems to have been confined mainly to London owners and it is doubtful whether it exercised any very marked influence on the conduct or fortunes of the industry during the war period. It is clear that as a channel for communication and negotiation between the shipping industry and the State, its importance at this period was much less than that of Lloyd's.

All through the Eighteenth Century the volume and importance of marine insurance had been steadily growing. The great increase in the total value of the hulls and cargoes at risk, the increased average age of ships and the greater value of individual cargoes combined to emphasize the importance both to the nation and to the individual merchant or shipowner of a system whereby "upon the losse or perishing of any Shippe there followeth not the undoing of any Man, but the losse lightethe rather easilie upon many, than heavilie upon fewe."[1] Especially was this so in time of war, when the risks of capture or destruction by the King's Enemies were added to the manifold perils of the sea.

The utility of insurance, however, depended on the stability of the underwriters, and this, in the earlier French wars, had not always proved equal to the strain. Two black days in particular long remained in the memories of business men. In 1693, when the news of Tourville's great stroke against the "Smyrna Fleet" was received in London, it is recorded that many merchants left the Royal Exchange with the faces of men under sentence of death. The insurance market at that date was quite unorganised, underwriting was not yet a specialised business, and many of the merchants and speculators who engaged in it lacked the necessary resources to stand up to such a blow. A large number of insurers failed and the resultant commercial crisis severely shook the credit of the Government.[2]

---

[1] Preamble to the Act establishing a Court of Assurances, 43 Eliz., c. 12.

[2] One of those who failed was Daniel Defoe.

By August, 1780, when Cordova captured fifty-eight out of sixty-three ships in the combined East and West India convoy, "New Lloyd's" in the Royal Exchange had become the recognised head-quarters of marine insurance and many specialists of long experience, sound judgment and large resources were to be found in the Subscribers' Room. Nevertheless, the losses, estimated at £1,500,000, were sufficient to break many of the weaker or less prudent operators, and thirty years later, at the height of the Napoleonic Wars, the tragedy was still bitterly remembered.

The stability of the marine insurance market was to be still more severely tested during the years 1793-1815. That it stood the strain was due mainly to the rapid growth of Lloyd's in membership, resources and organisation.

Lloyd's Coffee House as it was established in the Royal Exchange in 1774 was something more than a rendezvous for underwriters and insurance brokers. The house was the property of the Subscribers, the Masters being merely tenants at will. The control exercised by the Subscribers themselves in general meeting was supplemented by the more continuous supervision of the Committee, and both the Committee and the General Meetings soon began to concern themselves with matters of greater import than the provision of accommodation and the regulation of admission to the rooms. The revision of the standard form of marine insurance policy, carried out by a special Policy Committee and confirmed by a General Meeting in 1779, was a clear indication of the part Lloyd's was to play, not merely in providing facilities for marine insurance, but in regulating its processes.

The growth of Lloyd's in membership, organisation and influence was stimulated by the war itself. The rapid growth of British shipping and commerce during the war years and the severity of the risks to which they were subjected led to a great increase in the demand for insurance and the high rates of premium held out the prospect of big profits to successful underwriters. So great was the number of those who wrote risks either for themselves or as agents that Lloyd's became inconveniently crowded and in the year 1800 a series of regulations were introduced which had the double object of effectively excluding non-subscribers from the Rooms and imposing some qualification test for the admission of new subscribers.

It appears from evidence given before the Marine Insurance Committee of 1810 that there were then between 1,400 and 1,500 subscribers, of whom two-thirds were regular or occasional underwriters; the others being brokers who were not underwriters, or men who had retired from active business. The active underwriters in regular attendance, who did the bulk of the business, numbered probably about 500. Among the leading men who gave tone to the market many were specialists in insurance whose interests were wholly or mainly confined to writing policies as underwriters or showing risks as brokers. Others were also merchants or bankers, but as the Act of 1720, establishing the two Corporations, prohibited all other underwriting in partnership, their insurance business was kept entirely distinct from the transactions of the mercantile houses in which they were partners, and the balance of premiums due to them was free from any liability in respect of partnership debts.

The ruling spirits of Lloyd's were men of great ability, integrity and large resources—John Julius Angerstein, the friend and financial adviser of Pitt, still fondly remembered as the Father of Lloyd's; Sir Francis Baring, "the first merchant in Europe"; "Dicky" Thornton, "good for three millions," and others of similar calibre. There was as yet no provision of deposits under the control of the Committee as a guarantee to the assured, but the wealth of the men who took the largest risks and fixed by their example the rate of premiums, together with the high standard of integrity which they set, proved no small protection to the public.

The London insurance market included in addition to Lloyd's, the Royal Exchange and London Assurance Corporations, and a number of private underwriters who wrote policies at their own offices, at the Jamaica and Jerusalem Coffee Houses, or at the Coal Exchange, where the business was presumably confined to the insurance of Colliers. The two Corporations, however, were now mainly concerned with life and fire insurance, and the total volume of marine business carried on by them and by the unorganised private underwriters was trifling in comparison with the transactions at Lloyd's.

Marine insurance, however, was not confined to London. Private underwriting was busily carried on at Liverpool, where the Liverpool Underwriters' Association was formed in 1802, at Glasgow, at Bristol, at Newcastle and at Hull, where a good deal of the coasting and short sea trade was insured.

There were, moreover, especially in the north, a number of ship-owners' clubs, foreshadowing the Protecting and Indemnity Societies of today, which insured hulls on a market basis. Their operations, however, were confined mainly to coasters and to the marine risks on transports, the war risks of which were accepted by the Government.

Taken as a whole, it is clear that at least three-fourths of the total marine insurance of the country was effected in London—the proportion was probably much higher for the foreign trade—and that London, in this connection, was practically synonymous with Lloyd's.

The risks covered included a large proportion of neutral as well as British commerce. Many companies were formed during the war at Hamburg, Copenhagen and other European ports, and in the United States, for the insurance of ships and cargoes; but their business was confined mainly to transactions forbidden by law to English under-writers—insurance of enemy property and of neutral property against British capture. It was not a very profitable business, and by 1810 all but five or six of thirty-one companies formed at Hamburg had closed down.

The position of the East India trade in this, as in other respects, was exceptional. The East India Company carried its own risks. Many private ships from India were insured at Lloyd's, but others, together with practically the whole of the Indian coasting trade and the cross-trades in the Indian Ocean, were insured by companies formed in India itself. The reason for this was simply the slowness of communications, and for similar reasons a large part of the cross-risks in the West Indies were insured in the United States.

The marine insurance market, as thus constituted, proved fully capable of providing the cover required. In London alone the risks covered during 1809 amounted to well over £100,000,000. Nor was there serious difficulty in placing big individual risks. The record figure was £656,000 on specie in the *Diana* frigate from Vera Cruz, of which one of the Corporations took £25,000 and Lloyd's the rest. Richard Thornton alone once wrote £250,000 on a shipment of gold to St. Petersburg and offered to deposit Exchequer Bonds as security until the risk was run off. These were exceptions; but evidence given in 1810 showed that £40,000 could be placed without difficulty on "a good ship from Tonningen," £69,000 on a West Indiaman and cargo, £200,000 on a regular fur ship from Quebec, and £250,000 on "a ship or ships" from the East Indies.

To what risks was the property covered at Lloyd's and elsewhere exposed? The answer is not easy. In the coasting trade and the trade with Ireland, the Channel Isles and Man (then included in the "Foreign Trade") the losses were comparatively small. Any attempt to work out a percentage of losses to sailings or to tonnage on the Register for the foreign trade proper, is complicated by the absence of information as to the number of cross voyages, the difficulty of ascertaining the number of ships actually employed in foreign trade and the frequent impossibility of ascertaining a vessel's employment, definitely, from the returns of losses in *Lloyd's List*. An estimate of losses in the foreign trade proper of Great Britain which was prepared for *A History of Lloyd's* gives the following results for the period 1793-1801, in which the second column represents net losses, after deducting ships recaptured:

	GROSS	NET
Percentage of Losses to Sailings	3.44	2.75
Percentages of Losses to Round Voyages ..	6.88	5.50
Percentage of Losses to ships on Registry employed in foreign trade	7.72	6.17

Admittedly, this is nothing more than an estimate, but it is probably not far from the truth.

Losses by marine risks were at least as numerous as losses by enemy action; but of these a far higher proportion was, almost certainly, incurred in the coasting and Irish trades. The risks covered, however, included also many cargoes in neutral ships, and in some instances the risks of seizure after cargoes had been landed at European ports. Moreover, the real test of the stability of the market was its ability to stand up, not to the average rate of risk, but to the accumulation of heavy losses at times of crisis. Of these, five were considered at

Lloyd's as occasions of peculiar anxiety. In 1794 all Dutch ships and cargoes in British ports were seized on the outbreak of war with Holland and the underwriters were compelled to meet very heavy claims under policies effected before the outbreak of war. In 1795 Richery captured thirty ships, mostly laden with silk, out of a convoy from the Levant. In 1797 a great number of American vessels, mostly insured in London, were seized and condemned in French and Spanish ports. In 1799 came the seizure of all British ships in Russian ports, and although they were subsequently released on the death of the Emperor Paul, a total loss had already been paid. Finally, in 1810, came the wholesale seizure of ships in Baltic ports.

Nevertheless, the evidence given before the Select Committee on Marine Insurance in 1810 shows conclusively that the strain was well met. There were, undoubtedly, a considerable number of failures, especially among speculative operators with no great experience who obtained business by under-cutting rates. Among the leading professional underwriters, who did the bulk of the business, the standard of stability was proved by the evidence of leading brokers to be very high. A typical experience was that of James Barnes who, during six years, had collected £280,000 in claims and lost only £300 in bad debts. Angerstein, during twenty-two years had recovered £490,000 for a single firm and lost only £1,100. Two other brokers who gave evidence relating to risks amounting to £11,000,000 or £12,000,000 had lost less than £1,600 between them. It is at least equally significant that, although sweeping allegations as to the prevalence of failures were made by the enemies of Lloyd's, they were in no one instance substantiated by figures, and witness after witness admitted under cross-examination that his own losses had been negligible.

Without adequate cover and a high level of security, the great expansion in trade and shipping that took place during the war would, indeed, hardly have been possible, and if the cost of insurance was high, so too were the profits of war-time trade. What that cost was has to be gathered mainly from the evidence of two or three underwriters' risks books that have happily been preserved. They show, as might be expected, very wide variations in the rate of premium as between trade and trade and very rapid fluctuations from time to time.

In 1805, for instance, Villeneuve's arrival in the West Indies sent up rates on homeward voyages from the Islands from an average of 8½ per cent. to 15 or 16 per cent. In the same year Baltic risks could be covered at three to five guineas. In 1808, with the Continental System in force, as much as 40 per cent. was paid on cargoes in neutral vessels bound to Baltic ports in French occupation; and the average rates varied from £11 in summer to £13 6s. 8d. in the winter months. In 1810, the *average* premiums received by Mr. George Hobson for Baltic and Scandinavian voyages were 21.5 per cent. out and 17.2 per cent. home. By 1814, with the liberation of the Continent, these averages had sunk to 3.55 per cent. and 4.7 per cent. respectively. From January to May, 1812, the homeward passage from Jamaica could be covered at an average of 6.8 per cent.; from June to December, with American frigates and privateers joining in the attack on British trade, the figures rose to 11.1 per cent.

It must be remembered that these figures include the normal premium for marine risks, which would seem to have varied from about one per cent. to two per cent. according to trade, and further that they were usually subject to agreed returns, sometimes amounting to one-third or even one-half of the total in respect of ships sailing with convoy and arriving safely.(¹) In the safer trades the premiums were comparatively low. Mr. Hobson's yearly averages show that voyages between London and Ireland would usually be covered at from 2½ per cent. to 3½ per cent., and coasting voyages at 1½ per cent. or less. For all risks accepted, coasting and foreign, his yearly averages from 1810 to 1814 work out at 7.0, 6.2, 6.6 and 6.76 and 5.37 per cent. respectively. So far as conclusions can be drawn from the fragmentary data available, it would seem that the prevailing rates of premium were adequate to the risks involved, but not extortionate, having regard to the uncertainty which attended the calculations of the ablest underwriters in those days of slow communications.

The supremacy of Lloyd's in the world of marine insurance and the inclusion among its active figures of so many of the leading men

---

(¹) The underwriters preferred this system of "Returns" to the quotation of differential rates for sailing with convoy because it gave them an advantage in respect of ships which were captured after parting company.

in commerce and finance were alone sufficient to give weight to the Committee's influence in maritime affairs; but this influence was incalculably increased by the peculiarly close and confidential relations between Lloyd's and the Admiralty. The goodwill which the Navy itself bore to the Subscribers—expressed with particular warmth by Nelson—arose mainly from the fact that "Lloyd's Coffee House" played the part of the Mansion House today in raising subscriptions for the relief of the wounded and the dependants of those killed in action. This culminated in the establishment of the Patriotic Fund in 1803.([1]) To the Admiralty, Lloyd's represented, first and foremost, a source of intelligence and an instrument for shipping control.

From the days of Edward Lloyd himself it had been the boast of Lloyd's Coffee House to provide its customers with early and accurate news of sailings, arrivals, marine casualties and naval or political developments affecting trade and shipping. This intelligence system was greatly and rapidly extended during the war, especially through the efforts of John Bennett, junior, both before and after his appointment as Secretary to the Committee in 1804. A digest of all such news as could properly be made public was posted up daily in the Coffee House and published twice a week in *Lloyd's List*. Confidential items were reserved for the books in the Subscribers' Rooms; but everything which could have political or naval importance was sent on at once to the Admiralty, who frequently received in this way the first news of political events abroad and of the movements of enemy warships as well as of British merchantmen.

The national value of this intelligence was even greater in those days of poor and slow communications than that of the similar services performed by Lloyd's today. Moreover, the necessity of marine insurance in foreign trade made Lloyd's, in the circumstances of the time, the best channel of communication between the Admiralty and the shipping community as a whole and the best means of

---

([1]) The Patriotic Fund was founded at a meeting of subscribers to Lloyd's, held on 20th July, 1803, and was intended "to animate our defenders by sea and land," and for "granting pecuniary rewards or honourable badges of distinction, for successful exertions of valour or merit."

bringing pressure to bear on owners or masters who disobeyed instructions.

From the outbreak of war all complaints by escort commanders of masters breaking convoy were sent on to Lloyd's for transmission to the owners, who seldom failed, under pressure from the Committee, to take appropriate action. The owners, for their part, frequently sent in complaints by shipmasters of negligence or tyrannical conduct on the part of officers commanding escorts, and these were duly forwarded to the Admiralty for investigation.[1] From the ship-masters themselves came letters of thanks for the protection provided, and requests for its extension.

As the war went on it became more and more an established practice for the Admiralty (and occasionally for Commanders-in-Chief on Foreign Stations) to consult the Committee on such questions as convoy regulations, ports of assembly and sailing dates, and for the Committee to volunteer suggestions on matters of trade defence. Notable instances were their successful protest in 1804 against the practice of despatching convoys with a single ship escort[2]; their influence in the establishment of coastal convoys in 1810 for the protection of ships falling out of, or sailing to join, the big convoys; and their co-operation in the working of the system of coast signals established in 1805 for the purpose of giving warning of enemy cruisers. Both the Minute Books at Lloyd's and the correspondence between Lloyd's and the Admiralty preserved at the Public Record Office[3] bear evidence of a close and continuous co-operation which was of incalculable value in the defence of British trade. Had some of its results been studied in time, they might have proved of as great value in 1914-18.

One further service performed by Lloyd's may be mentioned, for the light it throws on the difficulties of foreign trade during the later stages of the war. Under the Berlin and Milan Decrees, any neutral

---

[1] Complaints might also centre on the inadequacy of the naval escort, see pages 236, 237, Chapter X on the fate of H.M.S. *Wolverine* when on convoy duty with the Newfoundland Trade.

[2] Arising from the loss of the *Wolverine*. See James, *Naval History*, vol. III, pp. 255-6.

[3] Secretary's In-Letters, Letters from Lloyd's, Ad.1/3992.

ship guilty of trading with Great Britain became liable to seizure by French cruisers or by the port authorities in France and the countries dominated by France. At the request, therefore, of the Board of Trade and Plantations, it was arranged, in April, 1806, that while the destinations of such vessels continued to be correctly recorded in the confidential books, they were shown in *Lloyd's List*, which circulated on the Continent, as arriving at European or American ports.

Apart from its war activities, Lloyd's earned the gratitude of the seafaring community by the part which it took, from 1802 onwards, in the establishment of lifeboats round the British coasts. Its relations with the shipowners themselves were normally, but not uniformly, friendly.

In many respects the interests of shipowners and underwriters co-incided. The Committee of Lloyd's took part in promoting the Act of 1803 for preventing the wilful destruction of ships([1]); they defrayed, in certain instances, the expense incurred by shipowners in prosecutions for fraudulent stranding or scuttling; the Agents whom they began to appoint in 1811 at British and foreign ports were instructed to render British shipmasters every service in their power; a short code of signals for ships in distress, invented by a Mr. Bracken-bury, the Liverpool Agent, was approved by the Admiralty and the Trinity House in 1812. In 1808, when the West India Dock Company were endeavouring to obtain legislation to limit their liability, Lloyd's cordially supported the Shipowners' Society in their opposition.

It was another matter when it came to the question of the ship-owners' own liability. By the Acts in force at the beginning of the War, the liability of owners for goods embezzled by masters, or for damage due to acts of the master and crew without privity of the owners, was limited to the value of the ship and freight.([2]) In 1812-13, the Shipowners' Society sought to extend this limitation to all cases of collision or unseaworthiness. So far as collision was concerned, the Committee of Lloyd's were prepared to admit the justice of the claim. But they were utterly opposed to any limitation in cases of unseaworthiness and their opposition was successful.

([1]) 43 Geo. III, c. 113.   ([2]) 7 Geo. II, c. 15 ; 26 Geo. III, c. 86.

A more lasting cause of friction between underwriters and ship-owners was the question of classification of shipping. The Society of Underwriters formed in 1760 to publish a Register Book of Shipping had never been formally incorporated with Lloyd's, but its members were practically all subscribers to Lloyd's and the book was published entirely in the interest of insurers; so much so that access to its contents was jealously restricted to subscribers to the book or to Lloyd's. Like the Lloyd's Register of today, its importance lay in the symbols which denoted the classification of ships according to build and upkeep.

The trouble arose in 1797, with the adoption of new rules for classification which the shipowners declared to be unjust. They had two main complaints. As regards build, they maintained that the classification depended entirely on the place where the ship was built; and, in particular, that it gave an unfair preference to Thames-built ships. As regards upkeep, they complained that the classification depended solely on age, and that an old ship, however good her state of repair, was unfairly penalised in comparison with a more modern vessel which might be less carefully looked after.

These complaints may have been exaggerated, but there was point in them and when they failed to produce any effect, the leading ship-owners co-operated in promoting the publication of an opposition Register, which came out in 1798. Its success was such that Lloyd's found themselves obliged to admit the Society of the Shipowners' Register as a Subscriber to the Rooms; but the underwriters complained bitterly of its unreliability, alleging that its management sought popularity with the shipowners by lowering the standards of classification.

This competition between the "Green Book"—the Underwriters' Register, and the "Red Book"—the Shipowners' Register, went on until 1834, when the two societies were fused in the present Lloyd's Register. Its effects were wholly bad. Both Societies were carried on at a loss and, what was much more important, neither Register Book commanded general confidence, or was able to exert adequately that influence in favour of a high standard of safety for life and property at sea which was especially necessary at a time when the State did not concern itself with such matters.

It will be seen that the British shipping industry at this time was curiously compact of strength and weakness. On its purely business side it was vigorous and progressive, with a growing flexibility of technique. As regards the upkeep of the ships and the treatment of those who officered and manned them, its standards were low. Its organisation for dealing with questions affecting the industry as a whole was hardly more than embryonic, though this defect was in some part made good by the widespread influence of Lloyd's. With all its defects, it showed at least no lack of individual enterprise, and backed by a strong and now well-organised marine insurance market, it stood up well to the heaviest strain to which it had ever been subjected.

CHAPTER II

The Seaports

(i) LONDON ..	..	*C. Northcote Parkinson*
(ii) LIVERPOOL ..	..	*A. C. Wardle*
(iii) BRISTOL ..	..	*Professor C. M. MacInnes*

IN a work attempting to describe British Overseas Trade it would be absurd to omit all mention of the seaports on which that trade was based. It would be impracticable, on the other hand, to describe them all. Rather than reduce this chapter to a mere gazetteer, it has been thought best to deal with three of the ports—London Liverpool and Bristol—and ignore the remainder. Those chosen are not necessarily the first three in order of importance. It is clearly recognised, moreover, that Hull, Newcastle, Sunderland, Glasgow and Whitehaven—to name only a few—are fully as worthy of study. It must be remembered, however, that it is foreign trade with which we are concerned; and that, too, in time of war. Some harbours, important in themselves, were more often filled with coasters than with ocean-going ships. Without going into any detailed comparison of tonnage, it may be said that the three ports described are fairly representative of the period. Bristol typifies Eighteenth Century Commerce, firmly and prosperously established. Liverpool is the symbol of a new commerce which a growing industrialism was already beginning to create. London belongs to both past and future and is large enough to include elements of each.

The period with which we are dealing falls within the Canal Age. The four great river systems of England, the Thames, the Severn, the Mersey and the Humber, were being linked to each other largely in the way that Brindley had planned. The Severn had been connected with the Trent in 1772, the Trent with the Mersey in 1777, and the Thames with the rest in 1805. The result was that the Industrial Midlands were given a choice of outlet, the subsequent growth of seaports depending largely on the direction in which the exports tended to flow. For a number of reasons, Liverpool exerted a stronger attraction than Bristol or Hull, a stronger pull, even, in some respects,

D

than London. The early construction of the Mersey Docks at once symbolised and hastened a process which mainly geographical factors had already begun. The immediate future lay increasingly with Liverpool and Clydeside. But it must not be assumed that the other seaports were, for that reason, on the decline. Bristol certainly was not: its growth was merely on an Eighteenth Century scale. Hull was growing, too, but was on the wrong side of England for the oceanic trades and well-placed only for the trades which the war tended to interrupt.

From the point of view of the seaports, the main feature of this period is the enormous increase in the tonnage to be handled. Ships were tending to increase a little in size, but far more were they increasing in number. Many of the old ports, even where not dependent—as in Devon or East Anglia—on declining or vanished industries, were simply too small for the needs of the day. With vessels still relatively small, the problem was, in the first place, one of area: the problem of depth came later. This was a period, therefore, in which the growing seaports were primarily intent on increasing their harbour capacity. On their success in this much of their future development would depend.

I. The Port of London

LONDON was, throughout our period, the most important harbour in the British Isles. The tonnage of shipping entering the river had more than doubled since 1750, with the result that, by 1794, the number of voyages made from London numbered nearly 14,000 a year. Coasting voyages accounted, admittedly, for more than 10,000 of these entries, but a total of 3,663 foreign voyages, including 2,219 by British vessels, was far beyond what any other Port could boast. It was greater, in fact, than London could accommodate. The vessels, especially the coasters, would not all be in the river at the same time. Even so, in summer, when the ships in foreign trade were in, the congestion was appalling. At a busy period between May and October the shipping in the river might include:

  (a) About 433 West Indiamen of 200-500 tons, bringing 122,000 hogs-
      heads of sugar.

(*b*) Some 428 Timber Ships, of which 250 would discharge their cargo into the river and take up twelve times their own mooring space.

(*c*) Over 300 Colliers, out of an existing total of 431; each one surrounded, on an average, by 13 barges.

(*d*) Over 50 East Indiamen, mostly below Deptford, and

(*e*) About 3,500 barges, lighters, hoys and punts; 500 being for timber and 1,180 for coal.

The above list, which ignores all but the largest trades, gives only a faint idea of the problem. Traders to Prussia, Holland, Ireland, Hamburg, Russia, Portugal, and the United States might all be there, with coasters bound for anywhere between Sunderland and Greenock. For this mass of shipping, when our period begins, the mooring space consisted of the Pool of London (Upper, Middle and Lower), extending from London Bridge down to Horseferry Tier; Limehouse Reach and Deptford Reach. In practice, however, the lower Reaches were used only by East Indiamen and by ships under repair. Vessels that were loading and unloading crowded into the Pool so as to be near London, with resulting confusion, collisions, delays and damage. The only wet docks in the river were the Brunswick Dock at Blackwall and the Greenland Dock at Rotherhithe. The former belonged to Perry the Shipbuilder and was used only by East Indiamen. The latter, Howland's Dock, had been dug between 1696 and 1700, and had been used by the South Sea Company's Whalers. Neither of these docks could appreciably relieve the congestion in the river.

As inadequate as the mooring space was the quayside accommodation. The Legal Quays, as they were called, had been defined in an Act of 1558. They numbered twenty; seven between London Bridge and Billingsgate, eight between there and the Custom House, and five (including the Custom House Quay itself) from there to Tower Dock. All imports subject to Duty, except those of the East India Company, were supposed to be unloaded at one or other of these. In practice, the goods on which lighter duties were payable were allowed "on sufferance" to be landed at what were called the Sufferance Wharfs. All but five of these were on the Surrey side—several round St. Saviour's Dock(1)—and were to that extent inaccessible

---

(1) "Dock" in eighteenth century terminology normally means dry dock—a dock drying out at the ebb. These were unsuitable for laden vessels over a certain size.

from the City. Numbering only twenty-one in all, they did not wholly solve the problem. There were inevitable delays in unloading cargo; delays which, in turn, added to the congestion.

The situation was well summarised by Mr. Graeme Spence, Maritime Surveyor to the Admiralty:

> ... when full of Shipping ... [London] ... is infinitely the noblest and largest Port in Britain; yet for want of sufficient Room, it is perhaps as inconvenient a one as any in it; nay the Confusion is greater than in any Port I ever saw, for it is often so crowded between the Tower and Lime-house that a Wherry sometimes is scarce able to pass with Safety between the Tiers, much less a Vessel. At such times, the Damage which Vessels do to each other ... is extremely hurtful to them and injurious to Property. [1].

Resulting partly from the practice of unloading goods into barges and lighters and partly from the length of time which might elapse before goods were unloaded at all, there had grown up an astonishing system of pillage. A swarm of water thieves, sub-divided and specialised, raided the ships and lighters by day and night. The total population officially employed in the Port of London numbered, it was thought, 120,000; and of these a fair percentage were known to be in league with the thieves. Others among those employed in unloading—"a Description of Persons called Lumpers"—were themselves guilty of pilfering. Mates, watchmen and Revenue Officers were often bribed, and the river swarmed with gangs of Night Plunderers, Light Horsemen, Mudlarks and Scuffle-Hunters. Ten to eleven thousand people, it was estimated, [2] took part in or connived at this system of pillage. Sugar, rum and coffee being among the chief objects of plunder, it was the West India Merchants who suffered most. It was through their support, therefore, that the River Police came into existence in 1798. But the effects of the River Police were confined to the one trade, or to such shipowners in that trade who would avail themselves of the protection offered. The evils of plunder and pillage were only partly checked in 1798, and before that date they were widespread and notorious.

The movement to provide the London River with wet docks owed its origin, partly, to the lack of mooring space near London; partly to

---

[1] Evidence given before the Parliamentary Committee of 1796. See also Plate 2, which shows the congestion still to be seen in 1803.

[2] Colquhoun. *Treatise on the Commerce and Police of the River Thames*, 1800. The loss amounted to £350,000 a year, or more.

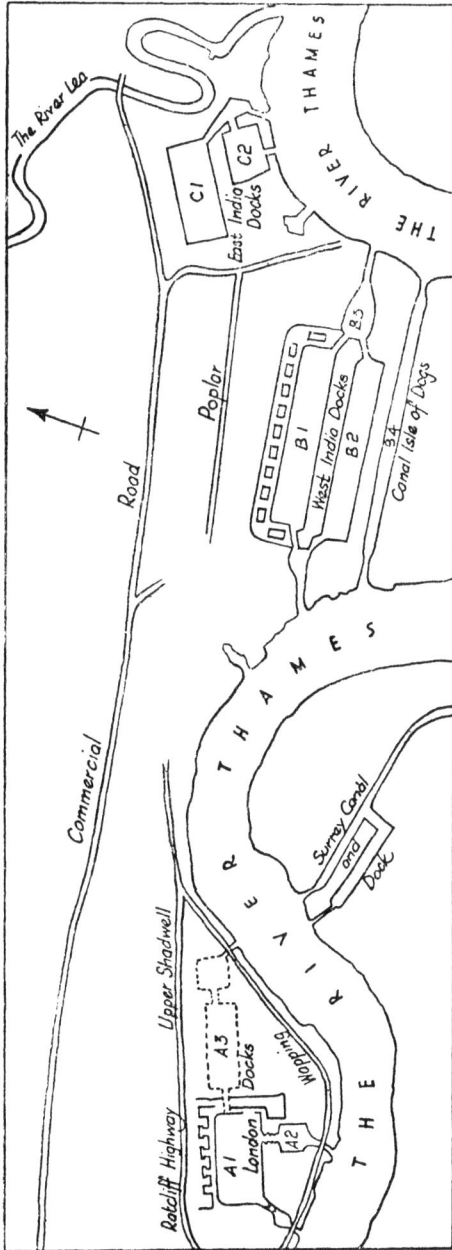

PLATE 3. Plan of the Docks at London, 1808

the pillage to which cargoes were exposed. It also owed something
to the example of Liverpool, where wet docks had already proved a
success. Agitation, which had begun before the war, resulted in the
appointment of a Parliamentary Committee "to enquire into the best
Mode of providing sufficient Accommodation for the increased
Trade and Shipping of the Port of London." The Committee, of
which Pitt himself was a member, reported in 1796. They had discussed eight different plans for improving the Port, together with the
objections raised to some of them in petitions to the House. No
positive recommendations were made but some of the plans were
declared, on the evidence received, to be inadvisable. These projects
fell into two categories: those proposed by commercial groups—the
City of London, the Merchants and the Inhabitants of Southwark—
and those put forward by individual engineers. It was the former
which had the more serious consideration. The most interesting
proposals, however, came from an individual, Mr. Reveley, the
architect. He had three alternative schemes, the most ambitious of
which involved diverting the river into a straight channel and leaving
the existing bends or loops to form the docks on either side.(¹) "The
Principle of these Plans" it was admitted "is novel, grand and capti-
vating." It was a principle which failed to captivate the Elder
Brethren of Trinity House. With some relief, the Committee turned
to less frightening proposals. The Merchants wanted a dock at
Wapping, as near to the City as possible, but connected by a canal
with Blackwall. The Corporation of the City of London wanted
docks in the Isle of Dogs, opening into the river at either end and
especially suited for the Colliers, on which London relied for its 300
cargoes a month. The Inhabitants of Southwark wanted a new dock
at Rotherhithe. No one plan, as we have seen, was chosen by the
Committee; the apparent result being that all three plans were
proceeded with, providing London with as much dock space as it
would need for the next half century.

The West India Merchants, who perhaps stood most to gain from
dock construction, had made no proposal to the Committee of 1796.
It was they, nevertheless, who now took the lead, acting on a plan

---

(¹) See Plate 4.

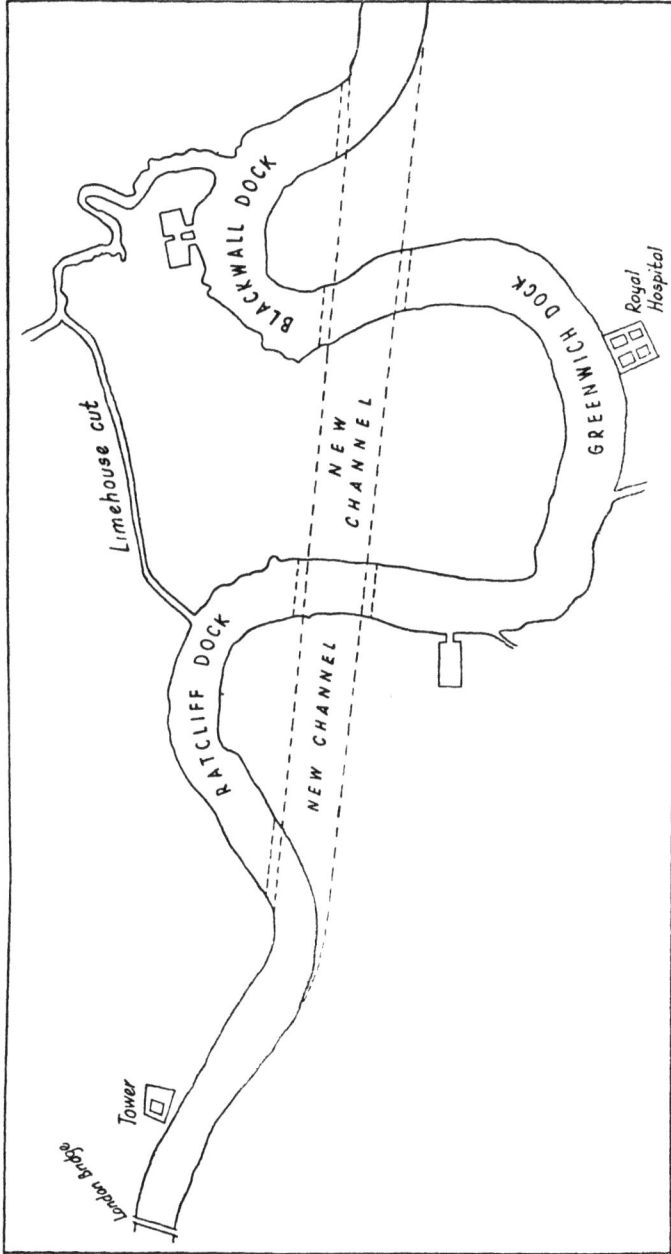

PLATE 4. Proposed Diversion of the Thames

resembling that put forward by Mr. Wyatt. The West India Dock Company was formed by Act of Parliament in 1799 and work was begun in the following year. With a capital of £1,380,000, the Company excavated an area of 295 acres in the Isle of Dogs, making accommodation for 600 vessels of 250–500 tons. The docks, with their adjoining warehouses, were surrounded by a wall and ditch. There was a guard-house at the gate and a system by which eight sentries (soldiers) would each sound a bell at intervals to prove their vigilance. The West India Docks were opened by Mr. William Pitt in 1802. The Corporation of the City of London, meanwhile, adhering to its own plan but moving in a more stately fashion, dug a canal across the Isle of Dogs to the South of where the West India Dock Company was at work. The original intention was to encourage ships to use this as a short cut and so avoid the river's detour round by Greenwich. No such result was achieved, but the canal, completed in 1806, proved useful. It came to be called the South-West India Dock and was ultimately taken over by the West India Dock Company itself.

Simultaneously, as from 1800, the Merchants' Plan (but without the proposed canal to Blackwall) was being carried out at Wapping. This was a built-up area and the project, although relatively small from an engineering point of view, was disproportionately costly. A capital of £3,238,310 was raised, mostly to be spent in the purchase and destruction of the 1,300 houses which covered the site. A further £700,000 had to be subscribed before the docks were opened in 1805. The London Docks, as they were called, were intended for the more valuable imports—wine, brandy and tobacco. They included vast warehouses and one of these, for storing tobacco, covered as much as five acres. St. Katherine's Dock, even nearer the City, and intended for even more specialised cargoes, such as indigo, tortoiseshell, marble and scent, was not completed until 1828. It forms, nevertheless, a part of the same attempt to bring the costliest goods—and not merely the smallest vessels—within easy reach of the Exchange.

One advantage of wet docks is that they enable a system of bonded warehouses to grow up; a system by which import duties are paid when the goods are sold, not when they are landed. Such a scheme—for the promotion of which Sir Robert Walpole was almost driven from power by merchants who had discovered how to avoid paying duties at all—was introduced in 1803 (43 Geo. III, c. 132) while many of the docks were still being built. The one interest which it did not affect was that of the East India Company, which already enjoyed that privilege at its warehouses in the City. The East India Ship-owners, however, had also been subject to pillage in a certain degree, and they launched a modest scheme of their own. Their task was simplified for them by the existence of Perry's Dock, which they proposed to incorporate, and the Company's warehouses, which they did not mean to supersede. With a capital of £500,000, they began work in 1803 and had completed the docks by 1806. The main peculiarities of the East India Docks, apart from the absence of ware-houses, lay in their depth of water (23 feet) and in their distance from London (4¾ miles). But the distance was, of course, something to which the East India Company was accustomed. Their ships were mostly too large and too deeply laden to come any further up the river. For the rest, the docks were well defended and the goods landed there went on to London in closed and locked waggons.

South of the river the Southwark investors divided their energies between the Surrey Canal Co. and the old Greenland Dock. The latter was acquired and extended by the Commercial Dock Co., formed for the purpose in 1807. These docks were intended primarily for timber and grain. They were not united with the Canal Company, to form the Surrey Commercial Dock Company, until 1864.

From the foregoing accounts it will be seen that the period 1800–1815 was one of enormous activity in port improvement. And if Liverpool led the way, and if Hull and Bristol were not far behind, London's achievement was not unworthy of its commercial supremacy. Without perhaps consciously planning for a future expansion, the Londoners did, in fact, provide themselves with a system of docks which needed little improvement until after 1850. In 1793 the Port of London was a length of tidal river, packed tight with shipping, a scene of continual groundings and collisions and a battlefield on which honest men fought a losing battle against piracy and pillage. By 1815 the docks had been built. The shipping had quitted the river and no longer needed to unload into barges. Ships no longer stranded in the mud or settled, with the ebb, on top of their own anchor flukes. The river was patrolled by constables and the docks watched by sentries. The thieves had turned to some other business and the Port of London had been reduced to order.

II. Liverpool

ALTHOUGH Lord Erskine, visiting Liverpool in 1792, indulged in hyperbolical compliment when he said that the town was "fit to be a proud capital for any empire in the world," there was then no doubt as to its firm status as a thriving and progressive mercantile community. Its 8,000 houses held a population of 80,000, mostly engaged in vocations concerned with overseas trade.

As pioneer of the wet dock system (the first Liverpool dock was completed in 1715), the port boasted a number of docks, each well equipped to provide modern services such as few of the older sea-trading centres could offer. In addition, there was the extensive canal system of South Lancashire, which afforded a cheaper mode of inland transport for coal and Manchester goods than did the indifferent roads of the period. Merchandize was thus delivered alongside or on board the export ships in the Mersey at more economical freights than elsewhere—a factor which had much to do with Liverpool's mercantile development in the eighteenth century.

At the outbreak of the French War, the merchants of Liverpool owned 572 vessels totalling 90,004 tons, manned by about 10,000 seamen, and in that year more than 4,000 vessels, equal to 400,000 tons, entered and cleared from the port. More than a hundred of the Liverpool-owned ships were employed in the slave trade, i.e., the triangular voyage which began with the freightage of English manu-factures to the west coast of Africa, there to be exchanged for a ship-load of African negroes. This cargo was freighted across the Atlantic to the West Indian islands or Demerara, and there sold in exchange for a cargo of sugar, rum, molasses or cotton, which was brought back to the Mersey. It was a threefold transaction which proved most lucrative to the Liverpool, Manchester and Birmingham capitalists concerned.[1] In 1793 Liverpool's foreign trade, in order of tonnage, was with the following countries: British West Indies, Russia, Prussia and Poland, Africa, United States, Denmark and

---

[1] See Chapter VIII, page 164, and Chapter XI, pages 258, 259.

Norway, the Mediterranean, and the British and Greenland fisheries. In addition, there were 2,300 clearances for Ireland, and a substantial coasting trade with other parts of the British Isles.

There was no direct trading with the East Indies until after 1813, but Liverpool enjoyed quite an importation of goods from the Far East, brought round by coasters from the Thames. There was an excellent warehousing system, which was expanded in 1805, when the town was made a warehousing port.([1]) It was not until 1814 that Liverpool merchants were allowed to engage directly in the Far Eastern trade. In that year the ship *Kingsmill*, 516 tons, owned by John Gladstone (father of the statesman), was despatched, and she was soon followed by other vessels from the Mersey.

Few Liverpool-built ships of those days exceeded 500 tons, but the whole fleet of the port gave ample employment to ship-carpenters, sailmakers and the other vocations ancillary to shipbuilding and ship-owning. Local shipbuilding and fitting-out was extensive, and during the period under review the number of shipwrights on Merseyside doubled itself, such was the war demand for tonnage and repair. It is curious that no ships were built at Liverpool for the Royal Navy during the wars of 1793-1815, although quite a number of the King's ships had been built there during the fifty previous years. Several fine vessels of 600 and 800 tons, however, were constructed for the East India Company. In 1793, a large number of Liverpool vessels were commissioned as privateers, and their manning, outfit, and main-tenance gave substantial employment to local craftsmen and seamen.([2])

Despite the hazards of war and the impressment of seamen, the trade of the port was well maintained.([3]) The principal local industries were shipbuilding, rope-making, sugar-refining, salt-making, pottery, watchmaking, and the loading of bulk cargoes (such as coal) brought down by canal. Liverpool also had a good trade in naval stores—a trade which began in the late seventeenth century—and always held large stocks of tar, hemp, turpentine, iron and timber, imported from the American plantations and from the Baltic States.

([1]) Under the Act of 1803. See page 56.

([2]) See Gomer Williams' *Liverpool Privateers*.

([3]) For a typical year, see Appendix to this Chapter, page 63.

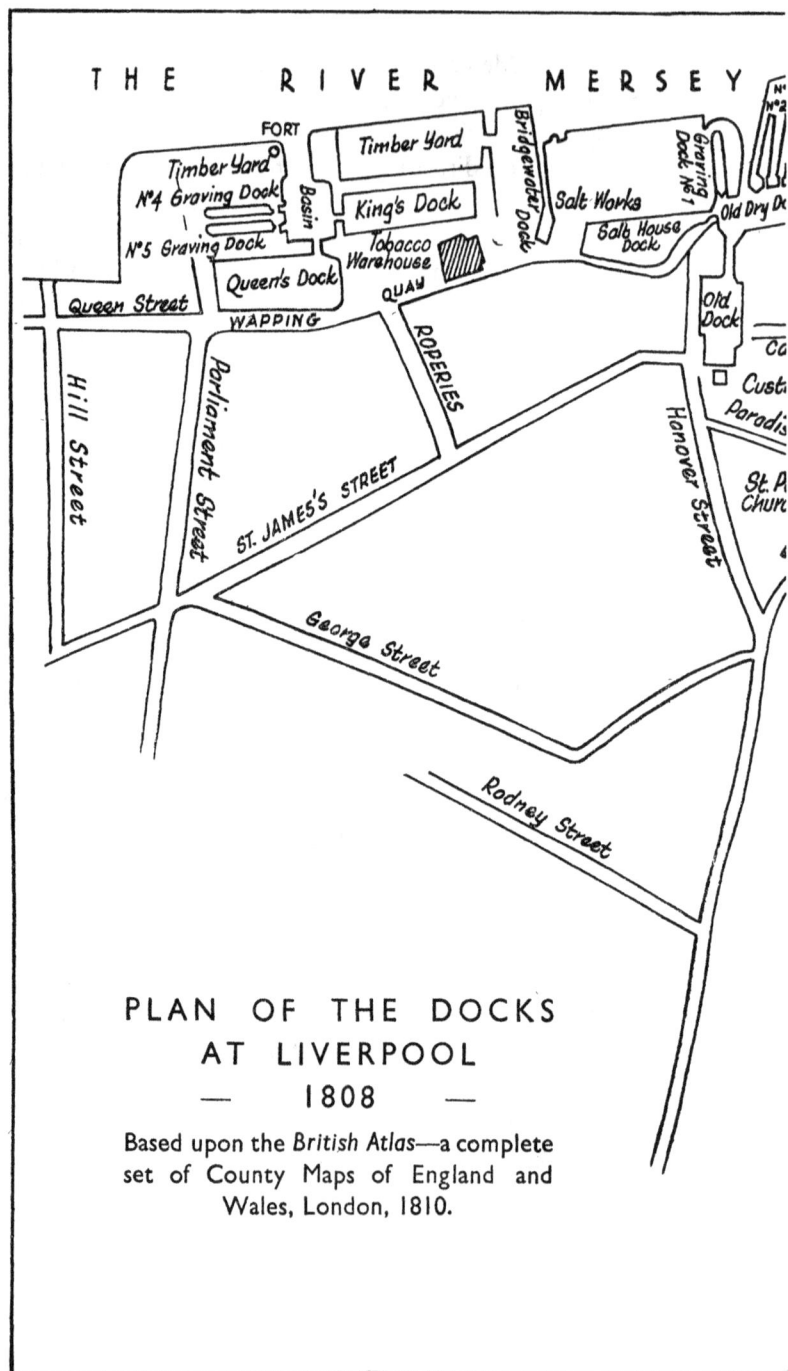

THE   RIVER   MERSEY

FORT
Timber Yard
Nº4 Graving Dock
Nº5 Graving Dock
Timber Yard
Basin
King's Dock
Tobacco Warehouse
QUAY
Queen's Dock
Queen Street
WAPPING
Bridgewater Dock
Salt Works
Salt House Dock
Graving Dock Nº1
Old Dry Do
Old Dock
Nº
Nº2

Hill Street
Parliament Street
ST. JAMES'S STREET
ROPERIES
Hanover Street
George Street
Rodney Street

Cust
Paradi
St. P
Chur

PLAN OF THE DOCKS
AT LIVERPOOL
—   1808   —

Based upon the *British Atlas*—a complete
set of County Maps of England and
Wales, London, 1810.

PLATE 5.

60

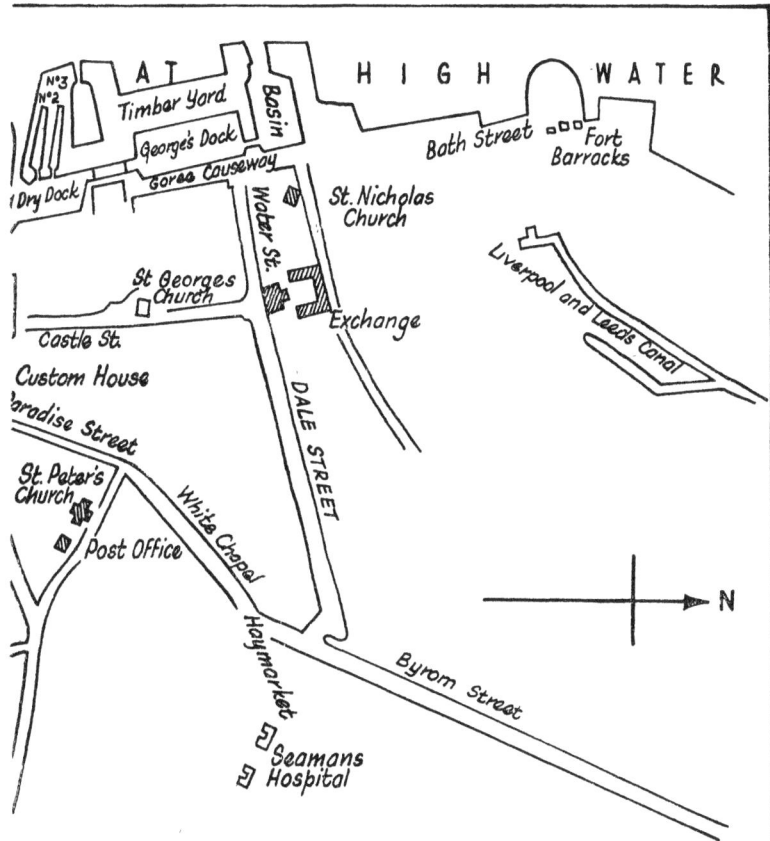

AT   H I G H   W A T E R

Nº3
Nº2
Timber Yard
George's Dock
Basin
Dry Dock
Gores Causeway
Bath Street
Fort
Barracks
St. Nicholas
Church
Water St.
St Georges
Church
Castle St.
Exchange
Liverpool and Leeds Canal
Custom House
Paradise Street
St. Peter's
Church
White Chapel
DALE STREET
Post Office
Haymarket
Byrom Street
N
Seamans
Hospital

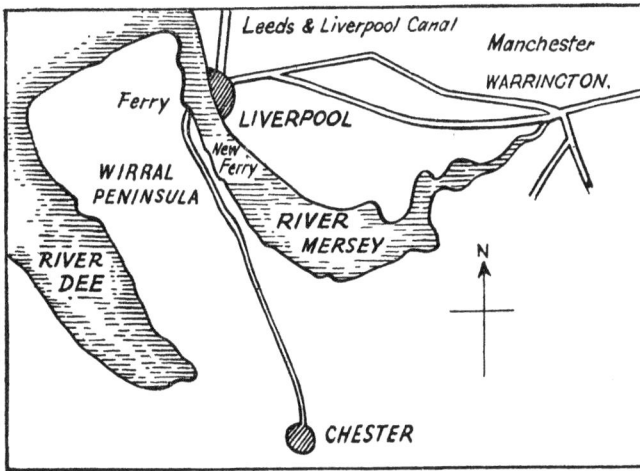

Leeds & Liverpool Canal
Manchester
WARRINGTON.
Ferry
LIVERPOOL
New
Ferry
WIRRAL
PENINSULA
RIVER
MERSEY
RIVER
DEE
N
CHESTER

The volume of trade fluctuated considerably during the war years. Despite smuggling, the Continental blockade brought about a great shrinkage in trade, which by 1807 had declined by 25 per cent., causing serious distress among the poorer classes in Liverpool. Outbreak of war with America also proved disastrous. The number of ships entering the Mersey sank from 6,729 in 1810, to 4,599 in 1812. These diminutions of local commerce did not, however, affect the determination and loyalty of the citizens. The American trade soon rehabilitated itself on peace being made with that country, and the tonnage entering the Mersey port had, by 1814, risen by 25 per cent.;([1]) while Liverpool-owned tonnage reached, by 1800, a total of 796 ships of 140,632 aggregate tons. In 1798, the slave trade—in spite of war conditions—reached its peak, 149 Liverpool ships carrying 52,557 slaves across the Atlantic. This trade, however, was abolished in May, 1807.

The value of the dock estate, in 1800, was about £24,000, while the dock revenue increased from £28,365 in 1801, to £59,741 in 1814. An indication of the values and variety of the colonial and foreign produce handled at Liverpool during the war years may be gained from the fact that when the Goree warehouses there were burnt down in 1802, their contents comprised sugar, coffee, cotton, grain, spices, hemp and other goods to the value of £300,000. It is interesting to note, moreover, that the insurance risk on this produce was carried by the merchants themselves.

The naval defence of the port consisted primarily of the guardship, H.M.S. *Princess*, but there was plenty of local man-power to call upon in case of need. As in 1715 and 1745, and in subsequent years, they raised volunteer battalions of infantry, the merchants equipping and arming these units largely at their own expense. The shore defences were strengthened, and their guns manned by seamen from the merchant ships in port. In 1804, no less than 180 officers and 3,686 men paraded as volunteers, including a complete artillery corps comprised of the boatmen of the Mersey. In addition, a unit of regular troops was raised and equipped by one wealthy local merchant at his own expense. The whole male population of the town

---

([1]) See Chapter IX, pages 205 and 226.

| | INWARDS | | | | | | OUTWARDS | | | | | |
| | BRITISH | | | FOREIGN | | | BRITISH | | | FOREIGN | | |
	Ships	Tons	Men	Ships	Tons	Men	Ships	Tons	Men	Ships	Tons	Men
Africa	7	940	90	1	116	11	105	25,459	3,461	7	1,812	209
America, viz., British Colonies	39	8,195	411	305	78,024	3,562	143	22,632	1,407	309	77,066	3,674
United States	36	8,717	629	2	307	16	23	6,166	294	1	168	8
Azores	2	207	10	11	2,379	110						
Batavian Republic												
British Fishery	12	515	49									
Denmark	2	246	13	4	475	31	40	9,461	429	46	8,090	384
Caracas				1	250	14						
Germany	8	1186	62	14	1,685	102	17	3,806	179	31	5,554	246
Gibraltar	2	276	15				5	539	42			
Greenland	5	1,596	247									
Guernsey	2	158	10				4	551	29			
Honduras	2	545	26									
Jersey	2	219	15				2	153	9			
Ireland	711	67,777	3,685				1,041	38,670	4,896			
Isle of Man	59	2,266	161				93	5,007	348			
Italy	1	128	8	8	1,163	70	1	128	9	3	444	29
Iceland										2	431	21
Isles of France				1	212	17						
Madeira	5	683	103	1	224	11	3	573	99	2	237	16
Malta							4	480	33			
Norway	6	647	37	10	2,144	111	6	830	45	15	3,156	160
Portugal	70	10,980	630	13	1,368	91	16	2,832	166	13	2,113	119
Prussia	42	9,702	442	144	41,062	1,694	10	2,526	123	119	37,748	1,399
Russia	76	18,437	880	1	300	18	101	22,794	1,088	11	3,635	126
Sicily	4	644	38	8	1,534	83	3	392	26	3	461	27
Spain				10	1,634	93				17	3,546	165
Sweden	1	158	9	13	2,504	149	1	158	8	31	4,235	230
South Whale Fishery							1	180	35			
Vera Cruz				2	342	26						
British West Indies	217	56,691	4,244				118	34,798	2,700			
Foreign West Indies	15	3,716	303	2	587	25	1	200	12	1	147	9
	1,304	194,629	12,123	551	136,510	6,234	1,738	228,335	15,438	611	148,840	6,822

was registered, and those between the ages of 16 and 60 held liable to be called out in case of need.

Liverpool was never, in fact, seriously threatened. Enemy ships, French and American, often entered the Irish sea and occasionally intercepted Liverpool ships before they had joined or after they had parted from their convoy, but the "Liverpool-man" could generally give a good account of himself. Except when the French landed at Fishguard, there was never much cause for alarm. The overseas trade continued, and on the resumption of normal business activities at the close of the war, it was found that the trade of the port, as reflected by the dock dues and the number of vessels using the Mersey, had almost trebled itself.

III. The Port of Bristol

At the end of the eighteenth century Bristol was a town of about 100,000 inhabitants, drawing on a wide area for her exports and despatching the goods which were landed on her quays to almost every part of the country. Down the Severn there came to her trows and small vessels laden with the products of Gloucestershire and the western midlands. Coastal vessels brought to her quays manufactured goods and other produce from the West country and from Wales. Her merchants, such, for example, as John Pinney, had business connections, not only with the West of England but with London, the Midlands and places as distant as Glasgow, whence they purchased salt herrings for the use of the slaves in the Sugar Islands. Besides her sea-borne and river-borne traffic, Bristol carried on a flourishing import and export trade by road transport with inland districts. John Pinney, for example, sent his clerk to Bridgwater Fair each year to do business with the Somerset clothiers, and he frequently purchased cloth from such places as Kilve and Wiveliscombe for export to the West Indies. As road transport was still slow and expensive, it is not surprising that the people of Bristol showed a keen interest in canal projects and in the work of Macadam.

The industries of the city were as varied as its imports and exports, though they tended to be specialised in the direction of the plantation trade and the building and maintenance of ships. Great quantities of brass were produced at Baptist Mills. This was either drawn into wire or formed into battery, as it was called, for use in the Guinea trade. Glass-making, however, was perhaps the chief manufacture carried on in the city at that time.

> The great demand for glass bottles for the Bristol Water, for the exportation of beer, cider and perry; for wine, and for the use of Town and Country, keep the various bottle glass-houses here constantly at work. The call for window glass at home, at Bath and in the Towns about Bristol; in the Western Counties, Wales, and from North to South wherever Bristol Trade extends, and the great quantities sent to America, employ several houses for this article. Here are likewise two houses, in which are made white or flint glass, and phial bottles.[1]

The Bristol Sugar Refineries were, of course, famous,[2] and it was natural that a distilling industry should have grown up alongside them. Bristol spirits were in great demand both for home consumption and for export to Africa, and, under this one item, Bristol each year paid thousands of pounds in excise. From the middle of the seventeenth century a great tobacco manufacturing industry had existed in Bristol. During the French Wars this was in a flourishing condition. Soap had also been made in the city since the sixteenth century, and there were iron foundries and lead works. Cloth, silk, lace, sail-cloth, toys and earthenware completed the list of manufactures.

The chief imports came from Newfoundland, Virginia and the West Indies, though other sources were substantial, and the export trade was as extensive. Newfoundland, Quebec, Nova Scotia, New York, Maryland, Virginia, the Carolinas and Florida received goods from Bristol, which were later disseminated throughout the vast continent of North America in return for fish, timber, furs, deerskins, indigo, logwood, tar, cotton and rice. From the West Indies, in

---

[1] *Matthews's New History of Bristol, or Complete Guide and Bristol Directory for the Year* 1793-4, p. 40.

[2] See Shiercliff, *The Bristol and Hotwell Guide*, 1793, p. 18.

E

addition to sugar, came molasses, rum, cotton, dyewoods and mahogany. Until interrupted by the war and Napoleon's Continental policy, Bristol also carried on a considerable trade with Holland, Hamburg and Scandinavia. Russia sent her deals and the Mediterranean countries their fruit, wine and oil in return for English cargoes from Bristol. Each year numbers of vessels belonging to other British ports, as well as many foreigners, entered the Avon, and it was said that the port itself owned 300 sail which were engaged in the colonial and foreign trade.(¹) One of the most important branches of the city's commerce, as it was one of the oldest, was the traffic with Ireland; indeed, in European trade, it came only second to that of the Iberian Peninsula. The long period of war affected the trade of the city grievously, and this in turn gave still further impetus to a tendency, already well-marked, which impelled the merchants of Bristol to concentrate their attention on the West Indian trade. Nevertheless, in 1814, Bristol imported from the Iberian Peninsula some 4,000 bags of Spanish wool,(²) and as soon as the war was over the European trade began to shew signs of recovery, as did also the temporarily interrupted trade with the United States.

Though the commerce of the city was thus widely extended, it is still a fact that it had become perilously specialised, for it was to a very large extent confined to the West Indies. From Bristol there went to the Islands, as the papers of such men as John Pinney show, every conceivable article of wearing apparel, together with household furniture, food for masters and slaves, plantation implements, building materials, weapons, ammunition, Hotwell water and quantities of bottled liquors and wines.

The following figures illustrate the state of the trade of Bristol in 1801 and 1815, but unfortunately no records remain of the tonnage represented in the various branches. It was usual for those engaged in the Newfoundland Fisheries and in the Guinea Trade to prefer relatively small vessels, while the West Indiamen were relatively large.(²)

(¹) Shiercliff, op. cit., p. 14.   (²) Evans, *The Picture of Bristol*, p. 76.
(²) See Chap. VIII, p. 180.

PORT OF BRISTOL

SHIPS IN AND OUT, 1801 AND 1815[1]

	SHIPS IN		SHIPS OUT	
	1801	1815	1801	1815
Channel Isles	17	8	20	16
Europe	93	190	38	86
Ireland..	116	154	109	122
Isle of Man	2	—	5	—
West Indies	70(²)	54	73	53
North America	85	34	63	76
Africa	2	—	6	—
Southern Whale Fishery ..	1	—	—	—
TOTAL	386	440	314	353

One of the oldest, as it was one of the most important of the city's industries was ship-building. In the period covered by this book, 43 vessels left the stocks on the Avon. Of these, many were small craft. But the number included ships such as the *St. Vincent*, launched in 1804 and described as the largest West Indiaman which up to that time had appeared in the port. She registered 493 tons. But the *Nelson*, launched three years later, was spoken of as the largest vessel that had so far been built in Bristol, and was "a monstrous three-decked vessel of 600 tons."[3] The ships built included privateers, and Powell enumerates sixty-three such vessels belonging to the port between 1793 and 1815. By far the best-known and largest of the shipbuilders was J. M. Hillhouse, Son & Co., but there were other well-established shipyards, such as that of Sydenham Teast, near Canon's Marsh; Nicholas Blanning, at Redcliff, and William Blanning, at Wapping.

In Bristol the merchants were frequently shipowners and planters as well. Thus, for example, John Pinney, who owned large estates in Nevis and later set up as a West India merchant, ordered a ship, the

---

(1) *Bristol Imports and Exports.*

(2) Of these, two were from "Africa and Demerara."

(3) Powell, J. W. Damer, *Bristol Privateers and Ships of War*, p. 317.

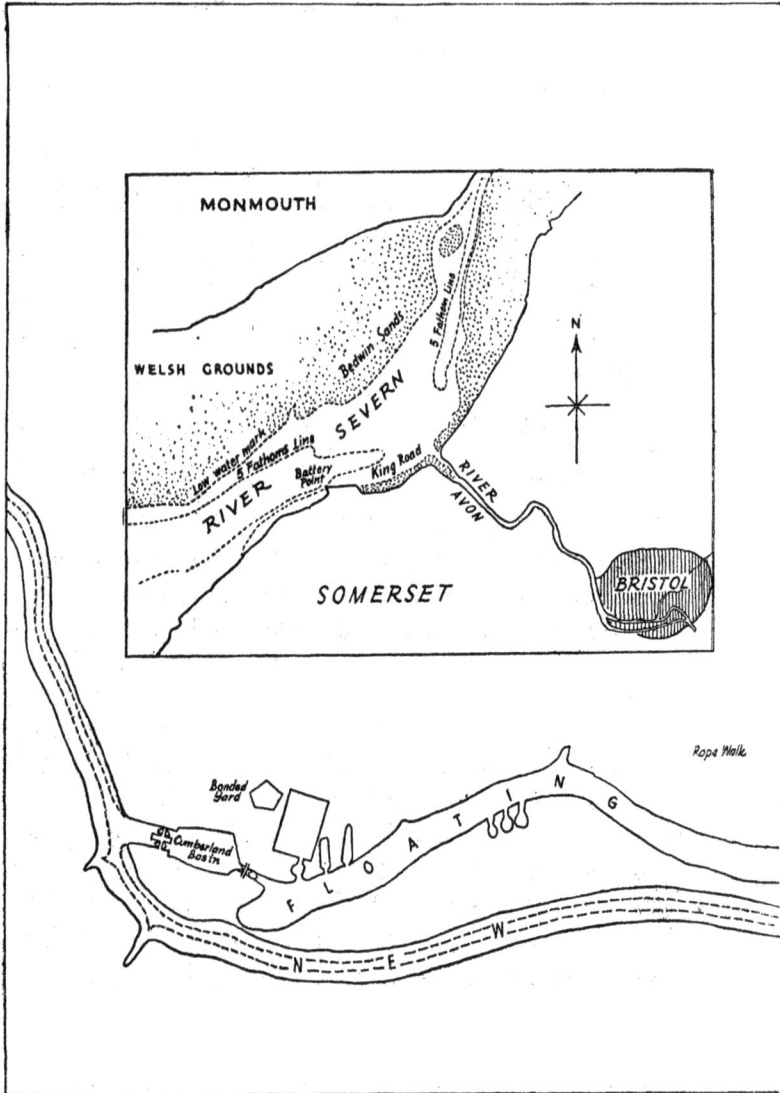

PLATE 6.

THE CITY AND SUBURBS
OF BRISTOL
— 1825 —

Based upon Mathews' new and correct
plan.

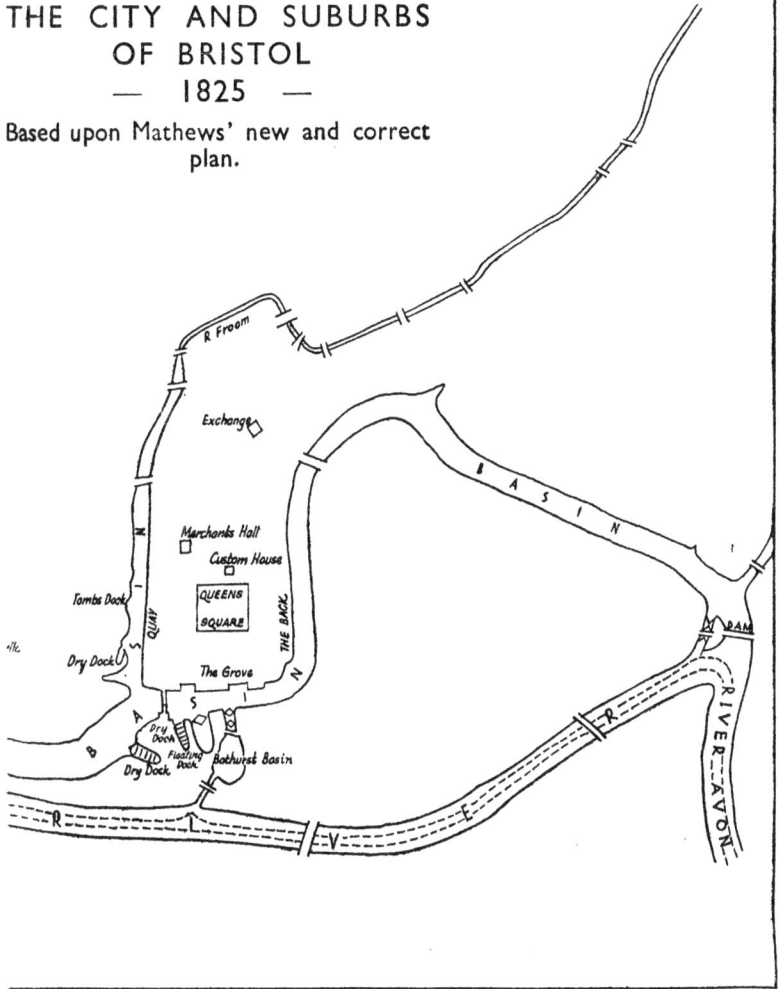

R Froom

Exchange

BASIN

Merchants Hall

Custom House

Tombs Dock

QUAY

QUEENS
SQUARE

THE BACK

Dry Dock

The Grove

DAM

RIVER—AVON

Dry Dock

Floating Dock

Dry Dock

Bathurst Basin

FR

R—————V—————E———L

Nevis, to be built as soon as he was established. Later on he and his partner also owned the *King David*. It thus came about that in Bristol there was not as much specialisation in the different branches of the shipping industry as existed in London. In his letters, Pinney frequently stresses this point and beseeches his correspondents in Nevis and elsewhere not to forget that, unlike the merchants of London, who very often had no interest in ships,[1] the merchants of Bristol usually owned those that carried their goods. His letters show, incidentally, more than a trace of that enmity between London and the Outports which had been so acute in previous centuries. Bristol men could not forget that their city had recently been the second in the kingdom.

Besides the machinations of wicked Londoners and the catastrophic falls in sugar prices, the Bristol merchants were troubled by a strike among the working shipwrights in 1794. These showed "dangerous revolutionary tendencies."[2] Later in the war there was similar trouble with the mudheavers—a most important group—and also with the merchant seamen themselves and their officers, all wanting some increase in pay. The merchants' other worries included the commandeering of their ships as transports and the dangers resulting from the press-gang, at the approach of which ships were often deserted. And then there was convoy. Pinney and his brethren were for ever moaning about delays, the incapacity of naval officers and the horrible waste of money consequential upon being held up for weeks is such places as Cork Cove. Though the merchants were anxious to show they did not wish to subordinate public to private interest, they contrived to convince themselves that in furthering their own commercial ends they were acting in response to the dictates of the finest patriotism.

When such matters were not under discussion, the wicked intentions of the Government with respect to the Slave Trade could always be counted upon to provide abundant material for dissatisfaction. After all, these men were true Britons, and as such were never happier than when they had some grievance, real or imaginary, to air. From

---

[1] Pinney Papers, Business Letter Books. B.6, folio 188.

[2] Merchants' Hall. Book of Proceedings, No. 12, 1789-1797, folio 345 ; also Merchants' Hall, West India New Society, July 19th, 1800.

time to time, they sent up loyal addresses to the King expressing their gratification at some recent victory. Though not too eager for it, they even collected money for the wives and families of disabled soldiers. But, on the whole, a vastly more pleasant occupation for them took the form of remonstrances addressed to the Government in which they denounced the neutrals who, contrary to the law, were cutting into their own cherished West India trade. According to their own story, they were all, collectively and individually, ruined several times in each year. But the readiness with which they raised the great sums required to complete the Floating Harbour,[1] their investments in the funds and in the various canal undertakings, the luxurious houses they built in Bristol and their purchases of large country estates, together produce an impression of solid and established wealth.

---

[1] Bristol had always relied principally on two anchorages, Kingroad off Portishead and Hungroad off the left bank of the Avon, above Pill. Then there was the great Quay, upwards of a mile in length. But the trouble about this wharf was that the ships there were immobilised twice a day on the mud. Two wet docks, capable of holding fifty sail, and one dry dock were constructed, but these were insufficient. A plan was made to deflect the Avon into a new cut and so turn a stretch of that river and of the Frome into a Floating Harbour of 80 acres in area. Work began in 1804 and was completed, at a cost of £600,000, in 1809. See Plate 6.

CHAPTER III

The Employment of British Shipping

by C. ERNEST FAYLE

lately Lecturer at the College of Imperial Defence. Author with Charles Wright, of "A History of Lloyd's." Author of "A Short History of the World's Shipping Industry," and other works

THE fields of employment open to British shipping in 1793 may be grouped under five main heads:

A. The foreign trade proper of Great Britain.

B. The trade between Great Britain and Ireland, the Channel Islands and Isle of Man; then included in the returns of "Foreign Trade," but sometimes separately referred to as the "Foreign Coasting Trade."

C. The trade of Ireland with countries other than Great Britain.

D. Cross-trades between ports (British or foreign) outside the British Isles.

E. The coastal and local traffic of Great Britain and the British Possessions.

Of these, groups B and E, with a large part of A and C, were reserved, under the Navigation Acts, to vessels on British register.

The total number of vessels so registered in September, 1792, was 16,079, of which 12,776 were owned in Great Britain, 1,558 in Ireland, the Channel Islands and Isle of Man, and 1,745 in the Colonies. The large majority of these, however, were small craft employed in coasting and local traffic or inshore fisheries. How many were actually employed in foreign trade cannot be stated with any approach to certainty, but the table given below gives some indication of the employment afforded by the Foreign and Foreign Coasting Trade.

NUMBER OF BRITISH SHIPS ENTERED AND CLEARED AT PORTS
IN GREAT BRITAIN, 1792 :

	ENTERED	CLEARED	AVERAGE TONNAGE
1. LONG DISTANCE TRADES :			
Asia	28	36	707
West Indies, British and Foreign	705	603	233
United States	202	223	221
British North America	219	383	147
Africa, excluding Egypt	77	250	202
TOTAL	1,231	1,495	
2. SOUTHERN EUROPE AND MEDITERRANEAN :			
Spain, Portugal, Atlantic Islands,			
Malta and Gibraltar	975	615	126
Italy and Austria ..	138	215	143
Turkey, Levant, Egypt	38	48	224
TOTAL	1,151	878	
3. SHORT SEA TRADES :			
Russia, Scandinavia, Baltic and			
Germany	2,746	1,367	186
Holland and Flanders	1,603	1,734	117
TOTAL, N. Europe ..	4,349	3,101	
France ..	1,413	1,317	73
4. Greenland and Southern Whale			
Fisheries	160	135	270
TOTAL, Foreign Trade proper ..	8,304	6,926	
"FOREIGN COASTING TRADE" :			
Ireland ..	4,194	6,354	75
Channel Islands and Man ..	532	611	47
TOTAL	4,726	6,965	
TOTAL, Entrances and Clearances ..	13,033	13,891	

It will be noted that, on a mean of entrances and clearances,
"Foreign Coasting" accounts for over 43 per cent. of the total movements recorded as "Foreign Trade." In many years the proportion
was higher, and it is essential to keep this fact in mind when attempting to work out any ratio of losses to sailings in the Foreign Trade
proper.

Any estimate of the actual number of ships engaged in the Foreign Trade proper must be largely guesswork. We know, however, that the East Indiamen ([1]) went out one year and came back another ; that the round voyage to China might occupy as much as three years; that whalers might be one, two or three years away from port, and that few ships in the other long-distance trades accomplished more than one round voyage a year. In the European trades repeated voyages were more common, but both passages and turn-round in port were extremely slow by modern standards and it is probable that an average of one and a half round voyages a year in the Southern European trades, two in the Baltic and Scandinavian traffic, three or four in the trade with Holland, and four in that with France is a reasonable assumption, although packets and some fast-sailing merchantmen would, no doubt, show a better record.

On this basis it would appear that somewhere about 5,000 British ships may have been normally employed in the true Foreign Trade of Great Britain. About another 300 should probably be added for the Foreign Trade of Ireland—the statistics for which, though very imperfect, suggest that British entrances and clearances for ports outside Great Britain seldom averaged over 400 or 450. For the Cross-Trades no reliable statistics exist, but the numbers of ships lost, with such other evidence as is available, make it reasonably clear that, on any given date, several hundred ships would be making passages between overseas ports. Many of these passages, however, would represent the middle part of a triangular voyage originating or terminating in Great Britain. While it must again be emphasised that any estimate must be largely guesswork, it would be reasonable to suppose that, in the year preceding the outbreak of war, 5,500 British vessels or rather more were engaged in some form of foreign trade, leaving over 12,000 for the "Foreign Coasting" and coasting traffic of Great Britain, the inshore fisheries and the local traffic of the West Indies and North American Colonies. The "Country Trade" or local traffic in Asiatic waters is not included, as it was carried in India-built

---

([1]) The East India Company's ships actually at sea usually numbered between seventy and eighty during the period 1800-1810. Including those under repair, and the "extra ships," East Indiamen numbered altogether about a hundred.

For NEW YORK
The fine American Ship
FAIR AMERICAN
CHARLES CLASBY, Master
Burthen 245 tons, will positively fail, wind and weather permitting, in ten days, for freight or paffage apply to the Captain on board in the King's Dock ; or to WILLIAM BARBER *and* Co. Liverpool, 9th October, 1804.

For BARBADOES,
The ship SOVEREIGN,
GEORGE CUNNINGHAM, Master
Intended to fail with the next convoy from Cork. For freight or pafsage apply to
HENRY PARRY, Junr.

For BARBADOES,
The ship MAXWELL,
Captain EDWARDS
Intended to join the next convoy from Cork, appointed to fail the 16 *November.*
And the ship IRLAM, Captain KEYZAR,
Of 24 guns, 9 18-pounders and 50 men or up-wards, carries letters of marque, with liberty to chace, capture, and man, prizes and it is intended to fail in all October. For freight or pafsage apply to
BARTON, IRLAM and HIGGINSON
(One property)

For SALE
The Ship WESTMORLAND,
EDWARD KELLY, Master,
lately arrived from Barbadoes and now in the Queen's Dock.

	feet	inches
Length aloft	113	0
Extreme breadth ..	19	2
Burthen per Register ..	406 tons	

For inventories and further particulars enquire at
BARTON, IRLAM and HIGGINSON

For SALE by PRIVATE CONTRACT
The fast-failing, Bermudian-built
Brig, HAWKE,
PETER JACKSON, Master,
With all her materials as she lately arrived from St. Thomas, burthen per regifter 135 *tons. For inventory and further particulars apply to*
TAIT and Co.

WANTED TO CHARTER
AN AMERICAN VESSEL
Of about 150 *to* 200 *tons burthen, a faft failer and in every refpect well found to load immediately with dry goods for New Orleans and to return from thence with a cargo of cotton, &c.*
Apply to BARCLAY, SALKELD and Co.
Brunswick Street

STEAM ENGINE
*T*O *BE SOLD, a STEAM ENGINE on Boulton and Watt's principle of eighteen horfe power which may be seen at work in Prefton, by applying to Mr. Walker, bookfeller at that place.*
The Engine has only worked three years, and will be delivered to the purchafer in two months from this time.

LEEDS and LIVERPOOL CANAL and
DOUGLAS NAVIGATION

TALBOT INN, AND
GENERAL OFFICE FOR TRAVELLING,
The following MAILS and POST COACHES
Set out from the above INN, viz.

*T*HE LONDON ROYAL MAIL, *every Night at a Quarter paft Nine o'clock, in* 29 *Hours.*
The LONDON LIGHT COACH, *every After-noon at Four o'Clock, well lighted and guarded.*
The LONDON and PORTSMOUTH COACH *every Night.*
The YORK and HULL ROYAL MAIL, *every Morning.*
The BIRMINGHAM and OXFORD COACH, *every afternoon at Four o'clock.*
The MANCHESTER and LEEDS ROYAL MAIL, *every Morning at Half paft One o'clock.*
The BIRMINGHAM, BRISTOL, EXETER and PLYMOUTH EXPEDITION COACH *every Afternoon at Four o'clock.*
The COMMERCIAL COACH, *to the Pot-teries, Newcaftle, Stone, Stafford and Wolverhamp-ton, to Birmingham every day.*
Performed by ANDERSON, EVANS and Co. Who refpectfully inform the public they will not be accountable for any package whatever above 5*l value, unlefs entered as such and paid for accordingly.*
Pafsengers finding themfelves fatigued from the length of the journey, may reft upon the road and pro-ceed without additional expence. (One property)

COMMODIOUS AND EXPEDITIOUS
CONVEYANCE BY WATER.
*C*UFFIELD *& Co, refpectfully inform all Merchants and Shippers of Goods, that their Flats load every day at their Wharf South end of the Parade, George Dock Liverpool and arrive the day following at Chefter.*
At Chefter every Wednefday and Friday for Manchefter, where they arrive on the fucceeding Friday and Monday ; the Flat which arrives on Friday leaves Manchefter on Saturday, and arrives at Chefter the Tuefday following.
At the fame place for Warrington every Satur-day, where they deliver goods on the Tuefday following.
The Proprietors folicit for the above eftablifh-ment the favour of the public, and as the whole is under the conftant attention and direction of princi-pals the utmoft care may be depended upon.

YELLOW FEVER
NO. 40 CHARING CROSS, LONDON
*D*R. WILLICH, *late Phyfician to the Saxon Ambafsador at the Court of Great Britain and Author of the Domeftic Encyclopaedia, treatife on Regimen and Diet, &c., &c., approves and recommends to the immediate notice of the Public at large (and thofe in particular who are going to the Weft Indies, America, or any other part of the World that may be or has been fubject to Peftilential Difeafe) the Remedy which is Sold at the Proprietor's Warehoufe No.* 40 *Charing Crofs.*

ships not on the Register; although this trade added, of course, to the responsibilities of officers commanding on the East Indies Station.

The long-distance trades, especially those with the East and West Indies and the United States, were the pivot of the whole commercial system. The United States was the most important single market for British products. From America and the Indies came not only many luxuries and some important articles of general consumption, but essential raw materials, notably cotton, for the rapidly expanding British industries, the products of which were in increasing demand on the Continent. The entrepot and re-export trade in Eastern, Colonial and American goods was among the most lucrative and jealously protected branches of British commerce. Apart from the direct losses incurred, any interference with these trades would strike at the roots of a large proportion of the traffic with European countries. Finally, these trades, with the exception of the American, were strictly confined to British ships.

In time of war they were exposed not only to the depredations of privateers and isolated cruisers, but to a more concentrated attack in the Atlantic approaches by light squadrons and even by battle fleets issuing from the French and Spanish ports. Their importance and the routes they followed combined to make them the chief commercial factor in the disposition of our naval forces. They have, therefore, been made the subject of separate consideration in the later chapters of this book.

From the point of view of shipping, the East Indies Trade was chiefly remarkable for employing vessels of an average tonnage about three times that of the normal merchantman. Such ships, however large, had to be numerous, too, owing to the length of the voyage. They were wholly confined to the East Indies Trade and were too large and costly to be employed elsewhere. The East Indiamen were built, owned and run on a system peculiar to the trade, and were sharply differentiated from all other tonnage on the Register.

The Whaler, again, was a type apart, built for a particular trade and unsuited to any other. With them, too, the length of the voyage, especially in the Southern Whale Fishery, involved the employment of more ships than were annually cleared; but they were too specialised to be available as part of the general pool of tonnage.

This pool included, on the other hand, the shipping normally employed in the United States trade. Even the "constant traders" on this route were perfectly well suited to other employments during a time of need; and most of them were, in fact, drawn elsewhere during the war, to be replaced by American vessels. The West India-men occupied an intermediate position. Most of them were built for the trade, sluggish sailers, designed solely for big cargo capacity. But there was nothing in their size or build to exclude them from finding employment on other routes or in the cross-trades. Indeed, there were fast, well-armed ships among them, built as "runners" (vessels licensed to sail without convoy), which would have little difficulty in securing a charter elsewhere when the West Indian freight markets were dull. Nor was there anything to prevent ships employed in other trades—if on "Plantation Register"—from picking up a cargo in the West Indies when the demand for tonnage was brisk.

The two remaining long-distance trades, the African and the British North American, were, in 1792, of lesser importance, and are not made the subject of special treatment here. The majority of the ships cleared for "Africa" were slavers and on a triangular voyage which is fully described in Chapter XI and mentioned in Chapter VIII. The direct trade with the Guinea Coast and Barbary States was not large. There were valuable imports of ivory and palm-oil from Guinea, fruit and wine, wax and gums from North Africa. These were mostly paid for in cheap textiles, arms, liquor and inferior gunpowder—a dirty, profitable, but not extensive trade.

Trade with British North America was on a larger scale, but was remarkable for the low average tonnage of the ships and the great discrepancy between the clearances and entrances. The explanation of both these characteristics is to be found in the large number of small vessels which left West Country ports to fish on the Banks of Newfoundland, many of which subsequently disposed of their cargoes in Spain or Portugal.(1) Some larger vessels were employed in taking out supplies for the fishermen, and the direct trade with Canadian ports employed ships similar to those which traded to the United States. They took out British manufactures and re-exports

---

(1) See Chapter X on the Newfoundland Fisheries, especially pages 231 and 232.

such as tea and sugar, bringing home in exchange furs, skins, a little grain and an occasional cargo of timber. By far the most valuable cargoes were those of the fur ships from Quebec.

The European Trades, considered as fields for the employment of British shipping in peace and in war, were sharply differentiated in more than one respect from the majority of the ocean trades. In the first place, they were mostly outside the protective ring-fence of the Navigation Acts and were, even in time of peace, largely dependent on foreign ships. In the second place, some of them, notably the traffic with France, Holland and Flanders, were carried on by small vessels, only otherwise useful in the Irish or Coasting Trades. The ships which sailed to the Baltic and Scandinavia were much larger, but many of these were prizes or purchased foreign-built craft, allowed to accept charters for Spain or the Mediterranean but rigidly excluded from the "Plantation Trade." On the other hand, there was a close connection between both the Baltic and Southern European Trades and one very important branch of the coastal traffic. The supply of London with coal from Newcastle and Sunderland employed vessels at least as large as those engaged in the majority of the ocean trades. In 1797 the average size of the colliers entering London was 220 tons—and many of these ships were as readily available for cargoes to Cronstadt, Lubeck or Barcelona. Indeed, they were sometimes employed in the ocean trades. A series of voyages performed during the years 1781-1788 inclusive by the ship *Forester*, of Shields, is well worth summarising as an illustration of the flexibility of shipping at this date; as also the importance of cross-voyages and the impossibility of drawing any hard-and-fast line between the ships engaged in various trades.

VOYAGES BY *FORESTER*, OF SHIELDS, 1781-88

(From *A Mariner of England* : William Richardson)

1781-2 (a) Shields—London with coal.

(b) Shields—Lubeck with coal; in ballast to Cronstadt; thence to Hull with iron, hemp and tallow. (War conditions, nine months round voyage.)

1783 (a) Shields—Wyborg in ballast; Wyborg—Newcastle with deals.

(b) Shields—Cronstadt with coal; Cronstadt—Newcastle with iron, hemp and tallow (three months round voyage). Laid up for winter.

1784   (a) Several trips, Shields—London with coal.

(b) Shields—Archangel in ballast; Archangel—Shields with 1,600 barrels of tar. (Not laid up.)

1785   (a) Shields—London with coal.

(b) To Memel in ballast; Memel—Lynn with timber.

(c) Shields—Marseilles with coal; Marseilles—London with cotton and sarsaparilla.

1786   (a) Shields—Gibraltar and an Algerian port with coal, gunpowder and lead.

(b) Barbary—Gibraltar for orders, with wheat, beeswax and sheep. Sent to Cadiz.

(c) Cadiz—Konigsberg with salt; to Memel in ballast; Memel—Corunna with spars; Corunna—Exmouth—Shields. Laid up.

1787   (a) Shields—Cartagena with coal; Cartagena—La Matt, near Alicante, in ballast; La Matt—America or Ireland, as winds might prove favourable, with salt. Went to Philadelphia.

(b) Philadelphia—Santander with flour and biscuit. Santander—Shields in ballast.

1788   Shields—Bordeaux with coal; Ile de Ré—Philadelphia with salt; home with Nicaragua wood (dye-wood) to London.

During the war, the trade with Southern Europe was exposed to the same dangers as the ocean trades. The North Sea, Baltic and Coasting Trades were, on the whole, subject to less interference at sea; though their losses were serious enough. What differentiated the experience of the European traffic from that of the Ocean Trades was that both in the North Sea and Baltic—as also in the Mediterranean—the chief menace came from the French armies rather than from their cruisers and privateers. It was not the sea risks but the extension of French control along the European coast-line that sent up insurance premiums to fantastic heights, and even threatened many branches of commerce with complete extinction.

The European trades are too complex, however, for detailed discussion in the present work. The Foreign Trade of Ireland, on the other hand, hardly appears to call for separate treatment. The bulk of it was carried on with Northern and Southern Europe, especially the former; but there was also some direct traffic with North America and the West Indies. The conditions of trade and the dangers to which the ships were exposed in war were much the same as in the Foreign Trade of Great Britain. As regards the Cross-Trades, enough has already been said to emphasise their importance in minimising ballast voyages and giving flexibility to the employment of British shipping.

It remains only, in the present chapter, to say a few words on the way in which the employment of shipping as a whole was affected by the war. For this purpose it will not, fortunately, be necessary to discuss in any detail the economic policies of the belligerents. Despite the bewildering inconsistencies presented by their utterances and actions, the dominant motives of the British and French Governments are tolerably clear. Both based their policy firmly on mercantilist theory. Both regarded the expansion of the export trade as a primary object of policy, and imports—especially from a political or commercial rival—as, at best, a necessary evil. Both desired to draw gold from the enemy country as a means of crippling its war finance. Both looked to tariffs and trading-licence fees as a means of providing the sinews of war.

Actuated by these motives, both Governments were intent on stopping the enemy's export trade and on interrupting the supply of raw material on which his exporting industries depended; as also the colonial produce he might re-export. The stoppage of imports for home consumption was not, in general, a serious object of policy, though a real effort might sometimes be made to intercept special categories of goods, such as naval stores or foodstuffs consigned to overseas bases. The main object of economic policy, in war as in peace, was the expansion of a country's own exports at the expense of rivals, and the attainment thus of a "favourable balance of trade." To compel the enemy to accept one's own goods and pay for them in cash—this was regarded as a master-stroke.

On paper, both Governments prohibited practically all intercourse with the enemy; but the Traitorous Correspondence Act of 1793 and the more drastic Orders in Council of 1807 were used less for the prevention than for the regulation of trade. The main object of the British Government was to force British goods into Continental markets, including the French, and to exclude from those markets, so far as possible, all foreign competitors. Paper blockades and sweeping decrees of non-intercourse were the foundation of a gigantic system of special licences which enabled Great Britain, in large measure, to control the trade of the Continent.

French policy was even less consistent with French professions, because it was more affected by sheer fiscal necessity. When Napoleon licensed shipments of corn to Great Britain from Holland, the Mediterranean, and even France itself, he was doing nothing irreconcileable with the economic doctrines of the time. Licences to import British manufactures and re-exports were another matter. His determination to exclude British goods from every European State which could be brought by persuasion, threats, or conquest within the circle of French domination was wholly sincere. If it was imperfectly carried out it was not through any weakening of his will to strike at the resources which sustained not only Great Britain, but also, to a large extent, her allies. The failure of the "Continental System" was due, in the first place, to the corruption of his marshals and officials, combined with the self-interested passive resistance of his allies and vassals. But in the last years of the war, as the French finances became more and more crippled by gigantic military expenditure, coupled with the strangling of French overseas trade, Napoleon himself was compelled to shift his policy from the exclusion of imports to their regulation by license, for the sake of the revenue derived from duties and license fees.

These ideas and necessities of the belligerents inevitably affected their attitude towards trade carried on in neutral ships, though such trade remained liable to attack when not covered by special license. And indeed the doctrine of contraband was pushed very far by both sides. The attack on belligerent shipping was, of course, subject to no restriction. It was pursued not merely as a naval measure but as an intensification of the commercial rivalry of peace; as a means of popularising naval service by the opportunities afforded for gaining prize-money; and as a means of enriching the mercantile and shipping community through the activities of privateers.

In one respect the Traitorous Correspondence Act marked a definite step forward. In the earlier eighteenth century wars the insurance of enemy ships and property had been passionately defended as a means of draining France of gold—since the premiums received were assumed to leave a substantial balance over losses paid—and as a

F

source of information with regard to the movements of French shipping. Towards the end of the War of Austrian Succession an Act prohibiting the traffic had been passed against strong opposition, which did not come solely—or even chiefly—from the underwriters. All the evidence suggests that it was a very effective blow at French commerce, but it was not revived during the Seven Years War. In 1793, for the first time, the insurance of enemy ships and of enemy property in neutral ships was prohibited from the beginning of the struggle.([1]) There is evidence that such transactions were still carried through furtively, but the prohibition seems to have been generally and progressively effectual.

In the defence of British trade, the convoy system, then as now, played a preponderant part. It would be foreign to the purpose of this book to enter upon an examination of the naval aspects of convoy, but a word must be said as to its commercial effects. From this point of view the application of the system was much easier in 1793-1814 than during the Second World War. The prompt arrival of cargoes was not, as is the arrival of foodstuffs and raw materials today, essential to national existence. And in the trades where, on an average, but one round voyage was made in the year, the delays inseparable from the system were of comparatively small importance. The owners and masters of fast-sailing ships, eager to forestall the market, were often impatient of convoy restrictions, but to the nation and to the commercial community as a whole, the delay of a month or two while awaiting escort, and the subordination of speed to keeping company, were matters of indifference. It was thus possible to economise escorts by moving the trade in big fleets, at long intervals, without causing any serious commercial dislocation. In the Baltic and Scandinavian trades, where repeated voyages were normally more common, the inconvenience was greater; but the difficulties created by the military and political situation were so serious that a slowing down of trade must, under any system, have been inevitable.

In these circumstances there was little effective opposition to the

---

([1]) Where the property in the goods had not already passed, the prohibition of insurance on the cargoes of neutral ships bound to French ports extended only to certain specified categories of goods.

Act of 1798 which made convoy compulsory, with certain exceptions, for all ships employed in foreign trade.([1]) The East Indiamen, the Hudson Bay Company's ships, and vessels bound for Irish ports were specifically excepted and in all trades licences "to run"—that is, to sail independently—could be obtained from the Admiralty for fast ships, sufficiently well armed to offer effectual resistance to an attack by a privateer.([2])

No system of defence could prevent heavy losses; but these losses, together with those caused by marine perils, were more than made good by new building and by prizes added to the Register, with the result that, in striking contrast with the experiences of 1914-18, the tonnage on the Register was substantially higher at the end than at the beginning of the war. The actual figures are as follows:

	1792		1814	
Owned in	Ships	1,000 tons	Ships	1,000 tons
Great Britain ..	12,776	1,187	19,585	2,329
Ireland, etc. ..	1,558	250	1,665	84
Colonies	1,745	103	2,868	203
TOTAL ..	16,079	1,540	24,418	2,616

This increase was spread fairly evenly over the war years and would suggest at first sight a great increase in the volume of trade carried by British ships. The figures of entrances and clearances tell a different story. It is true that there was an increase in the volume (and a still greater increase in the value) of trade and that this is reflected in some increased movements of shipping; but when we turn to the movements of *British* ships, we are confronted, for almost every year of the war, by a decline on the peace figures, and this decline is still more strongly marked in the figures for the Foreign Trade proper. This decline was greater in number than in tonnage owing to the complete cessation (so far as British ships were concerned) of the short sea trades with France, Flanders and Holland. Taking, however, as

---

([1]) 38 Geo. III, c. 76.
([2]) As from about 1779 many British merchantmen had been substantially strengthened by the introduction of the Carronade.

an example the five years 1802-1806 inclusive, the average tonnage of British ships cleared for countries outside the British Isles was only 917,000, as against 1,040,000 tons in 1792; a reduction of nearly 12 per cent.

Naturally enough, the effect of the war on the employment of British shipping varied widely as between route and route. The East Indies and West Indies trades were still jealously restricted to ships under the British flag, and the volume of traffic in both trades expanded during the war, partly as a result of the capture of the French West Indian Colonies. Trade with the United States fell more and more into the hands of the American shipowners, who had already captured a large part of it before the war.

The route to British North America gained greatly in importance. During the first or Revolutionary phase of the struggle, the clearances on this route fell away heavily, owing to the closing of Spanish ports to the products of the Newfoundland fisheries. When, however, Spain became an ally of Great Britain during the Napoleonic War, this part of the trade recovered. What was still more important, the difficulties of the Baltic Trade led to an unprecedented demand for North American timber.

So late as 1801, the imports of squared timber from the British Colonies amounted to no more than 3,000 loads, against nearly 159,000 loads from Europe. The war, however, increased the demand for timber, and at the same time the extension of French influence to the Baltic coasts made it impossible to satisfy this demand wholly from Northern Europe. In order to stimulate further the Canadian timber trade, heavy differential duties on European timber were imposed in 1806, and the effect of these duties, coupled with high freights and premiums in the Baltic trade, led to a notable re-direction of the traffic. By 1811 the imports of squared timber alone from British North America amounted to more than 154,000 loads, as against about 125,000 loads from Europe, and the imports of masts and deals from Canada showed a similar increase. Ships built in Nova Scotia and New Brunswick had a share of the traffic, though many of them, built hastily of green wood, were of such "short duration" that the underwriters refused to insure them for a second voyage.[1]

---

[1] Hist. MSS. Com., Vaux Collection, VI, 221.

Taken as a whole, the figures for the ocean trades show that, despite the infliction of heavy losses, the enemy fleets and privateers failed to restrict seriously the movements of British shipping. To the European trades the chief menace was not so much attack at sea as the triumphs of French arms and French diplomacy ashore. From the beginning, not only the French but the Flemish and Dutch ports were closed to British ships, and the trade with Spain was also lost to them for over a decade. At various periods, and in varying degrees, most of the Mediterranean and North Sea ports and many of those in the Baltic were similarly closed. Yet the Continent was always hungry for British goods and British merchants were not slow to take advantage of the opportunity presented by the elimination of French competition. In the later years of the war there was actually a great increase in the number of British clearances to Baltic and Scandinavian ports, and as the number of repeated voyages was reduced by war conditions, this represented a still larger increase in the number of ships employed. From the first, however, a very large proportion of the trade with Northern Europe was carried on under neutral flags.

The general position in the later stages of the war was that tonnage in the ocean trades, other than that with the United States, remained all British; while about 90 per cent. of the trade with the United States, and about half the traffic with both Northern and Southern Europe was carried in neutral ships. A table for the years 1802-1811, inclusive, which unfortunately includes the "Foreign Coasting Trade," shows the proportion of British entrances and clearances to the total tonnage as 65.3 per cent. and 65.8 per cent. respectively. Of the tonnage entered "with cargoes," only 62.5 per cent. was British, but the vast and complicated system of trade control was used to retain as much as possible of the export trade for British ships, so that in tonnage cleared "with cargoes" the proportion rose to 77.8 per cent.

How many British ships were actually employed, under war conditions, in the Foreign Trade proper of Great Britain, it is, of course, impossible to state. A calculation made by Commander J. Cresswell, R.N., gives the total for 1797 as 2,872.(¹) This, however,

----

(¹) *British Shipping at the End of the Eighteenth Century*, Commander Cresswell. *Mariner's Mirror*, XXV, 2nd April, 1939.

was a year of very disturbed trade, when the mean of entrances and clearances amounted only to 2,847, as against an average of 3,985 for the years 1793-1801 inclusive. This has been taken here as representing an average of about 3,550 ships for that period.([1]) To this must be added at least 600 or 700 vessels employed in the Foreign Trade of Ireland or on cross-voyages. Very extensive sampling of the losses recorded in *Lloyd's List* for the years 1795, 1797, 1798 and 1799 reveal the losses of ships on cross-voyages to be about one-quarter of those suffered in the Foreign Trade of Great Britain, but this certainly exaggerates the proportion of shipping employed in the cross-trades, as the incidence of loss in some of these trades would inevitably be high, and many of the passages were incidental to voyages starting or terminating in British ports.

At the highest, it is difficult to estimate the average total number of ships employed in some form of foreign trade during the years 1793-1801 as more than about 4,200 to 4,500. During the second phase of the struggle, the number was, undoubtedly, substantially higher, so far as can be judged from the figures of entrances and clearances. It may have amounted to something between 4,250 and 5,000 in the Foreign Trade of Great Britain alone. Even so, it is clear that the foreign trades could not absorb anything like the whole of the great increase in tonnage on the Register.

A large proportion of the small vessels displaced from the trade with France, Flanders and Holland were no doubt absorbed by the Foreign Coasting Trade. The traffic with Ireland, which was becoming more and more important as a source of food supplies, increased steadily throughout the years of the war, and there was also a great increase in the traffic with the Channel Islands, which became a busy centre for the distribution of prize cargoes and for semi-legalised smuggling to and from the Continent. For ocean traders a new source of employment was provided by the opening of South American ports to British ships; but the greater part of the tonnage added to the Register must have been required to make good that withdrawn from commercial employment by the popularity of privateering and the demands of the transport service.

([1]) *A History of Lloyd's*, Appendix A.

CHAPTER IV

Ships of the Period and Developments in Rig

by BASIL LUBBOCK

Author of "The China Clippers," and other works

IN considering the merchant ship of the Napoleonic era there are
certain facts which we must remember in order to get our per-
spective right. The first of these is the smallness of everything
compared to the present day, the smallness of the known world, of
the man-power of different nations, and above all of the long-voyage
merchant ship. If we examine the registrar's figures for 1800 and
compare them with the present day, we find that in 1800 the average
tonnage of ships registered in Great Britain and Ireland was 113 tons,
compared to over 3,000 in the year 1938. Yet there were over three
times as many British ships sailing the seas in 1800 as there were in
1938, the exact figures being 14,363 ships in 1800, as compared with
4,405 ships in 1938.

Next, we have to realise that our ancestors' idea of speed was very
different from ours. Ten miles an hour was a good average for an
express coach on land, and half this amount was good going for a
ship on a deep water voyage. Yet for all that, a coach on a galloping
stage or a sailing ship rolling along with all her flying kites([1]) set
before a trade wind gave one a greater idea of speed than a train or
motor of the present day making 60 miles an hour.

Turning to the factor of size it is easy to prove that not only
Englishmen, but their European neighbours (both friends and
enemies), were smaller than their grand-children and great grand-
children. The evidence of this is not only shown by old uniforms and
clothes, but by the length of old beds and the height under the beams
in the 'tween decks of even the largest ships of the Napoleonic era.
In fact, compared to the present day, not only were men and women
smaller themselves, but their conception of size was very much less
than ours. It should be realised that as long as wood was the only

---

([1]) This and other technical terms used in this chapter and the next are explained in a
glossary. See page 291.

material used in shipbuilding a limit was set and the extreme of this limit was reached by the first-rate ship of war, such as the *Victory*. The largest merchant ships in 1793 were those in the service of the Honourable East India Company. To modern eyes, even the finest of these ships would have appeared extraordinarily short and tubby or barrel-shaped, for they had what was called "great tumble home," having more breadth at the water line than at the deck level. These Indiamen, in fact most merchant ships of that era, had only 3½ beams to length.

The finest and fastest ship in the East India employ in 1793 was probably the *Nottingham*, of 1,152 tons. This vessel was said to have been copied from a Swedish ship, the *Gustavus III*, a well-known trader to China, which had a great reputation for speed, and though she had a complement of from 160 to 170 men, could only stow 1,230 tons of tea. The *Nottingham* was built at Clevely's yard in 1786, had a length of 130 feet and beam of 40 feet. She turned out to be a very fast, successful ship. She was well manned by 104 British seamen.

The largest ship employed by the Company in 1793 was the *Royal Charlotte*, of 1,282 tons, but by 1804 she had given place to the *Marquis of Cornwallis*, of 1,360 tons, which was called the Company's frigate. This vessel, and the 1,200-ton *David Scott*, a very well-known Indiaman, proceeded no further than Bombay.

The crack ship of the East India fleet during the early years of the nineteenth century was the *Royal George*, of 1,200 tons, commanded by Captain Timmins, which bore the brunt in Commodore Nathaniel Dance's action with the French squadron in February, 1804. Admiral Sir Edward Pellew, Commander-in-Chief of the East India Station, once sent the following message to this ship:

"Tell the captain if he had not his main topmast staysail in the brails I should have taken his ship for a frigate."

This smartness is not surprising, for Captain Timmins began life in the Royal Navy, being a midshipman in the *Experiment* when she captured the *Belle Poule*. In 1807 he sailed from Plymouth to Madras with a ship's company of 660, including over 500 soldiers. In a five-months' passage the *Royal George* had no punishments, very little illness and only one death. In 1808 she again took out troops, and, according to the *Naval Chronicle*, was armed with 62 guns. She is not to be confused with the other *Royal George* in the East India Company's service, which was destroyed by fire whilst lying at Whampoa on December 25th, 1825.

The sailing dates of the East Indiamen were arranged so that the China ships could take the S.W. monsoon up the coast and the N.E. for the return passage, thus an average voyage took about eighteen months. The India ships were able to make the voyage in less time, but the affairs of the Company were conducted in such a leisurely and lordly fashion that it was seldom that a ship took much less than eighteen months on the round voyage.

A number of first-class ships were built in Bombay dockyard by the famous Parsee family of Wadia: *Scaleby Castle*, 1798; *Bombay*, 1807; *Charles Grant*, 1809; *Earl of Balcarres*, 1810; *Abercrombie Robinson*, 1811; *Herefordshire*, 1812, and *Buckinghamshire*, 1816. The largest of these, the famous *Earl of Balcarres*, was of 1,406 tons, and proudly showed two lines of ports like a line-of-battleship. George Cupples' description of a Bombay-built East Indiaman in that classic, *The Greenhand*, is something of a caricature:

" '*The Seringapatam*—do you know her?' I said. 'Ay, ay, sir, well enough,' said he, readily—'a lump of a ship she is, down off Blackwall(1) in the stream, with two more—country-built, and tumbles home rather much from below the plank—sheer for a sightly craft, besides being flat in the eyes of her, and round in the counter, just where she shouldn't, sir. Them Parchee Bombay shipwrights *does* clap on a lot of onchristien flummeries and gilt mouldings, let alone quarter-galleries fit for the king's castle.' 'In short, she's a tea-waggon all over,' said I, 'and just as slow and as leewardly, to boot, as teak can make her?' 'Her lines is not that bad, though, your honour,' continued Jacobs, 'if you just knocked off her poop—and she'd bear a deal o' beating for a seaboat'."

Nothing shows the inbred conservatism of British sailors more than their contempt for that lovely wood teak. Somehow or other, teak-built ships were given a reputation for being heavy and slow, but a ship built of the finest Malabar teak was almost everlasting. (When the old *Pique* frigate was broken up at Falmouth a few years

(1) East Indiamen moored well down the river. See Chapter VII, page 150.

before the war I had some of her teak put into a little yacht, and it was just as good as when it was first cut, some eighty years before.) The *Earl of Balcarres* was a case in point. After over fifty years of active service she served as a hulk on the West Coast of Africa. Another well-known example is the *Java*, the most interesting and longest-lived of the many famous coal hulks at Gibraltar.

Besides the East Indiaman, there was one other trader in Indian and Chinese waters which flew the British flag; this was the Indian country craft or wallah, which was Indian-built and Indian manned, though commanded and officered by Europeans. The Indian ship-builder had been quick to realise that his designs were not so well-fitted for long voyages as the European, and right back from the days of the Portuguese he commenced to build ships which were almost exact replicas of the old carracks and galleons, and owing to the fact that he built with imperishable woods, ships which looked as if they had come straight out of the Elizabethan Age were to be seen in the Indian Ocean, using the same winds as the composite-built tea clippers and even the great wall-sided iron carriers of Victorian days.

All East Indiamen were ship-rigged and it may perhaps be convenient to discuss, at this point, what the term "ship" can be taken to mean. For the traditional seventeenth-eighteenth century sail-plan was already very modified. In 1793, for example, there were still ships afloat with the long lateen or mizen yard, but in practically all British ships this lateen yard had been replaced by the modern gaff, fitting to the mast with jaws and hoisted by throat and peak halliards from the deck. There was some confusion in the development of this sail; at first it kept its own name of the mizen, and a more or less rectangular sail (which was set outside it by a halliard leading through a block at the end of the gaff, and which in the days of the clippers was called the ringtail) was first of all known as the driver. This driver developed into what came to be known as a large mizen or spanker, the old mizen having been furled along the gaff. This new sail was hoisted up to the gaff by means of three sets of halliards. In the later Blackwall frigates it was the custom at one time to sheet down the spanker to a bumpkin poking out over the taffrail, but in Napoleonic times it was the uniform practice to have a long boom extending for perhaps one-third of its length over the stern.

Modern squaresails are very nearly rectangular, but this was far from being the case in the days of wood and hemp, when the sail plan was very much narrower, the width being gained (along with an additional 1½ knots in speed in a fresh wind) by the studding sails, or steering sails, as they were mostly called at that time. As showing the way a sail plan tapered in 1800-and-war-time, a topsail had over one-third more cloths in its foot than in its head; the only exception to this tapering being the forecourse, which conformed to present-day practice and was slightly shorter on the foot than on the head.

With regard to reefing, a course had two rows of reefing points, a topsail four, and the topgallant sail of a first-class ship three. One should remember that wire rope had not been invented and that even chain was used very sparingly, thus the clews of sails consisted of eyes in the bolt rope, not spliced, but merely seized together to make a loop. The topsail sheets were rove through these eyes from foreward aft, with a double wall double crowned as a stopper on the end.

The leach of an old-time topsail contained no less than eight cringles, one for each reef band, one for the reef tackle pendent, and three bowline cringles. A course had four additional cringles along the foot called the buntline cringles. It did not have three buntline cringles but two, known as the upper and lower buntline cringle.

Staysails seem to have been very popular, there being always four and in lofty ships, sometimes five staysails between the fore and main masts, namely: the main staysail, main topmast staysail, middle staysail and main topgallant staysail, and even royal staysail. Except for the main staysail these sails had a length of luff extending down the topmast and lower mast. The mizen topgallant staysail was a queer-shaped sail, being sometimes almost square. This was due to the head of the mizen topgallant mast being nearly on a level with the main topmast cross trees, thus the stay was sometimes almost horizontal.

The spritsail and spritsail topsail were two important sails during the Napoleonic era. These sails, which had been set on a small mast at the end of the bowsprit during the latter half of the seventeenth century, were now set underneath the bowsprit and jibboom. When these two sails fell into disuse, racing ships, like the tea clippers, were to have recourse to a single sail setting under the bowsprit and jibboom, which, for some long-forgotten reason, was called a Jamie Green.

The canvas used by British merchantmen, in fact all European merchantmen, and men-of-war, was made of flax, but American merchantmen used cotton canvas. It is not certain how early this cotton canvas came into use on the other side of the Atlantic, but it was a common means of identifying American ships in war-time.

In the Middle Ages the flax for weaving sail cloth was grown chiefly in Somerset, and the great weavers of early days were mostly Flemish and Huguenot settled in that county. The sail-making tradition continued but there was a great improvement made in sail canvas by Richard Hayward, at Crewkerne, who founded the modern firm of Richard Hayward & Co. about the year 1790. About that same date a sail-maker of Cowes, called George Rogers Ratsey, started making sails out of the Hayward canvas, these sails being very much better cut and less baggy than was usual at that date. The great advocate in the Navy of flatter sails was Lord Cochrane, but he was one of those sailors who was in advance of his time in every way. Of the sails of the Napoleonic Wars it is probable that only one remains, and that is the *Victory's* topsail, which reposes, or used to repose, in the *Victory* museum at Portsmouth. In a lecture on sail-making, the late Thomas W. Ratsey speaks of another sail, that on which Lord Nelson died and which was stained by his blood. This sail was kept at Greenwich for many years and the name of its makers, the famous firm of Baxter Brothers, of Dundee, was stamped upon it.

American writers in the days of the clipper ships were wont to compare the gleaming white cotton canvas of their ships with the rather dingy baggy-looking flax canvas of the British and other nations. Flax canvas, however, had its advantages, being very much more pliable and easily handled in wet and frosty weather than cotton canvas, which, under such conditions, became as hard as a board. The United States Navy, unlike the United States Merchant Service, never deserted flax for cotton, and right up to 1914 purchased its canvas from Baxter Brothers.

The rigging of British ships at this date consisted almost entirely of hemp, and even hemp cables were still in common use for some years after peace came; for it was some time before seamen were able to trust very much to chain cables, and in early logs there are constant entries of links breaking and chains being lost. The hemp cable of a first-class Indiaman took up the whole of her forehold, being over eight inches in diameter and tested up to a strain of over 50 tons. One hundred fathoms of this huge cable weighed between six and seven tons. The great wooden-stocked anchors, weighing over five tons, were fitted with specially large rings two feet and more in diameter to which these cables were bent, great care being taken to prevent chafe. The rings of the cable itself was served with "keckling" and then well marled with canvas.

Next to the cables the largest rope in the ship was used for the stays and shrouds of the lower rigging. One of the most important pieces of seamanship in the days of rope rigging was the constant setting up (in landman's parlance, tightening) that was needed. When it is recognised how much stretch and shrinkage there is in hemp and how much it is affected by dry or wet weather, one realises that the task of an old-time bos'un in keeping his masts properly stayed must have been unending.

Of the smaller stuff used aboard ship, such as gaskets for making the sails fast, row bands or rovings for making the sails fast to the jackstays on the yards, and nippers for frapping the cable to the messenger (or viol, as it was called, owing to its being led through a block which was lashed to the mainmast and in shape and size was something like a bass viol) were made aboard, and the spun yarn winch was rarely idle during fine weather.

The merchantman of the Napoleonic Wars was what the sailors call a heavy working ship; that is to say, not only was her gear heavy, but the ropes worked stiffly through the blocks. This was entirely owing to the two pet theories of the British seaman. The first of these was that weight meant strength, and the second was that big clumsy-looking blocks took away from a vessel's smartness and ship-shape appearance. The Americans fell into neither of these mistakes; their ships could be worked by half the men required in English vessels owing to the fact that they used smaller ropes and bigger blocks, so that all their running gear worked easily. They also took care not to use a three-inch rope where a two-inch one would suffice.

In size and importance the West Indiamen came next to those of the East India Company.([1]) A very excellent example of one of these ships is shown in Cooke's etching of the *Thetis*. Though his well-known etchings were published twelve years after peace had been proclaimed, the *Thetis* is a very good example of the war period. To the eyes of a modern seaman her length of mast seems to be entirely out of proportion, but Cooke is usually accurate; no marine artist was ever more careful to be correct in the delineation of ships. Owing to a very short-sighted tonnage rule the untaxed factor of depth of hold kept British merchantmen, West Indiamen included, too deep and narrow. There were certain conventions also about masting and sparring in relation to a ship's dimensions that conformed to no reason; the dictum "what was good enough for our fathers is good enough for us" being a very favourite one in British ports.

Next to the West Indiaman came that most important nursery for seamen, the whaler—both Arctic and South Sea. Whilst Hull was the largest port for Arctic whalers, London was specially interested in the new venture of hunting the sperm whale. It was during the American War of Independence that London first succeeded in getting hold of American mates and harpooners for the South Sea fishing. These Americans had taught the trade of Cachelot hunting to English seamen by the outbreak of the Napoleonic Wars, and during these wars the London whalers belonging to Messrs. Enderby & Son were not only working round the Cape into the Indian Ocean, but round the Horn as far north as the Galapagos Islands and the Mexican Coast.

The Southseaman differed from the Greenlandman in her brick tryworks necessary for boiling the oil out of the blubber. Neither the appearance of the Arctic nor the South Sea whaler varied from that of the ordinary merchantman except for one item. It will be seen in many pictures of Arctic whalers that the clews of the foresail were made fast to a light boom which was sheeted in the ordinary way. This innovation was for the sake of handiness, for a whaler's safety often depended on her ability to manœuvre. It was often necessary for her to keep backing, filling and twisting about on her heel in order to avoid a squeeze or to work through heavy ice.

([1]) For the tonnage of West Indiamen, see Chapter VIII, page 180.

Even ships as small as 150 tons were ship-rigged at the beginning of the nineteenth century, and the barque and barquantine were a very much rarer sight at sea than they were fifty years later. Two-masters, on the other hand, were common and the rigs of the two-master were very numerous, each slight technical variation in rig being differently named according to locality. Most of the colliers and Baltic traders were brigs or snows. The fruiters, racing from Smyrna and the Greek ports with oranges and raisins, were topsail schooners; that is to say they had three and often four square yards on the foremast with full suits of stunsails. To show how little was needed to alter a vessel's description, one of the differences between a topsail schooner and a brigantine was that a topsail schooner set her square foresail flying, whereas the brigantine had it properly bent to the foreyard. There are probably few people today who can say what was meant by a butter-rigged schooner. A butter-rigged schooner set her topgallant sail flying; the topgallant yard had no lifts, and when the sail had to be taken in the yard was lowered down on to the topsail yard, and the sail furled in with the topsail. According to Clark Russell the term "butter-rigged" was derived from the fact that numbers of schooners so rigged used to trade to Holland for butter. The topsail schooner rig always seems to have been the most popular one in the Channel, just as the brig or snow was the chief trader in the North Sea.

The brigantine or (as the Americans called it), the hermaphrodite, was never quite as numerous as the topsail schooner, but both types had probably evolved from what at one time was called the two-topsail schooner. This vessel set two light yards on her mainmast and was especially popular in American waters, some of the finest American privateers being so rigged. Mr. H. I. Chapelle, in his *History of American Sailing Ships*, gives the sail plan of the famous American privateer schooner, *Prince de Neufchâtel*, which shows the square sail set. A few pages further back in the same book is a repro-duction of one of Roux's drawings, showing the French *La Gazelle* of 1821 with main topsail and topgallant sail, the topsail having two rows of reef points. This vessel was called a brig-schooner (brick-goëllette) by the French. Mr. Chapelle calls it an hermaphrodite.

It was, of course, necessary for all merchantmen to proceed under convoy, but the daring captains of the fruiters (especially those who picked up oranges in Spain and Sicily), knowing their own speed—they had vessels which even the smartest Dunkirker found it difficult to catch—often broke away from their convoys and came racing up the Channel—sometimes half a dozen in a bunch, and every one of them striving to be first on the London market. That was the time when water sails, jib-o'-jibs or jib topsails, not to mention tremendous gaff topsails, were to be seen.

The brig rig was most popular with the Geordie collier. The only difference between the brig and snow rigs was an extra mast alongside the main, which simply served the purpose of carrying the hoops of the hoisting spanker. The East Coast colliers were tough customers, and the most dashing of French privateersmen often found them more than he bargained for. There was no speed to them, of course, for the bow of one of these brigs often consisted of a solid balk of oak rounded like a barrel, to which was nailed a ledge supporting a short figurehead, often the bust of the owner, his wife or daughter. These collier brigs, however, were as handy beating up the London River on the tide as the Hull Greenlandmen were in the Arctic. A typical Blyth or Newcastle brig is to be found amongst Cooke's etchings. There was nothing very distinctive about her rig; a full outfit, however, of stunsails and staysails was carried. Some of these vessels were of great age (such as the famous *Cognac Packet*), and it was a common saying that it was difficult to wash down their decks owing to the ups and downs in the planking. Another very old collier was the *Brotherly Love*, which was afloat in Cook's time, and was always reputed to be the ship in which he first went to sea. This mistake occurred owing to confusion of names, for it was the *Freelove*, of Whitby, which was Cook's first ship. The *Brotherly Love* was sunk in collision off Harwich in 1887.

Most of the cross-channel traffic and also the coastal passenger traffic, such as from the Northern ports to London, was carried on in smart cutters. The cutter had a rig and a type of hull which had been especially developed by the English, just as the favourite of the French was the lugger and of the American the fore-and-aft schooner. So distinctive were the hulls of British cutters that even vessels rigged as brigs and schooners were spoken of as cutter-built when their hulls conformed (as they often did) to the cutter type.

Very much like the cutter was the hoy. This craft came originally from Holland and had the usual spritsail and leeboards, but in English waters it was transformed into what the Americans call a sloop. The Thames hoy has, of course, been immortalised by Charles Lamb; this was the passenger craft that took people from London for a joy-ride to Margate or Ramsgate before the days of the paddle-steamer.[1] In February, 1802, the hoy *Margate*, bound to London with twenty-four passengers, struck upon the Reculver Sand and most of her passengers were drowned.

The cutter rig was also common amongst the larger fishermen. It was not until well after the mid-Victorian decade that the North Sea and Brixham trawlers were lengthened into ketches. All round the coast small luggers of varying types were used for hand-line and trammel net fishing; and the lugger, a craft that could generally be beached, was the vessel par excellence of the smuggler. Our long-shoremen in those days were very tough customers and were never averse to a bit of smuggling or even wrecking, and they went astonishing distances in even the ordinary open pulling boat. In Southampton Water there were especially fast pulling boats in which the longshoremen thought nothing of rowing across the Channel and back again with cargoes of brandy, silk and tobacco.

So far as is known there were only two four-masted ships afloat during the Napoleonic wars (if we exclude Chinese junks). Both of these were experimental ships, the first was English and the second French. The English ship, which was named the *Transit*, was built at Itchenor from the designs of Captain Richard Hall Gower, who had resigned his appointment as chief mate of the East Indiaman *Essex* in order to give his whole attention to his new invention, which, he contended, would possess great advantages over ships of normal design.

Originally rigged as a five-masted barquentine, the *Transit* had an unusual amount of deadrise; but after her trials the fifth mast was removed and the foremast placed further aft, thus turning her into an

---

[1] Pleasure craft were quite common. They are not included in the total of barges, hoys, etc., given on page 51.

efficient four-masted barquentine. The sum of £8,000 was subscribed to build and equip her, Gower, her inventor and commander, taking ten shares; the rest being taken up by John Blades, her managing owner, four master-mariners, seven gentlemen, one clergyman and two maiden ladies. Her registered tonnage came out at 195 and her length was 98 feet.

On proceeding to London to load, the *Transit* gained great praise from the pilots owing to the ease with which she turned up the river to Blackwall, where she was taken into Perry's Dock.([1]) The popular interest in this revolutionary vessel was very great, and she was visited by Pitt (the Prime Minister), Earl Spencer (the First Lord of the Admiralty) and a number of naval officers. Captain Gower hoped that his ship would be given employment by the Admiralty, but in those days most naval officers were more conservative even than naval architects, and the *Transit* did not, apparently, meet with their approval. Whereupon Captain Gower loaded a cargo for Lisbon and sailed on September 18th, 1800.

In the Channel heavy sou'-westerly weather was met with. The *Transit* nevertheless succeeded in beating down to within seven miles of Portsmouth. Captain Gower, however, decided to put back as several of his small light sprits, as they were called, had carried away. These sprits were rigging spreaders to give support to the three after masts which, except for a boom running from the head of the fore-mast to the main (which seems to have been horizontal), were not stayed together in any way. On arriving in the Thames, Captain Gower gave up his charter, trans-shipped his cargo and remodelled his sail plan, doing away, as already stated, with the fifth mast and so placing the fore-mast that it could be stayed in the usual way to the bowsprit. The *Transit* when re-rigged was painted by T. Whitcombe, and there is a reproduction of J. Jeakes's engraving in the *Mariner's Mirror* for July, 1933 Vol. XIX, No. 3).

As soon as she was re-rigged, Captain Gower sought employment for her as a packet ship, both from the Post Office and the East India

---

([1]) Perry was a shipbuilder and his wet dock had not, at this period, been purchased by the East India Dock Company. It could be used, therefore, by any vessel. See page 51.

Company, (¹) but was obliged in the end to load a cargo of shot and saltpetre for the Portuguese Government. There was the usual delay in assembling the Lisbon convoy at Spithead, but Captain Gower took advantage of this delay to exhibit the sailing of his strange ship; and on July 2nd actually sailed round the Royal Yacht whilst she was lying in Christchurch Bay. By this date the Earl of St. Vincent had succeeded Lord Spencer as First Lord of the Admiralty, and both he and the Chairman of the Honourable East India Company informed Captain Gower that they were ready to purchase the *Transit*. Whereupon it was arranged that the *Transit* should be tested in the Channel against a fast sailing sloop-of-war. Her cargo was discharged and the Deputy Master Attendant of the East India Company boarded her for the trials. The *Osprey*, a 383-ton sloop-of-war built in 1798 from the lines of a French corvette, was selected to test her.

The trials took place off the Isle of Wight, and the *Osprey*, which had the reputation of being a very fast ship and had had great success in ridding the Channel of many notoriously speedy Dunkirk privateers, was beaten on every point of sailing. In spite, however, of the *Transit's* success neither the Admiralty nor the East India Company went further in the matter, and Captain Gower was obliged to re-ship his cargo and sail with the convoy. The *Transit* was eventually employed in the Turkish trade and she more than once ran the gauntlet of the Spanish gunboats which cruised off Gibraltar and Tarifa on the lookout for vessels sailing without convoy, but her speed invariably brought her out safely. The end of this remarkable ship was recorded in *Lloyd's List* as taking place during the autumn of 1810, when on a voyage from Haiti to Smyrna she was wrecked off the south-west end of Heneaga.

The other four-master was a square-rigged French privateer, of 24 guns and 210 men, captured on her first cruise, nine days out from Bordeaux. This valuable prize was sold at Plymouth in October, 1801, and in the Bill of Sale the following particulars of her are given :

> "To be sold on Friday, October 9th, by ten o'clock in the forenoon, the handsome ship, *L'Invention*, of the following dimensions: Length on lower deck, 135 feet 5 inches; ditto of keel, 121 feet 3 inches; breadth, extreme,

---

(¹) The East India Company employed a few Packet Ships, usually in connection with the overland route to India.

27 feet 5 inches; moulded, 27 feet 1 inch; height between decks, 4 feet 9 inches; depth in the hold, 9 feet 4 inches, and measures 486 tons.

"She is quite new, and was built at Bordeaux, under the immediate care and inspection of Citizen Thibault, a celebrated member of the Society of Arts and Sciences and Belles Lettres: and fitted with four masts, which have been found to answer extremely well, in her sailing, even before the wind: she is allowed by the first Master Builders, by whom she has been examined, to be an exceedingly well and fine built vessel, of a beautiful Form and Model: her superiority of Sailing has enabled her to elude the Vigilance of our best Frigates, and she was only taken after a Chase of ten hours, and the loss of topmasts in a fog and heavy sea, which also prevented her escape by her Sweeps, worked by an entire new and novel machine of singular simplicity and effect; she abounds in stores, which are all new and of the best materials; has a neat Figure Head; a deep Waist; and is full coppered to the Wales. Mounts 24 guns, and appears well calculated for an East India Packet, the Southern or Whale Fishery, or Straits Trade, or any other business in which Safety and Dispatch are requisite, and is a prize to His Majesty's Ship of War *Immortalite*, Henry Hotham, Esq., Commander, taken in sight of the *Arethusa*, Thomas Wolley, Esq., Commander, and now lies in the Hamoaze, and will be there delivered."

Some enterprising merchants of Guernsey bought *L'Invention* and employed her in the Straits trade. Though all but four of her guns were removed and she carried a crew of only thirty-one men (two mates, twenty-one seamen, five boys and three petty officers) instead of two hundred and ten, she was granted a "Letter of Marque." An engraving of this ship appears in the seventh volume of the *Naval Chronicle*, and there is believed to be a painting of her in existence which was done at Naples in 1803.

L'Invention is shown under all plain sail with royals on fore, main and mizen, but only topsail and topgallant sail set besides an enormous spanker on the jigger mast. She is given a tremendous jibboom, setting four head sails, and staysails are set on every available stay between the masts, which are of unequal length, the main being the highest, fore and mizen about equal, and the jigger truck reaching about as high as the mizen topgallant yard. In order to give spread to this sail plan the foremast was raked slightly forward and the jigger mast aft.

On her first voyage under her new owners she arrived at New York on 20th October, 1802, forty-four days from Leghorn and thirty from Gibraltar. This was a fast passage for those days, and indeed all her passages seem to have been well above the average, witness the following taken from some of her log books which are still in the possession of a grandson of her Guernsey skipper:

Left Gibraltar	April 7th,	arrived	Virginia	May 14th,	37 days
„ Norfolk	June 22nd,	„	Leghorn	July 31st,	39 „
„ Leghorn	September 12th,	„	New York	October, 26th,	44 „
„ Norfolk	November 29th,	„	Leghorn	January 8th,	40 „
„ Guernsey	June 13th,	„	St. John's, N.B.	July 3rd,	20 „

This last was a very exceptional passage for a West-bound one across the Atlantic. *L'Invention* was eventually lost off the River Plate soon after her Guernsey owners had sold her.

From their records these two four-masted ships, *Transit* and *L'Invention*, deserve to be classed amongst the clippers, but they seem to have had no effect on contemporary shipbuilding design. Revolutionary changes were imminent, but the prototypes of the clipper ships came neither from Itchenor nor from Bordeaux. They came, in the form of schooners and brigs, from the Baltimore shipyards; and they came unnoticed until, right at the end of our period, the American privateers proved so difficult to catch.

CHAPTER V

Seamen

by BASIL LUBBOCK

Author of "The China Clippers" and other works

THE seaman of the Napoleonic Wars lived a life that was so divorced from the land that it was not possible to mistake him. In physique, in his outlook upon life, in his clothes and even in his very speech he was unmistakable. In the technique of his craft the sailor who had voyaged with Hawkins and Drake would have found no difficulty aboard an East Indiaman. Indeed, he would have found little to worry him in the handling of a twentieth century four-masted barque; and it was not until the middle of the Victorian era that the man-of-warsman differed in any way from the merchant seaman.

During those long years of war, which came to be called "1800-and-war-time," the proper handling of a ship's armament was as much a part of a sailor's education as the handling of her sails. The seaman had to know how to fight a broadside gun, whether it was a long gun or a carronade. Though he was not expected to be a marksman he had to be conversant with the use of the musket and pistol. The favourite weapon, however, of the British tar was undoubtedly the boarding pike; a weapon which accounted for the successs of many a gallant boarding affray and many a defence against overwhelming odds.

Captain William Nugent Glascock, R.N., the author of *The Naval Sketch Book* (published in 1826), thus describes the sailor:

> "Sailors are a remarkable, plain, downright race, as no man acquainted with their character would deny. Devoid of all guile, the seaman never thought to disguise his object, though he might sometimes be found 'veering and hauling' to get rid of some difficulty which he imagined lay in his way."

And Nelson is supposed to have said, "Aft the more honour, forward the better man."

The British seaman was, as a rule, drawn from the sea ports and coastal towns, and from the lower strata of society, and he was extraordinarily ignorant of civilised life and the ways of the land. Nevertheless, the captains and officers of all merchant ships (except those in the employ of the Honourable East India Company) had risen from the fo'c'sle; the common expression for the successful seaman's life being: "in at the hawse hole and out of the cabin window." There were several drawbacks to officers of this type. To begin with, they were seldom more than rule-of-thumb navigators, for the man who had had to teach himself to read and write, once he had learnt the use of the three "L's"—log, lead and latitude, was generally content with his qualifications as a navigator. Then again, the man who rose to command from the ranks had lived a life of such hardship and of such rough treatment that in most cases the fibre of his character had been hardened, and this often made him a cruel task-master without any bowels of compassion. Here is a quotation from a short essay on the character of sailors in the *Naval Chronicle* of 1807:

> "Inured to hardships, to dangers and to a perpetual change of companions the seaman contracts a species of stoicism which might raise the envy even of a Diogenes. 'Avast there!' cried a sailor to his comrade, who was busy in heaving overboard the lower division of a mess mate, just cut in halves by a chain shot, 'Avast! let us first see if he has not the key of the mess chest in his pocket'!"

Anecdotes of this sort, of course, could be quoted without end.

Another class of anecdote about the sailor, which was a great favourite with eighteenth century editors, was that which dealt with Jack ashore on the spree, throwing his hard-earned guineas about, riding horses facing the tail, etc. Here is an example of this type of story (taken from the *Naval Chronicle* of 1808). It describes the character of British seamen in a work called "Letters of England," said to be translated from the Spanish but rather believed to be the production of Mr. Southey, the poet; the correspondent ended up:

> "As for fear it is not in their nature. One of these men went to see a juggler exhibiting his tricks; there happened to be a quantity of gunpowder in the apartment underneath, which took fire, and blew up the house. The sailor was thrown into a garden behind, where he fell without being hurt. He

stretched his arms and legs, got up, shook himself, rubbed his eyes, and then cried out (conceiving what had happened to be only part of the performance, and perfectly willing to go through the whole), 'Damn the fellow! I wonder what the devil he will do next'!'

Many of Jack's sprees ashore ended, of course, in the law courts, and his defence of his own case often gained him an acquittal. Here is an example (also from the *Naval Chronicle* of that year):

"A short time ago, a seaman, who seemed to have stowed away more grog than he could steadily carry, was brought before the sitting alderman, at the Mansion House, by a publican, at whose house he lodged, charging him with having broken his windows, and assaulted him. Honest Ben, a veteran near 60, who appeared to have weathered many a hard gale, and was a good deal shattered, both in hull and rigging, after hearing the charge against him, and being asked what he had to say in his defence, turned his quid, hitched up his trousers, and addressing the worthy alderman in the true forecastle dialect, said, 'Why, your honour, belike I might have come athwart this here man in a breeze, and mauled him a little, fore and aft; but he has forgot to tell your honour as how he began first; so your honour must overhaul him a bit before you send me to the bilboes. Your honour must know, I am a customer at his house, and take my berth there, and he's my purser, and all that; but he has forgot to tell you as how that he hove me overboard last night, and shattered my head rails and lower timbers before I begun and stove in his lights. And does your honour think that I, who have been a seaman in his Majesty's service, man and boy, these 40 years, will ever take such rough hauling from e'er a lubber in Europe, without giving him a battle? If I do, then I say I am no seaman.' This harangue produced a good deal of laughter, and honest Ben was dismissed, upon a promise that he would not strike his landlord again, unless his landlord struck him first."

It has been contended, especially by the late R. C. Leslie, the author of *Old Sea Wings, Ways and Words*, that the sailor of the days of sail was of far finer physique than the landsman of the same date. Leslie exhibited a picture in the Academy entitled *A Sailor's Yarn*, which emphasized the difference in length of limb and breadth of shoulder between the seaman and the landsman. This picture had the honour to be inspected by Turner at the Academy, who, after looking at it intently for a moment, exclaimed: "I see, a gull; I like your colour." The gull, of course, was the least important part of the picture.

A naval officer, writing his reminiscences of the Leeward Station during the war, gives the following description[1] of a seaman aboard a man-of-war brig:

"There was a seaman of herculean frame in her, whose strength was

---

[1] Nautical magazine.

in proportion to his bulk, and whose mildness was equal in degree to his great muscular power and courage. His name was Ogden, or Ogburn, I forget which; and he alone managed the foremast gun, a carronade upon a carriage;(¹) when this gun became heated it repeatedly upset, but was instantly righted by him, apparently without much effort; it was a curious sight to see the earnestness and ease with which this single *homo* performed his part, loading, priming, firing, spungeing, and running out his piece, without the slightest assistance from any other person; and all executed in equal time with the others! He performed the feat of lifting up a carronade (I believe, a 12-pounder), from the hold, placing it on his shoulder, and ascending with it in that position, up the ladder, to the deck!"

He goes on:

"In the whole course of my experience, I do not recollect to have seen but one deformed seaman; he was 'hump-backed,' was a gunner's mate, and a valuable man: the only piece of vanity I observed in him was the extraordinary care he took of his huge 'pig-tail,' or queue, without exception the most monstrous I have ever seen belonging to the genus."

The sailor was a much more national character right up to the end of the nineteenth century than he is at the present day. The nautical character in the drama is now a rarity, but was very common in the eighteenth century. Again he was the hero of much doggerel and a great deal of satirical verse. Such prints as *The Sailor's Farewell, The Sailor's Return, The Contented Waterman, Pretty Poll and Honest Jack, Tom Truelove's Knell, Lovely Nan,* and *The True British Tar,* illustrated many popular songs about the sea service.

Going back a few years into the eighteenth century there was a still greater vogue for prints with a feminine interest, with such nautical titles as *A Man-of-War Towing a Frigate into Harbour,* and *An Engagement Between the "Heart of Oak" and "Charming Sally";* another was entitled *Jack on a Cruise.* There were, of course, innumerable ships and sailors immortalised on pottery. Unfortunately, mugs, plates and punch bowls are easily smashed. Comparatively little of this pottery has survived to the present day, and it grows rarer, of course, as time goes on.

It is only natural that the nautical fiction of the period should be centred upon the Royal Navy. Indeed, the greater part of it was the work of naval officers, and the Merchant Service was sadly neglected. Later writers, however, such as Cupples, Captain Marryat and Clark

---

(¹) Carronades were often on a fixed mounting and recoiled on a slide.

Russell have pictured life aboard an East Indiaman. Clark Russell also wrote a privateering yarn named *An Ocean Freelance*, which gives a very clear and correct picture of a privateersman's calling, and is undoubtedly one of his best books.

In reading Marryat's amusing books, such as *Peter Simple* and *Mr. Midshipman Easy*, many have thought that he was caricaturing the British seaman, but as a matter of fact there was little exaggeration in any of his characters. After long years afloat it is not surprising that the seamen of that date went in for wild orgies of drinking when ashore, and indeed it is to be feared that drink accounted for more than half the shipwrecks and sea tragedies of those days. Too often when a man gained command of a ship and for the first time in his life was his own master, the temptation of the bottle proved more than he could resist, and ruin and degradation sooner or later was the result.

There were no qualifications or, indeed, examinations, for the officers in the Mercantile Marine, except in the service of the East India Company. The Company offered a career which was very much sought after, and it was preferred in many cases to the Royal Navy as offering better opportunities of making a fortune. This, in spite of the known fact that many a commander of a flash frigate or smart gun-brig made a tidy little sum out of his prize money during the long years of warfare.[1] At a period when noble birth and rank were almost worshipped there were practically only five careers considered fitting for the younger sons of the nobility and landed gentry. These were: the Royal Navy, the Army, the Bar, the Church, and last, but by no means least, the Merchant Service, as it was called (this was, of course, the East India Company's service). Not only were half-pay naval officers found in the Company's ships, but at the end of the war there was a general rush of unemployed lieutenants and midshipmen to join the Company's service.

If the privileges and opportunities of making money were great, the expenses were also great. To quote from the unpublished auto-biography of a commander of the East Indiaman, *Royal George*:

"I had no family friends, and hardly one in the world of any power, but

---

[1] Admirals made even more through having a share in every prize taken by every ship under their command.

my old commander, Lord Torrington, and I appealed to him when I received an Admiralty order to return to the Jamaica station on promotion, which after what had occurred I had no great heart for, and also I began to look the position of a lieutenant in the Navy at £120 a year for life in the face.

"The world was tired of war, so I thought I might do something better, and I went down to his lordship's seat in Kent to talk the affair over. Of course, he was angry and much against my leaving the service, but he yielded, and I pointed out to him the Honourable East India Co. service was open to me. He then gave me letters to a very rich and powerful East India Company house of the firm of Alexander & Co., they appointed me third mate of their ship, the *Royal George*, but when I got on board, to my grief, I found their uniform was more expensive than the Navy and their mess expenses twice that of H.M. ships.

"I could not return to Messrs. Alexander again to give up my appointment without writing to his lordship to explain the situation. I found myself thanking him gratefully for all he had done for me, but under the circumstances I must return my appointment to Messrs. Alexander & Co.

"Two days later a man came on board with a letter from his lordship enclosing a cheque for £200, and then he said, 'I am his lordship's tailor and have his orders to fit you out for the voyage.' Rest assured I was grateful, and nine years after, when I commanded that ship on my return home from that voyage, I had to my credit on their books £15,000."

It should be explained that the owners of the ships (usually called the "ships' husbands,"(¹) but entered in the Honourable Company's books as the "managing owners") were responsible for all the appointments of officers and crew, even including the "guinea-pigs," as East India midshipmen were nicknamed. But the promotion of officers was strictly regulated by the Company itself. From cadet to commander the Company's officers had to serve a stated period in each rank before gaining promotion to a higher one.

The following regulations were established by the Court of Directors at the end of the year 1793 in this Minute:

RESOLVED :

THAT a Chief Mate shall have attained the full age of twenty-three years, and have performed a voyage to and from India, or China, in the Company's service, in the station of Second or Third Mate.

That a Second Mate shall have attained the full age of twenty-two years, and performed a voyage to and from India, or China, in the Company's service, in the station of Third or Fourth Mate.

That a Third Mate shall have attained the full age of twenty-one years,

---

(¹) See Chapter VII, page 146.

and have performed two voyages to and from India, or China, in the Company's service.

That a Fourth Mate shall have attained the full age of nineteen years, and performed one voyage to or from India, or China, in the Company's service.

N.B.—Every person previous to his being first appointed a Sworn Officer must produce a certificate from the parish-register, or other satisfactory proof, of his age.

At the same time the commanders, officers and petty officers, including even the ship's cook, were granted the privilege of occupying a certain amount of space in the ship for their own private trade, and were also allowed to carry out bullion for their own purposes.

For a ship of 755 tons or upwards, the space allowed was as follows:

PRIVILEGE OUTWARDS :

	TONS	FEET		TONS	FEET
Commander.. ..	56	20	Four Midshipmen, each	1	10
Chief Mate	8	0	Coxswain		10
Second Mate ..	6	0	Six Quarter-Masters,		
Third Mate	3	0	each	1	10
Purser	3	0	Captain's Steward ..		10
Surgeon	3	0	Ship's Steward ..		10
Surgeon's Mate ..	2	0	Captain's Cook ..		10
Fourth Mate.. ..	2	0	Ship's Cook		10
Fifth Mate	1	0	Carpenter's First Mate		10
Sixth Mate		10	Caulker		10
Boatswain	1	0	Cooper		10
Gunner	1	0	Armourer		10
Carpenter	1	0	Sailmaker		10

BULLION OUTWARDS :

	£			£
Commander	3,000	Surgeon's Mate		100
Chief Mate..	300	Fourth Mate		100
Second Mate	200	Fifth Mate		50
Third Mate..	150	Boatswain		50
Purser	150	Gunner		50
Surgeon	150	Carpenter		50

In addition, the commanders of China ships were allowed to carry £3,000 in bullion (i.e., silver) for the purchase of gold.

The private trade allowed in India and China was in coral, amber, coral beads, amber beads, pearls, emeralds and any sort of precious stones; the commanders and officers being obliged to pay to the Company the same duties and commission as ordinary traders.

Privileges homewards from China consisted of:

			TONS					TONS
Commander	..	..	38	Surgeon's Mate	..	..	2
Chief Mate..	..	..	8	Fourth Mate	..	..	2
Second Mate	..	..	6	Fifth Mate ..	..	..	1
Third Mate	..	..	3	Boatswain ..	..	..	1
Purser	..	..	3	Gunner	..	..	1
Surgeon	..	..	3	Carpenter ..	..	..	1

Privileges homewards from India consisted of :

				Surgeon's Mate	1 ton	24 feet
Commander	..	30 tons	32 feet	Surgeon's Mate	1 ton	24 feet
Chief Mate	..	6 „	16 „	Fourth Mate ..	1 „	24 „
Second Mate	..	4 „	32 „	Fifth Mate ..		32 „
Third Mate	..	2 „	16 „	Boatswain ..		32 „
Purser ..	..	2 „	16 „	Gunner.. ..		32 „
Surgeon	..	2 „	16 „	Carpenter ..		32 „

The private trade was mostly in china ware, silk, musk, camphor and arrack. Even though Custom's duty, Company's duty and hire of warehouse room from the Company had to be paid, these trade allowances often netted a handsome profit for the senior members of an East Indiaman's complement.

There was one other privilege allowed the captain, and that came under the heading of dunnage for the protection of cargo and stores. Commanders made this the opportunity for bringing home large amounts of rattans, wanghees, canes, bamboos and other valuable wood, and so much space was taken up unnecessarily under this denomination that a regulation had to be made confining this so-called dunnage strictly to the amount necessary for its ordinary function. Nor was this the commander's only privilege, for he was allowed to import two pipes of Madeira wine,([1]) and what was known as the flooring chop of teas was allowed as commander's privilege. This was limited to a height of 13 inches, and not allowed to exceed 20 tons in an 800-ton ship, 30 tons in a 1,200-ton ship and 40 tons in a 1,400-ton ship.

Besides these trade allowances the commander of an East Indiaman received primage and passage money, though it was his duty, of course, to provide provisions and stores for the passengers. The

---

([1]) East Indiamen called at Madeira on the outward but not on the homeward voyage. The wine had therefore to travel out to the East and back. See page 152 and the front end-paper.

passage money alone on an average voyage came to £1,500, and Lindsay gives an instance of an East India commander making no less than £30,000 out of the round voyage from London to India, from India to China, and home; and £10,000 a voyage was quite usual for a commander with a good business head. Passengers who wished to mess at the captain's table on the outward passage paid as much as £100 extra for the privilege.([1])

The extra allowances for officers were laid down at the same liberal rate; the commander, for instance, was allowed 11 tons of liquor, wine, beer and spirits, reckoning 36 dozen quart bottles to the ton. In the cuddy the chief officer was allowed 24 dozen of wine and beer, the second officer 20 dozen, the purser 16, and the surgeon 14. In the gun-room mess the third mate was allowed 16 dozen, the fourth mate 12, the fifth mate 10, the surgeon's mate 12. In addition, each of these messes was allotted a puncheon of rum. There was another descending scale of allowances in the matter of groceries; the chief officer, for instance, being allowed two firkins of butter, one cwt. of groceries, four cwt. of pickles and one cwt. of cheese. Every officer and petty officer, moreover, was allowed his own servant, and the captain two servants.

As regards the uniform, the captain's uniform coat was of blue cloth with black velvet lapels, cuffs and collar of gold embroidery, the buttons being stamped with the lion and crown of the Honourable East India Company. The waistcoat and breeches were of deep buff; his neck was throttled in a huge black stock, and on ceremonial occasions he wore a cocked hat and side arms.([2]) In the East he ranked on an equality with a post-captain in the Royal Navy.

The pay of an able seaman was 35s. per month, with two months' advance, which was handed over to his boarding master, usually a Ratcliffe Highway Jew. In order to cash their advance notes seamen were obliged to put up with high rates of discount from the slop shopkeepers and others who made this their business. There were no shipping offices in those days and the crews were selected by the first and second officers and the boatswains before the ships hauled out of

---

([1]) For further details of the messing arrangements, see Chapter VII, page 154.

([2]) See frontispiece. Sir Nathaniel Dance, Commodore in the action between the China Fleet and the French Admiral Linois in 1804, is shown in the East India Company's uniform, but wears no stock.

dock. It was of the first importance in an officer to be an expert judge of sailormen.

Since Elizabethan days the chief nursery of seamen has been on the East Coast serving aboard the colliers and Baltic traders. These hardy North Countrymen were perhaps one of the earliest communities to form a Labour Union. This Union, however, did little towards improving their lot aboard ship or the standard of their wages. Its chief aim was to maintain a high quality of seamanship. In those days seamen were apprenticed to the sea, and before a man was allowed to serve as an able seaman he had to pass a *viva voce* examination in seamanship before a committee of experts and prove that he was able to perform any rigging work that could possibly be required aboard ship. Few seamen of the present day could pass one of these examinations. Not only had the candidate to answer questions on how to handle a ship in any given circumstances (even to "club-hauling" off a lee shore), but he had to be able to demonstrate the sail-maker's art before his examiners, such as putting a clew or a cringle into a fore-and-aft or a square sail. He had to be able to graft, make Turk's heads, whale knots, rose knots, and point ropes' ends. He had to turn in a deadeye neatly, strop a block, make long and short splices, make a Carrick bend with two ends of a hawser, rig a topmast stunsail boom, and so on.

The usual apprenticeship indentures were concluded between the apprentice, with the advice and consent of his father, and the merchant or mariner. For four years, it was agreed, the apprentice

"shall faithfully serve his master, keep his secrets, gladly do his lawful commands, waste not his goods nor lend them unlawfully, shall not commit fornication nor contract matrimony, shall not play at cards nor dice tables, or any other unlawful games without licence of his said master; should neither buy nor sell; shall not haunt taverns, nor playhouses, nor absent himself from his said master's service day or night unlawfully, but in all things as a faithful apprentice shall behave himself. In consideration of which the said (name of master) for himself, his executors and administrators doth covenant promise and agree shall teach and instruct by the best means he can his said apprentice in the art of a mariner, finding the said apprentice sufficient meat, drink, lodging and all other necessaries except wearing apparel."

The apprentice was generally paid at the rate of £7 for the first year, £8 for the second, £10 for the third and £12 for the fourth by decent owners, though it is to be feared that the apprentice saw little of this money, being usually in debt to the ship at the end of the voyage.

One of the greatest nurseries of seamen was that of Arctic whaling,([1]) and the Greenlandman, like the South Sea whaler, had always a number of green hands aboard learning the craft of whaling. During the war years the protections granted the Greenlandmen were often little heeded by the commanders of men-of-war, and the officers engaged in pressing seamen. As a result there was very bad blood between the Greenlandmen and the men-of-war on the North Sea Station, and there were several instances of the former resisting the press. The chief grievance of the whalers was that on their return from the fishing, men-of-war sent their boats aboard them off the coast, and even the guard ships off White Booth Roads boarded them for the purpose of pressing seamen.

In 1798 the crew of the returning Hull whaler *Blenheim* fought off the boats of the sloop-of-war *Nautilus* with their long lances and harpoons. Having taken the precaution of securing her master and pilot in the cabin the angry Greenlandmen refused to heave to, but unfortunately got their ship aground at the entrance to the harbour. Whilst other man-of-war boats lay off and kept up a musketry fire, the launch of the guard-ship *Nonsuch* (commanded by Lieutenant Bell) attempted to board. The man-of-war's men were received with a load of grape shot from a swivel, and when at close quarters found that a harping iron wielded by a wild-looking whaleman was a terrible weapon. Indifferent to the bullets whistling over their heads, crowds of people watched the fight from the Humber Street ship-yards and from the garrison side. The boat was beaten off with the lieutenant a casualty and two men so badly wounded that they died shortly afterwards in hospital. No sooner had the boats cleared off than the crew of the *Blenheim* slipped ashore and went into hiding. Although £100 was offered for the apprehension of the men who had killed the man-of-war's men no information came forward.

It was about this date that a man-of-war's men attempted to press the local strong man, William Kerr, who stood 6 feet 4 inches and weighed 24 stone. After a terrific fight against tremendous odds Kerr

---

([1]) One of the enterprises, originally, of the South Sea Company. See Chapter III, page 73 for the numbers and tonnage of ships employed.

was overpowered and carried aboard the boat. The story goes that he sat quietly until the boat was well on her way to the ship, then, with his back against one gunwale and his feet against the other, he began to push without being noticed. Suddenly the boat split in two and sank, whereupon Kerr swam ashore and returned without saying a word to his blacksmith's shop. According to local tradition all the other occupants of the boat were drowned. Many other exploits are told of this Blythe Hercules, such as carrying a heavy anchor across his shoulders for half a mile, and jumping a five-bar gate with an eight-stone woman under his arm.

There are innumerable stories of Greenlandmen and French privateers. In 1794 the Hull whaler *Raith* was captured near the Shetlands when returning to Hull from the fishing. A prize crew of sixteen Frenchmen was put aboard her and her own crew, with the exception of the mate and one seaman, were carried aboard the privateer. As was often the case with wild privateersmen they celebrated their capture by a carouse. Soon the watch below turned in to a drunken slumber, and the watch on deck clambered into a whale boat hanging from the quarter davits and were soon snoring like their fellows. The mate and seaman of the *Raith* were quick to take advantage of this. Having cut the falls and let the boat drop into the sea with its nine drunken Frenchmen, they then nailed up the companionway, thus confining the seven remaining men below deck. After this they successfully navigated the *Raith* into Lerwick.

Another recapture that year was that of the South Sea whaler *Chaser*, of London, which was coming north-about, fearing to risk the English Channel. She was captured on July 19th off the Orkneys by an 18-gun privateer. She was recaptured by the second mate and three boys, the rest of her ship's company having been removed aboard the privateer. In this case also she was safely navigated into port, reaching Peterhead eight days later.

Another instance of gallant recapture was that of the *Harmony*, of Hull, which was one of the Baltic convoy which left Elsinore on December 12th, 1803. On December 17th she was captured by a Dutch privateer which, as was usual with privateers, took out her master and crew, with the exception of the mate and two hands. A prize master and five Dutchmen were put aboard to navigate her to

Holland. On December 26th the three Englishmen recaptured the ship after a terrific fight which lasted for half an hour, in which one of the Dutchmen was killed and the Dutch commander and two others were wounded. Before the intrepid three could get the *Harmony* into port they had to weather out a bad gale. Nevertheless, though the ship was damaged in her rigging they succeeded in gaining Balto Sound in the Shetlands on December 31st. After being refitted the *Harmony* eventually reached Hull on February 8th, having been given up for lost when the convoy arrived without her. At Hull her recapture was reported in the news sheets as "an enterprise which for daring had been seldom known, and merited reward from the owners and underwriters."

Of all British seamen Greenlandmen had the reputation for being the toughest, and, as a rule, French privateers fought very shy of such ugly customers. Amongst seamen a Greenlandman's galley was considered to be "lowest in the scale of vulgarity," its inmates being more wild and uncouth, more rough and blasphemous in their speech and more swayed by superstition than any other seamen under the British flag. After a visit to Lerwick in 1814, Sir Walter Scott wrote:

> "Here's to the Greenland tar, a fiercer guest
> Claims a brief hour of riot, not of rest;
> Proves each wild frolic that in wine has birth,
> And wakes the land with brawls and boisterous mirth."

It was the custom for Greenlandmen to put into Lerwick on their way to the fishing in order to take aboard a number of Shetland seamen, who were cheaper than the more skilful English and Scottish seamen, as well as steadier.

The last of the *Centurion's* crew, George Gregory, who had been pressed from the collier brig *Mary*, of North Shields, when in the Downs, died at Kingston on 13th February, 1804, at the age of 109. He had begun his sea life as a ship's boy of fifteen as far back as 1714. By far the most interesting account, however, of a sailor's life covering this period is the autobiography of John Nicol, who dictated his story to John Howell, of Edinburgh, who, besides the *Life and Adventures of John Nicol* (published by Blackwood in 1822), wrote the *Life and Adventures of Alexander Selkirk* (published in 1828).

Nicol was born in 1755, went to sea in 1776, and after serving in men-of-war, Greenlandmen, South Seamen, East Indiamen, convict ships and in a discovery ship, ended up his sea service aboard the *Goliath*, in which he was present at the battle of St. Vincent and the Battle of the Nile. Nicol was a very steady, careful living sailor for his day. His father was a cooper by trade, and for practically the whole of his time at sea Nicol acted the part of "bungs," as the cooper was always called. But he was one of those seamen on whom officers could depend, and thus he was always somewhat of a privileged man and was often given such enviable jobs as brewing spruce beer.[1]

Not the least interesting of his experiences was service aboard a convict ship, the *Lady Julian*, bound to New South Wales with female convicts. Contrary to the usual belief there was no ill-treatment of these convicts, and the worst punishment was called the "wooden jacket." This was an old barrel with a hole cut in the top for the head and one on each side for the arms. Though a hardened woman convict treated this as a joke at first, she soon wearied of it as she could neither sit nor lie down. The discipline on a female convict ship seems often to have been fairly lax, and the women were allowed full liberty aboard; each one, indeed, being allowed to choose a temporary husband from the crew.[2]

An interesting diary of an able seaman aboard a convict ship was published in the "Blue Peter" in 1930. This diary was just 100 years old, but conditions in 1830 were, if anything, worse than they were twenty years earlier. The convict ship, which was the *Kains*, of 353 tons register, built in 1816, and belonging to Kains & Co., of Shields, took her live freight on board off Woolwich; Charles Picknell, the diarist, making the following entries:

> 29th June, took in all prisoners from Horsemonger Prison.
>
> 30th, took in all prisoners from Newgate Prison, all ironed and acrying.
>
> July 1st, 1830, took in prisoners from Liverpool and Manchester, heavy irons.
>
> 2nd, took in prisoners from Birmingham and City of York.

---

[1] An antiscorbutic. See Chapter VI, page 125.

[2] This state of affairs was not invariable. See page 116.

3rd, a Sunderland brig drove athwart us and carried away our main topsail yard in two pieces.

4th, Scotland prisoners took in.

5th, Irish prisoners took in.

7th, all prisoners and free women aboard. The Quakers came on board praying with them and giving the prisoners all kinds of useful things.

8th, a.m., 1 o'clock, we sail from Woolwich. 10 o'clock at the Nore. Prisoners came on deck, little thought where they were.

2 p.m., off Margate.

4 p.m., off Broadstairs. Fired a bull-dog (salute) to the Captain's father.

8 p.m., let go our anchor in the Downs.

According to our able seaman there seems to have been more trouble with the crew, from the mate downwards, than with the convicts. The mate spent half his time in confinement, chiefly for being drunk. The second mate was also continually confined to his cabin, and the ship was only a day out from Plymouth when six able seamen were put into irons and lashed down to the poopdeck for two days for the crime of talking to the women. On the same day an apprentice, Frederick Smith, was tied up to the larboard main rigging and given six dozen lashes for saying: "You and I can't ist [hoist] this punchin of wine alone." A week later the chief mate was confined for getting drunk and encouraging his watch "to sing saucy songs." And so the voyage went on with always some of the crew in irons and an equal number in the doctor's hands owing to the poor food. The menu was certainly not ambitious, but may be taken as typical of the period except in that the quality was below average. The diarist complains bitterly and gives the weekly allowance as follows:

Sunday	..	..	Junk, duff
Monday	..	..	Hog, peas, sup [soup]
Tuesday	..	..	Bread, junk
Wednesday	..	..	Hog, peas, duff
Thursday	..	..	Junk, duff
Friday	..	..	Hog, peas, sup
Saturday	..	..	Junk, bread

He ends up his log by giving five verses of a typical sailor's song, of which the following are the first and last verses:

"I was paid off at the home
From a voyage to Sierra Leone;
Three pounds monthly was my pay.
When I drew the cash I grinned,
But I very soon got skinned
By a lass who lived in Peter Street called Ray."

"Oh my charming Nelly Ray,
They have taken you away,
You have gone to Van Dieman's cruel shore;
For you've skinned so many tailors,
And you've robbed so many sailors,
That we look for you in Peter Street no more."

When cooper of the East Indiaman *Nottingham* Nicol experienced one of the sailor's worst hardships of war-time. When the ship reached the Downs from Canton she was boarded at once by man-of-war boats and her whole crew pressed into the service, and the *Nottingham* had to be taken up the river to Blackwall by ticket-porters and Greenwich pensioners. Nicol also gives us, incidentally, a glimpse of soldiers aboard ship in those days of cramped accommodation. The poor soldier had a bad time of it, and Nicol remarked, "Every morning we threw overboard a soldier or a sheep."

Except in the service of the Honourable East India Company there was no uniform in the Mercantile Marine. Nevertheless, the clothes worn by the sailor were distinctive and unmistakable, and, whether supplied by a ship's slop chest or by some Jew slop shopkeeper from Ratcliffe Highway, conformed to the same pattern, and in this there was no distinction between the man-of-war's man and the merchant jack. In one of Thomas Dibdin's songs there is the following verse:

"'Tisn't the jacket and trousers blue,
The song or the grog so cheerly,
That show us the heart of a seaman true
Or tell us his manner sincerely."

And in another he puts the following words into the mouth of a
sailor's sweetheart:

"Aboard my true love's ship I'll go,
    And brave each blowing gale;
I'll splice, I'll tack, I'll reef, I'll row,
    And haul with him the sail:
In jacket blue and trousers too,
    With him I'll cruise afar,
There shall not be a smarter chap
    Aboard a man-of-war."

From these verses it would seem that the blue serge of the present
day was even then in general use, but the innumerable prints of the
period show that this was not so. A white cotton shirt with horizontal blue or red stripes, a neckerchief (usually black or dark blue)
in place of a collar, a short blue coat with fancy buttons, dungaree,
calico or white duck trousers (very often made aboard out of small
pieces of discarded lightweight canvas, for Jack was no mean tailor)
terminating above the ankles, and, lastly, white cotton stockings and
pumps with big brass buckles were worn on dress occasions and low
shoes (known as "purser's crabs") for ordinary use aboard ship,
though many foremast hands went barefoot summer and winter.[1]

The sailor's pigtail and his officer's neat club, tied in its black bow,
were almost universal in 1793, but had mostly gone out of fashion
before the end of the war. The pictures show the black tarpaulin hat
as Jack's usual headgear, but in the Merchant Service at any rate—
and also in the Royal Navy on the West Indies Station—beautifully-
made straw hats were the rule in the tropics; whilst in cold weather
knitted and soft cloth caps were sometimes worn.

Sailors slept in hammocks throughout the Napoleonic era, except
in the small, overcrowded privateers, in which there was no room
to stretch them. The need for light and pure air was not recognised
aboard ship until the nineteenth century was drawing to its close,[2]
and the atmosphere was often so foul below decks that a purser's dip

---

[1] See plate 11 for a seaman's dress as described.
[2] See Chapter VI, page 122.

would not keep alight. Even as late as 1853 the following evidence was given before a Royal Commission:

"In British ships the men are not treated as they ought to be. I have taken particular notice of their place of abode, which is in almost every ship of small size a small dark cave, without light or warmth, and not such a kind of place within which they may rest and repose themselves; and in point of size it is sometimes six or seven feet square, for six or seven men, stowed half full of rope and sails, damp and wet." These words applied equally to the war period, and it is evident from innumerable sailors' reminiscences that the deck was generally preferred, whenever weather permitted, to the sort of den they were usually allotted.(1)

Though the average seaman between our dates was the puppet of fate, serving now in the Navy, now in the Merchant Service, for one voyage in a whaler and the next perhaps in a slaver; being at one time a flying fish sailor or Sou'-Spainer, at another sugar-droghuing, coasting, or lumber-carrying up the St. Lawrence or Baltic, in each of these various types of sea life he found customs and usages which were peculiar to them.

The mercantile seamen who had the worst reputation during the Napoleonic Wars were those who manned the privateers, both British and French. Their discipline was considered negligible, their fighting powers very poor and their drinking habits beyond all reason, even in those days of gargantuan thirsts. They were thought, indeed, to be little better than pirates, all fish being considered good that came into their nets. No doubt there were many black marks against them, but wholesale condemnation, such as they received from the Royal Navy, was far from being completely justified. The merits or demerits of a privateer's crew necessarily depended upon the character of her commander.

Those with knowledge of the appalling cruelties of nineteenth century slaving might be tempted to suppose that the crew of a British slaver must have been less respectable even than that of the worst privateer. Such a theory would, however, be wrong. Before the transportation of slaves was forbidden it was a legitimate service, like any

---

(1) For the contemporary medical views on this matter, see Chapter VI, page 127.

other in the Mercantile Marine, and in the majority of English slavers the negroes were well treated, so that there was seldom any bad blood between them and their jailers. A case in point was the gallant affair in 1806 between the slaver *Mary* (Captain Adams) and a French frigate. Adams, backed up by his two hundred and fifty slaves, actually carried the deck of the Frenchman, but he was then killed by a chance bullet and the negroes, lost and bewildered without their leader, were driven over the side and lost what might have been their prize.

There are other instances of the like. On October 1st, 1799, in latitude 3° 30′ S., longitude 22° W., the slaver *Amelia and Eleanor* beat off a French privateer armed with eighteen six and nine-pounders. It was a hot affair, the slaver losing four of her crew wounded, one slave killed and four wounded, and the vessel itself so cut up that she was obliged to put into Barbados to repair.

Without a doubt the British seaman, whether he was in an East Indiaman, West Indiaman, Baltic trader, Whaler, Slaver, Collier or Coaster, was a very nasty customer to tackle, and never knew when he was beaten. Though a tower of strength at sea, he was a child ashore and the prey of every trickster that crossed his path. Unjustly treated by an ungrateful Government, after carrying his country's commerce and fighting his country's battles, he had little prospect in old age of being anything but a maimed beggar. He might consider himself lucky if he could keep himself alive by such trades as he had picked up at sea—such as cobbling, tailoring and the like. When the long years of war ended the number of maimed seamen begging in the streets was a national scandal; indeed it was stated that there was a continuous line of old seamen and soldiers singing choruses, and in other ways trying to earn sufficient to keep themselves alive, extending all the way from Liverpool to London.

CHAPTER VI

Health and Sickness

by J. A. NIXON, C.M.G., M.D., F.R.C.P.

Emeritus Professor of Medicine in the University of Bristol, formerly Consulting Physician to the British Armies in France. (Temporary Colonel, A.M.S.). Author of "Famine Dropsy," "Official Medical History of the War, 1914-1918," etc.

THE latter part of the eighteenth and the beginning of the nineteenth centuries represent a period during which sickness and deaths at sea reached their highest point. New countries were being opened up, British settlers, officials and troops were all making their way to distant lands. Trade and traffic on the seas increased. Yet sanitary science and preventive medicine lagged hopelessly behind. Accommodation on ship-board was insanitary and it was a lucky ship that cleared from an English port without some contagious sickness amongst the crew or passengers. At the time of the Napoleonic Wars no infectious disease could be controlled except, thanks to Jenner, small-pox. The mode of conveyance of the most fatal forms of transmissible disease was wholly unknown. It was not known until 1840 that enteric (or typhoid) fever was spread by human excretions, and the part played by lice in transmitting typhus was only discovered in 1909. Nor was the responsibility of the mosquito for conveying malaria and yellow fever recognised until 1897 and 1901 respectively. Even the infective nature of cholera and dysentery was in those days denied by the medical profession, although occasionally a shrewd observer like Captain King—who sailed with Cook—was "rather inclined to imagine that his people escaped the flux (i.e., dysentery) by the precautions which were taken to prevent them receiving it from others." Although tuberculosis or consumption carried off Captain Cook's own surgeon, Anderson, and one of his captains, Clerke, the view that it might be contagious (which had been suggested in 1689) met with no general acceptance.

Besides the pardonable ignorance of the transmission of infectious disease, accommodation and life on board ship were, except in fair weather, miserably foul and well calculated to produce sickness of all kinds. Ventilation in bad weather was difficult to secure. The bilge water could scarcely avoid contamination as well as developing the foulest smells. The victuals grew weevily, decayed and stank, and the drinking water, if it did not run short, became often well-nigh undrinkable. The number of privies in a ship was often hopelessly inadequate for the crew. In the Navy, especially, men were constantly being punished for absence because, owing to the scanty latrine accommodation, they went ashore without leave in order to find other accommodation.

The preservation of drinking water was one of the chief problems. According to Dr. Schoute, it was General Bentham who discovered that water would keep for years in wooden butts lined with tinned copper. In general, however, water was still kept in wooden casks, unlined, and always liable to "smell rather strong." The best remedy was that described by Lisiansky—taking the casks ashore and burning them out well. But he refers to another method involving a device called *Ostrige's purifying machine*. This must have been what Blane called "Osbridge's ingenious contrivance for sweetening water." "This consists," Blane continues, "of a hand pump which is inserted in a scuttle made at the top of a cask, and by means of it the water, being raised a few feet, falls through several sheets of tin pierced like cullenders and placed in a half-cylinder of the same metal. The purpose of it is to reduce the water into numberless drops, which being exposed in this form to the open air is deprived of its offensive quality. It is a machine very deservedly in common use . . . . " Another method, mentioned in Decker's report of 1768, was that of filtering, boiling and annealing. This last process was performed by opening the cask and exposing its contents to the air for twenty-four hours, after which a red hot iron was plunged into the water. The best method, however, of preserving water was to sail from Bristol where the local water was found to keep sweet for any length of time. "It is probably," Blane conjectured, "owing to the small impregnation of quicklime found in Bristol water that it is so incorruptible. It has the advantage of not being injurious to health, but on the contrary is rather friendly to the bowels, tending to prevent and check fluxes."

The commoner diseases at sea have been described by various authors. Lind (circa 1760) gives fever, scurvy, consumption, rheumatism and dysentery as the most frequent and fatal disorders in the Royal Navy. Blane, in 1782, gave as the most prevalent diseases of the English Fleet in the West Indies, fevers, fluxes, scurvy, ulcers, smallpox, rheumatism and pectoral complaints. It is interesting, as Rosen has pointed out, that whereas Lind found that scurvy accounted for 19 per cent. of the sick, Blane puts the figure at 6 per cent. On the other hand, Lind credited dysentery with 4 per cent., but Blane gave it 24 per cent. One of Lord Nelson's letters (to Dr. Baird, 22nd September, 1804) reminds us that consumption was also a very serious scourge at sea. "Of the few men we have lost," he writes, "nine in ten are dead of consumption." In 1772, Thunberg speaks of smallpox and measles as the most fatal distempers at the Cape of Good Hope. Occasionally, in a ship carrying many non-immune adults— in a slave ship for example—measles would prove severe and fatal, as it did when first introduced into Fiji.

The characteristic disease at sea, however, was scurvy, and we find mention of it at a very early date. It was Sir James Lancaster, commander of the first fleet sent by the East India Company to the East, who learnt—probably from the Dutch—how the disease could be prevented or cured. In 1599 he announced that oranges and lemons would do this, and that lemon-juice, moreover, could be shipped in casks and would remain drinkable and effective during the longest sea voyage. Despite this discovery and despite the later use of a variety of other (and cheaper) antiscorbutics, scurvy remained a common complaint. Writing two centuries later, Dr. Thomas Clark is puzzled by the prevalence of scurvy, which he knew Lancaster had overcome, and makes the reflection, "When we descend to modern times we find that we have not been more successful than our less-experienced ancestors." His wisest observation deserves, incidentally, to be preserved and handed on to all succeeding ages. "If the commanders of ships, the admirals, generals and officers of our fleets and armies were made responsible for any neglect in carrying out regulations of health . . . much human misery would be prevented. Our ships of war would not so often resemble floating funerals and our naval and military hospitals, pest-houses."

Blane has a good deal to say about scurvy and is one of the few writers who mention *night-blindness* as being sometimes associated with scurvy; as indeed it not infrequently is, although from a dietetic deficiency of a different kind. Scurvy is due to lack of Vitamin C, whilst night-blindness is due to lack of Vitamin A. These two vitamins are not found, as a rule, in the same class of food. Clark is very forthright about the prevention and cure of scurvy. "During the war the fleet was furnished with essence of malt: the powers of it were found to be so inconsiderable that some of the surgeons denied that it had any". "There is nothing yet known," Blane concludes," except lemon juice which possesses any certain and considerable curative power over this disease without the assistance of a proper diet." It is surprising to note that one of the greatest medical advisers of the Admiralty seems to have been unacquainted with the virtue of oranges, upon which the Dutch, no less than Lancaster, Woodall and Lind, laid such stress. It is still more surprising to find that Sir John Pringle, well known for his services to the Army, was an unconscious means of putting back the hands of the clock as regards scurvy and its prevention. At the Royal Society in November, 1775, he gave "a discourse upon some late improvements of the means of preserving the health of mariners." In this discourse he mentioned Lancaster, but made no reference to his cure for scurvy. Worse than that, he provided the Admiralty with an excuse for economising at the expense of their sailors' health. "I entirely agree with you, that the dearness of the rob [i.e., juice] of lemons and of oranges will hinder them from being furnished in large quantities; but I do not think this is so necessary, for though they may assist other things, I have no great opinion of them alone." These words are not Pringle's own. They are a quotation by him from a letter written by Captain Cook on July 7th, 1776. Whenever an attempt is made to give Cook the credit for overcoming the scourge of sea-scurvy this letter of his must be remembered, as also its influence when publicly quoted at the Royal Society by so eminent a man as Sir John Pringle.

There is evidence to suggest that certain other countries were ahead of England in the provision of antiscorbutics. Frederick Thomson, naval surgeon and author of *An Essay on the Scurvy* (1790), compares the British Navy unfavourably with the French. Like Blane, he mentions night-blindness as a symptom of scurvy. Recommending oranges, lemons and limes, he considers a pint of porter daily to be the best preventive of all. He ends, however, by quoting from the *Sentimental Journey*, published twenty-two years previously, "They order this matter better in France." More precise is our knowledge of the methods used by the Russian Admiral Krusenstern, who sailed round the world in 1803-6. He describes how his own ship, the *Neva*, anchored on August 25th, 1805, in the harbour of St. Peter and St. Paul. Eight weeks had passed since leaving Kamtschatcha. "In all our voyage," he writes, "we had not a single invalid, notwithstanding our total want of fresh provisions and that our antiscorbutic remedies were entirely exhausted." He makes a curious remark on scurvy that it had been thought impossible to prevent it as it originated in the sea air. "Nevertheless," he continues, "it is almost extirpated, means having been discovered of preventing it even on long voyages" by the use of potatoes, carrots and sourkrout, and by curtailing the excessive use of spirits. The *Neva* continued her voyage and arrived at Macao with her crew in the best possible condition. She had not lost a single man by sickness during her long stay on the coast of America (where no fresh supplies could be procured), nor on her passage to China. Krusenstern sums up his voyage, which lasted for three years and twelve days, by saying that his crew had "amazing good health throughout." His antiscorbutics were portable soup, essence of malt, essence of spruce or fir, dried yeast and mustard, sourkrout and cranberry juice. He apparently regarded tea as useful for the same purpose.

The account of Krusenstern's voyage was continued by Captain Lisiansky, of the Russian Navy, who sailed with him. Lisiansky records that their sourkrout was found in the highest state of corruption and that they were "deprived of a quantity of this valuable antiscorbutic that would have been more than sufficient for half the voyage." However, as an alternative, Lisiansky made spruce beer, "the essence of which," he says, "I had obtained in England." His other antiscorbutics included pumpkins, onions and essence of malt dissolved in hot water. At New Archangel (for his voyage took him into the Arctic circle) he laid in a stock of sorrel, prepared like sourkrout, together with hurtle berry juice and the berry itself packed in casks filled with water. "This," he says, "will keep a long time." Actually, thanks to his wise provisioning, he had no scurvy up to the time he was at New Archangel, but he was afraid of the length of the run thence to Canton. Lisiansky's plan was to vary his antiscorbutics and he used, on different days, his sorrel, his hurtle berry and his tea. He makes the curious observation that the Russians suffered from pain in the bowels when, after living on fish, they returned to bread.

The best way in which to carry preserved antiscorbutics was a matter of constant discussion. Gillespie gives some interesting details on this subject. "In the French Navy, sorrel is furnished in considerable quantity. It is beat up into a pulp of the consistency of an electuary (a stiff jam), a little salt added and put up into kegs, containing about twenty pounds. Thus prepared, it retains its virtues for twelve months and perhaps for a much longer time, and forms an excellent ingredient in soups for the convalescents and scorbutics." He describes the regular issue of lime juice in the British Navy, but adds that "Sour krout is no longer served in the navy, as the seamen make use of it with reluctance; yet there is very little doubt, that if cabbage were pickled with vinegar instead of being made into krout, the seamen would with avidity use the vegetables and the vinegar in which it had been preserved." The Dutch at Surinam were in the habit of preparing lime-juice with salt, "perhaps," adds Gillespie, "for medicinal use, which seems to be thus preservable for any length of time." "They also preserve limes," he states, "in a similar way, that is, the limes plucked before they are perfectly full, are put into a cask, and a pickle (most probably heated) somewhat stronger than sea-water is poured on them and the cask closed. Some prizes brought into Martinique from the port of Surinam were found to contain many casks of lime-juice and limes." Gillespie strongly recommends this method of curing the fruit.

Whereas scurvy was a complaint generally met with at sea, other diseases were peculiar to the Tropics or to particular parts of the world. Dr. Thomas Clark, in his book on the diseases which prevail in long voyages in hot countries, gives a Table of Diseases which occur on board ship. It is as follows:

Class I. Febrile Diseases: Remittent Fever, Hepatitis, Dysentery, etc.
Class II. Nervous Diseases: Apoplexy, Tetanus, Colic, Cholera

Class III. Cachectinal Diseases: Dropsy, Venereal Infection, Scurvy, etc.
Class IV. Local Diseases: Suppression of Urine, etc.

The classification of cholera as a nervous disease is a striking illustration of the amazing lack of observation which failed to notice the contagious character of this disease. But it was characteristic of the period, for in 1812, Mr. Ferguson, Inspector-General to the Army in Portugal, could report that "dysentery is in no case contagious"; an opinion which he shared with Sir John Pringle.

One problem bound to arise in the Tropics was that of ventilation between decks. It was generally believed that sleeping on deck, in the open air, would cause fevers and fluxes. On this last point, however, the contrary opinion was strongly held by James Johnson who, after sixteen years in the Navy, took up private practice and became Physician-Extraordinary to King William IV. In his book *The Oriental Voyager*, he publishes some "remarks on preserving the health of seamen in India." He speaks of the established regulation of making every man sleep in his proper berth and suffering none to be about the decks—"A system, in my opinion," he goes on, "very prejudicial to the health of ships' companies in India." Johnson draws a picture of a man turning into his hammock and falling fast asleep in a few minutes. At about eleven o'clock he awakes "in a deluge of perspiration and panting with the heat and rarified air; upon which he turns out and goes upon deck" to get a mouthful of fresh air. He gets up on the forecastle when the cool breeze from the shore immediately chills him and checks his perspiration. He is compelled by the regulations to go below and turns into his hammock; but during the course of the night he makes two or three more excursions to the deck. Such a ship's company will have a pallid, debilitated appearance and the sick list will be always crowded. He contrasts with this a ship where breach of the regulations is winked at by the officers. "If we look around us we shall see the forecastle, booms, waist-nettings strewn with sailors . . . in the ordinary dresses which they wore during the day . . . fast locked in the arms of Morpheus." This ship's company will look stout and healthy, there will be no long sick list or admissions to hospital. Johnson makes some exceptions when he would not allow sleeping on deck, such as during the rainy

season or when heavy dews fall during the night and, above all, "in
rivers and other situations where putrid exhalations are occasionally
blown off from the swamps or low muddy shores." We know now,
of course, that it was the mosquitoes not the putrid exhalations that
made these situations dangerous to sleepers on deck.

One of the most complete accounts of a voyage to India is contained in the observations of John Watson, surgeon on board the
Europa, which sailed from England to Madras and Bengal and back
again between January, 1792, and April, 1793. His account is exceedingly detailed and graphic. "Soon after the voyage began," he writes,
"an infectious fever broke out characterised by great thirst, nausea,
constipation, a hot dry skin and a rapid pulse. Wherever it appeared
it generally attacked nearly the whole berth or mess. Army recruits
were more affected than the ship's company because the former lived
on the orlop deck whilst the latter breathed a purer air. But they did
not entirely escape." The nature of this fever is uncertain. It was
evidently very benign, for he says that the ship's company on the
outward voyage numbered 103 and that, although 86 were sick, only
one died, and that as the result of a fall. The recruits and the passengers
from England, together with those who joined the ship at Madras
for Bengal, totalled 418. Of these, 264 were on the sick list, but only
one died. He gives the numbers (crew, passengers and recruits) who
were affected on the voyage to Madras as 350 out of 361 and comments that "with so many people confined in a small place with
fevers it will not appear extraordinary that one should die but that
so many should recover."

There were no orderlies or nurses on board, so that everything had
to be done by Watson and his assistant, Walker. "There was scarcely
a moment in which one or both of us was not employed in visiting
the sick, administering medicines to them, or in attending to other
duties equally necessary." Both surgeons frequently felt the effects of
the fever, "but aperients and occasionally a little bark kept them
well." As many of the sick as possible were brought upon the gun-
deck where a platform was erected for them and every mode that
could be devised to remove the foul air from them was made use of.
It must be remembered that the fever from which they suffered and
from which the "Jesuits' bark" (cinchona or quinine) protected

Watson and Walker was malaria: the cause of this fever was in those days considered to be as its name implies, "foul air."

"Cleanliness, good order and free circulation of air," says Watson, "are the first and great causes of health on board ship and without them medicine will avail but little." The *Europa* stopped at St. Iago, one of the Cape de Verde islands, hoping to obtain fruit and other fresh food. Owing to a drought which had lasted for three or four seasons there was no fruit to be had, and so the voyage continued to Madras without further stop. Several convalescents developed scurvy before Madras was reached, and during the ship's stay there the ship's company continued sickly. Madras was noted for its unhealthy situation and the principal diseases mentioned by Watson are remittent fevers or the marsh kind (i.e., malaria), bilious vomiting and dysentery. At Bengal the *Europa* turned round and sailed for the Cape of Good Hope. There were still fevers, and now with the returning passengers came dysentery and liver inflammations. Dysentery, we learn from another journal, sometimes made dreadful ravages amongst the ship's company. On one voyage in 1810 nearly seventy men died of it in nine weeks. This form of dysentery, with its liver inflammations, was almost certainly the *amoebic* form, since it could be cured by ipecacuanha enemata, as suggested by Thomas Clark, M.D., who was himself (as Trotter records) surgeon of an East Indiaman.

As the *Europa* sailed southwards scurvy appeared, especially among the convalescents from fever, contrary to Watson's usual experience that it was commonly on the run northwards from the Cape that scurvy occurred. After the Cape, however, the sick were plentifully supplied with vegetables and soup, so that Watson could record that "we became at length a healthy ship." After St. Helena there was very little sickness. Curiously, Watson does not mention any store of orange or lemon-juice as having been carried, although two hundred years earlier (in Lancaster's time) these had been part of the regular victualling of East Indiamen. There was a naval proverb of this period—"Work and keep scurvy out of your bones." Possibly, since orange and lemon-juice in casks was expensive, the Indiamen had abandoned their own sound practice of earlier times in order to fall into line with the Royal Navy.

I

It is noteworthy that the Dutch, although trading on a smaller scale with some twenty-five ships sailing and as many returning each year, had as serious a medical problem in Java as the English had in Bengal. Their voyages, moreover, were attended with such loss that Chief Surgeon Dekker, a man of international reputation, was instructed in 1768 to compile a memorandum of instructions respecting life on board ship. The figures of mortality at sea, which occasioned such alarm, have been preserved for the years 1766, 1767 and 1768. They are shown in the following Table:

Year	Ships	Deaths on voyage to Cape of Good Hope	Deaths between the Cape and Batavia	Delivered at Batavia Hospital
1766	25	368	207	819
1767	29	363	657	1,208
1768	21	362	554	921
Totals	75	1,093	1,418	2,948

The principal diseases were classified as:

(a) Catarrhal (which included sore throat, otitis or middle ear inflammation, pleurisy, pneumonia and ophthalmia).

(b) Fevers (including intermittent, the majority of which were malaria or else unidentified, but apparently contagious fevers—perhaps dysentery),

(c) Acute biliary fever (sometimes inflammation of the liver or gall bladder with jaundice, sometimes probably typhoid).

(d) Scurvy (which the majority of Dutch physicians at that time held to be contagious).

(e) Dysentery.

On some exceptionally favourable voyages there were no deaths at all, so that the sickness, suffering and deaths on the unfavourable voyages must have been appalling. It will be seen from the above figures that seventy-five voyages to and from the East Indies yielded a total of 2,511 deaths, an average of over thirty-three per ship.

Besides the diseases mentioned, broken limbs and injuries occurred and any surgical intervention was attended by the risks of sepsis prevalent in those days; in addition to which was the risk of gangrene, especially likely to occur in the presence of scurvy. The commonest casualties, as listed by Blane, were drowning, suffocation from foul air in the hold, poisoning (including snake and insect bites), frost bite, burns, wounds and lock jaw.

The Dutch were far from solving their problems in Dekker's time. On the contrary, in the five years 1770-1774, seventeen ships lost between them on the voyage to the Cape no less than 2,363 men. In 1772 the deaths in forty vessels amounted to 2,898, nearly all of a malignant putrid fever which was probably typhus. Between 1750 and 1800 the scientific and medical societies of Holland frequently discussed the problems of health and therapeutics at sea and in the Indies, but in the transactions of these Societies it is clear that the fundamental principles of the prevention of disease had not—except in the case of smallpox—begun to be appreciated. By 1823, however, a Dutch traveller, Dr. Waitz—a pioneer in preventive medicine in the Tropics and an advocate of abstinence from alcohol—could write that the dangers of sea travel had much diminished. He attributed this to the improved food, better drinking water, ampler airing and greater cleanliness. The two latter circumstances, he thought, were responsible for the disappearance of scurvy. But he also mentions that food was more varied owing to supplies being shipped of "preserved vegetables," such as leeks, onions, cucumbers, gherkins, French beans, cauliflower, mustard and apples. The art of canning food had actually been invented for Napoleon's armies but the good results at sea were not to be felt until after the period with which we are dealing.

As compared with the Indian Ocean, the West Indies presented a different problem. While they had a terrible reputation for sickness, the relatively short voyage to and fro was not exceptionally un-healthy. It was on land and in port that yellow fever made its ravages and gave the West Indies a bad name. The Journal of Rear-Admiral James throws light on the conditions there. "The dreadful sickness that now (1794) prevailed in the West Indies is beyond the power of any tongue or pen to describe. In a few days after I arrived at St. Pierre I buried every man belonging to my boat's crew twice and nearly all the third boat's crew in fever." Referring to the same period, Willyams, Chaplain of the *Boyne*, wrote that he had been

informed "by Captain Schanck of the Royal Navy, the agent for
transports, that during this expedition 46 masters of transports and
1,100 of their men died of yellow fever."

Yet, even at this date, the shrewd observation was made by Trotter
that yellow fever was produced by contact with the shore. "The
disease," he observed, "uniformly disappeared from ships as they
increased their distance from the West Indies. At 32° North no fresh
attacks were known." He relates, moreover, that "Vice-Admiral C.
Thompson, who lately commanded there, was so certified of this
from long experience and attention to the subject that he sometimes
insisted upon ships putting to sea when their condition otherwise
was most unfavourable." One captain hesitated to put to sea owing to
the distress amongst his crew, but the Admiral was firm, saying that
"if he did not see the vessel under weigh in an hour, the boats of the
Fleet should *tow* her out to sea." The ship went to sea and returned
after a fortnight's cruise in perfect health and free from the yellow
fever with which she had started. Trotter comments that, in his
opinion, "an imitation of this practice will always be attended by
salutary consequences." James Anthony Gardner, who had been
shipmates with Trotter in the *Edgar* (1787-9), speaks of him as "A
most excellent fellow with first-rate abilities, an able writer and a
poet." Whatever his literary gifts, Trotter was evidently a man
endowed with accurate powers of observation, not too respectful of
the opinions of the medical authorities of his time and capable (as his
reports show) of vigorous and independent thought.

One of the letters of Ann Gardner Brodbelt, whose husband was a
physician practising in Jamaica, to her daughter Jane, a schoolgirl in
England, confirms the view of Admiral Thompson as to the value of
putting to sea when yellow fever appeared.

"I am sorry to say," she wrote to Jane on 25th May, 1794, "that for
three or four weeks before the *Powerful* left Port Royal the yellow
fever had made such dreadful ravage among the officers and sailors
that they had buried upwards of a hundred of the latter besides seven
or eight officers, indeed had the London and Cork fleets not arrived
as they did (four days previous to their departure) they must have
put off sailing for want of hands to take the ships from the Island.
I sincerely hope that the change of situation from the harbour at Port

Royal to the free air which the *Powerful* will now enjoy by going out to sea, may be attended with every favourable change in the health of the poor people on board, and" (here follows a remarkably penetrating observation for those times) "that it will likewise prevent others from taking the infection." In another letter, however, of 15th June, 1794, Mrs. Brodbelt writes of the "dreadful devastation the yellow fever was making on board the *Powerful*"—even after that ship had left Port Royal. She mentions that some of the merchant ships with the Fleet were infected with this fatal fever; among others the *Simon Taylor*, on board of which a young lady went in perfect health and was a corpse in less than fifty hours after she was attacked by the fever.

It should perhaps be emphasized, in conclusion, that yellow fever usually began among seamen who had actually been ashore. Had it been possible—as it obviously was not—to avoid contact with the shore, a ship in harbour might have been relatively safe. Bancroft, writing in 1811 on "Yellow Fever and other Contagious Fevers," lays stress on the short distance some contagions could pass over the sea. He gives many quotations showing how short was the distance from shore that the malarial infection, for example, could travel, and observes that Blane put it at two cables length in Jamaica. Most of the evidence here quoted relates to the Navy, but it will be realised that greater risks, in proportion, were run by merchantmen, whose stay in harbour was (in the nature of things) more necessary and more prolonged.

In colder latitudes the risk of disease was very much less. Voyages into the Polar Seas were fairly numerous at this period, whether for purposes of exploration or in pursuit of whales, seals or furs. The two William Scoresbys, father and son, have left records of such voyages. Captain William Scoresby, senior, left seven log books, in one of which (for 1806) he records having reached latitude 81° 30′ N., or 519 miles from the North Pole. It seems that his ship, a Greenland whaler from Hull, was little troubled with sickness. William Scoresby, the younger, published in 1820 an account of the Arctic Regions, with a history and description of the Northern Whale Fishery. He speaks of the disease prevalent on these voyages—scurvy,

frost bite, intermittents, asthmas and catarrh—but adds that catarrhs
are rarely followed by any dangerous consequences.

One disease, however, against which a cold climate offered no
protection was typhus. What an epidemic of typhus fever was like
on board ship is vividly brought home in "An account of the fever
called the bilious remittent," by Sir William Burnett, K.C.B. This
deals with an outbreak in 1813-14 among the Russian Fleet then in
the Medway, and amongst the prisoners of war, chiefly Danish and
American, confined in prison ships at Chatham. "The fever," he
says, "was making rapid advances in each of the ships . . . the surgeon
who had been appointed to succeed Mr. Thomson (. . . an early
victim of the fever) was in so ill a state of health as to be unable to
perform his duty; and Mr. Johnson, the surgeon of the *Defiance*, was
. . . labouring under a severe attack of the prevailing disease . . . .
From the *Bahama* . . . and the *Defiance* I could get no satisfactory
account of the progress of the disease . . . but I found a large sick-
berth full of patients labouring under fever, most of them dangerously ill." To add to the difficulties, smallpox also broke out among
the Danes and Americans—fortunately without spreading to the
French prisoners in neighbouring ships. The severe weather (there
was a deep covering of snow) which prevented proper ventilation
of the infected ships, made matters worse. In the course of the
epidemic every medical officer—except Burnett himself and one
assistant surgeon—suffered an attack of the fever, from which one of
them died. The ships' crews and marines, as well as women on shore,
were attacked. Burnett records that, before March 6th, when he
arrived, out of 157 removed to hospital, 45 died; and, after March 6th,
out of 518 attacked by the fever, 61 died. Still Burnett visited the
ships daily. He appeared to be taking such risks that the executive
officers tried to prevent his going below, alleging that he would
either meet with personal violence or contract the fever. Nevertheless, he persevered in making his visits below without anyone
accompanying him, and by degrees restored order among the
prisoners. His exertions succeeded, as the figures already quoted show.

Prior to Burnett's visit to Chatham, James Carmichael Smyth had
made a great stir with his method of curing typhus fever and
"destroying its contagion." An experiment was made in the *Union*

Hospital Ship on typhus patients brought there for the purpose. The ceremony of fumigation was thus carried out. Half an ounce of concentrated sulphuric acid was heated in a small tea cup immersed in heated sand. To this, when hot, an equal quantity of pure nitre in powder was added. Pipkins containing sand were carried through the wards by the nurses and convalescents who occasionally put them under the cradles of the sick and in every corner where foul air was suspected to lodge. This fumigation was continued until the whole space between decks fore and aft was filled with the vapour, which appeared like a thick haze. The report mentions that it excited a good deal of coughing, as it might well do since the decomposition products of sulphuric acid and nitre are intensely irritating to the respiratory passages and are capable, in high concentration, of doing much damage. For this plan, nevertheless, the British Government voted Smyth a reward of £5,000. Some critics (amongst them Trotter) did not think he deserved it, but the Royal College of Physicians decided firmly in his favour.

There was another measure upon which Smyth insisted and one which was of more practical value. By his orders, body clothes and bed clothes of the sick were exposed to the nitrous vapour and all dirty linen removed from them was immediately immersed in a tub of cold water, rinsed out on deck and hung up till nearly dry. Then it was fumigated before being taken to the wash-house. Dr. Menzies, who conducted the experiment, was able to report that, since he began fumigation, none of the ship's company was attacked with the disorder, and none of the sick who had come into hospital since his arrival had died. Menzies had some glimmering notion that the Russian sheepskin coats or shubs were to blame as "nourishing the seeds of contagion." He wished to destroy them, but as the owners would not agree he had to content himself with fumigation.

Menzies' report contains a full description of the hospital ship—an old man-of-war partitioned into wards and staffed by a matron, a washerwoman, and fifteen women as nurses. But such luxuries as hospital ships were intended only for the Navy. It will be noted, incidentally, that this particular epidemic began among prisoners of war. Typhus could, of course, break out anywhere—there was an outbreak, for example, in the *Robust*, one of Sir Edward Pellew's blockading squadron off Rochefort—but prisoners were especially liable to certain complaints. Convict ships, therefore, are a subject in themselves, but one outside the scope of this book. It will suffice for the present purpose to quote a surgeon (Colin Brown) who, after several voyages to New South Wales, silenced critics with the following remark: "If the objectors to an adequate scale of rations desire the death of the convict, that can surely be secured without the professional attendance of a medical officer and by means less expensive to the country than the usual provision for a long voyage."

It will be seen that medical science was progressing during the period with which we have to deal, and that the surgeons were often conscientious, able, courageous and even distinguished men. It remains to see how far their services, in the merchant service, were in fact available. Foremost in this matter was the East India Company, which paid attention to health throughout its history. The Keeper of Records at the India Office writes that "There is a strong presumption that a surgeon was always carried in the East India Company's ships . . . from, and perhaps before, 1613." Apart from that, the published Court Minutes include a report from the Shipping Committee (30th November, 1677) in which the chirurgeon and his apprentice are mentioned as part of the ship's company. And, from 1760 onwards, Hardy's *Register* gives us the names of all the surgeons employed. It is clear that the medical arrangements in the East Indiamen were by far the best in existence, perhaps outrivalling those in the Navy. Surgeons in the Company's ships had all been examined before their appointment by the Surgeons Company in London or, after 1798, by the College of Surgeons at Edinburgh. Their duties and privileges—they were allowed three tons of cargo space—and even their berths (on the larboard side and opposite the third mate's cabin) were carefully regulated. It is interesting to note, in this connection, that the famous Sir Robert Wigram had first served the Company as surgeon, in 1764, of the East Indiaman, *Admiral Watson*. His influence on the Court of Directors must, in his later years, have done much for the health of crews and passengers.

As regards other ships, many were compelled by Statute to carry a surgeon. As early as 1629 the Charter granted to the Barber Surgeons of London by Charles I instructed them to examine the "Sea

Surgeons," and compelled any ship sailing from the Port of London to have a surgeon on board. Arctic whalers were compelled to carry a surgeon under an Act of Parliament (26 George III, c. 41) regulating the Greenland Fisheries. This is mentioned by the younger Scoresby in his description of "the mode of mustering Greenland ships." "The person nominated as surgeon," he writes, "is next called and strictly examined as to his abilities and qualifications; if he produces certificates, etc., of his having been regularly bred to that profession he is passed; if not he is rejected and another proper person is provided before the ship is suffered to clear out." A few years later (1789) it was enacted (29 George III, c. 66) that no slave ship should sail unless there was at least one surgeon on board, who must produce a certificate of having passed his examination at Surgeons' Hall or at some "Publick or County Hospital," or at the Royal College of Physicians or Royal College of Surgeons at Edinburgh. The proviso that the African Surgeon might pass his examination at a Publick or County Hospital is unique. No other sea surgeon could obtain his certificate in that way. Examinations were held regularly at the Liverpool Infirmary and probably (although no record of it exists) at the Bristol Infirmary.

The first separate Act for regulating passenger ships was 43 George III, c. 56. By this Act every vessel carrying fifty persons was required to carry a surgeon possessing a certificate of having passed his examination at Surgeons' Hall, London, or at the Royal College of Surgeons of Edinburgh or Dublin. Every surgeon was compelled on oath to have a medicine chest properly stored, and he was obliged to give bond in the sum of £100 to keep a true journal which was, on the return of the vessel, to be delivered to the Officer of Customs and verified on oath. As from about 1804, then, we may assume that most of the larger British merchantmen carried a surgeon. The Dutch East India Company went further and established two surgeons, or even more, in every ship they had—and were even discussing at one time the advisability of raising the number to four.

In vessels where no surgeon was carried the ship's officers did what they could. Fanning, an American in the seal fur trade from the South Polar Seas to China, speaks gratefully of Dr. G. Smith, of New York City, who sailed with him on one voyage, but then goes on to describe how, on another occasion, several of his crew were struck by lightning. They were attended, he relates, "by our first officer who possessed of all others on board the greatest knowledge in physics and surgery."

Lacking a surgeon—or even a first officer with medical leanings—a merchant ship might present a sad spectacle. In contrast, for example, with Fanning's well-equipped *Aspasia*, another American fur trader, the *Maria*, was considered by Krusenstern to be in very poor case. Of only about 150 tons burden, she carried a crew of seventy in addition to the captain, the officers, the Company's agents and other passengers. As she was fully laden, the twenty men who were sick had barely room to lie down on the deck. They had no hammocks and many, lacking shirts, were wrapped in greasy furs. Unwashed and with long beards, they all appeared to labour under incurable scorbutic and venereal sores. Such a sight as this vessel presented was, by 1805, a rarity. That it was so is the measure of the success achieved in solving problems which, a century before, had seemed insoluble.

PART TWO

CHAPTER VII

The East India Trade

by C. NORTHCOTE PARKINSON, M.A., PH.D., F.R.HIST.S.,

late Fellow of Emmanuel College, Cambridge. Author of
"Trade in the Eastern Seas," and other works

THE East India Company had a complete monopoly of British trade to the East until 1813. Not until the very end of our period was it legal for a British merchantman to round the Cape of Good Hope without the Company's licence; and only in exceptional circumstances was such a licence ever issued. As regards all seaborne trade between Asia and Europe the monopoly was fairly rigidly upheld. The trade, on the other hand, between different ports in the East, although covered by the terms of the Company's Charter, was not monopolised. Instead, it was open to the business enterprise of the white communities in India as well as to the natives. This "Country Trade," as it was called, was virtually assigned by the Company to its own servants and protégés in India. It was a flourishing trade, carried on in ships which were built, owned, manned and insured in India; ships which traded between one part of India and another, between India and the East Indies, between India and China. In this chapter, therefore, we are concerned with two different branches of trade; the Company's trade and its Asiatic offshoot. Only indirectly did the latter business form a part of British overseas trade. "Country" ships sailed, however, under the British flag. They will be dealt with, therefore, at the end of the chapter, which must be devoted mainly to commerce between London and the East; to the trade which was completely monopolised.[1]

A distinction must be made between the Company's trade with India and its trade with China. The former depended largely upon the surplus revenues, real or imaginary, of the Bengal Government; more goods being brought from India than were ever sent there.

---

[1] This chapter is based upon the writer's *Trade in the Eastern Seas* (1937)

Thus the outward-bound Indiamen were not heavily laden. They carried, sometimes, little but reinforcements, arms, ammunition and goods for the use of Europeans in India. Owing to mortality among the white population, consisting mainly of soldiers, a tenth of the number had to be replaced each year if the establishment were to be maintained. Of true exports to India apart from men, woollens and iron were the chief, the former under statutory compulsion and far from profitable. For iron there was a genuine demand, but the supplies available for export must always have been limited. From India, the principal imports were cotton goods, silks, saltpetre, indigo, sugar and rice; all mostly from Bengal. The other settlements, Madras, Bombay and Penang, were held more for strategic than for economic reasons. Each represented an overhead charge on the profits made in Bengal. The China trade, on the other hand, was a true exchange of commodities, the exports being woollens, tin and other goods from England, together with raw cotton and opium from India; the chief import being tea.

The Company's commercial profits were mainly derived from the tea-trade, which had become a matter of national importance as the fashion for tea-drinking grew. Its profits derived from tax collection in Bengal largely disappeared in time of war, swallowed up by the cost of defence. This was the cause of the financial difficulties which were ultimately to be solved by exposing the Indian cotton-weaver to that Lancashire competition from which the Company protected him as long as its monopoly lasted. To the question of what should be exported to India, cotton cloth was the eventual answer. It was a solution to which the Company would not resort, and the East India Trade remained during our period, one-sided and unprofitable.

The Company's fleet sailed from, and returned to, London; loading and unloading in the river at no great distance from the Company's headquarters, the India House in Leadenhall Street. Oddly enough, however, the ships did not, for the most part, belong to the Company. With few exceptions, they were built by contract for a ring of capitalists and then chartered by the Company for a stated number of voyages. The actual owners were known collectively as "The Shipping Interest." It was an expensive and complex system which could hardly have survived had not the shipowners also been shareholders of the Company, with great influence among the Directors. That the Company lost heavily by this system is clear; and the more so in that the shipowners formed an hereditary ring, claiming privilege by right of custom, forbearing to compete with each other and uniting to exclude any competition from outside. If costly, however, the system cannot be said to have produced bad ships. The East Indiamen were among the finest, as they were by far the largest, merchantmen to sail from a British port.

Nearly all Indiamen were built in the Thames at one or other of the dockyards situated between Limehouse and Blackwall. Comparatively few shipbuilders were prepared to build such large vessels; and it was the close connection which existed between the builders and "The Shipping Interest" which made the shipowning monopoly so hard to break. The chief builders were Randall's, Barnard's, Perry's, Pitcher's and Wells's. Other firms, better known towards the end of our period, were Dudman & Co., S. and D. Brent, and Curling & Co. All these yards were at Rotherhithe, Deptford, Blackwall or Northfleet. Perhaps the best known of these firms was Perry's, of Blackwall, later to become Wigram's, the firm which owned the Brunswick Dock and Masthouse, now absorbed in the present East India Export Dock. Occasional Indiamen were built outside the Thames, at Yarmouth, Liverpool, Ipswich and Buckler's Hard; but these contracts were, for the most part, incidents in a struggle to break the monopoly of the Shipping Interest. Several Indiamen were launched at Bombay, sometimes to be owned by the Company itself; but these, again, were exceptional. In the main, the Thames builders maintained a virtual monopoly. In the repairing and refitting of Indiamen—a more profitable business, it was thought, than the building of them—their monopoly was complete.

East Indiamen were either "regular" or "extra" ships. The regular ship was taken up for six or more voyages; that is, for twelve or fourteen years. She was employed, in fact, until judged to be worn out. The extra ship, also built for the trade, and often constantly employed in it, was taken up for one voyage only. It was by varying the number of extra ships that the Company's tonnage could be made equal each year to the expected demand. In extreme urgency the Directors could charter other vessels, whether in England or India—

vessels built for another trade—but this happened very rarely. All ordinary demands were satisfied by the regular and extra ships, the difference between the two classes being of less importance, in practice, than might be supposed.(1)

Despite the fact that Indiamen were chartered, not owned, by the East India Company, they were all built for the trade under contracts which ensured a measure of uniformity. Ships might vary somewhat, but only within definite limits—and especially within limits as to tonnage. The size of the Indiaman was determined, in part, by the depth of water in the Hooghly. It had long since been discovered that a large ship is more economical than a small one. On the other hand, it was problematical whether a large ship, comparable in size to a naval third-rate, could ever reach Diamond Harbour in safety. The larger ships were built, therefore, but confined to the China trade. Those sailing to India were of two fairly distinct types; the one class of ship being intended for the more valuable cargoes, piece-goods and silks, the smaller type destined to load the "gruff goods"— saltpetre, sugar and rice. The East India ships fall thus into three main classes, the 1,200-ton class employed in the China trade, the 800-ton class and the 500-ton class, both meant for Indian waters. The "Extra Ships" were nearly all of the smallest class; even these, however, being large enough as compared with the ordinary merchantmen of the day, which were mostly of 200 tons or less. The cost of shipbuilding rose during the war years. Generally speaking, a 1,200-ton Indiaman could be built and equipped for her first voyage at a cost of from £50,000 to £70,000; an 800-ton ship for from £30,000 to £50,000; a 500-ton ship from £20,000 to £30,000. The price per ton did not vary as between one yard and another. The variations indicated in the above rough estimates were due to rising prices and wages, the course of the war and the demands of the Admiralty. The cost of shipbuilding varied from year to year but with a general tendency to rise as the war went on.

The first characteristic of the East Indiamen was size. The second lay, perhaps, in their warlike equipment. Intended to defend themselves against pirates or enemy privateers; intended to serve, if need

---

(1) For lists of ships employed, see Charles Hardy's *Register of Ships*, with the East India Company's regulations for the Maritime Service.

arose, as men-of-war, East Indiamen were loaded with artillery and manned (in theory) by a numerous and well-armed crew. The China ships would carry perhaps thirty-six or thirty-eight guns, the 800-ton ships from twenty-six to thirty-two guns, the 500-ton ships from twelve to twenty. They all had, in addition, a generous allowance of muskets, bayonets, boarding-pikes, pistols, cutlasses and grenades. When properly manned, an Indiaman could be a formidable opponent. Some famous actions were fought by the Company's ships, which were often disguised as men-of-war without disgracing their borrowed colours.

Including "extra ships," the East India Fleet numbered round about a hundred sail. Of these rather fewer than thirty would be in the 1,200-ton class, thirty or more of the 800-ton class, and forty of the 500-ton class—perhaps half of these being "extra." These figures leave out of account the fluctuations both in the total number and in the numbers of each class. For our period, however, a hundred ships would be a fair average, with an aggregate tonnage of ninety thousand.

Structurally, the East Indiaman had certain characteristic virtues and defects. The virtues arose partly from necessity and partly from contact with Indian methods of shipbuilding. Necessity, in the form of timber shortage, was compelling the builders to use iron knees and standards, thus gaining greater strength, while at the same time saving both money and space between decks. Contact with India brought about two major alterations; the introduction of the flush deck[1] and the gradual disuse of the "tumble-home" side. The latter improvement increased the space available for cargo, made the ship stronger and easier to build, and gave a better spread to the shrouds. The former improvement, while getting rid of the deep waist and its obvious risks in bad weather, was apt to bring with it a new and scarcely less dangerous top-heaviness. This fault was not inherent in flush-decked vessels, but was rather a result of the failure to increase the breadth proportionately. This brings us to the characteristic failing of the Indiaman, more especially apparent in the 800-ton class. Owing to a faulty system of tonnage measurement, into which the depth of hold did not enter, there was perpetual temptation to sacrifice breadth in favour of depth. This was in order to evade the

---

[1] See plate 12, showing a flush-decked Indiaman, c.1800.

K

full payment of dues based on registered tonnage. It was a mischievous tendency as the long, deep and narrow ships thereby produced were all more or less crank. This defect was intensified by the introduction of flush decks. It was less noticeable, however, in the 1,200-ton and 500-ton classes. Generally speaking, it may be said that the East Indiaman was the largest, most costly, most heavily armed merchant-man sailing under the British flag; but not, in every respect, the most seaworthy and certainly not the fastest.

An East Indiaman belonged, as we have seen, to a member (or, more often, a group of members) of the Shipping Interest. When the ship belonged to a group or syndicate, one of the owners represented the others and was called the managing owner or ship's husband. The ship was chartered, nevertheless, by the East India Company. The ship's officers had, therefore, a divided loyalty. They were employed directly by the managing owner to sail the ship. They were employed by the East India Company to safeguard the cargo. Appointed by the managing owner (who was apt to sell the command to the highest bidder), the captain—or commander, as the Company preferred to call him—had to take an oath of fidelity to the Company. The pay of the commander and officers, which was nominal, came from the owner but was paid through the Company. The officers' actual remuneration lay in their privilege of trading on their own account, a portion of the cargo space being allotted them for the purpose. But here again they were under a dual obligation, for it was by the owner's generosity that the space was given them but only by the Company's leave could they put anything into it. This complex system, far more anomalous than can be described here, worked more smoothly in practice than might be supposed; partly because of the close relationship (family, social and financial) existing between directors, owners and officers.

The officers of an Indiaman consisted of the commander, the first mate, second, third, fourth, fifth and sixth mates, the surgeon, purser, and as many as five midshipmen.[1] Only the first four mates were "Sworn Officers," but all wore uniform of a semi-naval pattern, with sidearms for state occasions. In India the commander

---

[1] See page 107, Chapter V, for the Company's regulations governing promotion.

of an Indiaman was treated as a personage. He would land under a salute of thirteen guns from the battery and the guard would be turned out as he entered or left the fort. As regards the private trade of the officers, the Company seems to have resigned to them the entire business of supplying goods to the European population in India. In ships of 800 tons the commander was allowed some fifty-six tons for his private venture; and since the ship might be half-empty, he could often have additional space for the asking. This trade was limited, however, in extent by the demand in India, where the white population was not very large. It was important not to overstock the market. The other officers were allowed from one to eight tons each according to their rank; the boatswain, gunner and carpenter having their share and some twenty petty officers being allowed ten feet each. Captain and crew occupied nearly a hundred tons in private venture on the outward voyage.(¹) Space was allotted less generously when homeward bound, the captain having but thirty tons and the rest in proportion. Private investments on the return voyage consisted mainly of the same goods as imported by the Company—tea, piece-goods and the like, destined to be sold together with the rest of the cargo. In China ships, however, the officers had the privilege of importing, with the tea, the chinaware to drink it from; a trade in which the Company did not meddle and in which the officers had, therefore, a monopoly. The privilege of private trade on the homeward passage was continually abused, commanders often exceeding their allowance or even smuggling their goods ashore to defraud the revenue. Whether by legal or illegal means, they often made considerable fortunes. It does not appear that any officer below the rank of second mate—with the exception, perhaps, of the purser—profited greatly or even made a living. The mates lived rather in expectation of becoming captains in their turn.

The inferior officers—boatswain, carpenter and the rest—did not differ greatly from their counterparts in a man-of-war; and the organization of the crew was indeed much the same, except in so far as it was less numerous. Wages were, in time of war, higher than in

---

(¹) For a more detailed account see pages 108 and 109, Chapter V.

the Navy for able and ordinary seamen, not quite as high for some of the petty officers. Besides her six mates, surgeon, purser, boatswain, gunner, carpenter, midshipmen and surgeon's mate, an Indiaman would carry a caulker, cooper, captain's cook, ship's cook, two stewards, sailmaker, armourer, butcher, baker, poulterer, barber and six quartermasters. These, together with their mates and servants, and about fifty seamen, made a total of about a hundred. The 800-ton ships had about that number; the 1,200-ton ships having twenty or thirty additional seamen and the smaller vessels, if not in the regular service, having crews of perhaps fifty all told. Seamen were procured in the normal manner, through crimps. As the war went on, however, it became increasingly difficult to raise men and even more difficult to keep them. The Company was always trying to obtain protection for its crews but never with any lasting success. The press-gangs were often busy in London River. What was worse, and far more systematic, was the impressing of seamen in India. The squadron on the East Indies Station had no other means of replacing its appalling losses from disease. The China ships were less likely to fall into the clutches of the East India Squadron. These were, therefore, more popular and easier to man; and men from other Indiamen would sometimes desert to them.

East Indiamen left half-manned owing to impressment in India had to enlist native seamen, Lascars and Chinese, in order to reach home again. There was a regular system of supplying these. The following extract is taken from the *Bengal Hurkura* of April 23rd, 1805:

> William Vanzandts respectfully begs leave to acquaint the owners and Commanders of ships and vessels, and the public in general, that he continues to supply lascars for ships. Mr. Vanzandts trusts, from his knowledge of the country trade and of these men, to give satisfaction to those gentlemen who may please to honor him with their commands, and to prevent the numerous impositions that have prevailed amongst the ghaut Serangs, by their sending on board mere coolies in the room of good lascars, the impropriety of which has given numerous grievances to the Captains and Officers when at sea; and consequently a fraud on the owners. N.B.—Neither lascars nor seacunnies will be engaged without first being strictly examined in their respective duties, and approved of.

Such an Agency as this was intended to serve the country trade but must often have served East Indiamen as well. Strictly speaking, all native seamen were supposed to be shipped back to the East as supernumeraries. Many, however, died on the voyage or in London. It also became necessary sometimes to relax the rule by which Indiamen had at least to sail with a European crew. There could be no such pretence on the homeward voyage, when anything from thirty to seventy natives might be carried. The Lascars and Chinese seem to have made excellent fine-weather seamen. They were apt to be useless, on the other hand, in a gale or an action. Of the Europeans, a proportion would always be foreigners—Germans, Spanish, French and Americans.

Besides her crew, an East Indiaman bound for India (not China) would often carry passengers. These might be of several different categories. To begin with, there were units of the regular army, and detachments sent to reinforce the units already in India. Numbers in this category varied considerably from year to year, following events in India. Soldiers added somewhat to the strength of a ship, but their officers found difficulty in keeping their men (and themselves) occupied during the long voyage—as also in keeping the peace between redcoats and bluejackets.(1) As Marryat remarked, "I believe there are no classes of people who embark with more regret, or quit a ship with more pleasure, than military men . . ." Next, there were the recruits sent out to join the East India Company's own European forces. Of these there might be twenty or thirty at a time and hundreds in the course of the year. In smaller numbers were the cadets and writers destined to recruit the Company's establishment of officers and civil servants. There might be as many as a dozen of these, but more often fewer and sometimes none at all. These young men or boys could be, and usually were, a decided nuisance. Finally, there were the real passengers, from whom the captain might hope to make a profit. These might be high officials and officers returning from leave, lawyers and merchants going out under the Company's licence, wives rejoining their husbands and ladies joining their friends as a speculation in the marriage market. The passage-money payable by the Company's servants was fixed by regulation and varied,

---

(1) The Duke of Wellington, in his younger days, advanced some sound proposals for keeping troops occupied on a voyage. See his Supplementary Despatches, vols. I and II.

according to rank, from £95 to £250. No more could be charged
except for additional cabin-space. Private passengers, on the other
hand, had to drive their bargain with the captain or purser. These
might have to pay £500 on the outward voyage. Nevertheless,
captains did not expect to make much profit on the outward-bound
passengers. Their aim was rather to gain such a reputation for
hospitality as would ensure them the patronage of "Nabobs" returning to England.[1] The passenger outward-bound might choose his
ship by reference to the books at Lloyd's, but the same man coming
home would be more knowing. He might elect to sail in the ship he
had come out in; and then again he might *not*. This was a matter of
moment, for the passage-money paid by a well-to-do family returning to England with children and servants might run into
thousands. Fares were, in general, much higher on the return
voyage; but passengers, it should be remarked, were far less numerous.

The passage to India was a tedious business for all but the very
studious—who could pass the time in learning Persian or Hindustani.
There was card-playing and dancing sometimes, flirting often, back-
biting and quarrelling always. It fell to the captain to keep order and
preserve decorum. The penalty for failure in this was a disorderly
ship; the penalty for outstanding success was (possibly) a duel with
some offended subaltern as soon as the voyage was over. As a means
of avoiding such encounters—with pistols at fourteen paces—a wise
captain relied mainly on madeira and champagne. His trade had its
consolations as well as its dangers.

An East Indiaman's voyage began with her "coming afloat" after
refitting. This meant coming to her moorings at Deptford, Blackwall
or Northfleet, where she would be joined by some of her officers,
who would supervise her rigging and preparation for sea. Presently,
the cargo would arrive from up the river, carried in lighters or hoys;
the mates, or some of them, being always on board to oversee the
stowage. Then the ship would drop down to Gravesend, where she
would remain for about a month under the care of the chief mate.
It was during this period that the recruits would be sent aboard, as
also the bulk of the supplies, the goods in private trade, and finally

[1] Such as William Hickey, whose *Memoirs* throw light on the homeward voyage.

the water and livestock. The ship was, from this time, likely to be noisy.

> The poop, upon which you ascended by ladders on each side, was crowded with long ranges of coops, tenanted by every variety of domestic fowl awaiting, in happy unconsciousness, the day when they should be required to supply the luxurious table provided by the captain.
>
> In some, turkeys stretched forth their long necks, and tapped the deck as they picked up some ant who crossed it, in his industry. In others, the crowing of cocks and calling of the hens were incessant; or the geese, ranged up rank and file, waited but the signal from one of the party to raise up a simultaneous clamour, which as suddenly was remitted.
>
> Coop answered coop, in variety of discord, while the poulterer walked round and round to supply the wants of so many hundreds committed to his charge.(¹)

Of the passengers, most would come aboard at Gravesend. The "Old Falcon," on the east side of the Town Pier—an inn now to be demolished, but then famous for whitebait—was their rendezvous. They would come by coach from London, send their luggage on board, and then stay at the inn until the firing of a gun warned them that the ship was ready to sail. It was while the ship lay at Gravesend that the commander came aboard in person. Dignity required his absence until the last moment—an absence mitigated by periodic and fleeting visits. Soon after his appearance there used to be a farewell visit of the managing owner, whose business it was to pay the crimps and give the crew a part of their wages in advance. As soon as he had gone ashore again, the ship was ready for sea and might drop down the river to the Downs.

Passengers would sometimes elect to embark from Deal rather than Gravesend, with the object of shortening the voyage. It was from here, in peace time, that the voyage really began. In time of war it was more usual to sail from Portsmouth. This was because the Indiamen had to sail in convoy, with naval escort which would await them at Spithead. In that case, it was at Portsmouth that troops were embarked, when there were any; and it was there, again, that the mails would be shipped. From the moment of dropping anchor at Spithead, the East Indiamen collecting there were under the orders of the escorting man-of-war.

After the outbreak of war the sailing calendar had to be simplified

---

(¹) *Newton Forster*, Captain Marryat.

to suit the convenience of the Admiralty. In peace time the first ships to sail were the China ships, usually four in number, bound for Bombay and Canton. These used to sail in December, but war conditions led to the amalgamation of this division with a more numerous group sailing in February and mostly bound for India. A second division was dispatched in March, many of the ships on the "Coast and Bay" voyage to Madras and Calcutta. A third division sailed in April and normally included the ships bound for China direct, numbering about five or six. Sometimes these China ships were added to the March division instead. Two more divisions sailed in May and June respectively with an average of perhaps half-a-dozen vessels in each, nearly all bound for India but occasionally including one or two China ships—bringing the total number at Canton up to twelve or more. There was then a slack period of nearly three months, followed by the sailing in September of a final convoy for India, numbering eight or nine ships. Allowing for occasional packets and Indiamen sailing singly, without convoy, there would be a total of about fifty regular and extra ships sailing in any given year. A similar number, meanwhile, would be on the voyage homeward, the China ships sailing from Whampoa (probably together) in January and February, and reaching the Thames in July. Sometimes the China Fleet was in two divisions, one arriving as late as September. Convoys from India tended likewise to sail early in the year, reaching London River during what was the slack season for sailings; a system convenient for docking.

The course sailed by outward-bound convoys took them from the Channel—where they were apt to be windbound—to Madeira. This was fairly direct, but from there they steered over towards the coast of Brazil, actually sighting it in some cases but at any rate going as far westward as would enable them to cross the equator (with suitable ceremony) between 18° and 23° W. Then followed a tiresome delay in the Variables, ending only when the South-East Trade Wind was picked up. A course was then set with the primary object of gaining a latitude in which westerly gales might be expected, and without much regard to the distance covered. Once in latitude 30° or 40° S., ships would steer so as to run down their easting, ultimately approaching the Cape of Good Hope from the south or even from the south-east. The convoy bound for China direct, however, would remain in the prevailing westerlies (the "roaring forties") until nearing the west coast of Australia, then known as New Holland, when they would head for the Straits of Sunda. Most convoys called at the Cape, though; principally, perhaps, to check their position, but also to obtain fresh water and provisions. Indeed, for ships carrying troops and passengers this was all but essential.

Two months or more might be spent on the voyage to the Cape. From there various courses might be steered. Ships bound for Calcutta or Madras usually timed their voyage so as to have the Monsoon in their favour while sailing up the Bay of Bengal; otherwise the approach by the Outer Passage, round by the eastwards, might be extremely tedious. Ships bound for Bombay might take the Inner Passage by the Mozambique Channel and the Eight-Degree or Nine-Degree Passage; or else the Middle Passage to the eastward of Madagascar, which was preferable during the North-East Monsoon. The Outer Passage, still farther to the eastward, was followed on the return voyage during the South-West Monsoon. From India to China the usual route lay through the Straits of Malacca, the best season being towards the end of the North-East Monsoon. Then the navigator would have the South-West Monsoon to take him up to Canton.

Routine on board an Indiaman was regulated and more or less invariable for the six months of the voyage. The crew was normally divided into two watches, the starboard watch commanded by the chief mate, the larboard by the second mate. The officers were divided into three watches, two being on duty at a time with, probably, one midshipman to assist. A watch lasted four hours except for the dog-watches from 4.0 to 6.0 and 6.0 to 8.0 p.m. The day's work began at 5.0 a.m., the upper deck being swabbed at 6.30, hammocks were piped up and stowed in the nettings at 7.30, and hands piped to breakfast at 8.0. Dinner was served to the crew shortly after noon. The watch was set again at 8.0 p.m., and all lights had to be out by 9.0; or, in the cabins, by 10.0.

An inspection was held every Saturday, for which the decks were cleaned and holy-stoned. The commander then went over the whole ship, expecting to see everything in its place and alert for signs of dirt or disorder. When he had finished the drums beat to quarters and everyone on board (passengers included) had to hurry to action stations. Then the crew exercised with the guns and small-arms, male passengers often parading with muskets and boarding-pikes, to act as marines. A service was held each Sunday, weather permitting, and the crew (as opposed to the ship) was inspected immediately afterwards. The captain could be fined for omitting to hold a service. On the other hand, were any clergy carried, or any nonconformist missionaries, they were discouraged, as a rule, from any excess of religious fervour.

The day's routine for the passenger began with breakfast at 8.0—a meal of tea and biscuits which many people did not attend. Dinner was served at 2.0, the passengers and officers sometimes forming two messes, the inferior one under the presidency of the third mate. Dinner in the cuddy was a rather elaborate affair for which people dressed beforehand. When the ladies withdrew, the bottle was circulated two or three times, after which the captain rose to end the ritual. Men and women came together again for tea at 6.0, and a light supper at 9.0. Passengers were usually idle and discontented, given to eternal grumbling about their accommodation, about the food and about each other. Their fare at dinner could vary a great deal and might reach a low ebb in bad weather—when they were, most of them, past caring about it—or when the ship had been long at sea. But it was princely when compared with the salt pork and biscuit on which the seamen lived.

The return voyage did not differ greatly from the outward passage except in so far as the ships were fully laden, undermanned, and with few passengers or troops. Sailing in convoys, often with naval protection, the Indiamen would call at St. Helena for water, and so finally return to the Thames. Until 1806, when the East India Docks were completed, the cargoes were discharged into decked hoys which came alongside them at their moorings opposite Deptford, Blackwall or Northfleet. After 1806, the homeward-bound Indiaman was stripped to the lower masts, moved into the Import Dock and there unloaded at the quayside. The principal object of this was to prevent pilfering. The hatches were not even opened until the vessel was within the dock walls; and nothing could then be removed except in the locked waggons or "caravans" which came to carry the goods up to the Company's warehouses in the East End and City.

After unloading, an Indiaman would normally go to a builder's yard for repairs, which the East India Dock Company—a subsidiary of the East India Company itself—was forbidden by its charter to undertake. Repairs and refitting might take as long as three months. After that, the ship was ready to "come afloat" and might, after another three months or more spent in loading and rigging, begin her next voyage. Ships arriving in the summer or autumn generally sailed in the early months of the year following.

★   ★   ★

Before concluding this brief account, something must be said about the "Country Trade" between the Indian ports and from these to China.[1] This trade had two centres, Bombay and Calcutta. The Bombay merchants employed teak-built ships of European design, the work of Parsee shipwrights, to carry raw cotton to China. With the cotton went various other exports such as pepper and sandalwood and goods bought on the outward voyage in the Straits of Malacca. From China there came, in return, tea and china-ware, silks and satins. Some twenty-five to thirty large ships were employed in the trade, mostly of over 600 tons and several of nearly a thousand. They were owned, many of them, by British firms with Scottish partners and Parsee capital. Others belonged, more openly, to Parsees. In either case, it was usual for a ship to have about four European officers and a native crew numbering seventy-five or a hundred. From Bombay there was also a considerable trade to the Persian Gulf and Arabia. Little, if any, of this was in British hands. The China trade, however, was enormous in itself, the value of the goods exported amounting to ten million sterling in two and a half years, from 1806 to 1808. If the trade to the eastward was left in native hands this was partly due to self-satisfied prosperity. Mackintosh wrote of Bombay: "There is languor and lethargy . . . here to which I never elsewhere saw any approach . . ."[2]

---

[1] See, among other works, *The History of the European Commerce with India*, David Macpherson.

[2] *Memoirs* of the Rt. Hon. Sir James Mackintosh, 1835.

The Calcutta trade employed smaller ships in greater numbers. Some carried rice from Bengal to the Coromandel Coast, returning in ballast. Others traded to the eastwards, exporting opium in exchange for spices and China goods. The vessels numbered between seventy and eighty, more than half of them being of 300 tons and upwards. Few ships exceeded 400 tons, as they were intended to sail up the Hooghly as far as Calcutta. They were not as solidly built as the Bombay ships, being intended rather for speed. The shipwrights who made them were Burmese carpenters working on French models. Originally built in the vicinity of Rangoon, the ships latterly came more often from the Calcutta yards. The ships were teak-framed but often with some lighter wood for planking. Like the Bombay ships, they had European officers and native crews; but, being engaged in a more dangerous trade (smuggling in the pirate-infested waters of the Dutch East Indies) the Lascar crews were stiffened, for fighting purposes, by an admixture of armed sepoys.

The Country Trade was remarkable chiefly for the size of the ships employed and for the swift fortunes made, at considerable risk, by both shipowners and officers. By European standards, the Bombay vessels were enormous; while even the Calcutta ships were far larger than the average merchantman of the day. They were also, many of them, incredibly long-lived. A teak-built man-of-war, launched at Bombay in 1831, was still useful as a hulk in 1911. A country ship, built circa 1800, was still afloat in 1928 and much admired for her carving and gilding. The building of these country craft occasionally provoked nervous comment at home. Joseph Cotton contended in 1799 that "Ships of Force should be admitted only in the Company's Employ, and the Pre-eminence in Naval Strength ought to be European. If Vessels of Force are built in any Number, or navigated by the Natives, the Tendency cannot but be alarming. Imperceptible are the Steps from Weakness to Power, from Restraint to Independence." The danger was not generally appreciated. And yet jealousy was not altogether misplaced. For, whereas the East India-men of this period were, in one sense, the finest merchant ships afloat —being larger, more heavily armed and manned than any other merchantmen—they were bettered in design and construction, in speed and seaworthiness, by the ships of the Country Trade.

CHAPTER VIII

The West Indian Trade

LUCY FRANCES HORSFALL, M.A., Ph.D.

Lecturer in History, University of Glasgow

THE British West India islands lie scattered along the chain which fringes the Caribbean between the mouth of the Orinoco and the peninsula of Florida. At the time of the Napoleonic Wars nearly all the maritime nations of Western Europe had a stake in this part of the world. Spain had been the first-comer, but France and England quickly followed, first as corsairs and traders, then as settlers. By 1800 the Dutch, the Danes and the Swedes also had trading outposts in the chain of islands. He who commands the sea can command the islands also. During the Napoleonic Wars, Britain, which had bases to wind-ward and to leeward (that is, in the east and in the west), first defeated the naval power of France and Spain, and then conquered most of the insular possessions of her enemies, who included, during the course of the wars, all the other European nations with possessions in the Caribbean.

Trade winds and ocean currents have had great influence on the history of the Caribbean. The winds blow regularly during most of the year from the north-east or the east, so that all sailing ships from Europe entered the Caribbean from some point along the eastern chain of islands known to the geographers as the Lesser Antilles. The Spaniards left these islands uninhabited and settled in Cuba, San Domingo and Porto Rico, which are to leeward. But here in the north-east corner of the Caribbean the British established their first settlement in 1623 on St. Kitts. Other settlements, especially on Barbados, which is to windward of all the other islands, gave the British a strategic advantage. But the Lesser Antilles were more than a thousand miles from the Panama Isthmus, the great city of Cartagena and the silver mines of New Spain, on which the British had their eyes focussed. The next step was the establishment of a base nearer the heart of the Spanish Empire, accomplished by the capture of Jamaica in 1655. From the port of Kingston could be organised either raids or trading expeditions in almost any part of the Spanish dominions.

The best way for a sailing vessel to leave Jamaica and the western Caribbean is through the passage between Yucatan and Cuba and so along the Florida peninsula through the Bahama Channel. There is also the Windward Passage between Cuba and Haiti, but this is into the teeth of the trade wind, and for a long time the French fortress at Cape Nicolas Mole made it difficult for British ships to use this route in wartime. Ships from the eastern Caribbean left the chain of islands further to the windward.

Except for a short period in 1795 when insurgents in sympathy with the French held Dominica, Grenada and St. Vincent, the British West Indies remained secure under the British flag during the wars. The worst that the Leeward Islands had to suffer was a raid of Missiessy's squadron in 1805 when £31,500 were handed over to the enemy, and forty merchantmen were captured or destroyed. But it was different for the foreign islands, most of which were captured by the British. Some were taken because of their strategic, commercial or agricultural value, some merely to prevent the enemy making use of them as bases for privateers. By 1814, St. Lucia, Trinidad, Tobago, Martinique, Guadeloupe, St. Thomas, Curacoa, St. Eustatius, and the colonies of Surinam, Demerara, Essequibo and Berbice on the mainland had fallen into British hands. These were called "the Conquered Colonies" in the Customs House books. In most cases their produce was treated equally with produce from the British islands, but sugar and coffee from Martinique, captured in 1809, paid foreign duties.

The tropical lands of the New World provided a great range of commodities for the markets of Europe. Sugar, the principal crop grown in the Caribbean basin, had become a necessity of everyday life, and Great Britain alone imported about 19/20ths of her total supply from the West Indies. There was also a surplus for re-export to Europe, but before the war Britain had great difficulty in competing with sugar from the French West Indies. The negro revolt in Haiti, which stopped sugar production, provided boom conditions for the British producer, but even at that time the British shipper suffered from the competition of the neutrals, especially the Americans, who carried Cuban and French sugar directly to continental ports. British sugar, and indeed almost all the British islands' produce, had to go first to the United Kingdom, except when sold by special permission to the Americans. No goods from Europe entered the islands except in British ships and from British ports. Goods were subject to duties at either end and were liable to all the restrictions which made up the Navigation System.

The high cost of freight and insurance, and the additional duties imposed by the convoy and other acts were burdensome, but it was still possible to make money out of the West Indian trade. The first five years of the war saw a revival in sugar, but this was due more to the collapse of Haiti than to the existence of hostilities. At the turn of the century the long decline in prices began. Not, however, until 1815 did it become apparent that the downward movement was permanent. Even if there had been no war the competition of foreign plantations and the slavery troubles would have led to the ruin of the West Indians. But the heavy burdens of additional taxation, the admission of produce from the conquered colonies into the home market, and the difficulties of selling sugar abroad accentuated their distress.

The rich West Indians shared with the Nabobs from the East the position of *nouveaux riches* in English society. Their wealth seemed to be fabulous. Was it not George the Third himself who, passing a handsome carriage with outriders in livery belonging to a Jamaica merchant, exclaimed, "Sugar, sugar, eh?—all *that* sugar! How are the duties, eh, Pitt, how are the duties?" [1] Even at the close of the war, when the long decline had already begun, the legend of the riches of the West Indian persisted. Thackeray, writing of the time of Waterloo, painted a picture of the unfortunate Miss Schwartz, who, having more than a lick of the tar brush, had only her money bags to recommend her. Miss Schwartz had come from the West Indies, as did so many of the planters, to spend her money at home, and establish herself in English society. [2]

---

[1] Wentworth, T., *The West India Sketch Book*, II, p. 70, note.

[2] Thackeray, W. M., *Vanity Fair*.

The merchant who remained in England shared in the wealth that came from sugar. In many cases he was more fortunate than the planter. Residence in the capital, and the possession of a country estate, which introduced him to the best county families, gave him greater opportunities for making his way in the world. If he could prove that he had always resided in England there was no fear of that mixture of negro blood which was so undesirable.[1] In many cases, planter and merchant were one. A man who began life on an estate in the West Indies might end his days in England as a merchant. In other cases, firms might come into possession of plantations through inheritance or foreclosure. Brothers or members of the same family might carry on between them the whole business of cultivating, shipping and selling the tropical produce. Even where there were no family ties, the relationship between planter and merchant was usually a close one. The planter often placed all his concerns in the hands of the merchant. The latter acted as agent and banker, bought all the necessities for the plantation, arranged about shipping them out to the islands, received the return cargo, and disposed of any profits. More often than not the planter's account was overdrawn. When the planter's children were at school in England their bills were met by the merchant, and allowances were paid to dependents who were residing in England. In cases where the mercantile house was the real owner, an agent or manager paid by salary or commission was in charge of the plantations, and all business was naturally conducted by the merchant at home.

The wealth acquired in the West Indian trade brought power. Most firms were comparatively small affairs; a partnership perhaps between two friends or two brothers, which might be dissolved within their own lifetime. In order to exercise their power, therefore, the West Indians formed associations among themselves. There were innumerable societies and clubs throughout the country; numbers probably existed which have left no trace and no records. The larger cities had more permanent bodies. Glasgow, Liverpool and Bristol all had West India Associations. The more important bodies, how-

---

[1] John Pinney, merchant of Bristol, made a great point of his family having been settled in Somerset for generations ; see MacInnes, C. M., *A Gateway of Empire*, p. 324.

ever, were in London. There existed, during the war, two organisations, the Society of West India Merchants, and the Meeting of West
India Planters and Merchants, both separate in their constitutions, but
having much the same membership. A charge on trade, varying with
circumstances, was made to meet expenses. The Society of West
India Merchants was the body with which the Admiralty corres-
ponded about the appointment of convoys. Whenever a question
arose which affected only one branch of the trade, a meeting of those
interested would be called. Thus in 1787 a meeting of the Jamaica
planters and merchants discussed the Free Port Act relating to that
island, and their Minutes were incorporated in those of the Society of
Planters and Merchants.([1]) In 1811 the Admiralty wrote to Lloyd's
begging that the gentlemen engaged in trade with the Bahamas
would form themselves into an association and appoint a chairman
for correspondence with the Admiralty regarding convoys. The
Bahamas merchants do not seem to have had any association, but the
committee at Lloyd's were able to suggest one or two names. Mr.
James Stevens, a merchant resident in the city, consented to serve.([2])
There were probably other loose associations which have left no
record. By such means the West Indians and their representatives
were enabled to exercise a power, which singly, no firm could have
commanded. These societies accomplished for commercial life what
the West Indian interest in Parliament could do in politics. Many of
the Members of Parliament were themselves merchants and belonged
to one of the organisations. In the political sphere, as well as the
commercial, these bodies exercised their power. When Mr. Pitt
wanted to alter the duties on East Indian sugar, he had a conference
with the Standing Committee of the West Indian Planters and
Merchants to explain his ideas, and as a result of their arguments his
plans were considerably modified.([3])

All sorts and conditions of men had interests in the West Indies,
from the landed gentleman to the younger son who was sent out to

---

([1]) West India Committee, Minutes of the Standing Committee of Planters and
Merchants, vol. I, p. 64.
([2]) Admiralty 2/1108, Letters relating to Convoys, p. 320 and 347.
([3]) West India Committee, Minutes of the Standing Committee of Planters and
Merchants, vol. I, pp. 169-196.
Penson, L. M., *The Colonial Agents of the British West Indies*, Chapter V.

L

the islands to make his fortune. Many of the smaller men did not survive, or else they made money soon and retired from the scene. But there were others who made a name for themselves, and stood out as men of good repute and great influence. In some cases, family tradition assisted the struggle. The Longs, of Jamaica, for instance, were always represented in the London West India interests, and the two Beeston Longs, father and son, were in turn chairman of the West India merchants. Another planter from Jamaica, Richard Pennant, Lord Penrhyn, was chairman of the planters and merchants during most of the war. The Hibberts and the Lascelles were two other families whose power was strong in the city. The latter were the forebears of the Earls of Harewood. But these were not the only West Indians whose descendants acquired national fame. John Gladstone was one of the principal West India merchants of Liverpool during the Napoleonic Wars, and he handed on to his son a fortune capable of supporting the rising political aspirations of the future Prime Minister. Another notable figure of the nineteenth century, Cardinal Manning, was the son of a London merchant whose forebears had lived in Jamaica. Bankruptcy and dwindling fortunes were all too common at the beginning of the nineteenth century, but some firms managed to survive the worst, and lived to repair their shattered fortunes in more profitable fields of enterprise.

By far the greatest number of wealthy merchants lived in London, and this port ranked first among all those in the United Kingdom. The Customs returns for 1809, for instance, show that 324 vessels entered London from the West Indies, as against 211 in the outports.[1] In 1787 the number of ships entering London had been about equal to those entering all the outports, although the tonnage had been considerably larger, 70,000 as against 50,000 tons.[2] The capital had grown in importance since the beginning of the war. An examination of a quarterly shipping list from Kingston, Jamaica, gives some indication of the proportion of trade coming from each British port. Some of the colonies, especially Barbados and the Leeward Islands, sent fewer vessels to London than to the outports. But

[1] Customs 4/5, List of Imports by Countries, 1809.
[2] Young, W., *West India Commonplace Book*, 36.

the Kingston figures[1] are fairly representative of the trade as a whole. Of 101 vessels coming from the United Kingdom, 58 cleared at London, 25 from the outports, including 11 from Liverpool, and nine from Bristol. From Scotland came nine, mostly from Glasgow, and from Ireland nine, from Belfast, Dublin and Cork. There was much similarity among the cargoes carried although, naturally, Belfast specialised in linens, Cork in provisions like butter and beef, while through Bristol went the ironmongery of the Black Country. Return cargoes to the different ports were also rather alike, although towards the end of the period much of the cotton wool was sent to Liverpool for Manchester. Sugar and coffee to be exported could be sent most conveniently to London, the great port for trade with the Continent, or to Glasgow, whence the produce was taken via the Forth and Clyde canal to Leith for export to the Baltic. The great improvements at the Port of London (especially the West India Docks, opened in 1801, where all West Indian ships were obliged to unload), gave the capital advantages over the western towns. There were difficulties in making progress down Channel from the Thames, but in spite of this London continued to hold its place as the greatest West Indian port.

The cargoes which were carried back and forth between the West Indies and Great Britain comprised a large proportion of the total trade of the Mother Country. On the official books of the Customs the West Indian trade was estimated at about one-seventh of the total exports of Great Britain. But the imports were worth even more; in 1808 they were £9.5 against £27.8 millions official value.[2] Vessels leaving England for the islands carried out less than they carried home, so that on the Books of the Customs there was an unfavourable balance of trade against the Mother Country. The planting class appeared by the statistics to be the creditors, whereas in fact they were the debtors. A great deal of the profits from sugar were spent in England, and did not, therefore, figure among the exports to the West Indies. There were other ways in which returns for sugar were made, via Madeira, North America and, until 1807, the African slave

---

[1] C.O. 142/24, List of Ships entered at Kingston, Jamaica, from March to June, 1806.

[2] Customs 17/30, State of Navigation and Commerce, 1808.

trade. Ships from England went out laden with manufactured goods and bought slaves on the Guinea and Angola coasts, which were later sold to the planter in the West Indies. The slavers were then free to pick up a cargo of sugar and rum and return to England. All the gold and silver that did not come direct from Spain and Portugal (and this trade was much interrupted during hostilities) entered Great Britain from the Caribbean or from South America. During the war England needed very large supplies of bullion. The East India trade absorbed some each year; the British armies abroad had to be maintained; and there were subsidies due to various foreign governments. The mines of gold and silver in the New World were mostly in Peru, New Spain and Brazil; but in the process of trade, mostly contraband, quantities of bullion reached the British West Indies and were thence forwarded to England. So great was the need after 1808 that special agents were sent out on behalf of the Government to buy dollars from New Spain. These men were obliged to conduct their nego-tiations from Jamaica, and they spent most of their time waiting for the captains of frigates to return from Vera Cruz, usually after a fruitless mission.[1] Besides bullion, England was annually importing vast quantities of sugar. After the destruction of the French plantations in St. Domingue, the British West Indies accounted for a large proportion of all the sugar consumed in Europe. The competition of Cuba, Brazil and the East Indies did not become serious until after the war was over. It was this monopoly of the sugar industry which made the French and German chemists turn to the substitution of beets and grapes. There were also other commodities which brought wealth to England. It has only to be remembered that at this time the trade to the East had not been satisfactorily developed, that the North American colonies which had been a valuable part of the British imperial economic system had left the Empire, and that the great markets of the southern hemisphere had not yet yielded anything of value, to realise that the West Indian trade was the strongest and most flourishing of Britain's commercial ties with her overseas possessions.

The trade to the British islands was divided into two distinct parts.

---

[1] Langnas, A. I., *The Relations between Great Britain and the Spanish Colonies*, thesis in the Library of the University of London, Chapter III.
Admiralty 1/262, Admiral Rowley to Croker, Jamaica, 20th January, 1811.

There was, first of all, the intercourse with the plantations which furnished the sugar and coffee growers with all that they needed and carried away their harvests, and there was, secondly, the entrepot trade which supplied manufactured goods to the various foreign colonies, particularly the Spanish, through the medium of the British West Indies. Because this intercourse was of less value than the plantation trade, and because it was illegal, and therefore hard to assess, historians have paid less attention to it than to the sugar trade. It was an ancient form of commerce, however, and had existed during the days of the Elizabethan adventurers, long before the planting of sugar had been introduced. It continued to exist as long as the commercial regulations of the lands surrounding the Caribbean prohibited the entry of shipping direct from England.

The plantation trade was always larger than the entrepot trade, although the latter grew during the war; and of all the plantation products, sugar was the most important. All the islands except the Bahamas cultivated the sugar cane, and in many of them it was the only product of importance. A glance at the official records for the year 1808 will show the preponderance of sugar. It is true that these figures represent only the official value and therefore are not strictly accurate. They can be used, nevertheless, for purposes of comparison, since the same inaccuracies apply to all the other entries except coffee, which was said to be greatly over-valued.[1] The total official value of goods imported into Great Britain from the West Indies in 1808 was £7,067,626, of which sugar accounted for £3,867,704, coffee for £2,123,288, and cotton for £244,181.[2] The conquered colonies in the same year sent £2,479,251 worth of tropical produce, of which coffee accounted for £1,170,858, sugar £861,018, and

---

[1] Young, 101.

[2] Customs 17/30, State of Navigation and Commerce, 1808. Compare with the real values, including the duty, according to Sir William Young's calculations for 1804-5 :

Sugar, home consumption	..	£7,569,662
exported	..	3,950,924
Coffee, home consumption	..	146,985
exported	..	1,165,520
Cotton	.. ..	..	1,097,242
Total Value ..	..	£17,002,117

cotton £349,467. At that time, Martinique and Guadeloupe, two important sugar-producing colonies, were not in British hands.

The West Indians had been cultivating the sugar cane for over a hundred and fifty years, yet their methods were old-fashioned and wasteful. It was not until 1793 that the first shoots of the species of Bourbon and Tahitian sugar cane were introduced into the Leeward Islands from Martinique and Guadeloupe. These new kinds of cane were hardier than the former, and yielded one-third more sugar. But there were disadvantages attached to their cultivation. The soil became exhausted easily, and replanting had to be done more often.[1] Exhaustion of the soil was an evil against which the planter had to fight continually and, in the long run, the chief cause of the fall of the British planter was the competition of sugar from the virgin lands of the mainland—sugar which could be produced more cheaply than his own crop. Indeed, some of the British islands, like Barbados and Antigua, were already declining. Barbados produced, in 1800, barely half the amount of sugar she had grown in 1735.[2] Jamaica, on the other hand, was an example of a colony which was at the height of its development as a sugar producer. There were still quantities of land to be developed, and she was already producing more than half of all the sugar imported into England from the Caribbean. By contrast, again, there were islands which had not yet reached anything like their maximum production. Grenada and St. Vincent, for example, suffered from disastrous civil war during this period. In the former island the authorities were challenged by the French inhabitants and the free people of colour; in the latter, by the black Caribs. According to all accounts, there was little to choose between them for barbarity and destruction. By 1800 order had been restored and cultivation resumed. These events placed both islands in the position of "frontier" colonies, the potentialities of which were only partly developed. Dominica, because of its hills, never became a great sugar-producing colony. In 1815 she exported less than Nevis, one of the Leeward Islands, about one-sixth of her size.[3]

---

[1] Ragatz, L. J., *The Fall of the Planter Class in the British Caribbean*, 79.

[2] Young, 18.

[3] Ragatz, *Statistics for the Study of British Caribbean History*, Table XVI.

All through the wars the export of sugar to England went on increasing. Not only was the production of all but the oldest colonies expanding, but there were also the additional crops from the conquered islands and from captured territory on the mainland. Trinidad added only half the amount grown in St. Vincent in 1815, but Demerara was growing almost a quarter of the amount produced in Jamaica.[1] The West Indian planters were convinced that the rapid expansion of these conquered colonies was the chief cause of all their losses. Yet the ships of the West Indian fleets continued to carry home larger cargoes of sugar each year. In 1815, 3,381,790 hundredweights of British-grown sugar reached Great Britain from the Caribbean, an increase of a million over the imports of 1793.[2]

The West Indians were suffering, it is clear, from over-production of a product which could find no market in Europe. The British shipper and the British merchant, not to mention the Government, all benefited from the law which required all British West Indian produce to be landed in England before proceeding to a European port.[3] In developing their transit trade the English demonstrated their genius for making money on commission. When there was a scarcity the English merchant prospered, but after 1799 there was too much sugar on the market. The Parliamentary Committee of 1807, which reported on the depressed state of the West Indian islands, laid much of the blame on the state of the continental market, which, ravaged by war, was unable to cope with the bumper crops which had been arriving in Europe for the past few years.[4] There had been a sharp fall in prices, from 72s. per cwt. in June, 1798, to 38s. in December, 1806.[5] The French, incidentally, were fetching home their colonial produce in perfect safety, because they made use of neutral vessels. In 1806, in his pamphlet, *War in Disguise*, James Stephen wrote that "not a single merchant ship under a flag inimical to Great Britain now crosses the equator, or traverses the Atlantic."[6]

---

[1] Ragatz, *Statistics for the Study of British Caribbean History*, Table XVII.

[2] Ragatz, *Statistics*, Table XVII.

[3] The law of 1739 which had allowed the carrying of sugar to the South of Cape Finisterre was repealed in 1792, and not revived until 1822. Ragatz, *Fall of the Planter Class*, 207 and 324.

[4] *Parl. Pap.*, 1807 III (65).   [5] Ragatz, *Statistics*, Table III.

[6] Stephen, J., *War in Disguise, or the Frauds of Neutral Flags*, 68.

The unfortunate British planter was shipping his sugar in British merchant vessels, subject to all the expenses of delay while waiting for convoy, added to war duties, high insurance and freightage. With things at such a pass it is not to be wondered at that the West Indian trade suffered even more when the Continental System was enforced. It became extremely difficult to export surplus sugar to the Continent at any price. On the London market sugar fell to 32s. 9d. per cwt. in September, 1807, and did not rise above 50s. for the annual average until 1813, when the worst of the storm had passed.(1)

Sugar was sent to England after it had gone through the first process of refining, when it was known as muscovado. The sugar cane had been pressed in the wooden rollers, and the juice had been boiled down until the molasses had separated, and a mass of brown sticky substance was left. This was packed in barrels made of oak staves, which had to be especially imported from the United States or British North America. The Mother Country could never herself spare enough timber to provide all the barrels needed in the sugar islands. The yearly demand was said to be twenty million oak staves, an amount that would have seriously injured the timber industry, already experiencing a shortage.(2) If for any reason the supply of oak staves was inadequate, as happened during the war with America in 1812, or at the time of the Embargo Act, the sugar crop was in grave danger of being left in the islands to spoil. When the muscovado sugar had been packed in hogsheads, of about 13 cwt. each, it was ready for carriage to the nearest port, either by land or by sugar droghers, the small vessels which coasted around the islands between port and plantation. The sugar was still in such a liquid state that there was always a loss in weight during the voyage. Tare allowance of one cwt. per hogshead was made on its arrival in England.(3) It was this seepage which caused the appalling smell of which so many travellers complained.

Molasses was the first by-product of sugar and from this was made rum. The Americans were accustomed to buy much of their molasses in the Caribbean, and make their own spirits from it. But the British manufactured their rum in the islands and exported the spirits to

---

(1) Ragatz, *Statistics*, Table III.   (2) Young, 137.   (3) Ibid., 46.

England. During the war the islands made more than they could sell, for there was no market for this liquor on the Continent, the American market was limited, and in England the West Indians had the greatest difficulty in persuading the public to drink it. The planters came up against a more powerful interest than their own in the distillers, and were in the long run defeated. Sugar was for a time used in the distilleries instead of corn, but this was more because of the shortage of corn, than because of the surplus of sugar.[1] Ever since 1775 the Royal Navy had been a large buyer of rum, but the planters found that the contracts were not what they might be. In 1806 they raised a storm because the Victualling Board bought far more brandy than rum, 625,000 gallons against 250,000 gallons, in perfect indifference that the chief supplies came from the enemy, France. Brandy was imported by the neutrals and was cheaper than West Indian rum. In spite of all their efforts to popularise their product the West Indians never succeeded in making the ordinary Englishman drink rum, although they did manage to increase the supplies to the armed forces.[2] To this day rum is rarely drunk in England, in France it seems to be served largely for medicinal purposes, whereas in the American hemisphere it forms the basis of many cocktails and long drinks.

The West Indians had, on the whole, no greater success with their coffee. Although the coffee itself was excellent (the best in the world still comes from the Jamaican highlands), they never succeeded in making it a universal drink in England. When the occasion called for a drink that was not alcoholic, tea was usually served. Even the former fashionable habit of drinking chocolate had not become popular. In the face of high duties and the success of its rival, tea, coffee had little chance in England. It was a source of anxiety to the coffee planter of the West Indies that he had to rely on sales to foreign markets in Europe. Great efforts were made during the French wars to increase the consumption in England. Before 1783 the charge in duties and excise had been nearly five times its value, but in that year there was a reduction of duty, and the imports doubled. Duties

---

[1] Ragatz, *Fall of the Planter Class*, 290 and 318-9.
[2] Young, 63 ff.
 B.T. 5/16, Minutes of the Board of Trade, 1806, passim.

continued to remain fairly high, however, as protection to the tea trade, until in 1808 they were reduced to 7d. per pound.([1]) But even after this date coffee remained, as Sir William Young put it, "rather an article of trade and export than of national consumption."([2]) In 1814 only five million pounds were retained out of fifty-one millions imported, of which forty million came from the West Indies.([3])

Jamaica was the greatest producer of coffee, exporting in 1814 almost three-quarters of the total amount coming from the West Indies. But at the beginning of the war her share was not so large. It was not until after the revolt in St. Domingue that there was a great extension of coffee walks in Jamaica. Most of the increase was fostered by refugee French planters who brought their knowledge and experience to the aid of the British West Indians. None of the other islands had an export that amounted to anything until after the reduction of duty in 1808. Dominica and Grenada had sent home considerable amounts in the early years of the war, but cultivation declined later. By 1812, Barbados, St. Lucia and Trinidad, besides the expanding colonies of Demerara and Berbice, were all sending coffee to England.([4])

Coffee was a difficult article to pack and carry because it acquired the taste of whatever other commodities were in its neighbourhood. The flavour of the bean would be entirely spoiled, for instance, if coffee were stowed near rum. After the berries were gathered from the trees and dried in the sun, they were packed in bales or bags, and sent to the port for shipment. On arrival in England the coffee was sold for consumption, or (more often) warehoused ready for re-export to the continent.

Sugar, coffee and rum were the three great plantation products of the British West Indies. They were the only articles for which a monopoly of the home market was properly safeguarded. One of the greatest curses of agriculture in the islands was the predominance of sugar and coffee to the exclusion of other crops. When disaster came, either through hurricane, drought, low prices, or blockade, the planters had no other product on which to depend. Efforts were made

([1]) Ragatz, *Fall of the Planter Class*, 42. ([2]) Young, 76.

([3]) Ragatz, *Statistics*, Tables IV and V. ([4]) Ibid., Table IV.

from time to time to relieve the situation by encouraging other crops, but they were mostly unsuccessful. When the downfall of the planter class came about, it was largely because of the depressed state of these three staple products.

Other articles exported from the West Indies which were grown in the islands included indigo, cotton, dyewoods, pimento and ginger, of which the most important was cotton. In 1793 the United States was only just beginning its enormous export of cotton to Liverpool, and the British people were spending a good deal of time and thought on developing their own sources of supply. The market was capable of absorbing as much cotton wool as could be procured. True to mercantilist principles, the Government believed that it was preferable to depend on British colonies for supply rather than on foreign countries, and much was done to encourage cultivation in the West Indies. Several planters, particularly in the Bahamas, took up cotton-growing with enthusiasm. But it was at all times an uncertain crop. In 1789 the British West Indies sent twelve million pounds to Great Britain, almost half of the total supply, but of this at least a quarter, and probably more, was imported from foreign colonies, and was not grown in the British islands at all.[1] By 1807 the British islands, exclusive of the conquered colonies, were growing only five million of the seventy-four millions pounds imported into England. In 1815 imports of cotton from the British West Indies were only three million pounds. The conquered colonies, however, were sending over nine million pounds, about a tenth of the whole importation into Great Britain.[2]

Cotton was gathered in the spring between February and June. It was then roughly cleaned of seeds by a gin, a simple instrument consisting of rollers, and packed in bales of 200 or 300 pounds. Most of the cargoes of cotton were shipped to Liverpool and thence despatched to the mills of Lancashire. The cotton grown in the West Indies commanded a high price. It was a long staple variety, grown in sandy soil near the edge of the sea. Today the same kind is known as sea island cotton. The texture was good and very fine. On the

[1] Customs 17/11, State of Commerce and Navigation, 1789.
[2] Ragatz, *Statistics*, Table VII.

Liverpool market sea island cotton, grown in Georgia, as well as in the islands, fetched from 1s. 6d. to 3s. a pound at a time when the whole price range was 1s. to 3s. 2d. a pound.[1] Demerara cotton was usually better cleaned than the island kind, and being of a very good quality was sold at a higher price than that from Jamaica. The cultivation in the Bahamas from which so much had been hoped had declined almost to nothing by 1815.[2] Like sugar and coffee, cotton suffered from the competition of new lands on the mainland; in this case from the United States, as well as from Brazil.

Shipments of dyeing materials and spices were on a small scale compared with the staple products of the West Indies. The indigo trade had at one time flourished, but since the middle of the eighteenth century West Indian indigo had formed only a small part of Britain's supply. There was first the competition of the Carolina indigo, and then after 1790 the increased imports from Bengal. Even the small amounts coming from the West Indies were not, for the most part, the growth of the British islands. By 1808 nearly six million pounds were entering England, of which over five million came from the East and only 161,741 pounds from the West Indies.[3] The trade in dyewoods, especially fustic and logwood, was more important because although the amounts were not large, the West Indies furnished almost all the supply. Some of this was grown in the British colonies, and in the logwood swamps of Honduras Bay, but some of it came from the foreign islands. Small quantities were often carried in the home-going vessels, especially from Jamaica. The forests of Honduras were also producing mahogany, which was shipped home to be made into chairs and tables for the use of the new moneyed class. Miscellaneous imports included ginger, pimento, arrowroot, castor oil, drugs, and tortoiseshell.

In return for these plantation products, the outgoing vessels carried all manner of British manufactured goods, and some provisions. "Not a button or a shoe, a pocket handkerchief or a hat are obtained elsewhere than in Great Britain," wrote a pamphleteer, "London,

[1] Ragatz, *Statistics*, Table I.
    B.T.1.21 no. 14, Liverpool to —, 24th January, 1803.

[2] Colquhoun, P., Treatise on the British Empire, 323 and 381

[3] Customs 17/30.

Birmingham, Bristol and Carron supply alike the mill-work, the nails, the hoes, the tools, the utensils of domestic life, and the implements of husbandry: the ash-coppices fall to bind the casks, and six millions of hoops are annually split in the service of the planter."([1]) The planter, or the agent who was in charge of estates where the owner was an absentee, usually dealt directly with the merchant at home. This merchant received the sugar and rum, put it into the hands of the broker, and with the proceeds supplied his customers' wants. The plantation stores and necessities for the planter were bought, and arrangements made to despatch the goods and bring home the sugar. Vessels going out to the islands were usually no more than half freighted. They carried dry goods, hats, furniture and saddlery for the use of the planting class, negro clothing, blankets, linens and linseys, tools, copper boilers, nails and other ironware for the use of the plantation. The rest of the freight was made up of provisions. The Corn Laws had limited the export of corn, but an allowance was made for small shipments to the West Indies. Great Britain was the only place within the Empire at this time from whence corn and flour could be obtained, for the North American provinces were unable to supply any large quantities. By the end of the eighteenth century, however, Britain was herself beginning to import corn on a large scale, so there was thenceforward little hope of her being able to supply the West Indies. If corn could not be imported from England it must come from the United States. In actual fact, during most of the war, imports of flour from America were allowed in the islands, contrary to all the principles of the Mercantile System, because supplies from the Mother Country were uncertain and limited. The other great article of food exported from Great Britain was herrings from Scotland, of which amounts valued at £51,000 were carried in 1804.([2])

From Ireland went soap, candles, beef, pork, butter and linens, of which the most valuable were linens. One of the evils of the exclusive cultivation of sugar had been that too little land was given over to growing food. In Jamaica there were some attempts to raise stock,

---

([1]) Bosanquet, C., *Thoughts on the value . . . of the colonial trade*, 40.

([2]) Young, 97.

and grow Indian corn, breadfruit and plantains for the use of negroes. Barbados grew some fresh provisions for the use of the shipping. But in the other islands the inhabitants relied on the import trade for their food. In any time of shortage due to storms, privateers or irregular arrivals of ships, the plantation negroes faced starvation. The only source of staple foods was the United States, which also supplied livestock and timber. The whole question of the American trade had an influence on the trade between England and the British islands, because the shipping of sugar to England depended on the supply of timber and provisions from the United States.

Except for this dependence for food on a source which was outside the British Empire, the West Indian trade was regarded with favour by the mercantilists because it was complementary to the economic life of Britain. It supplied necessary tropical products and provided an outlet for the sale of British manufactures in a market which was closed to the foreigner. All the shipping and freight were in British hands, and the profits eventually returned to England, for the planter and merchant who made money out of the sugar islands came home to spend most of it in the Mother Country. Mercantilists were never tired of pointing out that in reality the West Indian trade should rank not as foreign but as domestic.[1]

In war-time the charges on exports to the West Indies were heavy. Sir William Young calculated that the freight charged on export was about a quarter of the invoice value. The merchant's commission was 2½ per cent., and to this must be added the convoy duty of 2 per cent., raised in 1803 to 3 per cent. Charges on the cargoes carried home, however, were more injurious to the planter than those on the outward voyage were to the manufacturer. Freight on sugar was raised during the war by almost 50 per cent. to 9s. per cwt. The duty, which was 15s. per cwt. in 1791, was £1 7s. in 1806, liable to fluctuation according to the price of sugar. The price of plantation stores had gone up, so that in 1806 the planter was receiving as his net proceeds about half of what he received in 1791. Insurance fluctuated according to the fortunes of war. Outward cargoes paid on an average a 10 per

---

[1] See especially Bosanquet, 40, and Edwards, B., *History of the British West Indies*, II, 532ff.

cent. premium, and sugar coming from the islands 5 per cent., but on occasion, such as the anxious months before Trafalgar, it rose to 20 per cent.[1] The fall in the price of plantation produce which occurred at the beginning of the century, and the high cost of bringing commodities to market, added to the difficulties of the planter who was already finding it hard to compete with the new fields of cultivation in the United States, South America and the East. Yet there was no decline in production. Ships went home as heavily freighted as ever.

Some of the outgoing and incoming cargoes included goods for the entrepot trade with the Spanish settlements. As has been mentioned before, this commerce had had its origins in the work of the Elizabethan adventurers, who, long before the plantation system had been established, had regarded the Caribbean as a rich store house. The intercourse was continued as a contraband trade after the capture of Jamaica, which, throughout the eighteenth century, remained the chief entrepot. By the time of the Napoleonic Wars, the trade had been made legal, at least on the part of the British. To the Spanish authorities it was always contraband. By Act of Parliament[2] small foreign vessels were admitted into British West Indian harbours, carrying the products of the foreign colonies. This was known as the Free Port System because certain ports in the British islands were allowed to import foreign goods in foreign vessels, which before had been rigidly excluded by the Acts of Trade. Elaborate precautions were taken to prevent the entrance of foreign manufactures which would compete with British, and of foreign sugar and coffee where there was danger of its spoiling the market at home for the British plantation product. The system was in operation before the American Revolutionary War, but it was revised and enlarged in 1787 and 1792, and continued to be improved throughout the Napoleonic Wars. Before 1793 trade to French islands had been almost as important as that to the Spanish, but war prevented its continuing. Hostilities with Spain, however, did not bring the Spanish trade to an end. Instead, an elaborate system of licences permitted the trade to continue. It was not until the opening years of the nineteenth century, when all manu-

---

[1] Young, 45-49.

[2] The principal Acts were, 27 Geo. III cap. 27, 32 Geo. III cap 43 and 45 Geo. III cap. 57.

facturing and shipping rivals in Europe were eliminated (owing to the war) that the system was really justified. Pamphlets, minutes and letters from members of the Board of Trade and mercantile men show how important the trade became. The growth of industries in England, and the necessity of finding markets overseas made it imperative to foster such an outlet for manufactured goods as was provided by the Free Port System.

The Custom House statistics make it difficult to distinguish between imports from British and from foreign islands, and almost impossible to separate the British exports destined for the islands from those intended for the Spanish colonies. The tastes and wants of British and Spanish were very much alike. Plantations in Spanish possessions demanded Sheffield cutlery and Birmingham hardware, sugar boilers and nails, just as did the planter in Jamaica; and the Spanish creoles wore beaver and felt hats, stockings, cottons, woollens and linens from England. Sometimes the merchant found that the Spaniard was less willing to put up with British goods than was his British neighbour. The Spanish demand for German linens continued unabated, even though a superior Scotch and Irish material was available. The British planter was willing to pay the higher prices that were asked for the British linen, but the Spaniard obstinately refused to be content with any other article than the cheap German cloth. The merchant was quite as a loss to understand why the foreigner should think differently from the respectable Jamaica planter. The only way in which he could settle the difficulty was by importing German linens for his Spanish customer, and so a transit trade in foreign linens developed between Leith and Glasgow.[1]

It would be easier to estimate the amount of West Indian trade which was in reality a trade with Spanish colonies if only the colonial Naval Officers' Accounts were accurate, but unfortunately this is far from being the case. The Spanish importer always hated entering his cargo, because he feared reprisals and punishment from his own government if it became known that he was selling to foreigners such contraband articles as indigo and bullion.[2] Frauds on the part of the

[1] B.T.5.15, Minute of 25th April and 24th July, 1805 ; B.T.1.25.no.30. Representation of James Buchanan, 1805 ; On the Policy of Throwing Open the Transit Trade in Foreign Linens, 1816.
[2] B.T.1.30, no. 10, Governor Hislop to Windham, Trinidad, 4th July, 1806.

Spaniards, and carelessness or slackness on the part of the Customs
official in entering goods which were duty free, have left accounts
which tell only part of the story. It is impossible, especially, to
estimate the value of manufactured goods exported from any of the
British islands. All we have to go on is the statement of the merchants
of Jamaica, that in 1808, before the great increase in trade, the total
value of the exports from the colony was five million dollars, over
one million pounds sterling.(¹) The Customs House accounts for the
same year show that Jamaica imported £2,962,429 worth of goods
from Britain, which may be estimated at £5,000,000 real value.(²)
Trinidad exported 528,803 dollars (£100,000) worth of goods to the
Spanish colonies, and imported from Great Britain £521,261, or
approximately £800,000 real value.(³) It must be remembered that
this period was not one during which the trade was at its height. A
few years later the free port trade at Jamaica was exporting over nine
million dollars worth of goods.(⁴) The time came when the merchants of Kingston could declare that this entrepot trade was the only
one of importance left to their city.(⁵).

Jamaica, which took almost half of the exports leaving Great
Britain for the West Indies, was by far the most important centre for
the free port trade. Almost all its ports were granted permission to
trade with the foreigner, and boats arrived from a wide circle of
Spanish colonies in the vicinity. The Spanish Main, Panama, New
Spain, and the island of Cuba all bought merchandise at the warehouses of Kingston. The free port at Nassau in the Bahamas also
traded with Cuba and the Gulf of Mexico. In the Lesser Antilles there
were several free ports of which the most important were Grenada
and Trinidad, which sent cargoes to the Main. Curacoa, after falling
into British hands, continued and developed a trade with Caracas.
Between them, the British West Indian islands could offer the
merchant at home a command of all the Spanish markets that

(¹) B.T.1.41, no. 14, Minutes of a Committee of Merchants of Jamaica on the Free
    Port Trade, 18th July, 1808.
(²) Customs 17/30, State of Trade, 1808.
(³) Customs House Papers, Trinidad, General Report of Imports, 1808 to 1822.
(⁴) Jones, T. S., *Historical Study of Anglo-South American Trade*, this in the Library of
    the University of London, 339.
(⁵) B.T.1.44, no. 32, Minutes of——

M

bordered on the Caribbean Sea. As long as direct trade to South America was impossible owing to the restrictive policy of the King of Spain, the British manufacturer had to rely on the free port trade to sell his goods in the Spanish provinces.

The returns of the free port trade came to be less important than the export of manufactures. At first the foreign islands had been expected to furnish valuable supplies of cotton wool and indigo, two commodities badly needed in the factories and not grown to any great extent in the British colonies. But the development of cotton growing in the United States and Brazil and of indigo in Bengal offered more reliable sources of supply than the backward Spanish colonies. By the end of the Napoleonic Wars the returns for manufactured goods were being largely made in bullion, with occasional shipments of drugs, dyes, sugar and coffee. Almost all these commodities were the same as those produced in the British islands, so that it is impossible to tell how much of the cargoes of tropical products were actually of British origin. In the case of sugar and coffee, however, entries coming from the West Indies which were the growth of the Spanish colonies were labelled foreign.[1]

All these articles of tropical growth, like sugar, coffee, indigo, logwood and tobacco, were on the enumerated list, and by the terms of the Acts of Trade could be brought only to Britain, and must enter in British vessels. No alteration in the law was required when the free port trade was introduced, for the foreign produce of the Caribbean could be taken to England in the ordinary way in British shipping. Indeed, the purpose of the free port system would have been destroyed if the monopoly of the carrying trade across the Atlantic had been abandoned. The planters felt no dismay at the introduction of foreign produce into their home market as long as the produce was limited to such commodities as indigo and tobacco, which they were not cultivating to any great extent. But the admission of sugar and coffee was another matter. It was impossible to develop a trade in foreign sugar and coffee except at places where no British sugar was

---

[1] Customs 17/22, Account of goods imported to Great Britain from Jamaica differentiates foreign from British growth, 1800.
Cotton, British, 1,228,834 ; Foreign, 4,077,019 lbs

grown. The ports in the Bahamas and Tortola were the principal places appointed from which foreign produce was sent to England. On arrival it was warehoused, and if taken out for home consumption, paid the foreign duties. The amounts imported were never very large, and the planters had no cause for complaint. If the cargoes had reached greater proportions, doubtless more would have been heard from the West Indian interests.([1]) As it was, West Indiamen were permitted to carry out goods both for the Spanish and the plantation markets, and to return laden with the produce of the Main and the British islands.

Vessels which went out to the islands in the time of the wars were usually "established" ships; that is, they had been chartered by the merchant to sail to a certain colony and bring home previously estimated cargoes of sugar. The merchant contracted with the planter, who either loaded his barrels into the vessel at one of the bays around the coast or sent them in a drogher to the port where the vessel lay at anchor. Sometimes the mercantile firm at home owned the vessel. George Hibbert & Co., of London, owned a fine ship of 610 tons, one of the largest in the trade, built at Rotherhithe, which was regularly engaged in the Jamaica trade.([2]) But more often the ships were chartered. Fixed rates of freight were drawn up and formally agreed to by both merchants and shipowners. These ocean-going vessels were not owned in the islands, except in places like the Bahamas, which were not the object of much commercial speculation. The "established" ships were often built especially for sugar. The trade was also carried on in "seekers," vessels going out on speculation in search of a cargo. The African slavers belonged to this class. When the "seeker" arrived in the islands the master bargained with the planters whose crops were not already consigned, or with the island merchants who had on hand produce either from British plantations or foreign colonies. If the "seekers" were runners, and came out without convoy, they were a boon to the islands, because they

---

([1]) See West India Committee, Minutes of Planters and Merchants, March, 1792, for their point of view.

([2]) C.O.142.24-5, List of Ships entering Jamaica, 1806-7.

imported fresh provisions at times when there was a scarcity, and did this without glutting the market.(¹)

For the most part the vessels employed in the West Indian trade varied from 200 to 500 tons burden. The average size of vessels in 1808 was 298 tons.(²) Of the 101 vessels entered at Kingston for a quarter of 1806, only 22 were over 400 tons and only two over 500 tons burden.(³) Most of the ships were built in Great Britain, and except for an occasional brig or snow they were almost all ship rigged. The Kingston shipping lists for 1806 show that vessels trading between Jamaica and Great Britain were built almost entirely in the British Isles. Rotherhithe, Whitby, Whitehaven and Bristol were the most usual places, but many other ports, especially in the North and in Devon, launched West Indian vessels in their shipyards. The shortage of oak timber and the cost of shipbuilding in the Thames had led, according to the *Quarterly Review*, to many West Indiamen being contracted for in the north, instead of at London. Certainly, the Kingston shipping list for 1806 shows that most of the Thames-built vessels were launched before 1800. West Indiamen built especially for the trade were designed to combine speed with the maximum carrying capacity. Most of them were broad in the beam, and the older ships were found to be very slow sailers, a great disadvantage when sailing in convoy.

While the ships were built especially for the trade, there were always some which had been converted from other uses. When James went out to Jamaica as a captain in the merchant service, he was in command of a ship, the *Maria*, of about 450 tons burden, which had been built for the government as an ordnance store ship.(⁴) The vessels which had been built for the trade were often considered to be very comfortable. Dr. Pinckard was delighted with the accommodation in the *Lord Sheffield*, which took him to Barbados in 1796. This vessel had been specially built for the West Indian

(¹) Allen, H., *British Commercial Policy in the West Indies*, thesis in the Library of the University of London, 18, quoting B.T.5/1, Minutes of the Committee of Trade, 1784.

(²) Customs 17/30, State of Navigation for 1808.

(³) C.O.142.24, List of Ships entered Kingston, Mar-June, 1806.

(⁴) Laughton, J. K., *Journal of Rear-Admiral James*, 177.

service, and everything was designed for the comfort of the passengers. After an uncomfortable sojourn on board an old frigate, Pinckard was pleased to notice that the sleeping berths were private apartments, not partitioned off by canvas as in the man-of-war, that there were awnings, scuttles and port-holes all designed for protection from the tropical heat, and that the cabin was large and fitted with a mahogany wainscot, pier glasses and a sofa. Life on ship-board could offer no more. There were even bathing tubs on deck in which the male passengers could have a morning plunge.(¹) On the voyage home these delights were tempered by the appalling smell of sugar which pervaded even the most elegant cabins. Lady Nugent complained that everything tasted of the smell of sugar and that the whole cabin was covered with a sort of leaden surface which came off on one's clothes.(²) Except for this unpleasantness the passengers' and officers' accommodation in the better-class West Indiamen was comparatively comfortable. Many commanders could depend on carrying from five to ten passengers both out and homeward bound, including very often members of the services, business men and mothers fetching or carrying their children to school in England.

The armament of West Indiamen seems to have been very inadequate, both for runners and ships sailing in convoy. Rather a large number of vessels carried no guns at all, 30 out of 101 in 1806, while 16 carried only two, a number which could have been little protection against privateers.(³) Ships that were runners depended for security more on speed than on their armament, and ships that sailed in convoy can seldom have needed their guns, except for signalling. West Indiamen were given a fresh coat of paint as they sailed down the trades, so that they arrived in the islands looking their best. Their sides were painted yellow or black, occasionally red, and the mouldings picked out in black, yellow or white; many were painted yellow all over.(⁴) The owner of a West Indiaman was always engaged in a fight against the worm, and against the growth of marine life on the

(¹) Pinckard, G., *Notes on the West Indies*, 143.

(²) Cundall, F., *Lady Nugent's Journal*, 310.

(³) C.O.142.24, Shipping List, Kingston, 1806.

(⁴) Ad. 1/316, no. 59, Admiral Gardner to Stephens, At Sea, 11th September, 1794, enclosing account of convoy.

bottoms. Vessels had to be careened at least once every voyage. Copper sheathing was a comparatively recent innovation, and there were still merchant vessels which were without its protection. Advertisements in the Bristol papers, however, show that the largest and finest West Indiamen were copper sheathed during the period with which we are dealing.(¹)

Although the West Indiamen were rather small in size, there were so many of them that their tonnage compared favourably with the total tonnage of Great Britain. Colquhoun estimated that in 1815 there were about 600 ships in the trade of an average tonnage of 300 tons each.(²) A Parliamentary return shows that in 1804 London despatched 326 of an average tonnage of 324, the outports 188 averaging 277 tons each, and Scotland 84 ships averaging 242 tons each.(³). The General State of Navigation drawn up for 1808 shows that over 650 vessels were employed in the trade to the British West Indies alone, and that another 220 were trading with the conquered colonies, which at that time included Demerara and Berbice, St. Lucia and Curacao, but not Martinique or Guadeloupe. A further 92 British and 48 foreign vessels were trading to foreign colonies in the Caribbean, and 15 British sail were sent to Honduras Bay. The total tonnage of British vessels sailing to the Caribbean was five times greater than that of vessels trading to Asia and New Holland, 28 times greater than that trading to Africa, and nine times the tonnage of both British and foreign vessels going to the United States. Only the trade in European waters surpassed that of the West Indies, and repeated voyages make it impossible to compare this trade accurately.(⁴) The mercantilists considered the small size of the West Indiamen to be an advantage, for the building of West Indiamen did not call for the largest oak timbers, then in great demand at the naval dockyards. Moreover, small vessels trained proportionately more seamen than did the large ships. The shortness of the voyage, moreover, brought the crews home again within nine months, hardened by a tropical climate, and ready for service in the navy in case of national danger.

(¹) Powell, J. W. D., *Bristol Ships*, 304.

(²) Colquhoun, P., *Treatise on the Wealth . . . of the British Empire*, 344.

(³) Young, 37.   (⁴) Customs 17/30.

Vessels made one voyage a year. The best procedure was to leave England in the autumn, and pick up a return cargo as soon as harvest was over, in May or June. If the ship left the islands before the end of July, the hurricane season was avoided, and cargoes of sugar reached home in time to be transhipped to Baltic ports before the ice set in. The first convoy of the season was supposed to leave England in October and November, in time for the negroes to receive their annual gifts of clothing and meat for the Christmas festivities. In actual fact the convoy was often delayed, and sometimes the first arrivals did not reach the islands until January or February. Vessels continued to leave England until April or May. If they sailed any later they arrived too late to obtain a homeward-bound cargo and escape the Caribbean before the hurricane season. After July insurance rates were doubled. The ordinary policy specified that ships must sail before the first of August.

The early part of the voyage was always the worst; the storms and contrary winds of the northern latitudes were the greatest source of delay. Mathew Lewis, in 1815, was lucky in passing the Scillys seven days after anchoring in the Downs. In his second voyage the ship did not reach the latitude of Madeira until thirty-four days after leaving the Downs, having been blown back to Plymouth once, and having spent ten days tacking in the chops of the Channel.[1] After reaching the latitude of Madeira things became more comfortable. Sometimes the vessels called here for refreshment and a cargo of wine. Madeira was almost the only wine drunk in the West Indies in large quantities. Occasionally the planter would offer beer or porter, rum punch or a long drink, but Madeira was the staple liquor. It was usually drunk as sangaree, a mixture of wine, water and lime juice.

The trade wind was picked up anywhere between Madeira and the 27° parallel. After this the sails were set, and hardly changed until Barbados was reached. From the point of view of passengers and crew, this part of the voyage almost compensated for the weary weeks of pitching and tossing about in European waters. The ship was painted, tarred and scrubbed, awnings were stretched on deck, under which the passengers could recline. The ship kept pretty well

[1] Lewis, M., *Journal of a West India Proprietor.*

on an even keel, which made everything easier, and the constant breeze relieved the heat of the tropical sun.

When the vessel crossed the Tropic, the ship was visited by Neptune and his consort, or by Mr. and Mrs. Cancer. The ceremony seems to have been much the same as that held on crossing the Equator. After a week or so the end of the voyage came in sight. During the war, especially if they were convoyed, most vessels called first at Barbados, where wood and water and fresh provisions were to be had from the swarms of pettiaguas and canoes that surrounded every vessel that dropped anchor. The harbour, Carlisle Bay, was little better than a roadstead, protected by the land from the prevailing north-east trade. It was indented about a quarter of a mile and was a mile and a half or two miles across. There was good anchorage within the heads of the bay. The harbour was protected by Fort Charles to the south, where there was a signal station, and Fort James to the north. Within the Bay were the barracks and the capital of the island, Bridgetown. At times the roadstead would be crowded with vessels; at other times, especially in the hurricane season, it would be practically deserted. When Pinckard arrived in February, 1796, there were only two full-rigged ships at anchor, and between 11th February and 9th March only two vessels arrived from England. Sixty vessels from a convoy anchored within the next few days.[1] From its position to windward of the other islands, Barbados was a sort of porter's lodge for the Caribbean, where almost all ships called for news and for provisions. It was the first port of call for the fortnightly packets from Falmouth. There is an old saying, still current in the island, "What would poor old England do if Barbados were to forsake her?"

In spite of its position to windward, the lack of a good harbour and careening place prevented Barbados being used as the naval base for the Leeward Islands squadron. This was at Antigua, almost four hundred miles away, which had a good harbour. Throughout the French wars, even after the final capture of St. Lucia, which had been the French base in the West Indies, the Admiral on the Leeward Islands station continued to use English Harbour, Antigua, as the

_____

[1] Pinckard, I., 400-2.

arsenal and dockyard. He was obliged to keep his squadron well scattered so that the port at Barbados should be well protected.

From Barbados the ships went up and down the islands to their destinations. Vessels bound to the Guianas usually left the convoy to the windward of Barbados, but if no men-of-war could be spared, they proceeded to Carlisle Bay and were sent to the coast under protection of a ship from the Leeward Islands squadron. If the ship was a runner sailing without convoy she often proceeded direct to her destination. The Jamaica vessels and those bound for Antigua kept further north and made landfall at Deseada off Guadeloupe or at Antigua. The best passage to Jamaica was between Antigua and Guadeloupe, thence straight before the wind to Alta Vela, a rocky island to the south of Hispaniola, which was sighted by most vessels, and thence in a day or so to the east end of Jamaica. The passage from the Leeward Islands might take about five days.

The entrance to Port Royal harbour, the principal port in Jamaica, was difficult but not dangerous. The best channel was to the east, but that to the south was also in use, especially when leaving harbour with the land wind. After passing the fort, there was a good anchorage to be had for any number of vessels, secure in all winds. Merchant vessels usually proceeded up to Kingston, the chief town, which was on the opposite side of the bay, about two miles away. The passage was under the guns of the fort at Port Royal, where was the naval establishment, and of the various batteries on shore. It was a well-fortified harbour, large and secure in all winds except hurricanes, against which there is no security. It could rank, along with Havana, as the finest harbour in the West Indies. (See plate 14.)

The procedure of entering any harbour in the British islands was much the same. Usually there was no traffic in or out between sunset and sunrise, and if vessels arrived in the night they had to lay to until daylight. Every vessel was signalled from the fort, and if she was the first arrival from Europe for some time, she was besieged at once by stranger and friend for news. The master was obliged to pay a fee to pass the officer of the fort at the entrance. There was also a gunpowder tax levied by the island legislatures for the defence of the colony. The vessel then proceeded up harbour and dropped anchor wherever it was possible. Not even at Kingston or St. George's, Grenada, where there were fine large wharves, could all the vessels lay along-side. Much of the business of loading and unloading was done in lighters. On arrival the captain went ashore to the Custom House and Naval Office where he entered his vessel and paid the fees and the small duties levied by the colonies. In Jamaica, in 1815, a vessel from Great Britain paid fees amounting to £8 15s. 0d. to the Customs officers on either entering or clearing. There were also harbour dues to be paid in Kingston of £1 6s. 8d. from a ship and £1 from a snow or brigantine. Fees for pilotage amounted to £3 in or out of Port Royal harbour, and an additional £3 for proceeding to Kingston. Each island had its own Customs duties, levied by the island legisla-tures. The Jamaica revenue law exacted £12 12s. per tun on Spanish and Madeira wine, £18 to £25 on other wines, £4 4s. on beer, ale and porter, and 13s. 4d. per gallon on spirits. Refined sugar paid 6d. per pound, and tobacco and snuff 4d. per pound.[1]

Vessels usually engaged pilots when approaching Antigua, Jamaica, or the other islands which were difficult of access. These pilots were negroes, often slaves, of a rascally disposition. They were skilled in their trade, and had great knowledge of the coasts and bays, but some masters found that they were careless, and few seamen relished being ordered about on board their own vessel by an overbearing coloured man. Michael Scott has left a description of the ordinary Kingston pilot, a slave well dressed according to sailors' standards, who resented being called "Blackie," and who ran His Majesty's cutter *Spark* dangerously near the shoals at the entrance to Port Royal.[2] Peter Mangrove, the lovable old darky who helped Tom Cringle out of many a scrape, was very proud of his title of pilot to His Britannic Majesty's squadron at Port Royal, but even he was known to have scraped the copper on His Majesty's Ships against the reefs of Port Royal harbour.

Vessels bound to Jamaica and to the Lesser Antilles followed much the same course on the outward voyages. But coming home they took quite different routes. It was rarely practicable (as will be seen) for ships from Jamaica to return to windward, so the two trades

---

[1] *Royal Register and Jamaica Almanac*, 1815.
[2] Scott, M., *Tom Cringle's Log*, Everyman edition, 105 and 119.

pursued different courses. Ships from the windward usually sailed north along the chain. From Tortola the course was clear of all islands. The convoys usually steered due north without trying to make easting until they reached latitude 30° in the region of Bermuda, and here any extra men-of-war left them to return to service on the Leeward Islands station. A runner could often get farther to the east before the thirtieth parallel, but in convoy allowance had to be made for dull sailers, and there was some danger of the fleet being scattered in variable and light winds. From Bermuda the course was N.E. to latitude 40, longitude 45 to clear the Bank of Newfoundland, where the prevailing westerlies could be made use of to proceed to Cape Clear and so to the Channel.

There were two routes from Jamaica to Europe, both of which were hazardous in time of war. The Windward Passage between Cuba and Haiti was the more direct, but the ship coming from Jamaica sails into the teeth of the trade wind in negotiating this passage. In the old days it was not unknown for square riggers to run back to Jamaica after beating about for weeks, because they had run out of wood and water. Besides the difficulties of navigation, the ships had to pass the French naval station at Cape Nicolas Mole which commanded the Windward Passage, and, after the French evacuated the island there still remained the danger of privateers. When the war first broke out and Spain was still friendly, it was more expedient to sail to leeward of Jamaica and go through the Gulf of Florida. The passage around Cape San Antonio was not difficult, provided vessels kept well out from the Cuban shore to avoid the current that sets strongly to leeward. The best thing was to follow the route of the Spanish pilots and sail north to the Dry Tortugas before attempting to get to the east. The current which sweeps fast through the Florida channel could be relied on to carry the vessels along even though they were proceeding almost dead to windward. This current was convenient, but it might cause disaster. There are many stories of ships being swept on to the reefs which fringe the channel, trying vainly to get away by the use of the sails. When Lady Nugent returned home in 1805 by this route several vessels were reported missing in the Gulf, some were cast on shore, some were taken, and some parted company in the heavy squalls which are common in

August in those latitudes.(¹) After clearing the Florida Channel it was plain sailing except for the danger of heavy seas and gales off the Newfoundland Banks. The fleets from Jamaica were most exposed to these, because it was more difficult for them to make easting than for the Leeward Islands fleets, which had started so much farther to windward.(²)

If the Gulf of Florida was impracticable either because of a strong Spanish force at Havana (which commanded the Channel), or for other reasons, the Windward Passage was used. While the British were in control of Cape Nicolas Mole, as they were from 1793 to 1798, the route was comparatively safe, though the difficulty of beating into the wind was still an obstacle. Once past the Mole the route lay through the chain of islands which form the eastern end of the Bahamas. The Crooked Island Passage was not easy, but it was preferable to the Caicos Passage because the latter was dead to windward of Cape Nicolas. From the Bahamas the course was due north as before. When it was practicable the Windward Passage was Preferred to the Gulf. It was an advantage to be clear of the islands five degrees further east than the latter course would allow, especially when dealing with a convoy. The danger from the French men-of-war was of little account while the British held the Mole, and after they evacuated it, the revolt of the negroes and the establishment of the Black Republic left the British fleets nothing to fear from the naval base.

In war-time the protection of ships at sea between the West Indies and Great Britain was a problem which constantly exercised the minds of the naval commanders, the Admiralty and the West India merchants. Rules and regulations were always being changed, and yet neither Admiralty nor merchants were ever satisfied. A convoy system was introduced as soon as the war began, but it was not until 1798 that an Act of Parliament, 38 Geo. III, cap. 76, made it illegal for a ship to proceed without convoy unless by special licence from the Admiralty. It does not seem to have been difficult to get licences. In the year 1811, only two were refused of the first 23 that applied. There were hundreds of applications a year, and about a quarter of them were

---

(¹) Cundall, 310 ff.　　　(²) Young, 198.

from masters bound for the West Indies. Many of these came from London, but more from the ports in the north, where it was more difficult to join a convoy. The Bristol ships often sailed by licence, as it saved them making the rendezvous at Spithead or Falmouth. A vessel had to be specially built to be a successful runner. She had to be a fast sailer, swift enough to avoid the enemy privateers in the Channel and in the Caribbean, yet large enough to cross the ocean with a cargo, and to carry an adequate armament. The Bristol papers were full of advertisements of fast sailing runners of about 280 tons, carrying about 20 men and 10 guns.[1]

Many of the ships for the outlying colonies sailed without convoy. If a vessel were bound for the Bahamas from Glasgow, it was much quicker for her to run than to find her way first to Cork, where she would be subject to vexatious delays, sail with the convoy, which could be relied upon to take eight weeks at least to reach Barbados (instead of the six weeks for a single laden ship) and then on arrival in the islands, make the best of her way to Nassau, another fifteen hundred miles away. The same was true of the ships for Berbice, Demerara and Surinam. The Admiralty ledger for 1811 shows that licensed ships might also proceed to Jamaica or the Lesser Antilles.[2] Ships going out under special licence from the Government to fetch bullion from the Spanish colonies, fortified of necessity by a permit from the King of Spain, were also in the habit of asking for a passport from the Admiralty.

Vessels for Jamaica and for the Lesser Antilles generally sailed together in one fleet from Great Britain, rendezvousing either at Cork or at Spithead. At Cork the shipping from the West of England, Liverpool and Glasgow collected, together with the provision and linen ships from Ireland. At Spithead the London shipping and occasionally the trade from the North assembled. In the later years of the war the Spithead fleet used to call at Falmouth for any northern ships which wished to take advantage of the southern convoy. The London ships were usually escorted around from the Thames, and the commanding officer was always instructed to wait for them

---

[1] Powell, 313 ff.
[2] Ad. 7/69, List of Applications for Licences, 1811.

twenty-four hours after the first fair wind. When the appointed day had come the commanding officer went the round of the fleet, giving private instructions to each skipper. There were signals to be used in case of meeting with any of His Majesty's ships, and signals to be used at night by which the fleet could be distinguished from strange sail which might have come among the convoy. The fast sailers often had to be prevented from going too far ahead. On the voyage home the ship-of-war on each quarter of the convoy (it was usual to have at least two escorts) had distinguishing rigs so that a vessel might know what position he was in in the fleet. During 1798 the usual thing was for the ships-of-war to hoist an English ensign at the main top-gallant mast and fore-topgallant mast respectively, and clew up their foresail and mainsail alternatively.(¹) Sometimes extra men-of-war accompanied the fleets from home as far as Cape Finisterre or Madeira. Two ships usually went all the way to the Lesser Antilles. The first port of call and division of the fleet was at Barbados. When the convoy arrived, the commanding officer reported to the Admiral on the Leeward Islands station, who heard complaints from masters of merchantmen against the commanding officer and arranged for the protection of the fleets to the leeward if none of the accompanying men-of-war were especially bound for the Jamaica Station.(²)

The Admirals on the two stations were responsible for the appointment of homeward-bound convoys. The fleets went home in two separate batches. The ships from the windward met at St. Kitts or Antigua under the eye of the Admiral. In the later years of the war the rendezvous was Tortola or St. Thomas in the Virgin Islands. An escort was provided for the ships coming from Demerara, from Trinidad and from the outlying islands. While Martinique and Guadeloupe were in the hands of the French the escorting was very necessary, for the privateers from these two islands commanded all the routes from the south. Ships from Jamaica met at Blewfields Bay, on the western coast, if the convoy were proceeding by the Gulf of Florida, and at Port Antonio on the north if the Windward Passage was to be attempted. The danger from privateers based on Cuba was

---

(¹) Ad. 1.231, Admiral Harvey to Nepean, Martinique, 8th April, 1798.

(²) Ad. 1.231, Captain Ekins to Harvey, Dominica, 30th January, 1798.

so great that a ship of war was sent along the north coast to collect the ships from the various harbours and conduct them to the rendez-vous. The greater part of the fleet sailed from Kingston a day or two before the appointed time of meeting in Blewfields Bay. Notice of the sailing of convoys was issued to the ports by the Admiral commanding the station, after consultation with the merchants. The usual time allowance for the merchant vessels to collect was six weeks.

The convoys sailed at most irregular intervals. One result was that each convoy was very large; (¹) far too large, one would have thought, for two ships of the line to protect adequately. The usual number of ships in a convoy was between sixty and ninety-five sail, but in 1798 one hundred and sixty vessels left for home from Jamaica, and Dr. Pinckard sailed with three hundred from Spithead. (²) It was pointed out that if regular convoys were despatched at more frequent intervals the task of protecting the trade would be considerably easier. (³) Fleets arrived at Barbados about four or five times a year. They were reported, for example, in December (1797), February, April, June and October (1798), avoiding the hurricane months of August and September. (⁴) There was always some sugar ready for shipment in April or early May, and this was the time for the first convoy to leave, but whereas in 1798 the fleet managed to sail, after some delay, on 15th May, in 1806 there was no sailing until 7th June. (⁵) There were usually four sailings home, in May, June, July and October. In 1806 two fleets departed after the hurricane season had begun, and the convoy originally appointed for November did not sail until 21st January. Sir William Young, among others, urged that the system must be amended, and that the sailings should be carried out at the time advertised. The London merchants were accused of causing most of the delay with the outward-bound trade. Being at the seat of Government, they had the ear of the Admiralty and were able to have a convoy delayed until their own ships could get around to Spithead. They took advantage of these delays, their

(¹) See plate 13, showing the Jamaica convoy, homeward bound.
(²) Ad. 1.248, Admiral Parker to Nepean, Cape Nicolas Mole, 29th May, 1798.
(³) B.T.1.37, no. 19, Leycester, MeColl and Cotter to Trail, Cork, 1807.
(⁴) Ad. 1.248, passim.   (⁵) Admiralty Digest, 1806.

provisions being a few weeks fresher than those on board ships which had been at Spithead on time. The consequence was that no merchant was ready to load his ships for the advertised time, but always expected a few weeks leeway.[1]

An additional danger caused by irregularity was that there were times when an inadequate number of ships of war were left to protect the West Indian seas. If convoys sailed close together, their protection might draw off all the available ships on the station. And the real problem of the navy during this war was the protection of trade in the West Indies from the innumerable enemy privateers. There were certain favourite tracks where the danger was greatest. The Frenchmen from Martinique and Guadeloupe cruised to windward of Barbados in the track of the outward-bound commerce. The seas around Cuba and Haiti were full of privateers using these islands as bases. The danger became so acute that the colonial assemblies in 1806 chartered small well-armed schooners to contend with the privateers. These vessels were offered to the Admiralty as adjuncts to the naval force, but the offers were refused and the use of the vessels had to stop.[2] It was just some such force that was needed, however, in order to make the trade safe, for the small sloops suffered greatly and this type of vessel was seldom granted naval protection. Young suggested the use of Bermuda-built schooners to serve both as cruisers and convoys among the islands. They might have proved the solution of a problem that occupied the Navy for some years to come, even after the capture of Martinique and Guadeloupe. But they were not used, and naval protection for the West Indian trade continued to be the chief problem for the Admiralty in those waters.[3]

The early years of the nineteenth century saw the beginning of the downfall of the planter class. In 1800 the trade with the West Indies was still the most important of all colonial commerce, both because it was worth more than any other and because it conformed so

---

[1] Young, 203.
[2] Digest, 1806 ; Ad. 1.328, Admiral Cochrane to Marsden, passim.
[3] Young, 204.
  James, III 510 and IV 335, made some scathing remarks about small schooners which had entered the service, many of which had been lost. But these vessels should never have crossed the Atlantic.

strictly to the ideas of mercantilism. Most of the money made in the sugar trade was spent in Great Britain; the voyage was suitable for the training of seamen; the trade left a favourable balance in Britain's hands; and was complementary to the British system, producing what was needed at home, and consuming manufactures exported. But in thirty years' time the situation had changed. By the time that emancipation came, the West Indies were already becoming unimportant. Their own decline, the rise of the dominions in the southern hemisphere, and the development of British trade with countries outside the bonds of Empire, materially affected the position of the West Indies. The last years of the war, when American competition was checked by blockade, and European rivals hemmed in their own continent, was the last time when the West Indian traders exercised the monopoly which had made them rich and famous. In ten years' time Huskisson's reforms and his reciprocal trade treaties had introduced foreigners into the carrying trade between Europe and the Caribbean. Before long, the expression, "rich as a West Indian" had become old-fashioned and obsolete. Never again was the wealth of the West Indian merchants to play an important part in the life of Great Britain.

CHAPTER IX

The American Trade

by HERBERT HEATON, M.A., M.COM., LITT.D.,

Professor of Economic History, University of Minnesota, U.S.A.

URING the decade that lay between the end of the American
Revolution and Britain's entry into the European conflict the
broad channel of Anglo-American trade became clearly and deeply
marked. That course it kept almost unchanged until it was dammed
up by the war of 1812, and resumed again when peace was restored.
True, it could not contain all the water—it never had done in colonial
days. Even before 1793 the stream of American trade, now free to
flow almost wherever it wished, cut for itself new river-beds that
did not run toward British ports, and during the war years America's
neutrality enabled her ships to traverse routes that were hazardous
for belligerent vessels, and to carry vast cargoes that were not
composed of American produce. Yet even in those fantastic years
when the value of American exports rose above the $100,000,000
mark—three-fifths of them re-exports from the West Indies—the
solid core of trade with Britain remained a vital part of the whole
economy.

We can best approach our study of the war years by an analysis of
the trade pattern in the early 1790's. By that time the Revolution had
sunk into the near background. The unpaid debts which American
merchants owed British exporters in 1775 had been paid in full,
compounded at a few shillings in the pound, or crossed off. The
inrush of imports which British traders sent over in 1783 and 1784
to restock empty shelves or which American importers had ordered
for the same reason lingered in the memory as a horrible reminder
of the fact that imports have to be paid for by exports. It took time
for American traders to regain old markets or find new ones in a
world in which their nation, as a group of sovereign states without
an effective central government, had to fight its own trade battles.

Sentiment might induce France and Spain to intervene in the British civil war; but there was little sentiment left over to mitigate economic imperial policies in favour of the new nation. In fact the only sentimentalists were the British. For a few months during the peacemaking period of 1782-83 it seemed possible that the United States might be given the run of the British Empire for her ships and goods as if nothing untoward had happened. There was talk in the highest places about intercourse "on the most enlarged principles of reciprocal benefit to both countries."(1) Such dreams were shattered by Lord Sheffield and the shipping interests; American goods or vessels—or both—were almost or quite excluded from the British West Indies and British North America; but the direct trade between Britain and the United States was treated with great liberality. Most kinds of American produce were admitted to British ports at the same customs rates as were charged on imports from British possessions, and could enter in American vessels without paying the "alien duty" charged on foreign ships. Most kinds of dressed or shaped timber were admitted duty-free, though competing wood from the Baltic paid a small duty. American tobacco consumed in Britain enjoyed the same preferential treatment that it had always enjoyed over Spanish leaf, and continued to do so until 1826. The only serious price which the United States paid in the British market for its independence was the treatment of its wheat and flour as foreign and the ban on the entry of its ships to the British register. Neither of these disabilities turned out to be heavy.

In August, 1789, the officers of the newly-created federal government went into action at the customs houses, and began to collect the customs and tonnage duties which had been imposed by Congress that summer. Clerks in the Treasury began to grind out statistical compilations and analyses from the returns which came in from the ports, and when they produced their first year's trade figures it was possible to see what had happened to American foreign trade in general and to that with Britain in particular. Of the exports—$20,000,000 in 1789-1790—about 34 per cent. ($6,900,000) had gone

---

(1) For a recent account of the discussions in Paris and in parliament, see A. L. Burt, *The United States, Great Britain, and British North America from the Revolution to the Establishment of Peace after the War of* 1812. (1940), chapters 1-4.

to the British Isles and 13 per cent. to the British West Indies. In all, the British Empire took nearly half the exports.

It is not easy to compare this situation with pre-revolutionary conditions, for quite apart from the shortcomings of earlier statistics there had been a heavy smuggling traffic with the foreign West Indies and some parts of Europe. The best possible estimate is that in 1769 about 54 per cent. of the exports went to the British Isles and a quarter to the British West Indies, leaving about a fifth for southern Europe and Africa. If we allow for the smuggling, perhaps two-thirds to three-quarters of the colonial trade had been within the Empire. Independence had apparently reduced the imperial share of American exports from that fraction to about one-half, and the share of the British Isles from a half to a third. The figures may be off the mark, but they certainly reflect the partial decline of Britain as an entrepot for such produce as tobacco and the opening up of new markets which had not formerly been served through London—as for instance, the Far East.

The commodities which went to Britain included what the statistician quaintly called Products of the Sea, of the Forest, of Agriculture, of Animals, and of Manufactures. The old colonial staples—tobacco, rice, and indigo—still stood high on the list. Tobacco accounted for two-fifths of the total exports, while rice and indigo combined to supply another fifth. But the relatively new exports loom large in the picture. There is a million dollarsworth of wheat and flour, produced largely in the "middle states" from Baltimore Town up to New York. This trade had been developed greatly by Irishmen since 1750, and in 1789-90 a quarter of America's exports of wheat and a seventh of those of flour went to the British Isles. Under the Corn Laws of 1773, 1791, and 1804 the duty on imports could jump from a very low rate to a prohibitively high rate if the price fell below a certain figure. In 1791, 1792, and 1793 the virtual prohibition was imposed; but from that time onward there was no hindrance to the import of American grain or flour until America began to impose obstacles of embargo or non-intercourse in and after 1807.

Another newcomer was potash, or its improved derivative, pearl ash. Since mid-century North American potash, made from the ashes of burned trees, had been steadily ousting the "ashes of Muscovy," both in the bleaching of British fabrics and in the production of soap. By 1790 this frontiersman's cash crop provided exports which were worth almost as much as were those of rice, or about $750,000 yearly. During the same period, Ireland's expanding linen industry had come to rely on flax grown in Ireland from American flaxseed.

For the rest, there was a good export of timber, chiefly in the form of barrel staves and head-pieces; of such naval stores as tar and turpentine; and of fish oil. There were modest shipments of furs, maize, iron in pigs or bars, and cotton. As yet cotton was not showing much sign of the rapid advance it was to make during the next two decades, and the 1,400 bales exported in 1789-90 accounted for only $47,000 of the total export figure. Finally, there were odds and ends —a few barrels of apples, five casks of beer and porter, 355 hats, 800 pounds of ham and bacon, and four kegs of pickled oysters, worth one dollar a keg.

For the westward journey Great Britain and Ireland supplied the overwhelming majority of America's manufactured imports. Most manufactured goods paid an *ad valorem* duty and their import value was therefore recorded. Of $15,500,000 worth of such articles the British Isles supplied $13,500,000, or 87 per cent. It is not possible to say what part of these commodities were re-exports of the industrial products of Asia or continental Europe. London was the best place in which to pick up such articles, and its merchants gave better credit terms than could be obtained across the English Channel or North Sea. Yet an examination of countless manifests and invoices suggests that non-British manufactures played a small part in filling the holds of vessels bound for American ports. This was particularly true of the ships which sailed from Liverpool, Bristol, Hull, Greenock, or Ireland.

In the *ad valorem* imports were all the familiar products of the expanding and changing British industrial system: the cloths (and clothes) of all fibres, kinds, and qualities; pottery ware—useful and ornamental—for every part of the American home, from the kitchen to the dining room, living room, and bed chamber; metalware of every kind, size, and shape from Birmingham and Sheffield; enough sheet glass to repair all the damage done in a dozen presidential elections; enough paint or white lead to give two coats to every building from Salem to Savannah; and a motley of books and binoculars, guns and glue, sealing wax and slippers.

Many imports, even manufactured products, paid a specific duty of so many cents a bushel, gallon, pound, or dozen. These were counted but not valued by the customs men. In 1789–90 there came 84,000 gallons of beer, ale, stout, or porter in casks, and 18,000 dozen bottles for those who liked British brands and wished to see the label on the bottle; nearly 700,000 bushels of salt to help preserve the beef and pork for the winter; 150,000 bushels of coal for the fireplaces of towns which had burned up their local supplies of firewood in a country where coal seams had not yet been seriously tapped; nearly 2,000,000 pounds of nails for the carpenters of the rapidly growing coastal towns; 86,000 pounds of cheese for those who liked their cheese to have a tang and bite; 18,600 packs of playing cards—but what were they among 4,000,000 people?—and 178 pounds of snuff; of which 91 were Irish.

This pattern of exchange of foods and raw materials for manufactured articles and this list of commodities persisted throughout our period, and far beyond. No matter how war changed the volume or map of commerce, the things which Americans and Britons bought from each other remained virtually unchanged whenever there was freedom to sell and buy. Perhaps we could work out an index of American prosperity by studying the fluctuations in the imports of liquid refreshments and playing cards; or of the cycle in the capital goods industries by tracing the variations in steel imports; or of the ebb and flow of Irish immigration by seeing how the demand for snuff changed. But there are more important aspects of the pattern to be explored.

Anglo-American trade was a combination of the direct and the triangular, or even the multilateral. Much of it was a simple barter of goods for goods, or for goods and services. Its symbol was the "regular trader" or "regular trading ship," built to ply between a British and an American port. The perennial round of these vessels—usually full-rigged ships of 250 to 400 or even 500 tons, or barques of 150 to 250 tons—was as fixed as were the seasons. They sailed into an American harbour in late April or May, laden with a ballast of coal or salt and a top-dressing of "fine freight" which might in extreme cases pay as much as $40,000 or even $50,000 in customs duties, and which might therefore be worth between a quarter and a half million dollars for a single cargo. Within a month or five weeks, but in boom days within a fortnight, they had unloaded, taken on an American cargo, and were eastbound once more. In Liverpool, London, or some other port, which they might reach within a month, they emptied their holds, filled up again with British wares, and landed back in America in September or October. A month was spent in port, and again they were off, to winter, refit and repair in a British port in preparation for the next spring journey westward.

This standard programme—spring and fall arrivals in America, summer and early winter arrivals in Britain, with two round trips a year and hibernation in icefree British ports—was the high-water mark of efficient shipping operation until after 1815. Given good luck, it was a programme comfortably capable of operation. Any attempt to improve on it by trying three round trips would be too risky, for delay in reaching port would make the cargo available only after the buyers who came to the coastal centres for fall and spring supplies had left for home. In times of stress or after an interruption to traffic a vessel might get back to its schedule by doing five trans-atlantic journeys, but no vessel did six until the Black Ball line of passenger and fine cargo packets began operations in 1818. Many vessels did not even attempt the two round trips, but were content with one, and then filled the remaining months with shorter journeys along the American coast or to the West Indies.

Every American port had its regular traders engaged in the traffic with Britain. Some of them had relatively long careers. For instance, the *Adriana* dropped anchor in the Delaware at Philadelphia almost every late April and September between 1789 and 1801 to unload a cargo from Liverpool or London. There was a *Pigou* which completed two round trips between London and Philadelphia almost every year from 1787 to 1804, a *Roebuck* which plied to and from Bristol between 1791 and 1801, and a *William Penn* which never missed a step in delivering two cargoes yearly at each end of its London-Philadelphia run between 1791 and 1797. Some of the traders made fairly fast round trips, especially during the summer, and wasted little time in port. The *Betsey*, for example, reached New York from London on April 1st, 1791, was off again by April 14th, and was back again from London by August 24th. This was probably well-nigh a record for the London route at that time, but the vessels which were making the shorter journey to and from Ireland often got back within less than four months of their departure. During the first decade of the nineteenth century some regular traders made occasional passages which were faster than those of the late eighteenth, and in 1811 the *Pacific*, one of the most famous New York regulars of that time, established a record of nineteen days from New York to Liverpool.

Speed was, however, probably much less important than certainty. If you could get away from port without such grievous delays as sometimes happened in the Mersey mouth and get across westward, without being fogbound or becalmed, in not more than forty days, you could hope to have your goods on hand for the spring and fall buyers. Much has been said about the "maddening uncertainty" of sailing ship movements. Yet the dates of arrivals of vessels do not vary greatly from year to year. For instance, the brig *Lively* reached New York from Bristol on April 22nd in 1790, on April 4th in 1791, and on April 23rd and 17th in the next two years. The *Draper* did even better, with four consecutive spring arrivals from Dublin dating respectively May 8th, May 6th, May 5th, and April 29th. But the *William Penn* was the real miracle-worker, for she arrived on October 13th from London three years in a row, 1794-6. In 1797 she was two weeks late, so the age of miracles had evidently come to an end.

Around the core of regular traders there gathered a less orthodox merchant fleet. Some pursued a set triangular route, with the British Isles forming one of the angles, and with the West Indies, southern Europe, or north-western Europe as the other. Some came into regular movement in good times, but went off free-lancing if greater profit seemed possible elsewhere. Some vessels were full-time tramps, moving wherever their owners or charterers sent them, and therefore making only occasional calls in Britain. And some which never went near Britain played a part in providing the cargoes that came from London and the provincial ports to the United States, for they helped to pile up that surplus of exports to some areas which was paid for by a surplus of imports from the British Isles.

In the Anglo-American exchange of raw materials for manufactured articles, the value of a full cargo taken to Britain by one of the regular traders would normally be far less than that of an even partly-full return shipment. The richest eastbound cargo I have been able to find was carried by the ship *Factor* from New York to London in July, 1799. It consisted of sugar, ashes, skins, furs, logwood, bark, tobacco, staves, mahogany, and indigo—obviously a mixture of American produce and re-exports. Its value was recorded on the manifest at over $146,000. Yet the average customs duty paid on the cargo brought back on that voyage and on the three preceding return trips amounted to nearly $40,000, which would mean that each shipment was worth at least $300,000. There were a few American cargoes worth over $100,000, but there were many westbound ones far above that figure. The *Fanny* was more representative of the general run of traders than was the *Factor*. Four cargoes which she took aboard in New York for Greenock between 1798 and 1800 were worth an average of less than $24,000 apiece; yet six of her westbound cargoes paid an average of nearly $30,000 in duties.

The national statistics of Great Britain and the United States reveal the disparity in exchange of commodities on a grand scale. Year after year the British figures record that the annual "official value" of goods sent to the United States is three, four, or even five times that of the produce brought from America. If we group the years into periods, we get the following totals:

Period	British Imports from U.S.A.	British Exports to U.S.A.	Ratio
1783–1792	£8,878,000	£25,943,000	1 : 2.9
1793–1801	£14,506,000	£51,782,000	1 : 3.9
1802–1807	£12,104,000	£40,691,000	1 : 3.4
Total for 24 years	£35,488,000	£118,416,000	1 : 3.3

The American measure of this disparity was best given in 1806. In that year Congress was getting angry because the British had changed their policy towards American trade with the enemy. Gallatin, the Secretary of the Treasury, was asked to submit a report on American commerce with Great Britain and her dependencies and with other parts of the world. On the first page of his report[1] he announced that trade between the United States and "the dominions of Great Britain in Europe (Gibraltar excepted)" was highly adverse according to the returns for 1802-1804. The annual average exports to those dominions in those years were less than $16,000,000, while the imports were over $27,000,000, leaving an adverse balance on direct commodity exchange of about $11,700,000. With dispassionate skill he showed that this situation was not quite as terrible as it seemed, partly because American values were in effect undervalued f.o.b.,[2] while the imports were overvalued c.i.f.,[3] and partly because the Anglo-American trade must be thought of in wider terms of triangular or even polyangular commerce, in which merchants' profits and ships' earnings had to be thrown into the scale as invisible exports.

Gallatin's points, and some that he missed, are worthy of a moment's attention. Triangular trade, and even triangular shipping routes, played a very important part in the British and American economies alike. Americans shipped more goods to continental Europe, to the British and foreign West Indies than they took in return. The balance, including the profits and shipping earnings, was often remitted to London, there to be spent on British manufactures. Continental Europe simply could not supply America with enough of her own industrial or less-finished products to pay for what she bought, and so we find Stephen Girard, the great Philadelphia trader, transferring to the Barings in London more than $1,250,000 collected for him by the Hopes, of Amsterdam, during 1809-1811. This practice was reflected physically in the movement of some ships from America to a continental port, followed by a visit to London or Liverpool, and then a heavily-laden westward passage. It was less obvious, but equally effective, in paying for part of the rich cargoes which the regular traders took home.

---

[1] Gallatin's report is in *American State Papers, Commerce and Navigation*, vol. I, pp. 640-666.

[2] Free on board.   [3] Cost, Insurance, Freight.

In part the Anglo-American balance of payments was helped by the heavy predominance of American ships in the trade between the two countries. When the customs officers began their work in 1789 they found a substantial part of America's imports were arriving in foreign ships. Of the 129 vessels which arrived in New York by the end of 1790 from British ports, 71 were British and 58 were American. For the country's foreign trade at large, 217,000 tons of British shipping entered American ports during 1790, against 460,000 tons of American.

This situation did not last long. Congress had already taken steps to favour American ships, for in July, 1789, it had imposed a tonnage duty of 50 cents per ton on foreign-built and owned ships, of 30 cents on American-built but foreign-owned vessels, but of only six cents on American ships. In August it had added 10 per cent. to the customs rates charged on goods imported in foreign vessels. These preferences hurt British shipping, but the shadow of war did more damage. In November, 1790, the American consul in Liverpool reported that even "Previous to the apprehension of war with Spain (over the Nootka Sound dispute), the American bottoms had the preference in this port for carrying to the United States, but ever since that period they have enjoyed these advantages almost exclusively." If the traffic between New York and Liverpool is a fair sample, the consul was certainly premature in his rejoicing, for British vessels far outnumbered Americans on the westward trip up to the end of 1791. In 1792 the picture changed, yet even in that year the British tonnage entering American ports had dropped only to 206,000 tons,([1]) and 40 of the 100 vessels entering New York from the British Isles flew the British flag. Not until the war with France began did the combined effect of preference and neutrality show large results. In 1793 the number of British ships entering New York from home ports dropped to 22, and in 1794 to 17. The total British tonnage entering the country fell to 100,000 tons in 1793 and to 37,000 in 1794. Henceforth the overwhelming bulk of Anglo-American trade was

---

([1]) Of this figure, 100,000 tons represents arrivals from the British West Indies and about 68,000 tons from the British Isles.

conducted in American bottoms.(¹) The earnings of those vessels paid for a lot of British coal and manufactures.

No satisfactory statistics seem to be available from which we can divide transatlantic trade between the chief ports on either side of the ocean, Some impressions can, however, be gained by examining such official registers of ships' movements as have survived or such lists as can be compiled from the newspapers.(²) The following Table gives the arrivals from British ports in Philadelphia and New York during the period from August, 1789, to the end of 1794:

From		To Philadelphia	To New York
Liverpool	.. ..	104	143
London	.. ..	72	115
Bristol	.. ..	35	68
Hull	.. ..	12	31
Rest of England	..	45	25
Scotland	.. ..	11	41
Ireland	.. ..	73	110
TOTAL	..	352	533

Liverpool supplied 30 per cent. of the arrivals in Philadelphia and 27 per cent. of those in New York. London came second, contributing 25 per cent. and 22 per cent. respectively. The comparison probably is not as good as it seems, and of course the whole table is weakened by counting all ships as equal, no matter what their size. The London vessels often appear to be larger than those from the other ports, and their cargoes often pay higher sums in customs duties than do the others. Those cargoes are a motley miscellany of products from the countless industries located in or near the capital, but there is still evidence of a substantial flow of wares from the provincial manufacturing areas, and some hint of re-exports of

---

(¹) In 1796-7 $25,000,000 of British goods paying *ad valorem* duties entered the United States in American vessels, but only $600,000 in foreign ships.

(²) Official lists are available for both outward and inward movements at New York during part of the period, for Philadelphia arrivals during the whole period 1789-1817, and for Baltimore arrivals from the end of 1804. Newspaper lists of arrivals and departures are not very reliable, since it is clear that ship reporters were satisfied if they got the truth about some vessels but did not bother to get it all.

continental wares. A typical vessel from London would deliver in New York paint, white lead, oil colours, copperas, vitriol, whiting, saltpetre, gunpowder and steel; cabinet-ware, furniture, chairs, mirrors, musical instruments, and an occasional carriage; hats, haberdashery, millinery, and other wearing apparel; sugar moulds, printers' type, paper, stationery, and books; china and glassware, watches and woollens, cannon and anvils, and always a good supply of stout, ale, and porter. London was evidently a general emporium.

By the middle of the first decade of the next century London's position in the American trade had deteriorated greatly.(¹) The port books show the following distribution of arrivals in Philadelphia, New York, and Baltimore, and the departures from New York:

FROM	ARRIVALS IN(²)			DEPARTURES FROM New York (1806-1807) TO
	Philadelphia (1806-1807)	New York (July, 1806-December, 1807)	Baltimore (1805-1807)	
Liverpool ..	68	156	76	Liverpool .. 178
London ..	22	36	21	London.. .. 36
Bristol ..	11	21	6	Bristol 17
Hull ..	3	18	0	Hull 11
Rest of England	7	8	5	Rest of England 12
Scotland ..	1	25	0	Scotland .. 31
Ireland ..	20	69	8	Ireland 137
TOTAL ..	132	333	116	422

Liverpool was now sending out half the ships that went to New York and Philadelphia, and three-fourths of those destined for Baltimore. She was receiving over two-fifths of the vessels leaving New York for Britain. London supplied only a sixth of the Phila-

---

(¹) London was at a disadvantage, in competition with Liverpool, because of the possible delays which ships might experience in the Channel. The earlier development of the Liverpool docks may also have hastened a process which the growth of industrial Lancashire had made inevitable.

(²) These tables are not comparable with each other, since they cover different lengths of time. The Baltimore figures are for three years, those of Philadelphia are for two, but the New York entries are for only 18 months. The New York departures are for two years.

delphia arrivals and about a tenth of those entering or leaving New York. The same pre-eminence of Liverpool was seen at Boston, where Liverpool provided 61 of the 94 vessels whose arrivals are recorded in the Boston newspapers in 1807, and was the destination of 12 of the 26 ships leaving that port for the British Isles. In the cotton-exporting South the predominance was even greater. In 1807 the Savannah papers list 40 arrivals from British ports, of which 34 were from Liverpool and only one from London. They record 57 departures for Britain, and 43 of them are bound for Liverpool, seven for Greenock, but only three for London. It would be interesting to consider how far this decline of London's stake in the American trade made the commercial and shipping interests in the capital indifferent concerning the effects of more restrictive policies toward American trade with the enemy and therefore more favourable to the imposition and retention of more rigorous Orders in Council. But that topic would take us too far afield.

Liverpool's advance probably checked the relative growth of Bristol and Hull as well as that of London. In the early nineties Bristol contributed 10 per cent. of the vessels bound for Philadelphia, but only 8 per cent. a dozen years later, while the percentage from Bristol to New York dropped from 13 to six in the same period. Nevertheless, there were regular traders between Bristol and American ports as well as occasional callers. In the 1790's the port received much flour, wheat, timber, pig iron, naval stores, tobacco and quite a bit of cotton. It was a good spot for shipping the West of England broadcloths and the tinplate, coal, and other products of South Wales. Improved river navigation and canals allowed it to pull in pottery and hardware from the West Midlands. Hence the manifests of the vessels which reached America from Bristol list a very miscellaneous collection of goods. Yet it is evident that Liverpool pulled harder as time went by in competition for the export business of the Midlands manufacturer, and as the growing influx of cotton brought more and more ships to Liverpool there were always more vessels there—on the whole probably better ones—than could be found in Bristol.

Hull also had to be satisfied with a minor role in the American trade. It was a good year that saw more than a dozen ships leave the

Humber for the United States. Improved rivers and canals had in the eighteenth century brought increased traffic from the Trent valley, the Sheffield area, and the West Riding cloth and metal-working centres; but as the water connections between these regions and Liverpool were completed, or drew near to that end, producers and merchants on the east side or bottom end of the Pennines turned increasingly to Liverpool as their outlet to the western world. Ships continued to leave Hull for New York, though few went to the other American ports. They carried large quantities of what the manifests call "draperies," as well as woollens, linens, hats, files, spades, saws, pans, iron, steel, lead, paint, alum, mustard seed, ale and Yorkshire or Newcastle coal. Yet by 1800 Liverpool had become the chief port of those who sought the American market for the knitted goods, hardware, and textiles of the north central regions.

In the tables given above, Scotland occupies a minor role, but Ireland looms large. The Scots-American trade was concentrated on Greenock, with cotton, ashes, timber and tobacco prominent on the inward manifests and cottons, hardware, glass, porter, and coal supplying the chief exports. Ireland's importance is overstated in the figures of ship movements, since the vessels in the Irish trade were usually smaller than those trading with Great Britain and the cargoes were usually less valuable. Yet with this proviso it is noteworthy that both in the early nineties and in the middle of the next decade about one-fifth of the vessels reaching New York from the British Isles came from Irish ports and that in the latter period one-third of those returning from New York were headed for Ireland.

America was a vital factor in the Irish economy. She supplied much of the flour that was imported and virtually all the flaxseed and potash. The incredible growth of Ireland's population from an estimate of 2,000,000 in 1740 to one of 5,000,000 in 1800 may have been due to American flour, to the spread of American potato culti-vation, to the absence of a serious famine—or to all three. The growing export of linen—threefold between 1740 and 1770—was checked by the American Revolution and then doubled again during the next twenty years. This expansion called for a wide extension of the area under flax, of the demand for seed, and of the use of potash in bleaching.

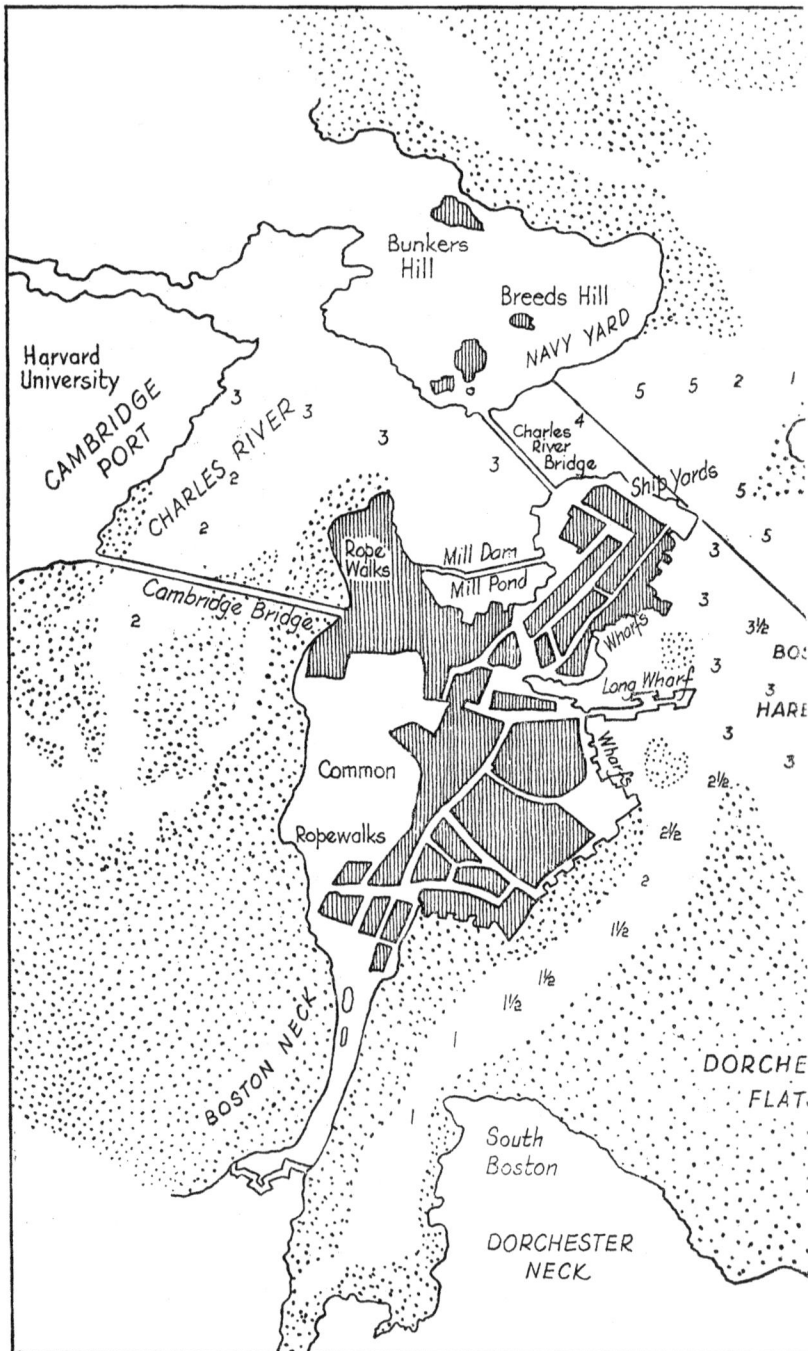

Labels on map: Bunkers Hill · Breeds Hill · NAVY YARD · Harvard University · CAMBRIDGE PORT · CHARLES RIVER · Charles River Bridge · Ship Yards · Rope Walks · Mill Dam · Mill Pond · Cambridge Bridge · Wharfs · Long Wharf · BOS... · HARE... · Common · Ropewalks · Wharfs · BOSTON NECK · South Boston · DORCHESTER NECK · DORCHE... FLAT...

PLATE 15.

PLAN OF THE PORT OF BOSTON

NODDLES ISLAND

1

2

2

3

5

6

5

TON

5   6

OUR

4

3½   2

3½   2   2

2

3½   4

3

3   4

3   3

3   3   4

3   3

3   3½

3½

Bird Island

3½

GOVERNORS ISLAND

2

3

3

FORT WARREN

✛

3

3

3

5

4

FORT INDEPENDENCE

✛

STER

O

The flax plant gives you your choice between seed and fibre. If you harvest it at the best time for getting good fibre the seeds are not ripe. If you wait until the seeds are ripe the fibre is poor or even useless. The Irish decided in favour of the fibre, and therefore had to buy their seed abroad. American flax-growers supplied it, by letting their seeds ripen to provide a cash crop which they sold to local merchants who sent it to the ports for shipment to Ireland. By the end of the eighteenth century nearly 300,000 bushels of seed were leaving American ports, and virtually all for Irish growers.

The seed was not ready for harvest in time to reach the ports before late autumn or early winter. If the Irish were to get it in time for the next year's planting, its carriers must cross the Atlantic during the winter, at a time when most other vessels were snuggling safely in a British or American harbour. An analysis of two hundred flaxseed shipments from New York between 1790 and 1801 shows that over forty began their voyage in late December, fifty in January, fifty in February, and nearly thirty in early March.

This seasonal pilgrimage had two interesting consequences. The seed was produced north and south of New York, and some of the best of it in Pennsylvania. But the Delaware, on which Philadelphia stands, was usually frozen over or blocked by ice during January and February, while the waters of New York harbour were open. New York therefore became the main port for the export of flaxseed, and this was one of the many influences which were leading to that city's rise to commercial pre-eminence.

The second consequence was the result of a piece of political timing. In 1807 Congress placed an embargo on the overseas departure of American ships. The law was passed on December 22nd, just as the flaxseed fleet was getting into its annual stride. Twelve ships had left New York before news of the embargo reached the city, and normally about thirty would have sailed during the next ten days. By picking December as embargo time, Jefferson and the legislators deprived the Irish of at least two-thirds of their seed supply for 1808. Further, the embargo was lifted in mid-March, 1809, which was too late to allow the Irish to get any of their seed for that year. Finally, the Non-Importation Act which Congress had passed in 1806 to bar the entry of many kinds of British manufactures became effective

about the same time as did the embargo. It wiped out imports of
Irish linen. Irish-American relations were thus exceedingly intimate.

The flaxseed ships returned to America in the early summer, just
after the spring fleet of regular traders had come to port. They took
on a cargo of potash, which would arrive in Ireland during the early
autumn and would be used during the winter to bleach the linen
made from the flax grown from the seed which had been imported
in the spring. Flour, timber, and miscellaneous items made up the
balance of the cargoes both in winter and summer voyages.

What of the westward cargoes? Ireland offered few commodities
suitable for the American market. True, there was linen; but you
could not fill all the ships with linen, and Irish exporters offered less
generous credit terms than did those in London or Liverpool. There
was some good glass, whisky, woollens, hides, goose feathers, and
jackasses. There was also some export of books, for Ireland was outside the scope of the British copyright law, and Dublin publishers were
therefore prompt to print pirated editions of eighteenth century best
sellers. But all told, it was hard to fill many vessels for the return
voyage. Some ships—perhaps a third of them—therefore went on to
a port in Scotland or England to pick up cargoes. Others returned
directly from Ireland in ballast, or carried such cargo as they could
procure, and added to their earnings by carrying great quantities of
one of Ireland's staple products—people. Whatever may be the fact
or fancy of Ireland's political and economic grievances, the harsh
reality was that in no conceivable circumstances could her natural
resources carry the population that she was piling on to them. When
she reached the five million mark, about 1800, she was asking every
square mile to support 150 persons, a burden very nearly as heavy as
that which had to be borne by the richer soil and vastly richer subsoil
of England and Wales. The export of human beings was, therefore,
the only possible Irish way of life, and America's exports of seed and
potash did much to provide the vessels which made that traffic
possible.

Irish emigration consisted of a fairly regular flow, swollen at times
by a flood of refugees. The refugees were especially numerous after
the abortive rebellions of 1798 and 1803, but the regular flow went
on all the time, though it might be checked somewhat when news of

a depression in America warned would-be emigrants that jobs were scarce and prices low across the Atlantic. Such depressions came in 1796 when a land boom burst and in 1802 when the Treaty of Amiens brought slackness to ports which had bulged with re-export business. But the revival of the war in 1803 restored prosperity, and the human tide flowed strongly westward until the embargo checked it at the end of 1807. The flow from England, Wales, and Scotland probably contained fewer fugitives, though there were some; in general, however, one gets the impression that those who left these countries did so because of the attraction of the new world rather than the repulsion of the old.

At each end of the journey the men who handled Anglo-American trade were a combination of native-born citizens and of temporary or permanent immigrants. When a vessel entered an American port the newspaper might report that her cargo was destined solely for the owner or charterer, for many a merchant owned a ship or two or hired them in order to integrate his enterprise or give variety to his capital investments. But when the regular traders came in they might bring goods for scores of importers, and a list of their names might occupy four or five inches of closely-set type in the shipping column.

If we penetrate behind that list we find every conceivable kind of commercial organization and practice. A merchant might receive goods he had ordered by mail, or through the American agent or partner of a British firm, or by word of mouth when he had made his last tour of the factories and counting-houses of the British Isles. He might receive goods which he had been commissioned to order by some trader who lived upstate or in a smaller port. Or the wares might have been consigned to him "on the account and at the risk" of some British merchant or manufacturer who wished him to sell them on commission. Sometimes they were addressed to a public auctioneer, who would sell them promptly, either for what they would fetch or subject to a minimum price-limit, at his "Public Vendue," would remit the net proceeds promptly to England, and would thus relieve the small-scale British exporter—whether manufacturer or merchant—of the need for having a full-fledged mercantile establishment or connection in the United States.

By 1800—and even long, long before—native-born merchants dominated the leading American ports. But those men were the descendants of immigrants, and the stream of commercial immigrants had by no means stopped. In 1812 there were 140 alien British merchants living in New York City, but there were probably at least another 140 who had come to America since the Revolution and had become naturalized citizens. Some had come to set up on their own account. Others had been sent by father, brothers, or partners to handle the American end of the business. Sometimes that business was an ordinary mercantile firm; but increasingly as we approach or pass 1800 it was a factory manufacturing enterprise which was building up its own selling organization overseas. Factories were by then seldom content to sell their goods to British merchants in the manner common during the days of domestic small-scale manufacture.

Most of these Britons came as young men, sometimes so young that, having learned the business in England, they apprenticed themselves for a few years to an American house in order to complete their training for the job to which they had been assigned. Some of them eventually went back to England to find a bride and settle; but many made their homes in the United States, and some were highly successful as merchants, shipowners, or eventually as manufacturers.[1]

The same diversity of organization was found at the British end of the trade. There were British merchants who spent part or all of their time sending goods to America on their own account or in response to orders they had received, and at the ports these men might also handle on commission the produce consigned them from America. In addition, Americans came to Britain for brief or long periods of residence. Liverpool especially swarmed with American merchants and commission houses sprinkled among the native firms. An American Chamber of Commerce was established at Liverpool in 1801, whose officers and rank and file were a solid international community.

[1] For a study of this topic see H. Heaton, "Yorkshire Cloth Traders in the United States, 1770-1840," in Thoresby Society's *Miscellany*, vol. 37, part 3 (1944), pp. 225-287.

The first chairman of the Chamber was James Maury, who had come to England from Virginia in 1786 to sell tobacco from Virginia and Maryland, naval stores and (eventually) cotton from further south, and to ship British goods to his native South. Before he left home he wrote to Washington, Madison, Jefferson and others asking to be given the handling of their tobacco exports and reminding them that he considered himself a strong candidate for a post as consul in London, Liverpool, or even on the continent, "provided the salary be competent to a support and [the post] does not debar me from trade." Washington said he was giving up growing tobacco; Madison gave him his business, and Jefferson later gave him the consulate in Liverpool. From that vantage point he saw and shared in the great expansion of cotton imports and of manufactured exports, welcomed distinguished American diplomats as they came through the port, viewed with alarm and regret the deteriorating political relations of the two countries after 1806, and served for forty years as one of America's most competent and faithful servants overseas.

Maury was never lonely for want of compatriots. In that respect he resembled those Britons who went to visit or settle in American ports. They could pass from city to city seeing old friends, hearing familiar accents, taking tea, eating Yorkshire pudding or mutton chops or slices of roast beef, drinking bottled ale, and feeling very much at home in front of a fire of Liverpool coal. The more one explores the activities of these British and American traders and watches some of them crossing the ocean every second or third year, the more one realises that the Atlantic was less of a great divide and more of a pond.

Until 1805 or 1806 the course of Anglo-American trade, and even of diplomatic relations, ran fairly smoothly. There is no time here to consider why they then began to run roughly, or why the increasing diplomatic difficulties rendered commerce hazardous and eventually impossible. The story has often been told, with its chapters on the impressment of American sailors, on the denial of neutral rights and claims, on Napoleon's Decrees and British Orders in Council. The central theme is that America tried to get what she wanted by fighting an economic war; and when that failed to achieve its purpose she turned to the other kind of warfare.(¹)

The effort to coerce Britain into mending her ways by hurting her manufactures, shipping, commerce, and credit began with the Non-Importation Act of April, 1806. This Act provided that a long but by no means complete list of British manufactured goods were to be forbidden entry. It was to come into operation on November 15th. This delay would give Britain time to negotiate an acceptable settlement of outstanding differences with a special American mission appointed for that purpose; and it would also allow the spring and fall cargoes of 1806 to get safely into American warehouses.

By mid-November no settlement had been reached, and the Act therefore went into effect, with a number of comic opera episodes. The *Olive* came into Baltimore soon after the fifteenth. She had been taking a cargo of flour to Ireland and then went to a continental port to pick up a load of salt. But the master had bought two pairs of Irish shoes in Cork as a present for a Baltimore friend. On his return he declared the salt and the shoes to the customs officers, and was informed that since any British import of which leather was "the material of chief value" was forbidden entry, the ship, shoes, and salt were liable to forfeiture. At almost the same moment the brig *Mars* arrived with a cargo of salt in bags made of hemp. The customs officer scanned his list and discovered that articles of which hemp was "the material of chief value" were also on it. Did that mean he must seize ship and cargo? If so, "this construction of the law would implicate almost all the goods imported from England which, particularly when in bales, are enclosed in hempen or flaxen linen." What about paper, rope and twine? All were made of banned materials. Gallatin's office was swamped with requests for instructions and interpretations. The Act was suspended in the hope that news of a successful settlement with the British might come from the mission in London, and did not finally come into effect until December 14th, 1807.

(¹) The best recent survey of the whole story will be found in A. L. Burt, *op. cit.* For a detailed account of the non-importation policy see H. Heaton, "Non-Importation, 1806-1812," in *Journal of Economic History*, vol. 1, pp. 178-198 (November, 1941).

Within eight days of that date the much fiercer Embargo Act was passed. The London mission had reached a settlement, but since it did not ban British impressment on the high seas, President Jefferson rejected it. The *Chesapeake* affair, in which a British warship fired on the American frigate, killed or wounded a score of her crew, and then searched her for some missing British seamen, created such a wave of anger that war seemed inevitable. Jefferson, however, kept his head, the British government expressed its anxiety to expiate the grievous wrong, and the war clouds slowly lifted. But meanwhile Napoleon's Continental System and the British counter-measures seemed to be making it unsafe for American vessels to enter the eastern Atlantic. Better therefore confine American ships and cargoes to their own ports. Thus would they be kept safe from seizure, and thus would the French and British be so seriously inconvenienced by lack of supplies from the western hemisphere that they would modify their policies to suit American demands. Of the two objectives the first sounded better, but the second was the more important. Economic coercion was being tightened another turn of the screw.

The Embargo ran its drastic and dismal course until March, 1809. The original Act was amended four times to plug up holes, and in its final form was ferocious in its provisions for stamping out original sin. It forbade American ships to go abroad, but allowed foreign ships to come in, subject to the condition that they took out no cargoes. It banned the traffic by sleigh, waggon, or packhorse with British North America since there was a certainty that some American goods might go out that way and some British goods come in.

The general story does not concern us here, except in so far as the combination of partial non-importation and complete embargo affected Anglo-American trade. Since New York had now become the chief American port for that trade, what happened there is a good measure of the general paralysis. In 1807, 226 vessels entered New York from the British Isles. During the Embargo period only 97 came. Most of these were American vessels coming home. At least a third of them did not know when they left Britain that they were to be locked up in their home ports. About a third of them did not return until the fall. All of them made the most out of the trip by bringing fat cargoes of the cotton pieces, cheap woollens, hardware, paint, crockery, salt and coal which were not on the non-importation black list. A few of them were British vessels which brought permitted imports; but since no outward cargo could be loaded, such ships would make no money on the return journey and therefore tended to avoid the American trade in favour of routes which the American ships had abandoned or in order to enter the Brazilian trade which had been opened up by the migration of the Portuguese royal family to Rio de Janeiro.

The number of sailings from New York to Britain dropped even more heavily. In 1807 it had been 211, but in the Embargo period it was only 13, all of them British ships. Only one of them went to Ireland.

In the other ports the same sad story was repeated. In Philadelphia the arrivals from Britain fell from 71 to 38. In Boston the newspapers record a decline from 94 entries to 36, while the departures dropped from 26 to four. Baltimore's arrivals slipped from 50 to 15, and those of Savannah from 40 to 14. In all harbours regular traders and tramps alike lay idle but safe. Some of them turned to coastal trade, some sailed illicitly beyond the coast to the West Indies or the Canadian Maritimes. But the number of embargo-breakers was relatively small. American shipowners gave the Embargo a fair trial.

In that trial it failed. True, it hurt the belligerent giants by depriving them of much produce. But it did not seriously injure their capacity for finding markets. Thanks to the returning American vessels, to the few British ships which were in the American trade, and to the exemptions from the non-importation ban, the "official" value of British exports to the United States in 1808 was half that of 1807 and the "real" value was about 45 per cent. of the figure for 1807. To keep half the United States market was a substantial achievement, especially when we remember that virtually all British goods were carried in American vessels. But for manufacturers as for shipowners relief from American pressure was found in the expansion of exports to other parts of America, especially South and Far North, and hence the figures of total British exports in 1808 were little different from those of 1807.

By the autumn of 1808 it was clear that the Embargo had failed. Throughout the winter Congress would spend part of the day discussing methods for making the ban more effective and then turn to consideration of its repeal. Meanwhile merchants and shipowners grew weary of paying the cost of Jefferson's sublime experiment, and when Congress proved slow in granting relief, an epidemic of transatlantic crossings broke out. By the end of March, 1809, Maury had noticed the arrival of forty embargo-breakers in Liverpool, and there may have been a smaller number in London and the other ports. Meanwhile, Congress finally made up its mind. The Embargo must go, but what should take its place? Complete surrender to London and Paris was out of the question, so the solution finally adopted in March, 1809, was that of permitting Americans to have intercourse with all the world except the belligerents. American ships could now go anywhere except to French and British ports, whether home, colonial, or controlled. American ports were closed completely to all British and French ships and goods, even though the latter came in neutral vessels. But the policy was baited with a promise of forgiveness if the Decrees or the Orders in Council were abandoned so far as they affected American trade and shipping.

The bait and the restricted freedom granted to American vessels wrecked the plan. Ships swarmed out as soon as the Embargo was lifted on March 15th, under bond to go only to a permitted port. Many of them declared they were taking their vast cargoes of cotton, timber, tobacco, and the like to Scandinavian ports, to a neutral West Indian harbour, or to new ports which suddenly emerged out of obscurity, such as Fayal in the Azores. Fayal had been almost unknown in the shipping lists for 1807, yet in the first three months of the new freedom, and from New York alone, ninety ships solemnly cleared for that island. In these strange places the Americans might transfer their cargoes to British vessels; but many of them wasted no such time and instead cleared again for Liverpool. By May Maury was sorrowfully reporting their arrival.

Meanwhile the bait seemed to have caught one large fish. In mid-April, Erskine, the British Ambassador in Washington, reached an agreement with the Secretary of State, by which the Orders in Council were to be inapplicable to American vessels. President Madison thereupon announced on April 19th that non-intercourse with Britain would end on June 10th. Shipowners jubilantly loaded their vessels and sent them off with instructions to hover off the British ports in order to be ready for entry on June 10th. At least fifty of them sailed into Liverpool on the 11th; vessels which had been sent to Fayal or Gothenburg were hurriedly informed to change their course, and Anglo-American trade boomed once more.

The boom was checked when in late July Washington learned that Canning had repudiated Erskine's pact. On August 9th Madison re-established non-intercourse with Britain, but it was impossible to make this effective at once. The vessels which were loading their fall cargoes or were already on their way west with them must be allowed to complete their trips. During the last four months of 1809 about 130 vessels reached New York with British goods, and every other port swarmed with heavily-laden ships from British ports. Hence the official value of British exports to the United States climbed to two-thirds of the level of 1807, while that of imports from the United States was over three-fourths of the pre-Embargo year. Of course, the real effect of revived non-intercourse would be seen in the spring shipments of 1810, but when that spring came Congress let the policy lapse, and trade became free.

Free, but for how long? Congress was loth to retreat entirely. It therefore tried another tack, in the hope that the new one might succeed where its predecessors had failed. It decided to allow full unfettered intercourse between American merchants or shippers and the British and French empires. But if either belligerent revoked his obnoxious policy towards American ships and goods, the President would "declare" this revocation, and the other power would then be expected similarly to mend his ways within three months of the declaration. If he failed to do so, his ships and goods would be barred entry as they had been in the former non-intercourse policy; but Americans would not be forbidden to enter his ports or to sell their goods to him. The unrepentant could thus continue to buy from America, but he could not sell or ship to her. The policy was not non-intercourse; it was only non-importation.

Napoleon promptly seized his opportunity. On August 5th, 1810, he dictated a note which his foreign minister delivered to the American ambassador in Paris. In it he announced that the Berlin and Milan Decrees were revoked as from November 1st, "it being under-

stood (*bien entendu*) that in consequence of this declaration the
English are to revoke their Orders in Council and renounce the new
principles of blockade which they had wished to establish, or that the
United States, conformably to the Act you have just communicated,
cause their rights to be respected by the English."

The gist of this letter reached America in late September, and
caused great rejoicing over the Emperor's apparent retreat. Madison
took it at its face value, and since Napoleon had fixed November 1st
as the death-date for the Decrees, he declared the fact on November
2nd, thus giving Britain until February 2nd to follow suit or face
non-importation on February 2nd, 1811. To deliver a ninety-days'
ultimatum to a government on the other side of the wintry Atlantic
and to get a favourable reply was cutting the time rather fine; but
since the British must have known the terms of the French note by
August they had ample time to make up their minds and to tell the
world that they were going to do what they had repeatedly said they
were willing to do if France was agreeable or would move first.

The news from France therefore caused scarcely a ripple of disquiet
on the water of Anglo-American commerce. Since May 1st the trade
had been booming, merchants showing an eager desire to make up
for lost time and so dispel some of the depression into which the
South American boom of 1808 and other factors had plunged the
British economy by 1810. Things were bad in America as well, so
the two countries had dire need of each other's help. Americans filled
mailbags with orders and climbed aboard eastbound ships and went
off to tour the British factories or warehouses, placing their orders on
the spot. Britons swarmed westward to re-establish old contacts or
to make new ones, whether as visitors or as members of the resident
colonies of Yorkshiremen, Lancashiremen, or Scots which crowded
many a boarding-house in New York City.

The shipping records bear evidence of the intensity of the traffic.
In spite of four months of non-intercourse at the beginning of the
year, 240 ships entered New York from Britain during 1810. This
was somewhat more than the arrivals in the good year 1807. The
autumn arrivals were especially heavy: 70 ships entered the port in
September, 55 in October, and 58 in November. The shipping
columns in the newspapers record the arrival of one ship bearing

1,115 casks, trunks, boxes, bales, cases, bundles, rolls, kegs, or chests of linens, woollens, cottons, ironmongery, hardware, etc., 195 crates of earthenware, 2,251 bars of iron, and 31 tons of coal from a list of importers that filled more than a quarter of a column. They tell of other ships with goods for seventy or even a hundred importers. And sometimes they give the names of the cabin passengers and the number of those "between decks." Only twice before—in 1801 and 1807—had the annual official value of the trade between the two countries been exceeded; and it is doubtful whether the stream of immigration had ever before flowed in greater volume.

Through the winter American traders waited for the news from London. But February 2nd, 1811, came round inexorably, and still no glad tidings of British compliance with the wishes of Madison and Napoleon. The British government, in fact, denied that Napoleon had done what he said he was going to do. They pointed out that there was no "authentic act of the French government publicly promulgated" to prove that the Decrees had been "absolutely and unconditionally repealed," and insisted that while they were eager to repeal their Orders they could not do so until some such document was produced. By implication they inferred that Madison had let himself be bamboozled by Napoleon's letter; that the treatment which the Emperor continued to mete out to American ships proved that he had not changed his policy; and that when Congress fortified the President's proclamation by passing a Non-Importation Act in March, 1811, it was letting itself be bamboozled as well.

The sad thing is that the British were right, and many Americans knew they were right. Not till May 20th, 1812, could the American attaché in London present the British ministry with any "authentic act." It took until June 23rd to get the British Orders in Council revoked—and five days earlier Congress had declared war.

Anglo-American trade therefore entered its last dreary period of peace-time restraint. American ships went off with their cargoes, but could bring no British home or colonial produce back, while British vessels were barred entry entirely into American ports. The only commodity that could be admitted from Britain was specie, for even coal and salt, the traditional ballasts, were kept out. Napoleon had at last won an associate whose strategy and tactics harmonized with those of his own Continental System, just at the time when that System was showing signs of breaking down in Europe. To the long European coastline, stretching from the Baltic to the Hellespont, along which British ships could wander vainly seeking a port and market there was now added the whole seaboard of the United States. The doom which Napoleon had sought to bring on Britain was now to be hastened, for if Americans continued to sell their wares to the British, yet bought nothing in return, the credit, not to mention the manufacturers and the merchant fleet, would be wrecked all the more easily.

The effect on British exports to the United States was soon apparent. The last ship to reach New York with a British cargo arrived on April 27th, 1811. From that date onward only 120 ships entered New York from the British Isles, compared with over 220 during the same period of 1810. Not one of them brought any goods. In the Customs House register there are 87 "ballast" entries in a row. The only variation is "passengers" or "passengers and ballast." Similarly, in Philadelphia, where the arrivals dropped from 62 in 1810 to 38 in 1811, the only change from "ballast" is "oatmeal in ship's stores" or "sundries in baggage."

The official value of British exports to the United States dropped in consequence by more than four-fifths. Yet the imports declined only one-tenth. Americans continued to send their cotton, tobacco and the rest to Britain, and in addition produce flowed to continental Europe, especially to Spain and Portugal where British troops were being fed largely with American flour. It was all, however, a one-sided business, mitigated immediately by the earning of immigrant fares and lightened by the hope that some day Britain would see the light and change her policy or that Congress would abandon coercion.

The revival of immigrant traffic had come during the free trade months of 1810, but during 1811 such traffic was more eagerly sought when there was nothing to put in the hold. It went on unchecked whenever ships were available until Britain heard that America had declared war. When the war began all alien enemy males, fourteen years of age or older, were ordered to register at the offices of the United States marshals. The registers for most of the states have survived, and from them it seems clear that there were about 12,000 enemy males, about 20,000 dependents, or a total alien enemy population of over 30,000. Not all the dependents had come from overseas, but over half of the wives and a quarter of the children were foreign-born. Of the registered males, nearly 5,000 had entered the country since the Embargo was lifted, but 1811 had been the big year. Depression at home made many of them eager to leave; and the energetic attempt to develop manufacturing industries in America (to produce the goods no longer imported from Britain) offered work for skilled textile or metal workers. For these the empty west-bound vessels provided a ready and cheap means of transportation.([1])

While the exporters kept busy and the passengers swarmed in, the importers were idle, except for occasional searching of the skies to see if there was any sign of a break in the clouds. Some had failed to receive goods ordered in the genial days of 1810, even though Congress had relented to the extent of permitting the entry of goods which had cleared from British ports before February 2nd, 1811. Large piles of these goods—bought and paid for—lay in warehouses in the British ports. To them were added still more purchases made during 1811 and early 1812 by Americans who wanted to be ready when the news came that Congress had relented or that Britain had revoked its Orders and that therefore the President had immediately lifted the ban on imports. And every British exporter had in his correspondence files letters from his American patrons telling him to make, buy, or despatch goods as soon as ever the Orders were abandoned, since he could then be sure that by the time they reached America the ports would be open to welcome them. Some fore-sighted Americans even ordered their goods to be shipped to Montreal, Quebec, Halifax, or a neutral island near the south-eastern States, there to have a good headstart when the race to the American market began.

The rest of that story is tragi-comedy. As Britain moved during the first half of 1812 towards revocation of the Orders, America moved towards war, and both reached their destination about the same time. On April 4th Congress imposed an embargo on the

departure of American ships, but scores of vessels scampered out of
port in order to escape incarceration, and thus added substantially to
the American merchant fleet that was abroad. Then, on June 23rd,
the Orders were revoked and British merchants swung into feverish
action. Virtually every one of them interested in the transatlantic
trade sent a letter, circular, or copy of the *London Gazette* to each of
his American patrons, and then rushed to get goods off to port and on
to a ship. Fortunately there were plenty of ships, for in Liverpool
alone seventy American vessels, escaping from the Embargo of April,
had come into port. By July 3rd the first of them, crammed with
cargo, was off for New York, and others soon followed. When in
late July news of the declaration of war arrived no one took it too
seriously at first. Surely when Congress heard that the Orders were
gone it would stop the war. So the ships continued to leave, the
British government let them depart with licenses to protect them
from seizure by British warships, and by the time the exodus ended,
goods estimated to be worth £4,000,000 had left Britain for the
United States.

Some of the vessels which carried them ran into the arms of
American privateers or warships. Others eluded capture and arrived
safely into port. There they found that the war had not been stopped
by the news from London, that the Non-Importation Act had not
been repealed, and that the cargoes were therefore seized for violating
that law. The importers protested to high heaven against this piece of
mass plunder. The privateers were forced to abandon most of their
claims, since they could not make war on American ships and goods.
The customs men had a better case, but it was not one that could be
allowed to stand in view of the vastness of the prize. Early in 1813
Congress agreed that prosecutions were not to be pressed against
those merchants who could prove that their imports had been
ordered or bought before knowledge of the war, or of America's
refusal to call the war off, had reached England. British aliens residing
in America were granted the same concession, but goods consigned
by British owners were fair forfeit or prize. The process of proving
ownership and date of order or despatch from England was slow and
cumbrous. It made the legal profession one of the most profitable
industries of the war years. But since the goods were badly needed by

the American public and since there were no public warehouses
capable of holding them until their fate had been decided the
merchants were allowed to get possession of them by giving bonds
to abide by the final decision of the Treasury or of the courts.

This mountain of manufactures, supplemented by the rising output
of American industry, served the country's civilian and war needs for
1812 and 1813. The last stragglers returned from Britain in early 1813,
and thereafter the only imported addition to the dwindling stock of
textiles or hardware was made when a merchantman bound for
South America was seized and her contents sold by auction. American
merchants turned to other lines of business, and the alien enemies who
were engaged in foreign commerce were interned forty miles beyond
tidewater. The gradual extension of the British blockade along the
southern and central parts of the coast checked traffic, even by neutral
vessels, with the ports of those areas. New England was not block-
aded, and neutral ships plied to Boston; but when they arrived with
cargoʾ ɔ of manufactured goods the customs officers often refused to
believe that the wares were Dutch or German in spite of all the
documents, and frequently seized them on the count that they were
British manufactures.

By early 1814 the country was badly in need of goods and of
customs revenue. On April 14th Congress admitted this fact by
repealing the Non-Importation Act. Henceforth, British goods could
enter the country in neutral ships from British home or colonial ports
or from neutral harbours. The only restriction on them was that they
must not be British property. Under this new policy British and
American vessels suddenly blossomed forth with such names as
Gustavus Adolphus and New England skippers adopted a Swedish
name and accent. They worked through Halifax, and though the
blockade had been extended to cover the New England coast in
April, 1814, cargoes of British goods seem to have been allowed to
pass through to Boston. But the most amusing aspect of the new
situation emerged when a customs collector on the Canadian border
wrote to Boston for advice. On and off he had been keeping British
wares out of the country since 1808. He could understand the stress
which had now forced the government to admit those wares in
neutral ships. But what about the neutral waggons, or about goods,

P

obviously of British origin, which were now coming to his post and for which admission overland was demanded on the ground that they were the property of Swedes?

Even with this new freedom and with the smuggling that went on between the United States and Nova Scotia, New Brunswick, Amelia Island and the West Indies, Anglo-American trade was a puny commerce during the war years. The destruction of the British records deprives us of any figures which might indicate how much was sent to the United States or received therefrom in 1813, but the figures must have been very small. Britain had to turn largely to other places for the timber, tobacco, and cotton that she needed, and America had to get along as best she could, expanding her manufacturing enterprise and doing without what she could not make for herself.

In the autumn of 1814 the collector of customs at Boston, following instructions from Washington, ordered all lighthouse keepers to "cause the Light under [their] care to be extinguished until further orders," since the only ships to which they were of any service now were British. On Saturday evening, February 11th, 1815, an envoy reached New York with a copy of the Treaty of Ghent, and in Monday's paper there appeared an advertisement announcing that a "fast sailing ship" would leave for Liverpool in a few days. On February 13th the envoy reached Washington and delivered his precious document to the President. On the 16th the Senate ratified the treaty unanimously. And on the 18th the Treasury sent a circular to all customs collectors, which read, "You will be pleased forthwith to cause the lights in the Light Houses under your superintendence to be renewed." The phrase "be pleased" was no idle form of speech.

CHAPTER X

The Newfoundland Trade

by A. C. WARDLE, M.I.EX., F.S.F.,

*Hon. Secretary, Liverpool Nautical Research Society. Author of
"Benjamin Bowring and His Descendants," and other works*

THROUGHOUT the eighteenth century, the settlement of Newfoundland was retarded by two restrictive influences. One was a domination by the west-country merchants of England, who considered the island to be for their own exploitation. The other was the traditional outlook of the home government which, while recognising the fisheries as a valuable trading asset, still continued to regard Newfoundland almost as a floating unit of the Royal Navy, capable of supplying both men and provisions to ships on the North American station.

The West-Country merchant and his servants monopolised the island's staple industry—the cod-fishery. In the spring of each year, according to the extent of his intended operations, the English merchant out-fitted his vessels for a voyage across the Atlantic to prosecute the fishery. The fish were caught, cured, and exported from Newfoundland chiefly by his servants, a small number of whom remained behind each year to winter upon the island. In course of time, a third class introduced itself. This comprised those seamen and fishermen who chose to remain ashore after their period of servitude to the merchant had expired. They and their descendants, in some cases, became planters, and procured all supplies and necessaries of life, including fishing gear, from the merchants, paying for them in fish and oils—a practice which obtained down to our own day.

This division of labour encouraged successful conduct of the fishery, for the merchant was thus left to concentrate on the commercial side of the industry. His function was to maintain supplies at St. John's and the principal outports, where he had his own establishments; and, in the autumn, to receive from the planters the fish and oil, which he sold and delivered to the European and West Indian markets. The planter, on the other hand, concerned himself solely with the catching and curing of fish, and in the manufacture of fish-oils—employment for which his habits peculiarly fitted him and made him diligent. This system so developed that towards the end of the century the quantity of fish caught by the servants of those merchants who conservatively followed the old practice became negligible as against the aggregate catch of the planters and *their* servants.

Such a system, however, was not without its defects. Attracted by stories of Newfoundland's prosperity, many useless persons were encouraged to migrate there from Britain and Ireland. They went ostensibly as servants for hire at the cod-fishery and, at the end of the season, became a burden upon the community. A large number, however, were incompetent for the work, and in certain Newfound-land ports as many as three or four hundred people would hide them-selves until all the ships had sailed for the fishery. Then they emerged, to be kept, and travelled from harbour to harbour, living in the most ramshackle huts and "tilts." They were never regularly employed, and lay as surplus population at St. John's, eventually becoming a social liability in one form or another. Even those who found seasonal employment constituted a problem, for the married men were accompanied by their wives and children, who often afforded a serious problem for Newfoundland's administrators. In 1804, the population at St. John's stood at 20,000, augmented by the arrival of 670 immigrants in the same year. Ten years later, however, as many as 10,000 of these immigrants, mostly from Ireland, reached New-foundland in one season, under conditions of Atlantic travel which must have rivalled in misery the middle passage of a West African slave voyage. A glimpse of those conditions is given in the records of a case tried at the Newfoundland court of assize in September, 1811, when James Lannon, master of the schooner *Fanny*, 101 tons, was charged with neglecting to provide sufficient water and pro-visions for passengers and crew, and for not having sufficient accommodation for the passengers. The *Fanny* had sailed from Waterford on 23rd April, laden with cargo, with 184 passengers and a crew of twelve. Several of the passengers had paid as much as six guineas passage-money, for a voyage which took forty-one days to

Bay de Verde, where twenty or thirty of them disembarked rather than go on to St. John's. Five passengers had died during the voyage, and a large number were landed in great ill-health owing to lack of food and water. Lannon's defence was that they had come on board his vessel "in such a manner as made it impossible to ascertain the number," and that he had no idea that the number was so great by seventy persons until the ship was three days out from Waterford. It was thus not difficult to visualise the lamentable conditions endured during a seven weeks' voyage. The jury found Lannon guilty of misdemeanour, and the judge sentenced him to pay a fine of £500.

Another aggravating feature of these years of the early settlement of Newfoundland was the constant menace of fire at St. John's, the capital. An unplanned concentration of wooden houses, out-buildings, fishing-rooms, and oil vats could be nothing else but a scene of frequent fires; and on occasion it became necessary for the whole garrison and the seamen to turn out and quench such conflagrations in order to save the town, but their labours were often seriously hampered by the mob, which was attracted thither by prospect of loot.

Such then was the industrial and social layout of Newfoundland in the days when the colony was still governed by the Naval Commander-in-Chief. Few colonial governors of the period had to face as many difficulties as did these naval officers, whose task was rendered no easier by the existence of a bitter sectarian feeling among the people. The only judicial system, moreover, prevailing upon the island was a legacy of the rough justice formerly meted out by the "fishing admirals" or principal servants of the old West-Country merchants, and the establishment of a court of civil jurisdiction by Governor Milbanke in 1791—the first measure of emancipation extended to Newfoundlanders—had scarcely had time to reveal its efficacy when the war began. The governor of the day, immersed in his dual task of political administrator and commander of an important naval station, thus became responsible for the internal peace and prosperity of a somewhat turbulent community, while at the same time caring for the naval protection of its coasts, fisheries and lines of supply.

Units of the Newfoundland squadron were called upon to patrol its bleak and rugged coasts and to protect its fisheries. The first of these duties was regarded unfavourably by most commanders, since it entailed dispensing justice at the various outports and settlements, where all disputes were "saved up" until the arrival of the man-o'-war. The work of the courts and the strain they imposed upon the naval commanders is amusingly described by an officer on the station at that period:

> "The judicature of this country is vested in the chief justice who, whilst personally presiding over the 'supreme court' in the capital, is assisted in the administration of justice in the distant districts by the naval officers employed on the station, who periodically visit the outports in his Majesty's ships for that purpose; a duty which excites no less apprehension from the dangers incident to so intricate a navigation, despite of all weathers, at fixed and stated intervals, than from the difficulties and serious responsibilities attached to the due performance of a task equally onerous and novel to mere naval commanders. For if, on the one hand, it requires considerable nautical ability to navigate a ship on this coast, from the uncertainty of the currents, frequency of the fogs, and the little dependence which can be placed on the lead; it, on the other hand, demands the exercise of a naturally sound judgment, and a more than ordinary discriminative faculty in a naval officer, to be able to wend his way through the devious intricacies of fraud, and avoid those rocks and quick-sands, too often interposed between the judge and the attainment of an equitable adjudication, by the partiality of official pilots (frequently in cases in which they themselves are concerned), or the craft or perjury of interested witnesses."

The naval officer goes on to describe a typical case:

> " . . . the court-house had undergone a singular, though here not unfrequent metamorphosis, having been a wooden storehouse for cured fish. Upon this store it was the bowman's duty, on reaching the beach, to hoist a spare ship's ensign, as a signal for holding court. Shortly after followed the captain's or lieutenant's coxswain, laden with a cloak-bag filled with books; the surrogate officer closed the train, attended by two of the resident magistrates, a couple of midshipmen, the captain's clerk as registrar of the court, and a few fishermen of the district as criers and tipstaves. . . . Proclamation is made for opening the court; the naval officer takes his seat aloft, arranging his gold-laced hat on one side of him on the bench, and his side-arm, as the sword of justice, on the other. The stores of Themis are ostentatiously spread before the court, to whose voluminous contents it is more than doubtful that either judge, magistrate, sheriff or any individual in court could possibly make a pertinent reference.
> "For several years these officers had not only to perform judicial, but divine duties; nor was it uncommon for a captain to marry a couple in the forenoon

—pronounce judgment upon a legal question in the afternoon—christen a child in the evening—and put to sea at midnight. This latter practice, though bold, is, in case the moon is up, proved by experience to be safe and judicious on this coast, from the general prevalence of fogs in the day-time, which are remarked to be less dense and frequent on moon-light nights."

The Colony's trade during the period under review shewed a preponderance of exports over imports. Fish was shipped to the islands of the West Indies in exchange for sugar, rum and molasses, while fish-oils, codfish and the products of the seal fishery were exported mainly to the United Kingdom which, in return, brought to Newfoundland cargoes of salt, bread, flour, beef, pork, cheese, woollens, fine goods, and hardware. Substantial shipments of codfish also found a ready market in Spain, Portugal and the Latin countries of the Mediterranean, these being paid for by the return of salt, fruits, wines, and olive oil to Newfoundland. In addition, there existed a substantial trade with the American mainland, which supplied Newfoundland with cattle, butter, oats, hay, beef, corn, bread and flour. Many of the voyages, however, were triangular. The merchant in England would load his vessel outwards with supplies or general merchandise for St. John's or the out-ports, from whence the little craft would proceed with a load of codfish to Spain or Portugal and return to her home port in the United Kingdom with a cargo of wines or fruit. Alternatively, after discharging her outward cargo at Newfoundland, she could take codfish down to the West Indies and then proceed home to England with sugar or coffee. Thus, the merchants enjoyed a lucrative business, with prospect of profit at each turn of the triangular venture.

The West Country supplied Newfoundland with serges and other woollens, ropes, nets and twines. Fine goods and continental wares were shipped from London, while Liverpool sent out bulk cargoes of salt and coals, in addition to the manufactures of the Midlands and Lancashire. Waterford, Cork, and other Irish ports shipped foodstuffs and a large number of emigrants.

Newfoundland's exports comprised codfish, cod oil, sealskins, seal oil, salmon, timber, furs and hides—and despite the hazards of war, the values of this produce increased from £590,000 in 1805 to £1,247,503 in 1815. Britain took Newfoundland's seal products, while fifty per cent. of her codfish was shipped to Spain, Portugal and the Mediterranean, twenty-five per cent. to the West Indies, and the balance to northern European countries. Codfish remained the staple export and was regarded almost as currency for nearly a century afterwards. The total exportation of fish increased from 661,177 quintals in 1804 to 1,150,661 quintals in 1815—and against these shipments, Newfoundland imported, in 1805, goods to the value of £231,000. Five years later, these imports had reached an annual value of £447,080, and in 1815 they were valued at £659,280. Among the British ports engaged in this trade were Bridport, Bristol, Dartmouth, Exeter, Greenock, London, Liverpool, Poole, Teignmouth, Whitehaven, and the southern Irish ports. The merchants of these ports had their own establishments or branches at St. John's or at the scattered outports, while the West Indian trade with Newfoundland was represented by such firms as Dunscombe & Harvey, agents at St. John's for the old Bermuda Company, which had maintained a branch in Newfoundland since 1767. Their mercantile successors are still in very active business in St. John's today as Messrs. Harvey & Company.

The cod-fishery, Newfoundland's chief industry, employed 20,000 men and, in 1814, reached a valuation of £2,000,000—a large sum for those days. This dried fish proved a convenient and staple item of food in many distant lands and found a ready sale, particularly in the Latin countries and warmer climes. During the Napoleonic wars, its value was enhanced by the food shortages resulting from extensive military operations. Its chief by-product, cod oil, which was sold by the tun of 252 gallons, also found great demand, largely in England, where it was known as train oil and used both as a lubricant and a luminant. On the Liverpool market the peak wartime price for cod oil was £40 per tun, but upon the introduction and extension of gas-lighting the price fell to about £20.

The industry next in importance at Newfoundland was the seal-fishery. In the early days, Fogo, Greenspond, and Bonavista were the principal centres, and for a long period the fishery was operated from the land in a rather primitive fashion, at varying times of the year. Benjamin Lester & Company, in 1778, were the first mercantile concern to encourage the spring fishery, by employing shallops. It was not until 1795, however, that the now-familiar fore-and-aft schooner made an appearance, the first decked sealer being the *Sarah Kempe*, 30 tons, built in Newfoundland by the Kempe firm. Two years later more craft of this type, mainly from Conception Bay, appeared at the fishery which, unlike its present-day concentration at St. John's, the capital, was then spread around the island, each of the leading out-ports sending out a small fleet to the ice. These schooners were described by Anspach and others as of 40 to 75 tons, strongly built and fitted with poles suspended at their sides as protection against ice. They carried a crew of up to 20 men and boys, and started for the ice on St. Patrick's day of each year.

In 1795, the St. John's sealing fleet could boast a total catch of only 4,900 seals, while a single schooner, the *Active*, 40 tons, of Brigus—one of the out-ports—brought in 7,500 seals. Six years later, however, the spring seal fishery as a whole was employing 140 craft of various tonnages and dimensions, manned by 1,639 men, and achieving a total catch of 81,000 seals. This fleet included as many as 30 shallops, a type of craft which was to disappear altogether within the next few years. In 1804 the spring and winter seal fisheries totalled 106,000 seals, which produced 1,500 tons of seal oil in addition to a valuable stock of skins, the value of which ranged from five to fourteen shillings per skin. Both skins and oil were readily bought at Liverpool and other centres in the United Kingdom.

There were also herring and salmon fisheries. Salmon were caught in small quantities at the several out-ports, barrelled and shipped to England. In 1813, 4,000 tierces of salmon were exported, valued at £16,000.

Newfoundland possessed ample supplies of timber, from which planters and fishermen constructed their houses, huts, fishing-rooms and flakes (the wooden stages on which the codfish were dried). There was also much shipbuilding activity, although this industry was not so far advanced as in other North American colonies. Ship-construction was undertaken in the period between the fishing seasons, when many vessels were constructed solely for employment in the cod and seal fisheries. Several larger ocean-going craft were built for the carrying trade. Newmans, of Dartmouth, built several fine vessels

at Gaultois, all highly commended by Trinity House for their stout
construction and fine model. The colonial records give several lists
of locally-built ships, a typical war year being 1804, when 30 vessels
were completed, totalling 2,300 tons. They comprised two ships,
twenty-one schooners, five brigs, one sloop, and one lugger, the
largest vessel being 232 tons, and the smallest 30 tons. They were
soft-wood ships and mainly designed for Newfoundland waters. A
number of war-vessels had also been built on the island, notably
the sixth-rates *Placentia* and *Trepassey*, launched in 1790, each of
321 tons, 14 guns, and a complement of 125 men.

Newfoundland proved an admirable outlet for Britain's manufactures, since the island's produce, both in peace and war, was highly
valuable to consumers in the British Isles and in Europe generally,
and thus afforded an excellent purchasing-power for the Newfoundlander. It is not surprising that the long arm of the Navy was generously stretched out to protect this trade—a duty which, in war-time,
imposed a strain upon a fleet almost wholly needed for offensive
operations. In the early spring of each year, Newfoundland merchant
ships sailed from England in company with the Halifax and North
American fleet, and the leading escort vessel usually took out the
Admiral-Governor of the colony, who was also Commander-in-
Chief, and who seldom wintered there but returned to England in
November or December. Successive, though smaller convoys
traversed the North Atlantic during the summer months, and the
final passages of the year were made towards December. Thus, the
risks of a northern winter and the ice-pack were avoided. Nevertheless, this convoy work called for the greatest seamanship and vigilance,
and proved a veritable nursery for seamen and future naval commanders.

Contemporary journals and periodicals give ample reference to
the convoy movements. The fleets consisted of hundreds of merchant
ships of all rigs and tonnage; and the voyages, while slowed down to
the speed of the poorest sailer, were conducted with a surprising
regularity. Most of the merchants and traders, at the outset of the
war, ranged themselves against sailing in convoy or company, but in
1798 the first convoy law was enacted, and the following letter from

Vice-Admiral Waldegrave indicates the difficulties under which regulated sea-traffic had to be enforced:

Agincourt,

SPITHEAD,

November 12th, 1798

SIR,

You have my permission to lay the accompanying papers before all those whom it may concern.

I am persuaded that the underwriter cannot fail to be much pleased with my new regulations respecting convoys, as those regulations evidently tend to lessen his risk, and I am equally persuaded that the liberal and active merchant who looks forward to quick returns and who in consequence makes a point of having his vessels well found can be no less pleased with my endeavours to shorten his voyage.

As to the censure that I am incurred from the little narrow-minded trader who makes no scruple to retard the sailing of a whole convoy for the want of his vessel being properly equipped and who perhaps even looks to his profit through her capture—I leave such censure to the contempt it deserves.

What led me to the forming the enclosed regulations respecting convoys was that some of the vessels that sailed under my convoy last year for Newfoundland, and others that sailed in this, were deficient in the complement of their sails.

As a proof of the efficacy of my newly-established instructions to the commanders of convoys, take the following fact: Two days previous to the *Latona's* sailing with her convoy from St. John's, Newfoundland, for the ports of Portugal, I asked Captain Sotheron if all the masters of the vessels had received their instructions? He replied, "No, they had not, as many of them were still very busy completing the complement of their sails." Can any proof of this be stronger? I seek no man's praise on this occasion; I fear no man's censure; I know my motive to be just, and as to the merits of the instructions I leave them to the decision of the impartial world and the test of time.

I am, Sir,

Your most obedient humble servant,

WILLIAM WALDEGRAVE.

To the Master of Lloyd's.

This was acknowledged by Lloyd's on 5th December, 1798, by an expression of appreciation, and a suggestion that the instructions might be extended to include an inspection of anchors and cables. History completely vindicated the wisdom of the convoy regulations, which still formed the base of the comprehensive code governing the protection of merchant shipping in the Second World War.

The Act(¹) imposed a convoy duty. No vessel was to sail from Britain without convoy, under penalty of £1,000. If any vessel, sailing under convoy, was wilfully navigated so as to separate, her master's share of insurance was to be void. To recompense the Government for the protection thus given, small duties were levied on imports and exports, in some cases by weight and in others by value, and trading ships were liable to tonnage dues which ranged from 6d. to 3s. per ton, according to type of voyage. The merchant naturally grudged convoy duty and high insurance premiums, but these complaints were slenderly based, since both charges constituted a levy on merchandise which was ultimately paid by the consumer at home or abroad. West-bound goods carried both insurance and convoy charges and although the latter enhanced their prices when charged to the Newfoundland dealer or fisherman, they eventually became a charge on the value of fish and oils exported to Europe, West Indies or North America. The foreign buyer or consumer therefore paid largely for the cost of British naval and insurance protection. In the case of triangular voyages, the resulting increased value of fish products gave the Newfoundland or English merchant a greater buying power in wines or fruits from the Mediterranean, and on rum or molasses from the West Indies.

Underwriters, however, at Lloyd's and elsewhere, ranged themselves firmly behind the system, and soon most of the trading communities appreciated its necessity. In the closing years of the century, substantial escort was provided for the Newfoundland ships, but later an increasing demand for frigates on more active operations resulted in the use of much smaller craft for escort duties, and brigs, sloops and armed schooners thenceforward constituted the main protection. As many as from 50 to 70 sail were often to be seen shepherded by a single brig or sloop, and the situation became so risky and the practice so prevalent that, in 1804, Lloyd's had to protest against the despatching of convoys under a single escort, and they pointed to the case of H.M.S. *Wolverine*. On March 24th, this sloop of 13 guns, en route to Newfoundland in charge of a convoy, sighted two strangers. They revealed an intention to attack the

---

(¹) This was 43 Geo. III, c. 57, but previous Acts had been passed during the War of American Independence.

convoy, and *Wolverine* accordingly stood to intercept them, signalling the convoy to escape as best it could. At 4 p.m. the larger of the
two enemy vessels, the French privateer *Alonde*, 30 guns, came
within range. *Wolverine's* armament consisted of two 18-pounders
and six 24-pounder carronades on the main deck, in addition to four
carronades on the quarter-deck and one on the forecastle, but on this
occasion one or two of her guns jammed, and so her broadside fire
was considerably reduced, while her opponent, being higher out of
the water, was able to use her 8-pounder guns at a longer range and
with greater accuracy. Both ships fought at 50 yards for an hour
before *Wolverine* lowered her colours. Her sails and rigging were cut
to pieces, her hull riddled between wind and water, and of her small
crew five were killed and ten wounded. Soon after the crew were
removed as prisoners she sank. Meanwhile, her convoy was attacked
by the second Frenchman and two vessels were sunk and the remainder escaped. There were other similar complaints of merchant
ships being left unprotected by escort vessels during an engagement,
but on many occasions the weather, rather than the enemy, caused
these separations, and even the larger warships had experienced
difficulty in holding on to their charges throughout a voyage. In
November, 1801, for instance, the *Camilla*, 70 guns, arrived at
Plymouth in thirty-one days from St. John's, Newfoundland, which
she had left in company with thirty vessels, but parted with them in
a gale and lost her own main-mast. At the entrance to the Channel
she was fortunate enough to fall in with six of her charges and brought
them safely into Dartmouth and Poole. In July, 1803, *Lapwing*,
which sailed that month from Portland for Newfoundland in charge
of a convoy, fell in with two Frenchmen, but was compelled to throw
her guns overboard, neglect her charge, and run for it.

Outbreak of war with the United States revealed the inadequacy
of convoy protection in a startling manner. During a period of three
years about 300 American privateers were let loose upon the British
trade routes, and as the nearest trading centre, Newfoundland, its
fisheries, and the supply routes to England, Mediterranean and the
West Indies, presented a tempting proposition to these corsairs. In
1812 the British North American station was strengthened to include
three sail-of-the-line, 21 frigates and 37 sloops, brigs and schooners.

A homeward convoy, in 1814, was deemed important enough to have the protection of four sloops, *Electra, Muros, Wanderer* and *Hazard*, all of 18 guns, and all specially detached from the squadron. Another convoy, outwards to Newfoundland, consisting of a hundred sail, proceeded from Cork under escort of *Crescent, Rosamund* and *Boxer*, and this measure of wider protection obtained until the war ended.

Nevertheless, the shipping annals of the period show extensive captures of Newfoundland merchant vessels, mostly victims to enemy privateers. In 1808, the *Alfred* and *Duke of Kent*, Newfoundland to Poole, with fish, etc., were captured by a French privateer but recaptured by H.M.S. *Melpomene* and taken into Oporto. The *Union*, Poole for Newfoundland with general merchandize, was captured and then retaken by H.M.S. *Plover*, while at the same time the Newfoundlander *Nancy* succumbed to a French privateer but was saved later by H.M.S. *Dragon*. The brig *Live Oak*, Newfoundland for Oporto, with fish, was captured by three Spanish armed row-boats and carried into Vigo, and the *Acorn*, Newfoundland to Oporto with codfish, was taken into Corunna. The schooner *Margery and Mary*, Newfoundland to Demerara, also surrendered in the same year to a French ship of war, and in 1807, the *Commerce*, a Dartmouth brig in the regular Newfoundland trade, fell to the Spanish privateer *Jesus Maria and Joseph*, but was fortunate enough to be recaptured by H.M. frigate *Virginie*. And so the catalogue of losses continues, and the American conflict produced still greater casualty lists. In July, 1812, the *Harmony*, of Newfoundland, *Berbice Packet*, of Teignmouth, and *William*, of Bristol, were captured by an American privateer off Sable Island, but the victor herself was ultimately captured by H.M. sloop *Indian* and taken into Halifax. During the same week, the *Ann*, Halifax to St. John's, Newfoundland, fell to an American raider. Such were the ravages of these American privateers that Newfoundlanders complained of "much annoyance from American armed vessels, and that the protection they have is totally inadequate to their safety." In the following September, the *King George*, from Liverpool for Newfoundland, was captured by the American frigate *Essex*, which vessel later compelled H.M. sloop *Alert* to capitulate after an obstinate engagement of 30 minutes, in which the *Essex* lost two men killed and six wounded, while *Alert's* casualties were five wounded. The British vessel was made a cartel and arrived in Newfoundland with her own crew and 50 other seamen from captured British merchantmen. In December of that year, the *Caroline*, of Newfoundland, was captured off the Banks by an American privateer, but master and crew later rose upon the Americans, captured the privateer, retook their own vessel, and brought both safely into Newfoundland.

There were also raids upon the Bank fishing fleets. Fishery protection vessels, and sometimes even frigates, spent much time searching for American raiders, one of which, in 1812, hovered for weeks off the south end of the Banks, capturing a number of west-country vessels sailing singly for Newfoundland, in addition to numerous fishing craft. The latter were usually burnt by the Americans as the easiest method of disposal, but the west-country ships were merely ransacked and the cargo thrown overboard, after the enemy had taken necessary supplies. Still, naval protection was generally maintained, and it is interesting to note that in 1812, on one occasion, no less than 23 American prizes were sent into St. John's, some with valuable cargoes, together with 230,000 dollars in specie. These were captures made by H.M.S. *Pomone*.

The rape of a convoy by French or American privateers was not the only hazard for the merchant ship or her escort. Newfoundland has long been termed the "graveyard of the Atlantic," and these northern waters and rugged coasts were ever ready to test the tautness of the ships employed and the skill of their navigators. In 1804 from 60 to 80 ships were lost by gales in a single day. The navy's casualties from marine causes were also heavy. In 1802, *Scout*, 18 guns, and *Fly*, 14 guns, foundered off the Newfoundland coast with all hands, and in 1812 a 16-gun vessel, *Avenger*, met her end in similar fashion. The *Tweed*, of 18 guns, became a total loss at Shoal Bay a year later, when all but 52 of her crew were drowned. Other instances might be quoted and, measured in lives, it is obvious that the strong arm of the Navy was extended at high cost to protect the Anglo-Newfoundland trade.

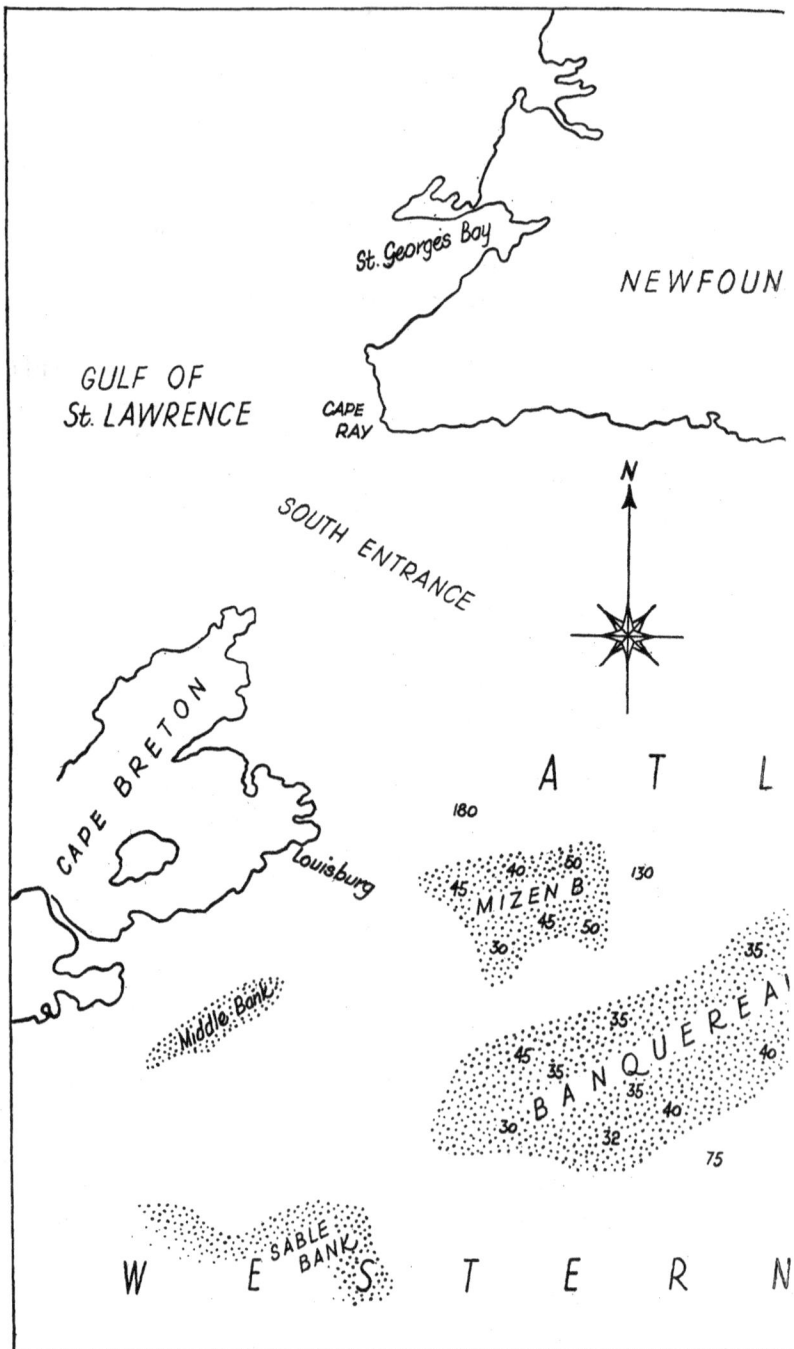

St. Georges Bay

NEWFOUN

GULF OF
St. LAWRENCE

CAPE
RAY

N

SOUTH ENTRANCE

A T L

CAPE BRETON

Louisburg

180

MIZEN B

40   50

130

45

45   50

30

35

Middle Bank

35

BANQUEREA

45   35

35

40

30   32   40

75

SABLE
BANK

W   E   S   T   E   R   N

PLATE 16. The Banks of

240

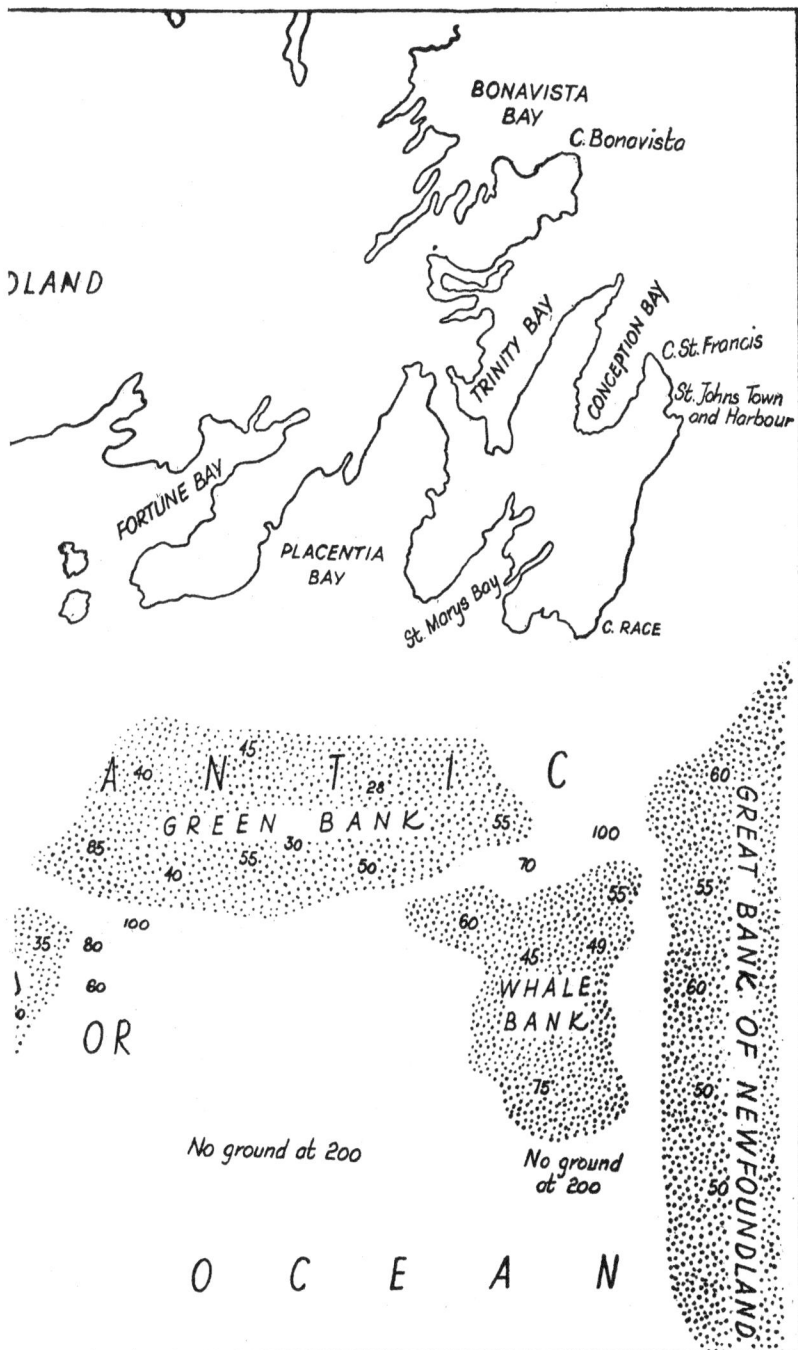

Newfoundland.

Q

Financial cost of the convoy system has been mentioned, but this was largely offset by reduction in war insurance premiums as a result of the escort work. After the introduction of compulsory convoying, the North Atlantic insurance rate dropped from six guineas per cent. to an average rate of three to four per cent. When war began with the United States the rate jumped to ten per cent., rising for a time to as high as nineteen. The risk of the West Indies run from Newfoundland is revealed by insurance rates which fluctuated from 15 to 25 per cent., although underwriters were willing to write the Newfoundland-to-Portugal risk at ten guineas. Nevertheless, without the compulsory convoy system, merchants would have been compelled to pay still higher rates, which would have rendered insurance, and perhaps trade, prohibitive.[1]

The Newfoundland fishery itself also required protection, a duty which fell to the warships on the station—a rigorous task which called for the highest standards of seamanship. So important was the Newfoundland cod-fishery regarded by the home government that, in the Trade Protection Act of 1803, the following clauses were inserted:

XV. Provided always and be it further enacted That it shall be lawful for any Ship or Vessel employed in the Newfoundland Fishery being wholly laden with Fish or other Produce of the said Fishery to sail or depart from any Port or Place within the said Island, or on the said Coast (except as hereinafter provided) without being accompanied with or being under the Protection of the Convoy, or without a Licence having been obtained authorising such Ship of Vessel so to sail or depart.

XVI. Provided always and be it further enacted That nothing in this Act shall extend or be constructed to extend to permit or allow any Ship or Vessel to sail or depart from the Port of St. John's in the said Island of Newfoundland without being under the Protection of Convoy or without Licence being first obtained for that Purpose during the Time any Admiral or other Person duly authorized by the Lord High Admiral of Great Britain or by the Commissioners for executing the Office of Lord High Admiral for the Time being, to grant licences for permitting Ships or Vessels to sail or depart without being under the Protection of Convoy shall be stationed or resident at the said Port of St. John's.

The vessels employed in the Newfoundland trade consisted of brigs, schooners, snows, sloops, and a few ship-rigged vessels. Their

---

[1] See also Chapter I, page 43, on the general rates of premium paid during this period.

tonnages ranged from the small schooner of 30 tons to several large
craft of 300 to 400 tons, but brigs of 100 to 150 tons preponderated.
The fleet included, also, a fair number of prizes captured from the
French and Spaniards. Liverpool and Greenock appear to have
employed the largest vessels in the Newfoundland trade. From the
records it would be difficult to set out an exhaustive and accurate
analysis of the craft employed throughout the war years. To illustrate
their distribution between the British ports, the following list shews
the result of a scrutiny of the shipping registers for the year 1807.
These vessels are shewn as prosecuting the Newfoundland voyage,
and the places named are their ports of registry:

Liverpool	..	60 vessels	Bristol..	..	12 vessels
Poole ..	..	58 ,,	Cork ..	..	6 ,,
Greenock	..	39 ,,	Topsham	..	2 ,,
Dartmouth	..	37 ,,	Waterford	..	2 ,,
Teignmouth	..	34 ,,	Dublin	..	1 ,,
London ..	..	23 ,,	Leith ..	..	1 ,,

Of these, the largest was the ship *Royal Sovereign*, 428 tons. Another
large vessel was the Liverpool-owned *Portland*, 372 tons, a 13 years'
old ship, armed with six guns. The smallest vessel in the trade was the
brig *Catherine*, 33 tons, Thomas Brown, master, owned by the firm
of Warren & Company, of Teignmouth. The foregoing distribution
may be taken as proportionately representative for the whole period
under notice.

The total number of vessels entering St. John's harbour each year
increased from 400 in 1794 to 852 in the year 1815. Of these, about
one-fifth were Newfoundland-built craft, the largest being 232 tons,
but small schooners comprised the majority. Six only of these locally-
built craft exceeded a hundred tons. The shipment of dry codfish,
etc., from Newfoundland to Europe afforded employment for at
least a hundred vessels. Ships engaged as ordinary cargo carriers to
and from the island were usually manned by seamen from their home
ports in Britain, but many of the west-country ships had their crews
augmented at certain times of the year by numbers of "servants" hired
for employment at the codfishery, many of these being picked up at
an Irish port on the way out to Newfoundland. Most of the smaller

and Newfoundland-built craft were owned by the planters themselves and manned by their servants. Liverpool vessels, sailing from
what had already become a most cosmopolitan port, carried mixed
crews which included numerous Irish seamen. These vessels usually
touched in at such ports as Wexford, Waterford, and Cork, and
there picked up a complement of emigrants or "servants."

A large number of the ships were armed for the voyage, Greenock
and Liverpool vessels being, proportionately, the most heavily
gunned. They would be licenced vessels, permitted to sail without
convoy, probably following a northerly course across the Atlantic
not likely to be frequented by French or American naval craft or
privateers. Armament varied according to tonnage. For instance, the
full-rigged ship *Star*, 464 tons, of Liverpool, carried twelve 12-
pounder carronades and four long 9-pounders; while such vessels as
Newman & Company's little Dartmouth brig *Dove*, 64 tons, carried
14 6-pounders, her small arms comprising 12 muskets, 12 pikes,
14 blunderbusses, 12 pairs of pistols and six cutlasses. She was valued
at £1,000 and carried a crew of 15.

Many vessels employed in carrying the bulk cargoes of fish, salt
and coals, were plantation-built, i.e., constructed of soft-wood in
Nova Scotia, Prince Edward Island, or Newfoundland. They were
mostly schooner-rigged, a typical example being the *Eagle,* 65 tons,
built at Barrington, N.S., in 1801, 56 feet length, 17 feet beam, with
depth of hold eight feet, described as a square-sterned schooner, with
one deck and two masts and having a raised quarter-deck, no
galleries, and no figure-head.

Of the southern English ports associated with Newfoundland, the
town of Poole, in Dorset, was one of the most important; and in the
season, when local merchants were fitting out their vessels, the Quay
at Poole must have presented a scene of great activity. These traders
had been long established in the business. The Slades and the Lesters,
of Poole, were settlers in Newfoundland in the opening years of the
eighteenth century. John Slade, who had a considerable establishment
at Twillingate, died in 1792, leaving estate valued at £70,000 derived
mainly from his trade with Newfoundland. It was Lester & Company
who first encouraged prosecution of the Newfoundland seal fishery
in the early days, with boats and shallops. Benjamin Lester, Member

of Parliament for Poole in 1830, was perhaps the most influential member of this affluent family. Other local names engaged in the Newfoundland trade were the Garlands, Kempes, Spurriers, Saunders, Neaves, and Torys, all of whom drove a thriving business throughout the Napoleonic wars. The difficulties of commerce in those days were not entirely confined to meeting enemy privateers or parting with a convoy on the high seas. Both the merchants and their employees had to put up with such obstructions as the press-gang, as is shown by the *Times* account of what happened to the *Maria*, brig, in 1794:

> "This morning (November 30th) arrived in Steedland Bay, the *Maria*, from Newfoundland, having some passengers on board, besides the crew; the officers of the impress service, expecting some resistance, had called for the military assistance, and twenty soldiers, armed, went on board the tender which went down to the harbour to meet the vessel; when coming alongside, and finding the people obstinate, orders were given to the soldiers to fire, which they did, the pilot (then at the helm) and two other men were killed on the spot, and seven others dangerously wounded, one of whom is since dead. Lieutenants Phillips and Glover, with all who were on board the tender, are taken into custody, and the whole town is in the greatest commotion."

Two days later *The Times* reported that a finding of wilful murder had been returned against the two lieutenants, who were eventually brought to trial.

In 1807 the largest unit of the Poole merchant fleet was the ship *Nancy*, 250 tons, owned by the Spurriers, who also built many of their own vessels at Oderin, Burin, and St. Lawrence in Newfoundland. Slade, too, built many small craft at his main establishments, Twillingate and Fogo, while Kempes constructed their own ships both at Poole and in Newfoundland. It was George and John Kempe who built the first decked schooner to be employed at the Newfoundland seal fishery.

One of the oldest firms engaged in the island's trade was that of Newman & Company, with headquarters at Dartmouth. They had factories at Port de Grave, Harbour Breton, and Gaulois, in Newfoundland, and their ships were usually named after aquatic birds, i.e., *Duck, Goose, Swan*, etc. In 1807, the Newman fleet consisted of two fully-rigged ships, 15 brigs, one schooner and two barques, and their trade extended as far as the East Indies. Their Newfoundland ships held government licence to carry arms. The brig *Dove*, 64 tons, for instance, was adequately armed, while the ship *Allison*, 259 tons, mounted twenty 6-pounders, and the brig *Active*, 127 tons, carried sixteen guns of similar weight. By an Admiralty order of 19th February, 1814, Newman's crews were held immune from the attentions of the press-gang.([1])

One of their brigs, the *Duck*, 64 tons, sailed from Newfoundland on 5th December, 1812, with a cargo of codfish for Oporto, and 17 days later was captured by a French frigate. Her commander threw overboard 900 quintals of fish in order to make room for a hundred British prisoners of war. The *Duck* was then despatched to England. Six months later, while on voyage from Waterford to Newfoundland, with 20 Irish "youngsters" or servants on board as passengers, the *Duck* fell a victim to the notorious American privateer schooner *General Plumer*, but was soon recaptured by the privateer *Sir John Sherbrooke*, of Liverpool, cruising in company with H.M. brig *Bold*. The next day, 27th May, 1813, the *Sherbrooke* came upon the *General Plumer* herself, crammed with prisoners and booty from a three months' cruise. After a long chase and a short fight, the American (being out-gunned) surrendered. She had 52 prisoners on board, and a crew of 34—far too many for the limited 'tween decks of the *Sherbrooke*. For two days the two ships kept close company, and then H.M.S. *Shannon* hove in sight. It is said that Captain Broke, of the *Shannon*, boasted an excellent crew, the result of six years of wholesome discipline and generous treatment, but it is typical of Broke that he should call for volunteers, and he accepted the pick of the Irish lads who had shipped from Waterford in Newman's brig *Duck*. Their adventurous voyage, however, was not yet completed, for within three days *Shannon* was in action against the American frigate *Chesapeake*, and the Irish "youngsters" behaved so well during this memorable engagement that Newmans were given the privilege of flying the white ensign at all their establishments in Newfoundland. Some of the Irishmen gave their lives in that fight and were buried in the old Dockyard Cemetery at Halifax, Nova Scotia.

([1]) Which other Newfoundland vessels were not. Their men were impressed in 1794 and in 1808. Some of them served at Trafalgar, and afterwards returned to the trade.

Another Devonshire port with extensive trade to and from New-foundland was Teignmouth, where the merchant families of Bulley, Bowden, Rowe, and Warren were established. One of the later partners in the Bulley firm was John Job, son of an English naval officer. Left an orphan, he was adopted by Samuel Bulley, of Teign-mouth, who had a planter's business in Newfoundland and a counting-house at Teignmouth, where John Job became an appren-tice. Eventually he was entered as junior partner and married Miss Bulley, the firm then becoming Bulley & Job. In 1778, John Job left for Newfoundland to take charge of the business there. He subse-quently made several voyages across the Atlantic, and in April, 1799, while on passage in his own vessel, the *Flora*, with other passengers, the ship was overhauled by a French privateer and captured. A diary kept by John Job has been preserved, and affords an interesting picture of a business man's experience in those days:

"We were captured 11th April, Lat. 48.08, Long. 18 by the Privateer *Role*, Captain Claud Digeaux, of Bordeaux, France. All the ship's crew and passengers were taken on board the Privateer except Mr. Payn, the cook, his son, Manley, and myself. We immediately stood to the eastward in company with the *Role* until Saturday, 13th. It being then more moderate, the boat came alongside with Samuel [a Mr. Bulley and John Job's brother-in-law] who took all his clothes, the quadrant and charts excepted. In the boats were taken several of the aforesaid passengers. Samuel was in good spirits and told me they were assured of kind treatment. This is the last I saw of him, as the *Role* stood immediately to the westward. May God grant us a happy deliver-ance ere long and a safe meeting with wife and children. Nothing particular happened until Friday, April 19th, 1799, when we anchored inside Isle de Re.

20th. We got into La Rochelle. The *Flora* was immediately hauled into the pier alongside the quay; hatches sealed, etc. Mr. Payn, myself and the boys were taken to the Commissary whence we were ordered after examina-tion to a place of confinement where I am now making this memorandum. Passed the night heavily. We left La Rochelle on the 27th April, travelled 20 miles. We were obliged to carry our baggage on our backs; roads very bad indeed; hearts heavy. We stopped the night at Sougeurs and got some refreshment at the prison-house. Accommodation very indifferent indeed.

28th. This day we left Sougeurs, travelled twenty-five miles, stopped at the village of Niort, at which place Mr. Payn became very ill and was obliged to get a Surgeon.

and so the diary goes on to record a journey on foot which lasted a fortnight before the prisoners reached their final rendezvous for internment. John Job's vessel, the *Flora* was impounded, but six months later he was released on cartel.

A few years later another vessel belonging to this firm, the *Hilton*, was fitted out at Teignmouth and, under Captain Bulley, despatched to Newfoundland. She fell in with a French man-of-war commanded by Jerome Bonaparte and was burnt on the spot, her crew being cast adrift in a boat, to reach the coast as best they could. Some years later, John Job gave up voyaging across the Atlantic and settled down at Liverpool, where he established the main branch of his business, a concern which still flourishes today under the old name and under the guidance of his direct descendants.

Liverpool's association with the Newfoundland trade reaches back to the late seventeenth century, and was probably stimulated by the refinery of Cheshire salt on Merseyside, a commodity of high value to the fishermen and planters in Newfoundland. As early as 1680, salt cargoes were loaded at Liverpool for the colony, but it was not until the close of the next century that the Mersey port participated to any appreciable extent in the trade with Newfoundland. The demand for salt cargoes, the cheapness of household coal as a result of the canalization of south-west Lancashire, and the proximity of the Midlands and the growing Lancashire industrial centres, probably induced a number of Newfoundland firms to transfer their headquarters from Devonshire to Liverpool or else to establish branches there. Enemy attacks on shipping leaving the west-country ports may have induced several of the prominent merchants to choose Liverpool as a centre, although both French and American privateers were fond of raiding the Irish Channel on occasion, and many a Liverpool merchant ship fell to them. As already mentioned, John Job settled on Merseyside in 1810, and other firms domiciled there during the period under notice were Hamilton & Graham, Ryan & Sons, Edward Hunt, T. Robinson & Company, and G. Neale, all of which had their own premises at St. John's and the out-ports of Newfoundland. Their business consisted in buying staple bulk commodities and manufactured goods for export to St. John's and Harbour Grace; and in selling at Liverpool the products of the cod and seal fisheries. In fact, the Mersey port became quite a centre of the Newfoundland fish-oils trade. It is to be noted, however, that Liverpool entered the trade at a date when actual fitting-out of vessels for the fisheries from this country was on the decline, most of the goods shipped from the Mersey being intended for sale at the merchants' stores in New-foundland for the fitting-out and equipment of vessels at St. John's and the out-ports. As the industrial revolution progressed in England, and the manufactures of Lancashire and the Midlands expanded, perspicacious merchants in the Newfoundland trade were quick to realise the value of the Mersey port as a centre and settled there in increasing numbers. Since those days, the Devonshire and west-country domination of Newfoundland has vanished; the once-flourishing trades of Poole, Dartmouth, Bristol, Exeter, and other English out-ports have disappeared, and today the Mersey remains the sole commercial link between Europe and our oldest colony.

Liverpool despatched some larger ships than those usually em-ployed by the west-country ports, and full-rigged vessels were frequently put on the berth to sail direct to St. John's, somewhat after the manner of the packet ships to New York. The following is a typical sailing notice of the period:

For ST. JOHN'S, NEWFOUNDLAND AND HALIFAX
The Ship *CHARLOTTE,*
William Fryer, Master;

Stands A.1 at Lloyd's, newly coppered and in every respect a superior vessel. Goods for Halifax by special agreement. Great part of cargo is engaged, and she will be despatched in a few days. For Passage, having good accommoda-tion, apply to the Master on board, West Side, Salthouse Dock, and for further particulars to Messrs. W. B. Cripps & Co. or EDWIN HUNT, Broker.
(From the *Liverpool Mercury*, 17th September, 1813.)

One of the leading Liverpool firms in the Newfoundland trade was Bulley & Job (formerly of Teignmouth, see page 247), whose vessels usually freighted the firm's own cargoes:

For ST. JOHN'S, NEWFOUNDLAND
The Coppered Brig *PENELOPE*
John Hanley, Master;

Burthen per register, 313 tons; has room for a few tons of goods, and is intended to join the first convoy from Cork. For freight or passage apply to Messrs. Bulley and Job, or N. HURRY and GIBSON, Brokers.
(*Liverpool Mercury*, 10th June, 1814.)

Another active Liverpool merchant was John Neale, who loaded vessels for Newfoundland:

For ST. JOHN'S, NEWFOUNDLAND
The Barque *EDWARD*,

Of 241 tons per register, has room for a few tons goods, provided an early application is made to

JOHN NEALE, Crooked Lane,

Who is in want of a first-class vessel of from 200 to 300 tons to take a cargo of measurement goods to Newfoundland. March 2nd, 1815.
(*Liverpool Mercury*, 3rd March, 1815.)

Other sailing notices might be quoted if space allowed, sufficient to illustrate the tendency of the Mersey port, towards the close of the Napoleonic struggle, to assume a lead in the Newfoundland trade, which afterwards so continued that finally almost the entire mercantile representation of the colony on this side of the Atlantic was domiciled at Liverpool.

CHAPTER XI

The Slave Trade

by C. M. MacINNES, M.A.

Professor of Imperial History, University of Bristol. Author of
"A Gateway of Empire," and other works
With an Appendix by Professor J. A. NIXON

THOUGH this chapter is concerned with the slave trade in the last years of its existence, it is necessary to make some reference to the contemporary movement which resulted in its abolition. Throughout all the years covered by this book those concerned in the purchase and sale of negroes were conscious of the growing hostility of the nation. Several years before the outbreak of the French war, Parliament intervened to ameliorate the lot of slaves on the Middle Passage by the passing of a regulative act in 1788, and down to 1807 there was always a vigilant party in England which was ready to denounce any who proved to be guilty of infringement of that measure. Shipowners, captains, planters, brokers and all concerned in this branch of commerce were never, in fact, wholly free from the fear of total abolition.

Though nothing could humanise the trade, still, the vigilance of Parliament, enlightened self-interest on the part of many of the merchants themselves and superior organisation in the conduct of the business combined to render the sufferings of the negroes less than they had been at any previous period. When the war with France broke out in 1793, the Abolitionist movement was already several years old, and in 1792 it had won a notable victory when the House of Commons determined that the slave trade should be gradually discontinued, and should cease altogether by January 1st, 1796. When these resolutions were sent up to the House of Lords the Bristol Society of Merchant Venturers petitioned that chamber against giving its sanction to so dangerous and mischievous a departure from established British commercial policy.[1] The outbreak

---

[1] *Society of Merchant Venturers. Book of Petitions*, fol. 109-110.

of the French war turned out to be fortunate for the trade, since it gave the House of Lords an excuse for doing nothing. The mind of the nation was now concentrated on the war, and so those who were only lukewarm friends of Abolition or concerned in the trade could conveniently forget the sufferings of the Africans which had caused such searchings of heart in recent years. Wilberforce, however, was determined that no such happy oblivion for the slave traders should supervene, and he went steadily forward on his great crusade. As highly coloured news from France horrified the nobility, gentry and wealthy middle-classes of England, and as the fortunes of war seemed to be turning against this country, the champions of this old-established commerce were able to enlist the horror of revolution on their side, for at a time when Jacobinism seemed about to engulf the world in ruin, sweeping reforms were out of the question. Many of his supporters deserted Wilberforce, and when he reminded the House in 1795 of the resolution which it had passed three years earlier to terminate the slave trade entirely by the first day of the ensuing January, and that as yet it had done nothing to carry that determination into effect, the slave interest was strong enough to induce the House to postpone a consideration of the proposal for Abolition for another six months.

In 1796 Liverpool petitioned against Abolition and two years later, the thanks of that city and a piece of plate valued at one hundred guineas was presented to Mr. P. W. Branker for his unremitting labours in defending the slave trade and for procuring its continued existence under reasonable restrictions. Another Bill for Abolition was before the House in 1799, and again Liverpool petitioned against it, but by then the zeal for the cause had greatly declined and the usual arguments were strengthened by references to the atrocities of rebel negroes in San Domingo, who, it was stated, inspired by Wilberforce and his dangerous intentions, had risen and murdered their masters. Indeed, at the close of the century, the trade felt sufficiently sure of itself to oppose a measure which was to provide still more improvements in the treatment of negroes during the Middle Passage. Shortly after this the tide turned again, and in 1804 Wilberforce carried a resolution in the House of Commons which called for the appointment of a committee that was to consider the propriety of abolishing the slave trade, but Parliament was fickle. In 1805, the House of Commons rejected a Bill for Abolition. This reverse proved to be temporary, however, for in 1807 Wilberforce, after years of ceaseless endeavour, at last achieved the purpose which had been the guiding motive of his life since that day, now so long ago, when he and his friend Pitt had discussed the woes of the Africans under an old oak above the Vale of Keston.

Throughout the course of this long controversy, which had roused the nation such as nothing else had done for over a century, the champions on both sides repeated their old arguments over and over again. The Abolitionists pointed to the undoubted cruelties of the trade. They denounced its lawlessness, and in the space of twenty years they familiarised the British people with the cruel sufferings of helpless Africans. Their opponents tried to minimise, for they could not wholly deny, the charge of cruelty, but they placed their main reliance on appeals to the sacred nature of private property. They stressed the national importance of the traffic and pointed out that it alone made possible the prosperity of the West Indian islands. For a century and a half England had not only tolerated the slave trade, it had gloried in it, and repeatedly declared it to be one of the mainstays of national greatness.

It was in London, Bristol and Liverpool, the three cities most concerned in it, that the slave trade found its most strenuous supporters. The metropolis, however, after the first few years of the campaign, played a very minor role in its defence, for after all, this branch of commerce was of slight importance to London compared with other trades. In its last years Bristol's share of the trade was also very small. Still, when the Abolitionist movement began, energetic opposition came from that city, and the petitions prove that the Society of Merchant Venturers and almost all the leading citizens of the place were ardent opponents of Wilberforce. It was, however, upon Liverpool, a city which virtually monopolised the carriage of slaves in the last years, that the chief burden of defence fell, and it was there, too, that the slave trade forces were mainly mobilised. In furtherance of this commerce alone, and with the encouragement and support of the whole nation, the citizens of Liverpool had invested vast sums of money. For it they had built docks, erected lighthouses and built up a great fleet, manned by thousands of men. Thanks to it, they had accumulated great fortunes which had enabled them to improve their city in all directions. To abolish this trade now, because of the alleged sufferings of negroes who, they were convinced, were scarcely human and certainly incapable of feeling pain in the manner of civilised Europeans, was a monstrous injustice. Such a revolution in British commercial policy, if carried into effect, could not possibly better the conditions of the negroes, who would still continue their own savage wars. Indeed, they would still be carried away into slavery by foreigners who possessed even less consideration for the feelings of their victims than the English. Thus, at a blow, the nation would increase the power and riches of her potential enemies and bring ruin upon those of her own people who for years past had done more than any other section of the community to advance the might and glory of England.

When, in 1806, it became clear that the slave trade was to be abolished, the merchants of Liverpool loudly demanded compensation for the losses which they would thereby sustain. Today, when the heat and fury of that bygone struggle are forgotten, it does not seem that this demand was wholly unreasonable. As the merchants declared, England had for over a century considered the slave trade as one of the most important branches of her commerce. To encourage merchants to invest their money in it and then suddenly to decide that it was wicked and must be abolished, and that no compensation should be paid to the dispossessed merchants, was neither logical nor just. These arguments, however, carried no weight in 1806. Wilberforce had the ear of Parliament and of the country, and with the Ministry of All the Talents in power, with Charles James Fox at its head, the slave trade could expect no mercy.

Although it took Wilberforce twenty years of ceaseless effort to carry his great crusade through to success, Parliament was not slow to recognise that grave abuses existed in the trade. In 1788, an Act was passed which was intended to eradicate the worst abominations of the Middle Passage as these had been laid bare in evidence recently presented before a committee of the Privy Council. The nation shuddered at the tales of fiendish cruelty which those who knew the trade had to tell. Many of the most glaring of these stories had never been contradicted, and while it was generally felt that Abolition would be an act of wanton interference with private property, there were good grounds for demanding reform. The Act of 1788, among other things, provided that:

> . . . In every ship, where the space between the two decks shall not be less than five feet in height, and where the cabin shall be fitted for the accommodation of the negroes, in the proportion of five persons for three tons, if the burthen of the ship does not exceed 160 tons; and of three persons for two tons, if the burthen of the ship does not exceed 150 tons; and in every ship where the space between the two decks shall be less than five feet, or where the cabin shall not be fitted for the accommodation of the negroes, in the proportion of one person for every ton burthen of the ship or vessel.(1)

It also provided that no surgeon should be employed as such in slave vessels unless he had a testimonial that he had passed a proper examination at Surgeons' Hall. However, the nation was content with formal recognition of these evils, for the penalty of £20 for every native exceeding in number the proportion directed, was so laxly enforced as to render the measure of little practical use to the tortured blacks. Though in the course of the next twenty years slave captains had to walk warily, it can, nevertheless, truthfully be said that the conditions which prevailed in many British ships in the last years of the trade's existence disgraced the name of England.

During the eighteenth century, Bristol, Chester, Exeter, Glasgow, Liverpool, London, Lancaster and Plymouth all participated in this commerce. From 1660 to the close of the war of the Spanish Succession, London predominated. Then in the next few decades, Bristol increased her share, till by the middle of the century she equalled and sometimes surpassed the metropolis in the number of ships she sent to the Guinea Coast. Liverpool, beginning in a very small way early in the eighteenth century, made amazing progress, and by the seventies was already competing for first place. In the last twenty years of the trade's history that port was unquestionably supreme. None of the other out-ports were ever of much consequence and in the period under review they seem to have dropped out altogether. In the years between 1793 and 1807, London each year sent a few ships to the African coast, but some, at least, of these took no share in the traffic

---

(1) *Annual Register*, 1788, p. 300.

in slaves. Some London ships returned direct from Africa with gold-dust, ivory, Guinea seeds, fruit, wax, gum, elephants' teeth, Guinea wood and palm oil. In furtherance both of this direct trade and of the triangular trade with Africa and the West Indies, London sent out a wide variety of articles. Coarse linens, woollen goods, iron, pewter, brass,(1) hardware manufactures, lead shot, swords, knives, firearms, gunpowder, glass and manufactured goods of all kinds appear in the list. After the merchants of London had recovered from the paralysing astonishment which first affected them when they heard that a movement was afoot to abolish the slave trade, they were active in its defence for a year or so. Gradually, with the development of new trades and problems connected with the French war, London appears to have lost interest in the carriage of negroes. So it was that in 1814 the capital was staunch for Wilberforce and petitioned Parliament to ensure that clauses providing for the Abolition of the trade should be inserted in the peace treaty.

In 1793, Bristol's interest in the carriage of slaves had greatly declined in proportion both to her own West Indian trade and to the share taken by Liverpool in the traffic in negroes. The city, however, was vitally concerned in the maintenance of plantation slavery. When, at the end of 1792, the Society of Merchant Venturers petitioned the House of Lords against the Abolition resolutions sent up to it from the Lower House,(2) no mention was made of Bristol's share in the slave trade itself. The Society was solely concerned with the disastrous effect of Abolition on the position of the West Indies. The trade with these islands was at that time the chief branch of the city's commerce, and the merchants of Bristol emphasised the supreme national importance of continued prosperity in the West Indies. Imports of sugar from the plantations enabled England to maintain a favourable balance of trade with foreign states. The shipping employed in this commerce added greatly to the naval strength of the Kingdom, and, indeed, all the well-worn mercantilist arguments were put forward to prove the importance of the Sugar

---

(1) See note on plate 18.

(2) *Society of Merchant Venturers. Book of Petitions*, fol. 119.

Islands in the imperial economy. West Indian sugar production depended upon slavery, for, as John Pinney said:

> Negroes are the sinews of a Plantation and it is as impossible for a Man to make Sugar without the assistance of Negroes, as to make Bricks without Straw.(¹)

Many of the citizens of Bristol, however, were already inclined to look askance at the actual business of carrying negroes from Africa to the plantations, and the writer of the *Bristol Guide for the Year* 1793 rejoiced in the outstanding virtue and self-sacrifice of his fellow-citizens:

> The Ardor for the Trade to Africa for men and women, our fellow-creatures and equals, is much abated among the humane and benevolent Merchants of Bristol. In 1787 there were but 30 Ships employed in this melancholy traffic; while the people of Liverpool, in their indiscriminate rage for Commerce and for getting money at all events, have nearly engrossed this Trade, incredibly exceeded London and Bristol in it, employ many thousands of tons of shipping, for the purposes of buying and enslaving God's rational creatures, and are the vendors (*horresco referens*) of the souls and bodies of men and women! to almost all the West Indian islands! ! ! (²)

This horror of the trade, however, had nothing to do with the fullest appreciation of slavery, for Bristol was deeply concerned in the management and control of sugar plantations. Long after the slave trade had been abolished, citizens of Bristol continued to derive their incomes from sugar estates worked by slave labour, and when the Emancipation Act was passed in 1833, many of her commercial houses received large sums in compensation, £55,178, £23,024, £19,867, £12,968, £12,357, £9,076, £8,092, £3,820, £3,572, and there were a large number under £3,000. It is stated that one firm, which had houses both in London and in Bristol received almost a quarter of a million pounds, but Mr. William Claxton, a member of the firm of Protheroe & Claxton, writing his son on matters of finance, said that he himself had been reduced to poverty through the Act and had lost £18,000.

While the smaller out-ports dropped out altogether and while only a few ships sailed from London and Bristol for Guinea each year

---

(¹) *Pinney Papers, Business Letter Books.*

(²) *Matthew's New History of Bristol, or Complete Guide and Bristol Directory for the Year* 1793-4, pp. 38-9.

R

in search of negroes, Liverpool's trade became enormous. In speaking of that city at the end of the century one writer says:

> This great annual return of wealth may be said to pervade the whole town, increasing the fortunes of the principal adventurers, and contributing to the support of the majority of the inhabitants. Almost every man in Liverpool is a merchant, and he who cannot send a bale, will send a bandbox, it will therefore create little astonishment, that the attractive African meteor has, from time to time, so dazzled their ideas, that almost every order of people is interested in a Guinea cargo.(1)

The capture of the French and Dutch Islands early in the new century led to an increased demand for slaves and this brought still greater prosperity to Liverpool. Lastly, when it became clear that the victory of Wilberforce was certain, the merchants on the Mersey made a supreme effort to wring as much money as they could from this doomed commerce before its extinction. Between January 1st, 1806, and May 1st, 1807, 185 vessels were despatched from Liverpool to the Coast with a combined tonnage of 43,755 tons, and in those last strenuous months they carried 49,213 slaves from Africa to the Sugar Islands, and so the slave traders of Liverpool made their *salut à mort*.

SHIPS WHICH CLEARED OUT FROM LIVERPOOL TO THE COAST OF AFRICA, 1793 TO THE TIME THE TRADE WAS ABOLISHED IN MAY, 1807.(2)

Year	Ships	Tons	Year	Ships	Tons
1793	52	10,544	1801	122	28,429
1795	59	—	1802	122	30,796
1796	94	—	1803	83	15,534
1797	90	20,415	1804	126	27,322
1798	149	34,937	1805	117	26,536
1799	134	34,966	1806	111	25,949
1800	120	33,774	1807	74	17,806

In its latest phase the Bristol and London trades seem to have been carried on by a number of small firms, each owning one or two

---

(1) *A General and Descriptive History of Liverpool* (1795) (anon.), p. 230.

(2) The majority of these were employed in the slave trade, the rest carrying woods and ivory.

ships. In Liverpool, on the other hand, most of the trade was controlled by a few large well-established houses, each of which owned several vessels, and in addition to these there was a varying number of small firms or individual merchants similar in economic standing to the slave traders in the other two cities. For the small entrepreneur the trade was a risky one, for in addition to the usual danger of storms, fires and shipwrecks, there were special features about the carriage of slaves which rendered it precarious. Large houses, however, which controlled a sufficient amount of capital to bear sudden and great losses could reasonably expect very large profits over a period of years. When the trade was well-organised and the ships were commanded by capable captains, who took a pride in reducing the mortality among the negroes to the minimum, the merchants might reasonably expect to reap three profits on their investment. The goods carried out to the Coast were exchanged for negroes at a profit, the blacks were marketed in the Islands at a profit, and the sugar or other tropical products brought home to England were sold at a profit. But still it was a speculative business, a fact which seems to be borne out by the high mortality which appears to have been characteristic of small firms in Liverpool.

Earlier in the century slave captains preferred small vessels, but before 1800 fairly large ones were quite common. Captain Crow, who commanded the last slave ship which sailed from Liverpool, gives the size of three of the vessels to which he was appointed at different times in his career. The *Will*, his first vessel, was about 300 tons burden, and carried 18 six-pounders besides small arms. His next ship, the *Ceres*, was of 400 tons burden and in 1805, he took out

> a fine new ship called the *Mary* . . . This vessel was nearly 500 tons burthen, and carried twenty-four long nine-pounders on the main deck, and four eighteen-pound cannonades on the quarter deck. We were manned by between sixty and seventy men, thiry-six of whom were qualified to take the wheel, being an uncommon proportion of able seamen, at a time when it was difficult to procure a good crew.[1]

The largest vessel engaged in the trade at the turn of the century was the *Parr*, of Liverpool, which was of 566 tons burden and was

---

[1] *Memoirs of the late Captain Hugh Crow, of Liverpool*, pp. 89-90.

launched in November, 1797. Still, it is significant that in the Act of 1788, which regulated the trade, reference is made to vessels of 160 and 150 tons and under. Thus, though larger ships were used in 1806 than was customary twenty years earlier, they were still on an average smaller than those that were at that time employed in either the East Indian or the West Indian trades. Slave vessels were of no particular rig, and references are to be found to ships, snows, brigs, and, indeed, to almost every kind of craft large enough to carry "a parcel of slaves."[1]

Grim things were told about the trade and of the manner in which the ships were manned. Clarkson was horrified at the scenes of degradation and debauchery which he beheld in the Bristol public houses he visited, but a pious young clergyman, unaccustomed to sailormen and the taverns they frequented, is scarcely a safe or impartial guide. On the whole, the mortality among sailors engaged in the trade was somewhat higher than among those in other branches of commerce, yet it does not appear to have been particularly unpopular among the seafaring population. The life of a sailor in any trade at that time was never distinguished by its comfort. Indeed, it was always dangerous and full of hardships, and the man who was seized in a quayside tavern and dragged aboard drunk would find it no more distasteful to die on the African Coast than to freeze on the Grand Banks. As a body the sailors engaged on the slavers' trade were a rough lot. Crow speaks of them as

> the very dregs of the community; some of them had escaped from jails; others were undiscovered offenders, who sought to withdraw themselves from their country lest they should fall into the hands of the officers of justice. These wretched beings used to flock to Liverpool when the ships were fitting out, and after acquiring a few sea phrases from some crimp or other, they were shipped as ordinary seamen, though they had never been at sea in their lives. If, when at sea, they became saucy and insubordinate, which was generally the case, the officers were compelled to treat them with severity; and, having never been in a warm climate before, if they took ill, they seldom recovered, though every attention was paid to them. Amongst these wretched beings I have known many gentlemen's sons of desperate character and abandoned habits, who had either fled for some offence, or had involved themselves in pecuniary embarrassments, as to have become outcasts unable to procure the necessaries of life.[2]

---

[1] See plate 17, showing a Liverpool Guineaman of the period.
[2] *Memoirs of the late Captain Hvgh Crow, of Liverpool*, p. 169.

Slavery was an established institution and these men believed that "niggers" were little better than monkeys, and whatever the defects of the trade might be, if it ensured a good and steady supply of old Jamaica rum at a reasonable price, it was well worth the sufferings it might cause to black heathen who probably did not have the sense to know when they were hurt. Still, while sailors had no particular horror of the trade, it cannot be said that they clamoured for berths aboard slavers. The voyages were usually long—twelve months was an average—and death among the crews was fairly common. As contemporary sailors sang:

> Beware and take care of the Bight of Benin,
> There's one comes out for forty go in,

and when all was said that could be said of it, the work of acting as gaolers to negroes was unpleasant. It would be quite erroneous, however, to impute the cultivated susceptibilities of the twentieth century to these rough sailormen of the eighteenth.

Normally, a Guineaman carried a larger crew than was customary in other trades. In Bristol it was generally the practice to carry 12 men for every 100 tons on vessels of 300 tons and over, whereas in the West Indian trade the number was seven for every 100 tons. In both trades smaller vessels carried a larger proportion of men to tons, though when Crow commanded the *Will*, of 300 tons, his crew numbered 50. Again, on vessels engaged in the slave trade, about two-fifths of the officers and men were able seamen, whereas in the West Indian trade the proportion was four-fifths. In time of peace the pay was about the same in both trades, but in war-time the Guinea sailors received about 5s. more than their fellows in the West Indian trade. Crow considered that the expense of manning an African ship was "excessive":

> The wages given in the *Mary* was ten guineas a month to the carpenter, nine to the cooper, seven each to the boatswain and gunner, six each to the quarter-masters, and six to every able seaman. Besides these expenses, three to four pounds was given as "crimpage" for able seamen.[1]

Bristol sailors were usually paid three months' wages in advance to enable them to equip themselves for the voyage, a practice which

---

[1] *Memoirs of the late Captain Hugh Crow, of Liverpool*, p. 90.

seems to suggest that the number of those who were forcibly carried aboard was not nearly so great as the Abolitionists declared. No further wages were paid on the Coast, but on their arrival in the colonial port they received half the wages still owed to them in the local currency at the rate of £1 colonial money for £1 sterling. This was a constant source of discontent among the men who, since the local money was invariably at a tremendous discount, complained that they were being robbed.

Slave ships carried a varied cargo when they sailed for Africa. It might consist of copper rods, various materials such as nicannees, Guinea stuffs, bafts, chintz, red and blue cotton romalls and choteas, cowrie shells, bars of iron, gunpowder, muskets, cutlery and drinking utensils, beads, brandy and other alcoholic liquors and fancy hats. Besides these trading articles, the ships carried the usual handcuffs, neck-rings, shackles, chains and other fetters with which to secure the slaves during the Middle Passage. An indication of the kind of articles taken to Africa is afforded by an advertisement for the sale of goods declared to be valuable in that commerce which were to be disposed of "under Prime Cost in Consequence of the Expected Abolition."

VALUABLE
ARTICLES
for the
SLAVE TRADE (¹)

To be Sold at and under Prime Cost in Consequence of the EXPECTED ABOLITION.

About Ten Million Dozen Negro Guns at 24s. per Doz.; About Three Tons Weight Hand and Feet Shackles and Thumb Screws, at 1½ per Pound; About Ten Thousand Fine Gold-laced Hats, at 10½d. each; Ten Thousand Gross Negro Knives, the whole Cast Iron, at 14s. per Gross; About Three Tons brilliant Diamond Necklaces, at 3s. per Pound; About Ten Thousand Pieces fine Negro Linen, at 5½d. Drawback 1½ per Yard. About Ten Thousand Doz. Negro Looking Glasses, at 3s. per Doz. And Five Thousand Quarters Horse-Beans, at a very reduced Price.

Enquire of the Slave Mongers

SPECIMENS of the WHOLE (except the Thumb Screws, the Sight of which it is thought would too deeply wound the Feelings of those not inclined to purchase) are NOW exhibiting on the Exchange.

(¹) Central Reference Library, Bristol. *Jefferies Collection*, vol. xiii, fol. 165.

Fortunately, it is not the task of the present writer to express an opinion on the amounts specified in this list, which is quoted merely as an illustration of the sort of goods which might be expected to be found in a Guineaman's cargo.

Before they sailed from their own ports captains received exact instructions from their principals as to the conduct of their trade. Owing to the character of the commerce and the length of the voyage a great deal was left to their discretion. Captain Caesar Lawson, who was appointed to the command of the *Enterprize*, of Liverpool, in 1803, was told to go to Bonny and barter his cargo for "prime Negroes, Ivory and Palm Oil."

> By Law this vessel is allowed to carry 400 Negroes, and we request that they may all be males if possible to get them, at any rate buy as few females as in your power, because we look to a Spanish market for the disposal of your cargo, where Females are a very tedious sale. In the choice of the Negroes be very particular, select those that are well formed and strong; and do not buy any above 24 years of age, as it may happen that you will have to go to Jamaica, where you know any exceeding that age would be liable to a Duty of £10 P head.

The owners also added directions as to the care of the slaves and crew.

> While the slaves are on board the Ship allow them every indulgence Consistent with your own Safety, and do not suffer any of your officers or crew to abuse or insult them in any respect . . . We request you will keep strict and regular discipline on board the ship; do not suffer Drunkenness among any of your officers or crew, for it is sure to be attended with some misfortune, such as Insurrection, Mutiny and Fire. Allow the ship's Company their regular portion of Provisions &c and take every care of such as may get sick. You must keep the ship very clean and see that no part of her Stores and Materials are embezzled, neglected or idly wasted.

As it was war-time, the owners of the *Enterprize* had taken out letters of marque against France and Holland, and Lawson was ordered to send any French or Dutch ships he might be so fortunate as to capture direct to Liverpool "under the care of an active Prize Master, and a sufficient number of men" and to put a copy of the commission aboard her.

> But do not molest any neutral ship, as it would involve us in an expensive Lawsuit and subject us to heavy Damages.[1]

The letter concluded with instructions to report to a certain firm in

---

[1] Williams, G., *A History of the Liverpool Privateers and Letters of Marque*, pp. 601-4.

Barbados to whom orders for the remainder of the voyage would be sent direct, and with arrangements for the payment of commission.

The first work to be undertaken on arrival at the Coast was the erection of barricades on the ship. Crow relates that on reaching Bonny in 1798

> one of our first occupations was the construction of a regular thatched house on the deck, for the accommodation and comfort of the slaves. This building extended from stem to stern, and was so contrived that the whole ship was thoroughly aired, while at the same time the blacks were secured from getting overboard. These temporary buildings would cost from £30 to £40, according to the size of the ship.[1]

During the last years of the trade ships from England were slaved on the Windward Coast, the Gold Coast, Whydah, New Calabar, Bonny, Old Calabar, the Cameroons and Angola.[2] Gold Coast and Whydah negroes found the quickest sale as they were hardier than the others. The Eboes, who were exported from Bonny, New Calabar and Old Calabar, were a superior people, much esteemed in the Sugar Islands for their fidelity and utility as domestic servants, though one writer complained that the men were inclined to be melancholy and to hang and drown themselves. They were not popular in Hava and Cuba, however, as they were not suitable for field work. The Quaws, who also came from Calabar, were, on the contrary, unpopular everywhere, for they were desperate and ferocious and foremost in any insurrection. Negroes from Angola and the Congo region were good, though not as hardy as those round Lagos.

When they reached the Coast the slave captains obtained their cargoes in various ways. If the supply of negroes was small they dealt with individual slavers who brought two or three slaves off to the ship in their canoes. Sometimes the ship's boat went ashore to trade in the native town or the Europeans went up the rivers in native canoes. The Royal African Company maintained forts where slaves were collected and made ready for exportation, and in places where the native ruler was powerful there was often a well-organised slave market. Native traders brought the negroes from the interior. These captives might be criminals who were sold by their own chiefs, or

[1] Crow, *op. cit.*, p. 66.
[2] See plate 18. The Coast from Benin Creek to the Cameroons.

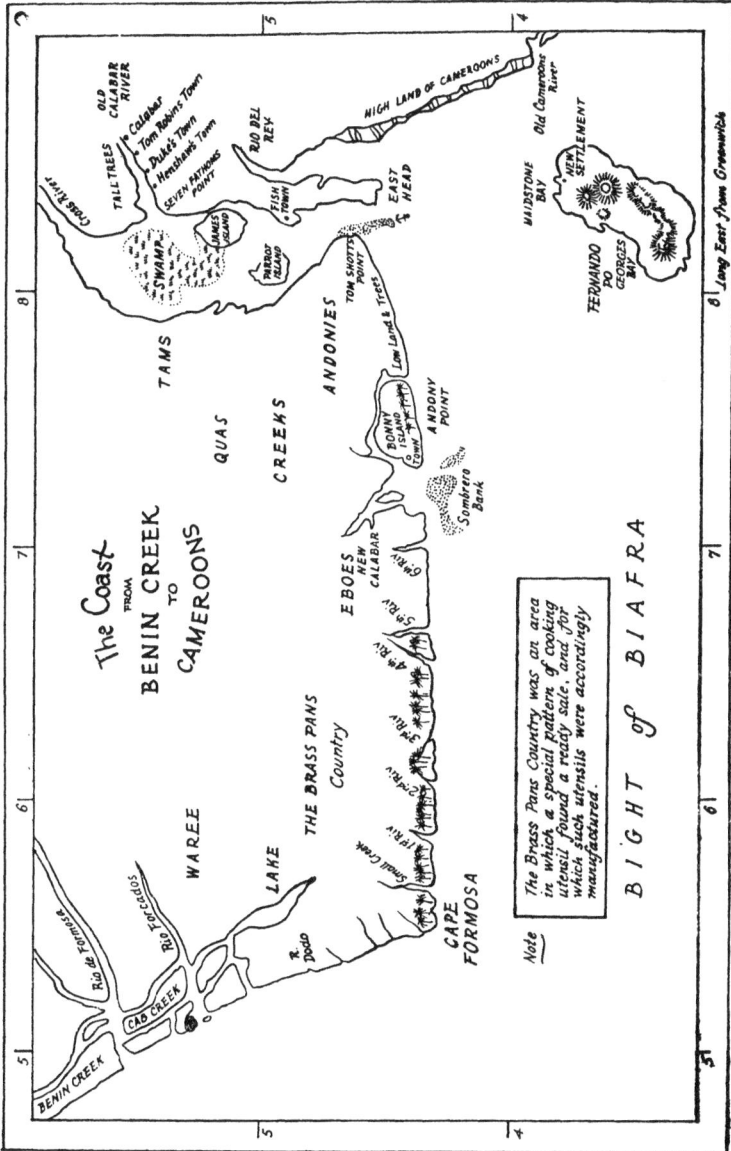

The Coast
from
BENIN CREEK
to
CAMEROONS

Note: The Brass Pans Country was an area in which a special pattern of cooking utensil found a ready sale, and for which such utensils were accordingly manufactured.

BIGHT of BIAFRA

PLATE 18.

265

collected by means of a "grand pillage." This was a raid executed by the soldiers of a local chief upon a neighbouring village. The soldiers set fire to the houses and seized the inhabitants as they fled. Other negroes might be prisoners of war, the war often having been brought about for the express purpose of supplying the trade.

A day was usually appointed for the buying of slaves and the negroes were herded into a large enclosed field, where the ships' surgeons examined them for physical disabilities and made them perform all manner of gymnastic feats. Boys and girls over ten years of age and young men and women were preferred, and the old and unfit were thrown aside to perish or become slaves to the Coast Africans. In the period under review varied prices were paid. Sometimes the bargain was effected by means of some recognised medium of exchange, such as "iron barrs," sometimes in goods on the basis of barter. Captain Crow gave the following list of goods for a slave at Bonny in 1801:

> One piece of Chintz, eighteen yards long;
> One piece of Baft, eighteen yards long;
> One piece of Chelloe, eighteen yards long;
> One piece of Bandanoc, seven handkerchiefs;
> One piece of Niccannee, fourteen yards long;
> One piece of Cushtae, fourteen yards long;
> One piece of Photae, fourteen yards long;
> Three pieces of Romalls, forty-five handkerchiefs;
> One large Brass Pan, two muskets;
> Twenty-five kegs of powder, one hundred flints;
> Two bags of shots, twenty knives;
> Four iron pots, four hats, four caps;
> Four cutlasses, six hundred bunches of beads, fourteen gallons of brandy.
>
> These articles cost about £25, so that the reader will see we did not procure negroes (as many have supposed) for nothing.[1]

In general, the price varied according to the season, the locality, the local political conditions, the health, sex, and age of the individual, and a hundred and one other things, but Crow refers to the

---

[1] Crow, *op. cit.*, p. 202.

payment of £25 per head as if it was quite usual to give that sum. His figures are probably perfectly reliable for specific transactions. At the same time, it should be remembered that he mentioned these sums in order to establish his contention that it would be absurd for slave captains to abuse slaves for whom so much had been paid. Throughout his book, he recurs to the point that good treatment was good business, since well-conditioned slaves would always command a good market price. Nevertheless, it is also true that during these two decades slaves were frequently purchased at figures very much under those mentioned by the redoubtable Liverpool captain. Once bought, the slave was branded on the breast and hustled aboard ship, for delay on the Coast involved additional costs and the possibility of insurrection.

When a ship was slaved the captain sailed with all speed for the colonial market. Though Parliament had intervened to soften the brutalities of the Middle Passage, a slave ship, under the most favourable conditions, must have been for the helpless negroes little better than a floating hell. Writing in 1807, in the year of the trade's abolition, Renny describes how men slaves were taken aboard in irons, every two of them fastened together with the right ankle of one locked by means of a small iron fetter to the left ankle of the other. If there was any sign of discontent or trouble, an additional chain was put upon their wrists. It was customary to send women and children aboard free, and later, after the African coast had faded out of sight and no danger was feared from the men, they also were liberated. Various descriptions have been given by the slave captains and others acquainted with the trade, of the conditions which pre-vailed on these vessels. Naturally, these writers vary widely in the pictures they draw, but it seems certain that in the later days the mortality rate fell considerably. Captain Crow was by no means the only commander who could report a voyage in which there had been no deaths among the negroes, all of whom had been brought to market in perfect health. This author gives a very pleasing, but probably highly-coloured, account of the living conditions aboard a slave ship. He describes their food as broth made from dried shrimps, yams, beans, rice, bread and coconuts, while the sick, he says, were given

> strong soups and middle messes, prepared from mutton, goats'-flesh, fowls &c. to which were added sago and lilipees, the whole mixed with port wine and sugar.([1])

All the slaves received a dram of brandy bitters before breakfast and they had three meals a day. Provision was made for them to wash themselves and even to take a daily bath, after which they were given palm oil, "their favourite cosmetic," and "chew-sticks" to clean their teeth. The day was spent in exercise and amusement, and the men had pipes and tobacco and the women beads.

Renny also speaks of the slaves spending their days on deck while their apartments were washed, scraped, fumigated and sprinkled with vinegar. According to him, they all had a bath each day before noon "than which nothing can be more agreeable, healthful or refreshing."([2]) This writer states that they were given as much as they could eat at each meal, together with an adequate amount of water, and if the weather happened to be cold or wet, drams also were served out to them. They were allowed pipes and tobacco whenever they wished, and between their meals, according to him, they were encouraged to dance to the music of their own native instruments. When this form of entertainment no longer attracted them, they played games of chance for which they were also supplied with implements of African make. He goes on to describe how the sick were taken care of, and concludes:

> Indeed, it is a fact, that at present, every scheme which can possibly be thought of for the preservation of the health, cleanliness, and cheerfulness of the Negroes is adopted during the voyage.([3])

Even this historian of Jamaica, however, is bound to admit that this charming condition of affairs was not always so, and there is evidence to prove that down to the very close of the trade, rapacious and cruel captains were not uncommon. Instances of wanton barbarity occurred which were a disgrace to humanity. A surgeon who made four voyages prior to giving evidence before the House of Commons

---

([1]) Crow, *op. cit.*, p. 146.   ([2]) Renny, *A History of Jamaica*, p. 173.

([3]) Ibid., p. 174.

committee in 1790 and 1791, said that after their meals the negroes were

> made *to jump in their irons*. This is called *dancing* by the slave-dealers. *In every ship* he has been desired *to flog such as would not jump*.
> . . . . on board his ship they sometimes *sung*, but not for their amusement. The captain ordered them to sing, and *they sang songs of sorrow*. The subject of these songs were their *wretched situation, and the idea of never returning home*.[1]

Though, thanks to parliamentary action, there was less overcrowding, the miserable slaves were compelled to endure six weeks or more of unmitigated misery.

The contention that even after Parliament had intervened the conditions were still appalling would appear to be borne out by the mutinies which sometimes occurred. Occasionally, however, such outbreaks, if not promoted, were certainly rendered possible by a momentary lack of vigilance on the part of the crew. In 1797, the *Thomas*, of Liverpool, was sailing from Loango to Barbados with 375 negroes aboard. While the crew were at breakfast on September 2nd two or three of the women slaves found that the armour-chest had been left open. They got into the after-hatchway, passed the arms to the men-slaves through the bulkhead, and about 200 of them ran up the fore-scuttles and put to death all the crew they met. Though the captain and a few men fought desperately, they were overpowered, and the slaves gained possession of the ship. Twelve of the crew escaped in the stern-boat, but only two reached Barbados. A few of the crew were kept to steer the ship back to Africa. Four of these escaped in the long-boat, and after six days and nights without food or water, reached Watling's Island, one of the Bahamas. Five of the crew remained on the *Thomas*. After six weeks of misery an American brig carrying rum came alongside, and the negroes overcame it and opened the rum casks. In the drunkenness which followed the remaining sailors of the *Thomas* recaptured the brig, set out for the nearest land and reached Long Island, Providence. The *Thomas*, with the surviving negroes, was later recaptured by H.M. frigate *Thames*, carried into Cape Nicola Mole and sold there.

Nevertheless, it was increasingly common before 1807 for ships

---

[1] *An Abstract of the Evidence . . .*, pp. 33-4.

to arrive in the plantations with healthy cargoes. Sir William Young, who visited the Sugar Islands in 1791 and 1792 speaks of newly-arrived slave ships he visited in Kingston harbour in which there were no sick aboard. The slaves had clean skins, their eyes were bright and, indeed, they bore every mark of health. In three voyages, one captain, who brought full cargoes with him each time, had lost only eight slaves and not one of his crew, and Captain Crow lost no slaves in three successive voyages. Young, describing a ship he saw in Barbados, said:

> The *Pilgrim* had not a scent that would offend, and was, indeed, sweeter than I should have supposed possible, in a crowd of any people of the same number, in any climate. A full half of either cargo consisted of children and generally as fine children as I ever saw from six to fourteen years.[1]

It can be said then, that before the trade was destroyed, conditions in the Middle Passage had been somewhat improved, but the journey from Africa to the plantations was still a melancholy business.

When the slaves arrived, sales were put through as quickly as possible. With luck, this could be done in one colonial port, but before a whole cargo was disposed of it was frequently necessary to peddle the poor creatures round from island to island, and in this way their miserable life aboard might be prolonged for weeks or even months. Advertisements of the sale of negroes constantly recur in the colonial papers of the time. Thus, on May 24th, 1803, the *Kingston Gazette* announced:

For Sale

On June 11th

302 Choice Young Eboe Negroes imported from Bonny in the ship *Otway*, Luke May, Master.

By Bogle, Jop & Co.,

while on another occasion, "fifty creole steers, most of them fit for the tongue," were offered for sale at Haddon, Penn. There are many difficulties in the way of stating an average price for which slaves were sold in the colonies. Their origin, condition, the state of the market, both in Africa and the New World, and the ability of the buyer and seller to bargain all affected the value of the cargo.

---

[1] Young, Sir W., *A Tour through the Several Islands . . . in the Years 1791 and 1792*, p. 269.

Bryan Edwards estimated that an able man in his prime brought in £50 to his captain about this time, while Pinckard gave the usual cost of a young, healthy man slave in the nineties as anything from £50 to £80, according to his age and strength. The 326 negroes which the *Louisa* landed at Jamaica about the turn of the century netted £19,315 13s. 6d., and other cargoes brought in much the same amount.

The voyage of the *Enterprize*, of Liverpool, 1803, may be taken as an unusually short and successful one. This vessel left the Mersey for Bonny on July 20th. During her passage to the Coast she detained a Spanish brig, recaptured the *John*, of Liverpool, and reached Bonny on September 23rd. She dropped anchor in Havana on January 9th, 1804, where the negroes she had aboard were sold. On March 28th she left Havana and reached Liverpool on April 26th, 1804. She delivered 412 negroes in Havana, although by law, as the captain's letter of instructions stated, the ship was allowed to carry only 400.([1]) This number was made up by 194 men, 32 men-boys, 66 boys, 42 women, 36 women-girls and 42 girls, and 19 died and one girl could not be sold as she suffered from fits. The equipping of the vessel cost the owners £8,148 18s. 8d., her cargo of trading goods was valued at £8,896 3s. 9½d., making a total of £17,045 2s. 5½d. The net profit on the round voyage, after selling the slaves, paying damages for detaining the Spanish brig and crediting salvage on the *John*, profit on teeth, logwood, sugar and so on was £24,430 8s. 11d.

Again, the *Fortune*, of Liverpool, which sailed from home on her first voyage on April 25th, 1805, arrived at the Congo on July 16th. There she was slaved and sailed from the Coast with a full cargo on November 10th for Nassau, which she reached on December 21st. She began her passage home on March 29th, 1806, and dropped anchor in Liverpool on May 2nd. For this voyage the original outlay, including the cost of the ship and her trading cargo, was £11,392 17s. 4d., and after all expenses had been paid, the sum of £13,270 0s. 1d. remained, which the owners considered to be a poor return on their investment. In this instance, many of the slaves were sold at credit and 100 still remained on the factor's hands on July

---

([1]) Vide supra, p. 19.

31st, 1806, and they were not all finally disposed of until September. This long delay in disposing of the cargo entailed much extra expense for rent of store, doctor's attendance, provisions, brandy, wine, tobacco, heads and offal, and oil for the slaves. It was, in fact, a disastrous voyage in many respects, for in addition to the great extra expenses and the small return, the third mate and six seamen died on the voyage, two sailors were drowned, the fifth, or trading mate and one sailor ran away and 34 seamen were impressed or voluntarily went aboard ships of the Royal Navy on the station. The result was that the captain found himself with men barely sufficient to work the ship home instead of the ample ship's company of 66 which had been in the vessel when she sailed from Liverpool.[1] To take but one more example, the *Louisa*, of Liverpool, sold 326 negroes in Jamaica for £19,315 13s. 6d., which, after all charges had been paid, represented a profit of £19,133 10s. 5d. on the original investment.[2]

In spite of the losses and risks which were characteristic of the slave trade, it was, none the less, a profitable one. Indeed, had it not been for the great rewards it yielded, it would never have found such stalwart defenders. At different periods it contributed materially to the prosperity of London, Bristol and several other ports, and in the last fifty years of its existence it caused a great and increasing stream of wealth to pour into Liverpool. No branch of commerce has ever received more unmeasured condemnation than the slave trade, both in its own time and since, and in the history of the world there can have been few trades that were more entwined with human misery, degradation and cruelty. But the guilt for these enormities must not be attributed to the slave traders only; it must be shouldered by the whole nation.

[1] Williams, op. cit., p. 604.   [2] Ibid., p. 605.

APPENDIX TO CHAPTER XI

Health and Sickness in the Slave Trade

by Professor J. A. NIXON, C.M.G., M.D., F.R.C.P.

of the University of Bristol

THE most important medical evidence concerning the Slave Trade is contained in the "Report of the Lords of the Committee of Council . . . concerning the Present State of Trade to Africa and particularly the Trade in Slaves" (1789). Many of the witnesses called were surgeons, but the most eminent medical witness was Dr. Spaarman, a native of Sweden and Professor of Physic and Inspector of the Museum of the Royal Academy at Stockholm. He had visited the Cape of Good Hope and had been on the West Coast (at Senegal and Goree) from August, 1787, until January, 1788. He had sailed from France and his voyage was undertaken partly for his health and partly (as he stated) from curiosity. He had not himself sailed in a slave ship but he said that they must suffer in the passage from what he had seen of the places where they lie. The French Captain had told him that they carry arsenic to get rid of the slaves in case they should run short of provisions and water. Spaarman did not think that the French ships were supplied with skilful surgeons.

Another witness, Mr. Wadstrom (whose name suggests a Scandinavian origin) gave somewhat similar evidence. The French Captains, he said, carry mercury and, if becalmed with provisions failing, they poison the slaves' food. The Captains considered it as an act of humanity because the negroes die without knowing what is going to happen to them, whereas the English Captains treat them with less ceremony and throw them overboard at once.

A French description of the trade, written by Saugnier and De Brisson in 1792, is of great interest, particularly in the instructions given to its agents on the Coast that slaves are to be well treated. "An agent should also be careful to prevent maladies of the negroes.

He should endeavour to discover the cause of their diseases and to apply the proper remedies; this is a most essential part of his study." "The care of slaves should not be left to ignorant surgeons nor to other understrappers. The surgeons," the agent is warned, "are for the most part young men without experience, a thing much to be lamented, for no voyage stands more in need of men of medical merit. It is true that surgeons of ability will not for a slight recompense undergo the dangers of an African voyage, but in order to induce such men to enter this service the trader should not begrudge to give a handsome recompense . . ." These authors give the *materia medica* of an agent and a list of five diseases that negroes are subject to: (1) Venereal Disease, (2) Ulcers, due to injury, (3) Scurvy, (4) The Itch, and (5) Worms.

It would seem that the British Slave Traders were less niggardly than the French for, despite the heavy mortality amongst officers and crews, medical men of high qualifications and talents sometimes volunteered for this service. Among them were to be numbered Thomas Trotter, Surgeon in the Royal Navy and one of the most distinguished names on the Admiralty Lists, who went a voyage in the African Trade as Surgeon of the *Brooke*, sailing from Liverpool in 1783; Robert Jackson, and Harrison, both, like Trotter, Doctors of Medicine; and two other Surgeons in the Royal Navy, Isaac Wilson and Ecroide Claxton. Others who showed their capabilities in various ways were Archibald Dalzell, who went out as Surgeon in 1763, and in 1770 was Governor on the Coast, and John Anderson, who first sailed as Surgeon and after a few voyages became master of a ship. The man whose name stands highest, however, for his work in the Slave Trade is Alexander Falconbridge, a Bristol Infirmary student, who sailed on four voyages with slaves, and published, according to Lettsom, "a sensible, well-written publication against the Slave Trade." He gave evidence at the bar of the House of Commons and contributed greatly to the trade's abolition.

Falconbridge's evidence was attacked vigorously before the Committee of Enquiry, but James Arnold, who had served for five years in the Navy as Surgeon and Surgeon's Mate, and had since made three voyages in Bristol Slavers (once under Falconbridge as his Surgeon's Mate), testified to the accuracy of his evidence. Arnold himself published a book on the Slave Trade in which he says that "the slaves are examined to see if they are physically fit, have healthy eyes, good teeth, stand over four feet high, and if men, are not ruptured; if females, have not 'fallen breasts.'" Many, he states, came on board wounded.

As shown elsewhere in this book,([1]) an Act of Parliament passed in 1789 required African ships to carry qualified surgeons; and these were under bond (39 Geo. III, c. 80) to keep a regular and true journal giving the greatest number of slaves carried at any time during the voyages and recording any deaths. It seems probable, however, that slave ships would have carried a surgeon in any case. One was needed to examine the slaves before they were purchased and branded. And if it was important to avoid paying more for the slaves than they were worth, it was at least as important to see that they survived the voyage. In general, it appears that, so long as provisions and water lasted, great care was taken of the slaves, and the Surgeon received a capitation payment of one shilling for every slave landed in good health. Falconbridge was so successful on one voyage that all his cargo of slaves were landed in good condition, and the owners made him a present of three slaves over and above his head money. The mortality among the slaves has often, perhaps, been exaggerated. Norris, one of the witnesses before the Committee, gave the following figures for some of his voyages:

				Number			Died
1. Crew	..	..	..	46	..	..	13
Slaves	..	..	..	380	..	..	100
2. Crew	..	..	..	40	..	..	4
Slaves	..	..	..	420	..	..	38 or 39

From figures such as these it is apparent that the crews might have —and in these instances had—a higher rate of mortality than the slaves. More significant still are the statistics available for the losses

([1]) See Chapter 6, page 137.

amongst crews of Liverpool and Bristol slave ships for the period September, 1784 to January, 1790:

Number of vessels	Original number of crews	Died	Brought home of original crews
350	12,263	2,643	5,760

The deaths, it will be seen, amounted to an appalling percentage—nearly 21.5 per cent. From 1750, similarly, the mortality among medical men described as "of Liverpool" was about ten times that among those of Manchester—the difference being partly due to the Slave Trade and partly to privateering. Anyone reading the evidence might conjecture that public animosity to the Slave Trade was as much aroused by the fate of our own seamen as by the traffic in negroes.

A part of the losses among the seamen can be attributed to the unhealthiness of the African Coast. As Captain Hills pointed out, merchant ships stayed longer in the river and went higher up it than a man-of-war would have occasion to do. He himself—the date of his voyage is uncertain—did not lose a man. But he attributed this to the precaution he took of making the men he sent on shore take "the bark" (i.e., Cinchona) before they went, and on their return, and he himself always saw them take it. It is obvious that other captains were less careful. And the surgeon, it must be remembered, had been engaged to look after the slaves and had no responsibility for the officers or crew. The evidence of other witnesses shows a horrible indifference on the part of the owners to the health of their seamen. As James Arnold remarks on this subject, "of all the treatment they received none was more shocking than when sick."

Apart, however, from disease, there is evidence to show that the seamen were often brutally treated by their officers. In the figures given above for the Liverpool and Bristol Slavers, it will be noted that, of the men who sailed, a large proportion died—but an even larger number, nearly 4,000, failed to return home. What happened was that the seamen, being "cruelly treated, whipped and beaten with very little cause, often without any" (Norris), deserted in the West Indies without receiving their wages. A new crew being shipped, the only wages the owners had to pay was for the homeward run from the West Indies to England. One seaman gave evidence that he was cruelly beaten both by the captain and the surgeon, that he was half-starved and that the surgeon neglected the sick seamen, alleging that he was only paid for attending the slaves. A rare pamphlet entitled *The Unfortunate Shipwright or Cruel Captain* contains similar accusations. The pamphlet was written by Robert Barker, late carpenter on board the *Thetis*, snow, of Bristol, in a voyage to the coast of Guinea and thence to Antigua. Barker says he was rendered blind "through the violent and wilful actions of Captain Robert Wabshutt and Doctor John Roberts, both of the City of Bristol." This was an instance, apparently, of the surgeon taking command of the vessel after the captain had died. This affair was hushed up at the time but it serves, with a great deal of similar evidence, to show that it was not only the slaves who suffered.

CHAPTER XII

The Post Office Packets

by ARTHUR C. WARDLE, M.I.EX., F.S.F.

Author of "Benjamin Bowring and His Descendants," and other works

IN its early days, the sea-carriage of mails was operated like other government services, under the "farming" system. This, together with the fact that the packets and their crews were mainly concentrated at Falmouth and a few other ports, rendered improvements both slow and difficult, but the outbreak of the French war coincided with attempts to bring about reform. Falmouth was perhaps the most important packet station, mainly because of its position, clear of the Channel and its headwinds. At that time there were about thirty of the regular packets stationed there,[1] of from 150 to 200 tons each, with other vessels hired when necessary. Manned by crews of up to 60 men, the ships were armed with as many as 18 guns. Each vessel was hired by the Post Office directly from or through the commander or master, and over these officers was appointed a Post Office agent, domiciled at Falmouth. He was independent of the jurisdiction of the local postmaster, and his duties were mainly concerned with the supervision of the foreign mails and the personnel of the packet-ships. He thus constituted the only link between the Post-Masters General and their Falmouth Packets. The hiring of craft was usually by contract for a period of seven years, with six months' notice of termination, and the post office carried the liability for loss of the vessels by act of war or other causes. Although no post office

---

[1] There were thirty-seven in 1808. They represented the bulk of the Packets (£60,444, for example, out of a total expenditure of £77,599 in 1796). The Packets were stationed, apparently, as follows:

    (*a*) *Falmouth*. West Indies, America, Lisbon, Corunna, and (after 1806) Gibraltar and Malta.

    (*b*) *Harwich* or *Yarmouth*. Holland, Hamburg and the Baltic.

    (*c*) *Dover*. Closed during the war. Packets transferred to Harwich.

    (*d*) *Weymouth* and *Southampton*. Channel Islands.

    (*e*) *Holyhead* and *Milford*. To Ireland.

servant was permitted to have any financial interest in the sailing packets, the conditions of service gave ample scope for the acceptance of bribes and for fraudulent practices. One flagrant defect in the system was the almost sinecure nature of the duties of the packet-commander himself. If he could satisfy the agent at Falmouth that he had good reasons (health or otherwise) for staying ashore, he might send his ship to sea without his presence and without a competent navigator. In an official minute of 1793 it was stated: "there are now twelve packets at sea; and no less than ten captains of them ashore." Five years later, while the country was engaged in grim warfare, one of the Post-Masters General was compelled to admit that one captain had been absent from his ship for many years, assigning no other cause than the death of his mother in 1792.

Another abuse of the service was the freighting of merchandise in the packet ships. Each vessel was built and hired expressly for speed and not required to carry any cargo other than the mails or specie. Each, however, was equipped with a spacious hold, obviously tempting to seamen of a trading nation. Each member of the ship's company, from the master downwards, really became a trader, to a greater or lesser extent, and openly stowed his ventures on board in the shape of merchandise to be exchanged abroad for goods which could command high prices and ready sales in Britain. The postal authorities seem to have winked at this practice for many years, and even went so far as to instruct their packet agents to ensure that cargo was not so heavy or so badly stowed as to prevent trim sailing or to interfere with the handling of the ship—with the result that the packets sailed with every available bit of cargo space filled, all the property of the master and his crew. Each man brought goods on board ranging from £500 to £5,000 in value, most of these wares being advanced on credit to the packet men by reputable London firms, some of which had their own appointed agents at the packet stations for this purpose.

These private ventures were covered by bona-fide insurances, and thus the packet-seaman was enabled to drive a lucrative trade, rendered all the more profitable by a maximum of smuggling. In peace-time, this ability to trade probably made for swifter ocean passages, as the participants would naturally work hard to speed their transactions and hasten to deliver the ship safe and sound at Falmouth. What proved an incentive for safe and rapid voyages in peace-time, however, became a menace during the war years. The risk of capture by enemy privateers or cruisers was not too great for these sea-traders who, being relatively well armed, were always ready to stand and fight to preserve their valuable cargoes, despite specific orders from the post office authorities instructing them, upon sighting enemy vessels and being pressed, to sink their mails if they could not show a clean pair of heels by out-sailing the enemy. There was also the incentive to make unprovoked attacks on smaller vessels, or ships not so well-armed, in the hope of plunder or prize-money, a practice which became so frequent that critics of the packet service at one time suggested total disarmament of the postal vessels.

The armament allowance granted by the post office was consequently reduced—a measure which certainly led to some change of tactics at sea. Merchants, whose sole interest in the service was the safe-carriage of mails, then began to notice that packet-ship after packet-ship was captured by enemy privateers, particularly while on the *homeward* run. Investigation pointed to the fact that such losses resulted in handsome profit to commanders and crews, since both were cautious enough to have their homeward trading ventures (which in some cases also included the profit on the outward transaction) covered by insurances. Alternatively, some of these seamen-venturers, after selling their wares abroad, would remit the proceeds home by mercantile drafts or letters of credit. They thus became indifferent to capture on the homeward voyage, and even claimed from the insurance syndicates for the loss of their goods purchased abroad. From this, it will be seen that the mails became a secondary consideration, and in several instances were consigned to the bottom of the sea almost when sighting the enemy.

Even those commanders who were strong enough to be above these temptations found themselves helpless, and many a packet-captain—when attacked—would have fought his ship with some reasonable chance of success had not his crew refused to work ship. There is an instance of one packet which was chased by the enemy during daylight until dusk, when she struck her flag, although the enemy ship was a mile away and had not fired a shot, and, in case the enemy had not seen the colours hauled down, the packet-master politely sent off a boat to inform the privateer that he had surrendered. It was later found that eight of the packet seamen who had refused to work ship had previously received value for insured goods in former captures; while the surgeon, who had urged the captain to strike colours, had been captured three times before and had claimed and received payment for goods insured on each occasion. The ship's steward also confessed to having taken out merchandise and failed to sell it abroad, had lost it by capture on a homeward run and was paid £250. Three of the deck hands had been captured for the fourth time, one of them receiving £200 on his last "loss."

At the outbreak of war, not one of the packets had received the armament requisite for prosecuting the service under war conditions, and within three weeks there was news that the Dover packet *Despatch*, while lying off Ostend, had been challenged by a French privateer, and her commander, having no means of resisting, was compelled to surrender and was carried into Dunkirk. This experience promptly resulted in arming the vessels. Those on the Falmouth and Harwich stations, being vessels of 50 to 80 tons, were given four 2-pounder guns. A few guns were allotted to the Holyhead ships, and eventually even the Milford packets were armed.

Under post office reform of the packet system, the regulations now demanded that the Falmouth packets should be of fixed design, about 180 tons each, to carry about 28 men and boys.[1] The armament laid down was four 4-pounders, two 6-pounders for use as chasers, and a quantity of small arms. This was designed to put them in a position to meet only the smallest of enemy ships. At the same time instructions were issued to packet-masters that they should run whenever possible, failing which they were to fight their ships and, when they could no longer fight, the mails were to be sunk with certainty before colours were struck. This ruling gradually put an end to the privateering ventures of the packet-men.

Despite this reform, the packet losses during the war were such as to arouse criticism and alarm. In March, 1798, out of 20 vessels on the Falmouth station, there was not one available in port to carry the Jamaica and Leeward Islands mails—the second instance of this

---

[1] See plate 19 for a typical packet vessel.

within a twelvemonth. The West Indian merchants in London and elsewhere consequently complained vigorously to the Postmaster-General, and an armed cutter was lent by the Admiralty to take out the mails. Between 1793 and 1798, 19 packet ships of the Falmouth station were captured by enemy vessels and had to be replaced by the post office at a cost of £50,000. Merchants now demanded that armaments should be increased, but the postmasters-general replied that they could do no more, and that their policy was to build the packets so that they could out-sail the enemy and not to equip them so as to engage him. The merchants thereupon submitted a memorial expressing some misgiving and pointing to the dilatory passages, the average voyage having been 45 days from Falmouth to Jamaica, and 52 days from Jamaica to Falmouth—long voyages for vessels specially designed for speed. The memorialists added that "in the mode of loading or navigating the packets some abuses exist sufficient to counteract the advantages of their construction."

The Falmouth packets at this period were usually three-masted vessels of excellent model, and their crews were picked young seamen. The crews being immune from the attentions of the press-gang, the packet service became popular, exclusive, and difficult to enter. Irrespective of the perquisites deriving from trade and from smuggling, the pay of the packet-men had always been good and certain, as compared with that of other seamen. Nevertheless, as in the case of most sheltered industries, much wants more, and the packet seamen saw fit, in 1810 and in 1814, to go on strike for increases in pay. The postal authorities dealt with the situation by transferring the Falmouth packets to Portsmouth for several months, while the second strike was brought to an end by manning the Falmouth packets with men from other ports.

Such is the unsatisfactory side of the picture, as gained from contemporary periodicals and other documents, and at first glance it would seem that the value of mail packets to the nation, particularly when at war on the high seas, was tremendously diminished by abuse and privilege. The war records also reveal, however, the many exploits of individual commanders and their crews which stand out in admirable relief against the stories of irregularities, smuggling and corruption.

The packet routes extended over practically all the navigated seas of those days, and the high importance of these extensive mail services, in war-time, cannot be too greatly emphasised. Their value as news-carriers was considerable. The packet-commanders had instructions to note in their logs and journals the news of all public and other happenings at home and abroad. Thus, officials and traders in distant parts of the empire were kept posted as to events in Britain; while London and the leading provincial towns received a constant and varied supply of commercial, social, and political news from all parts of the world, except the East, which was served by the East India Company's ships. This accumulated news was despatched from Falmouth and Harwich ahead of the mails, and lay at the London post office for inspection by merchants and newspaper representatives. Colonial governors and administrators were largely dependent upon the post office packets as the speediest conveyances for carrying important despatches and news, often preferring this mode of transit to sending by the safer, though slower man-of-war or merchant ship. Naval commanders on stations abroad also availed themselves of the service in rendering their home despatches. The packet-commanders were also in a position, from their own observation and experience, to report movements of enemy squadrons and units, their tonnages, armament and rating. They proved admirable informers for the British naval commanders, and their role during the Continental blockade was that of maintaining by written word, signal and confidential report the affinity which existed between the mercantile communities of the belligerent and neutral countries.

A most important sinew of war is finance and, as in our own day, the safe remittance of specie, credit and valuables was essential to the success of a campaign. On some occasions, men-of-war were utilised for this purpose, but many thousands of pounds' worth of gold and silver found their way to Europe by the packet ships, as revealed by contemporary records. For instance, the *Express*, Captain John Quick, sailed from Rio de Janeiro on 23rd March, 1813, carrying mails and despatches, together with specie amounting to £20,000. Upon nearing Cape Verde islands, she encountered the *Anaconda*, an American privateer, armed with 16 long 9-pounders and 120 men. After a long pursuit, the packet was brought to action. Then followed an hour's cannonading, during which "the packet's sails were cut in pieces fore and aft, the main and foremast very badly wounded, the main topmast shot away, four of the starboard guns dismounted, several shot between wind and water, three and a half feet of water in the hold, and the packet actually sinking." According to the *Liverpool Mercury* of June 4th, 1813, however, the ship herself was saved. The Americans plundered her and took the £20,000 in gold and then handed the packet over to her crew on parole, and she was brought into Falmouth on 19th May; oddly enough, with the mails intact.

Another adventure while carrying bullion happened to the packet *Francis Freeling*, which sailed from Lisbon on 1st May, 1814, and two days later sighted an American privateer schooner. The packet stood under easy sail, and the schooner soon brought her to action. After nearly two hours' fighting, broadside for broadside, the American sheered off to repair damage, but again attacked the packet from several different angles. After another hour of stiff fighting, the privateer was again beaten off, but made a third and similarly unsuccessful attack before turning her attention to an approaching merchant brig. The *Francis Freeling* then made sail and soon lost sight of the American, which is said to have mounted 16 guns and to have been manned by a very large crew. The packet ship, which had on board 130,000 dollars in specie, in addition to valuable mails and despatches, reached Falmouth within seven days of leaving Lisbon, and her passengers presented the master, Captain Bell, with a handsome sword and gave £100 for division among the crew, for their devotion to duty.

The packet mails contained a large proportion of documents such as drafts and letters of credit, without which British merchants might never have been able to conduct their trade and exchange, so indispensable to an island nation at war. It is to be noted that parallel with the packet service, a system of ordinary ship-letter system was introduced by the post office authorities. This was used by the merchants to a large extent, but the fleetness of the packet ships gave them superiority as the real arteries for the flow of commercial intelligence, finance, and news.

Mention has been made of the passengers carried by the post office packets, and an indication of the cost of such travel can be gained from a quotation of a few of the prevailing fares. For instance, the passage-money to Gibraltar was 35 guineas, to Malta 55 guineas, and to Jamaica 54 guineas—large sums for those days. Passengers consisted mainly of army officers, government officials, and merchants and their families. Usually, their behaviour when under fire was exemplary. On 15th June, 1813, the packet *Manchester*, under command of Captain Elphinstone, sailed from Falmouth with mails for Halifax. When ten days out, she encountered the American privateer *York Town*, a cut-down East Indiaman of 500 tons, with a bulwark of 14 inches solid timber, six feet high. She was commanded by a Captain Ricker, and mounted sixteen 12 and 9-pounders, and had a complement of 116 men. The *Manchester* carried ten 6 and 9-pounder guns and she was of 180 tons burden. After a stern chase of 38 hours, during which she maintained a running fight with the privateer, the *Manchester* was brought to a close engagement lasting over an hour, when Elphinstone and his crew behaved with great gallantry. They were ably assisted by their three male passengers, Captain Sabida, of the Royal Artillery; Mr. George Bell, merchant; and a Mr. Peter Snell. The last-named, and two seamen were wounded. With only two pounds of powder left, and the ship's sails, masts and rigging cut to pieces, Captain Elphinstone was compelled to throw the mails overboard and strike his colours.

A similar fate befell the *Princess Elizabeth*, packet, while on voyage from Malta to Falmouth. She was captured by the American privateer *Harp*, 110 men, 10 guns, after an hour's engagement, her mails being sunk before the ship struck. On this occasion, the Americans gave the packet ship up to her passengers, who brought her safely into Falmouth. Another action in which passengers participated was that of the West Indian packet *Portland*, Captain Taylor, which was lying becalmed off the island of Guadeloupe on 17th October, 1797, when a French privateer, *Temeraire*, bore down upon her. With the aid of a slight breeze the *Portland* was able to get off the land and, for a time, eluded the enemy, but he followed all night and at daybreak began to overtake the packet ship. Captain Taylor fired the first shot, which was immediately returned, and the privateer soon grappled the *Portland* and boarded her on the lee quarter. Lashing the jib-stay,

Taylor called upon his passengers and crew to open fire with their small arms. A fierce engagement ensued, favourable to the *Portland*, but a treacherous shot after the privateer had struck his colours carried off the master of the packet. Of the 68 men on board the privateer, about 40 were killed and wounded. The *Portland's* passengers comprised four British army captains, a surgeon from Antigua, and five West Indian merchants, all of whom took part in the fight and contributed in good measure.

As the packets always sailed singly, their various services to the government did not cost the country a penny for convoy escort. Operation of the service required, however, considerable organizing ability and skill. Irrespective of weather conditions, the packets were compelled to sail as soon as the mails were on board, and in such a service only a well-found ship could survive. The outfitting and maintenance of these craft therefore required all the skill of the best type of ship's husbandry, a task rendered the more onerous by the variety of the post office sea services. The chief packet stations during the wars were Falmouth, Harwich, London, Holyhead, and Milford, and from these scattered ports regular and frequent services were operated to Ireland, the Continent, Lisbon, Gibraltar, the West Indies, Brazil and Halifax; and in 1806, in deference to the wishes of the Mediterranean merchants, the Falmouth-Gibraltar service was extended to Malta—the first vessel being the *Cornwallis*, whose commander, Captain Anthony, however, had to run the gauntlet of Spanish gun-boats and was forced to ask Admiral Collingwood for convoy protection while passing through the Straits.

For the cost to the public of these services, let us take a typical year of the war period. The following were the rates of postage in 1813 for letters to:

The West India Islands and North America	2s. 3d.
Gibraltar, and the Squadron off Cadiz ..	2s. 11d.
Malta, Sicily and Mediterranean ..	3s. 3d.
Minorca	3s. 3d.
Brazils	3s. 7d.
Buenos Aires	3s. 7d.
Rio Janeiro	3s. 7d.
Madeira	2s. 8d.
Portugal	2s. 7d.
Spain	2s. 2d.

The Jamaica, Bahamas, and American packets were despatched monthly; Gibraltar, Malta and Mediterranean during the third week each month; Lisbon weekly; Cadiz once a fortnight; Gottenburgh twice a week; Spain and Portugal weekly; and the Brazils and Madeira packets sailed monthly.

The return of the packets was calculated as: to Jamaica and back, 17 weeks; America, 15 weeks; Leeward Islands, 13 weeks; Malta, 14 weeks; Brazils, 18 weeks; and Lisbon, four weeks. From November to February, the American packet landed a mail at Bermuda on each outward voyage, while the Brazilian packet, during the winter months, landed mails at Bahia on her outward voyage to Rio.

Postal costs thus constituted a heavy charge upon merchandise, and it is little wonder that the merchants became critical on occasion of the services provided. That they nevertheless used the packet system for most of their corresponding and remitting is revealed amply in contemporary records, while the general utility of the commercial intelligence transmitted by the packet ships may be gained from the various notices issued by the postmasters, of which the following (1813) is typical: "The Clerks in Waiting at the General Post Office, London, publish a Daily and Weekly Statement of the Sailings and Arrivals of the Packets; also a General Shipping and Commercial List, with necessary Information for the Use of the Mercantile World in their Foreign Correspondence."

Each of the war years saw an improvement and a tightening-up of the packet services, but the exigencies of war and an expanding trade gradually brought about a realisation that this method of carrying the mails was inadequate. For several years, another form of ship-mail service had been practised unofficially. The coffee-houses were in constant use as depositories for posting overseas letters. At these establishments, letters were picked up and delivered to ordinary merchant ships, the masters of which were responsible for handing them to a distributing agent at the port of destination. Not all ship-masters, of course, were diligent in the conveyance of these unofficial mail-bags and there were instances of the bags being dumped into the sea to avoid the bother of delivery. This clandestine mail-service was known to the post office authorities, and in 1799 they made an attempt to put the system upon a recognised and organised basis by

establishing the Ship-Letter Office. Letters posted at such agencies as
inns and coffee-houses were to be collected by the Post Office,
franked with an official stamp, sorted, and delivered to the various
merchant ships at time of sailing. This scheme, later improved,
rendered commercial intercourse more frequent and more widespread; but even such a concession was met by continuous complaints
from the mercantile community, of the nature expressed in the
following excerpt from the *Liverpool Mercury* of 23rd December,
1814:

> THE NEW SHIP LETTER ACT. It appears there is a new reading of this
> Act, for although in conformity with a *printed Notice circulated from the Post
> Office, all* Invoices have been exempt from Postage when forwarded by the
> same vessel as the goods; it has been ordered, within a day or two, that
> Invoices as well as Letters in general, must hereafter be stamped at the Post
> Office, and the Postage paid—We apprehend the Manufacturers will be of
> opinion that the Export Duty which they pay on the *value* of their goods,
> ought to be considered as a sufficient contribution to the Government,
> without the new Tax per *ounce* on the weight of the Invoice.

The 1814 Act, however, proved a failure, since it did not oblige
merchantmen to carry letters, nor did it oblige the East India Company's packet ships to convey or deliver them. A further Act, at the
close of the war, gave the Post Office power to establish a line of
packets to India and the Cape or to utilise ships of war for that
purpose, and it was also made compulsory for ordinary merchant
ships to carry mails whenever required by the Post Office. The official
responsible for this extension of the overseas mail services was
Francis Freeling, who served as Secretary of the Post Office from
1798 to 1836.

The tonnages of the packets varied according to the route on which
they were employed. The Harwich vessels, as we have seen, ranged
from 50 to 80 tons, but the Falmouth packets, which covered a wide
range of long-distance runs, were usually from 150 to 300 tons. All
were fast sailers, of a variety of rigs, i.e., ship, barque, brig and
brigantine, most of them built in the local yards of the south-coast
ports, although some were turned out from shipbuilding yards as far
north as the Mersey. Their construction was of a high standard, and
it is on record that several took as long as two years to build. The

soundness of their construction is confirmed by their length of commissioned service, and it may be noticed that Lloyd's register of 1835 shews such vessels as the *Redpole,* brig, 236 tons, built 1812; the *Nautilus,* brig, 235 tons, built 1814; and *Nightingale,* brig, 208 tons, built 1814, still in postal service.

They were manned, according to size, by crews of 18 to 40 in number—all well-trained seamen, and a proportionate number of boys, attracted to the service by the best of pay and emoluments. In addition to being excellent seamen, these packet-men proved very proficient gunners and experts in the use of small arms, and in the closing stages of the Napoleonic wars came fully up to British naval standards. In these later years on the high seas they had been compelled to meet the hardy American privateersmen, nurtured on the rigorous eastern Atlantic seaboard and accustomed to the handling of fast-moving sailing craft—but the packetmen proved their equal, as is shown in many stories dating from this period.

Armament of the packet-ships appears also to have varied according to tonnage. As we have already noted, the Falmouth packets mounted four 4-pounder guns and two 6-pounders as chasers; but Harwich packets carried only four 4-pounders; and the small Dover vessels were restricted to 2 or 3-pounder guns. The Irish packets were also armed, but there is no record of them being engaged in any close action. All were an attractive target for attack from boats and boarding parties, and in consequence each packet was furnished with ample supplies of small arms. At a later stage in the war, the Falmouth vessels had to be armed to better advantage. The *Townshend,* in 1812, mounted eight 9-pounders and one long 9-pounder—the latter being a brass piece of the type familiarly known as "Post Office guns." A Liverpool-built packet, the *Lady Frances,* 226 tons, fitting out at that port in 1800, carried fourteen 12 and 16-pounder guns, and was manned by 35 seamen. There were occasional shortages of ordnance, and in several instances the packets were forced to sail without their stern-chasers—a deficiency which proved fatal when they were brought to action.

As most of the Falmouth vessels were employed on the West Indian and South American voyage and thus came well within the range of American, French and Spanish privateers and cruisers, the

T

heaviest war losses were sustained by this branch of the packet service. These losses sometimes interfered with the flow of commercial correspondence and the remittance of funds, credit and bullion, as may be gathered from the collective complaints and petitions of the West India merchants. Thanks, on the other hand, to the good construction of most packet vessels and the excellent seamanship of their crews, normal marine losses were negligible in relation to the large number of vessels employed and the character of the voyages undertaken. Although many of the contemporary complaints were justified, it is evident that, generally speaking, the packets did good service. Despite the raging of the sea and the malice of the enemy, whenever the achievement was humanly possible, they delivered the mails.

Glossary

BACKING AND FILLING. An operation performed in narrow waters, when the ship has the tide in her favour and the wind against her.

BARQUE. A three-masted, square-rigged vessel, differing from the ship mainly in having no square mizzen topsail.

BARQUENTINE. The smallest type of three-masted vessel, square-rigged on the foremast, with square main-topsail, but with fore-and-aft mainsail and mizzen, the latter set on a short mast without a topsail.

BEND OR BENT (as used of a sail). To bend is to fasten. Bending a sail is fastening it to its yard or stay. Bending a cable was to tie it to the ring of its anchor.

BILL OF LADING. A document given by the Master of a vessel, acknowledging the receipt of certain goods on board, whereby he contracts to deliver the same in good order and condition at the port of consignment. One copy goes to the merchant to whom the goods are consigned, one remains with the exporter of the goods, and the third is retained by the Master.

BLOCK. The name given to a pulley or system of pulleys, mounted in a shell or frame and designed to increase the power exerted by the rope running through it. A block consists of the shell or outside part, the sheave (or wheel) or sheaves, the pin (axle) on which the sheaves turn, and the strap (of iron or rope) by which the block is made fast. Various blocks are shown in Plate 8.

BRAILS. The ropes made fast to the aftermost leech of the mizzen sail, and used for trussing it up quickly when not wanted. They were also used with the main-topsail and mizzen-staysail.

BRIG. A two-masted vessel of a typical North Sea rig, square-rigged but with a fore-and-aft mainsail. See Plate 9, figure 2, and compare with the definition of "Snow," as illustrated in figure 1.

BUMPKIN. A short boom, usually projecting from the bow of a vessel so as to extend the clew of the foresail to windward.

CAREENING. The process of heaving a vessel over on her side; more particularly, in the days of wooden ships, the process by which a vessel was beached and heaved over to enable the sea-weed and barnacles to be removed, by burning, from the ship's bottom or from the wooden sheathing by which it was protected. The introduction of copper sheathing largely did away with the necessity of careening, except for actual repairs undertaken in a place where no dry dock was available.

CARRICK BEND. A special kind of knot.

CARTEL. An agreement between two countries for the exchange of prisoners-of-war. A Cartel Ship was commissioned to convey and fetch the prisoners, or to carry any request or proposal as between two countries at war. A Cartel had to be unarmed, save for one signal gun, and unladen.

CHARTER PARTY. A contract between the freighter and the shipowner (or ship-master) containing the terms on which the ship is hired to freight. In it the shipowner covenants to deliver the goods, dangers of the sea excepted, at a place named, ensuring that the ship is properly equipped and manned. The merchant covenants to pay for this the sum as agreed.

CHART. A sea map showing coastlines, sandbanks, reefs and depths of water. See the plan of the Port of Boston (Plate 15) showing the anchorage and the leading marks for entering it.

CLEW. The two lower corners of a square sail. With a fore-and-aft sail or staysail, only the aftermost corner is called the clew. The other lower corner is the tack.

CLIPPER. The 19th century name for a merchant sailing ship designed to make fast passages on the transoceanic routes.

CLUB-HAULING. A method of tacking, by letting go the lee anchor as soon as the wind is out of the sails, which brings her head to wind, and as soon as she pays off, the cable is cut and the sails trimmed. It was only used in extreme emergency, usually on a lee-shore.

CRIMP. A landsman who kept a seamen's boarding house and who made it his business to provide seamen for ships in need of hands. Sailors were often deceived by crimps, being frequently taken off to ships while drunk or even knocked unconscious. Crimps were paid for their services at a recognised rate of so much a head.

CRINGLE. A small hole or loop in the bolt-rope of a sail; the bolt-rope being the rope by which the edges of sails were strengthened.

CUTTER. A small vessel of a characteristic English rig, as shown in Plate 9, figure 9, setting mainsail, square topsail, foresail and jib.

DEADEYE. A flat wooden block without a sheave, pierced with three holes and used in the standing rigging. One of these was made fast to the end of each shroud and another to the corresponding chain fixed to the ship's side. A lanyard was passed alternately through the upper and lower deadeyes until it became six-fold. Then it was drawn tight, tautening or "setting-up" the shroud. The shrouds were the ropes by which the masts were held laterally in position, and needed constant attention as the hemp swelled or shrunk. The system is clearly shown in Plate 11.

DOUBLE WALL DOUBLE-CROWNED AS A STOPPER. Stoppers were short pieces of rope, knotted at one or both ends. A wall-knot was a knot raised at the end of a rope by untwisting the strands and interweaving them amongst each other. Crowning was the finishing touch given to the work of art so produced.

FLUSH DECK. A vessel was flush-decked when forecastle and quarter-deck were joined together not by gangways and gratings but by a solid and continuous upper deck, strong enough to carry the longboat and to mount cannon. Such a ship, with raised poop but flush upper deck, is shown in Plate 12.

FLYING KITES. Light sails set "flying," i.e., without lifts or clews being lashed.

GAFF. The spar by which the head of a fore-and-aft sail (other than a staysail) is extended, e.g., the mizzen in a ship, the mainsail in a cutter.

GALLERIES (stern and quarter). Eighteenth century ships usually had quarter galleries, which were covered balconies built on either side of the great cabin and poop and communicating, especially in two-decked men-of-war, with a stern-walk. Quarter galleries were the officers' and passengers' latrines and often contained, in addition, a flight of steps. They can be seen in Plates 12 and 13. A stern-gallery is shown, in section, in Plate 1.

GANTLINE. A rope rove through a single block aloft, making a whip purchase; commonly used to assist in rigging the ship.

HALLIARDS. The ropes or tackles used to hoist or lower any sail, whether upon a mast or stay.

HAWSE HOLES. Holes cut through the bows of a ship, on either side of the stem, through which the cables passed when dropping or heaving anchor. They were plugged with oakum and wooden shutters when the ship was at sea, to exclude the sea. As this precaution seldom succeeded, the manger, a stout barricade built athwartships abaft the hawse holes, prevented the water penetrating any further aft.

HERMAPHRODITE. A two-masted vessel, with square topsails and topgallants, and fore-and-aft mainsail and foresail; a half-way stage between the Brig and the Schooner, and the American equivalent of what the English called a Brigantine.

HOY. A small vessel, with one mast and several varieties of rig, into which sea-going ships would discharge their cargo (especially before the docks were built) in the Thames. A Hoy is shown in Plate 9, figure 10, and several appear in Plate 2. Hoys were supplanted by Sailing Barges (Plate 9, figure 11), the ancestors of the Thames Barge now in use.

HULK. A vessel no longer sea-going, moored in harbour, usually without masts, and used as a floating barrack, prison or store-house. One is shown in Plate 10. A sheer-hulk was such a vessel specially equipped for hoisting lower masts into ships brought alongside for the purpose.

JACK-STAYS. Ropes stretched taut along a yard, to which the head of a sail could be bent.

JIBBOOM. A continuation of the bowsprit, to which it formed a kind of topmast and to which it was attached by boom-irons. Its appearance and purpose can be seen in Plate 17.

JIB-O'-JIB. The jib was a triangular headsail. The flying jib was set outside it, and the jib-o'-jibs outside that again.

KECKLING. Keckling was the art of winding old rope about a cable so as to preserve it from friction when rubbing against the bows or fore-foot. This might be done with iron chains to protect it from rocks, ice or shot.

KETCH. A two-masted vessel with a mainmast and mizzen. The rig is shown in Plate 9, figure 8. Bomb-vessels in the Navy were so rigged, with a large space forward of the mainmast from which mortars could fire without endangering the rigging.

KITES (see Flying Kites).

LATEEN MIZZEN YARD. The yard by which the old lateen mizzen had been extended, and which crossed the mast almost as shown in the Bilander illustrated in Plate 9, figure 7. By our period the lateen yard had been mostly superseded by the gaff.

LEECH. The perpendicular edges of a square sail, the fore- and after-edges of a triangular sail.

LEAD. The deep-sea lead was a sinker with a tallow-filled hollow at the base, suspended by a line of measured length, marked off in fathoms. It was whirled round and flung towards the bows of a moving ship so as to be as nearly as possible vertically below the ship when the bottom of the sea was reached. Hauled in again, the lead would show not only the depth of water but—from what adhered to the tallow—the nature of the ground, whether sand, mud or gravel. In soundings the lead might prove a principal means of ascertaining a ship's position, e.g., on the banks of Newfoundland (Plate 16). To heave the lead, the leadsman stood in the chains, the stout external platforms to which the shrouds were made fast. This process is shown in Plate 11.

LOG. As a means of navigation, the log was a method of calculating a ship's speed by noting how much of a line attached to a floating object thrown overboard was paid out in a given time. *Also*, the ship's journal, kept by the Master and recording her position, the weather experienced, the distance run and any noteworthy occurrences each day.

LUGGER. A lugger was a small vessel of one, two or three masts on which lug-sails were set. Of a characteristically French rig in origin, luggers were used for fishing, for smuggling and—by the French—for privateering. A lugger in shown in Plate 9, figure 4.

LUMPERS. Labourers used in loading and unloading merchant vessels in harbour.

MARLED WITH CANVAS. Ropes were sometimes protected from fraying by strips of canvas called "parsling." This was fastened on by marling, or winding with small line (marline, spunyard, twine) so that every turn was secured by a knot independently of the rest.

MASTHOUSE. A tall building overhanging the water, equipped with a crane for dropping lower-masts into position in vessels brought alongside for the purpose.

MESSENGER (or Voyal). A rope, a part of which was wound round the capstan and another part fastened to the cable by pieces of rope called "nippers." As the cable was too cumbersome to pass round the capstan, the capstan's energy was in this way transmitted to it.

NIPPERS. Lengths of rope yarn (9 or 10 feet long) used for fastening the cable to the messenger. Five or six were passed round the cable and voyal, the furthest aft being taken off as the cable approached the main hatch, others being fastened in the forepart of the ship. The ships' boys received the "nippers" and took them forward to use again. The name thus came to be applied to them.

PLAIN SAIL. A vessel was said to be under plain sail when she had set only the basic sails which determined her rig, without the extra sails (studding sails, staysails, skyscrapers and spritsail) which she might occasionally use. The frigate shown in Plate 13, which has the crippled *Lady Juliana* in tow, is under plain sail.

QUARTER-GALLERIES (see under Galleries).

REEFING. The system by which sail area could be reduced by taking in a part of the larger sails. The courses had, usually, one row of reef points, but the topsails, having a far greater area, had four.

ROBANDS OR ROPE-BANDS. Small pieces of yarn or spunyarn, used to confine the head of the sail to the yard or gaff.

ROYALS. The sails set immediately above the topgallants.

SCHOONER. A small vessel with two masts, fore-and-aft mainsail and foresail, which at this period normally set square topsails, as shown in Plate 9, figure 3.

SHALLOP. A sort of large boat with two masts, usually rigged as a schooner.

SHEETS. Ropes fastened to the lower corners of a sail, to keep it extended and in position.

SLOOP, NAVAL. A Sloop was a King's Ship too small to be rated and mounting fewer than 20 guns. A Sloop often mounted 18 guns with additional carronades which brought her real total up to 26. Sloops were rigged as ships or brigs and might measure about 360 tons. They were mainly used for trade-protection.

SLOOP. A small one-masted vessel with a gaff mainsail, similar to a cutter but with a proportionately smaller sail area. The Hoy shown in Plate 9, at figure 10, is sloop-rigged.

SNOW. A two-masted vessel, square-rigged on main and fore, with a square mainsail as well as a driver (or fore-and-aft mainsail, as in a cutter). To overcome the difficulty of setting these two sails on the same mast, snows often had a third embryonic mast abaft the mainmast. This was called a trisail mizzen, and is clearly shown in Plate 17; as also in Plate 9, figure 1.

STAYSAILS. Sails set between the masts. The Snow *Shaw* in Plate 17 has her main stay-sail set, for example. Other staysails were the fore-staysail and mizzen-staysail, the topmast staysails (fore, main and mizzen) and, on the main, the topgallant staysail, middle staysail and royal staysail.

STUDDING SAILS (or Stunsails or Steering Sails). Light sails set beyond the skirts of the principal sails and extended there by the stunsail booms by which the yards were prolonged.

TARE ALLOWANCE. An allowance made for any defect, waste, or diminution in the weight, quantity or quality of goods. Also, a deduction on account of the weight of chests, casks or bags.

TOPSAIL SCHOONER. The name now given to the old type of Schooner, which set a square fore-topsail or a square topsail on either mast. At this period such a craft was merely called a Schooner.

UNLOADING. Plate 8 shows one method of discharging coal. Four men hold whip lines attached to a rope which passes over a single pulley. A basket, fastened to the other end, is drawn, when filled, from the hold by the men's weight as they step down from the bench. But in a larger collier the men would jump down from a higher platform. This was termed "jumping" the coals.

VEERING AND HAULING. To pull a rope tight by drawing it in and slackening it alternately, used especially in hauling bow-lines.

WATER SAILS. A small sail set occasionally under the lower studding-sail.

Bibliographies and Lists of Sources

ARRANGED BY CHAPTERS

CHAPTERS I AND III

SHIPOWNING, INSURANCE AND THE EMPLOYMENT
OF BRITISH SHIPPING

ANON. *A Short Review of the History of the Navigation Laws of England.* 1849.
ANON. *The Important Trial at the Admiralty Sessions of the Persons charged with Sinking the Brig* Adventure *off Brighthelmstone, with intent to defraud the Underwriters,* 1802.
ANNALS. *Annals of Lloyd's Register,* 1884 and 1934.
ATTON, H. and HOLLAND, H. H. *The King's Customs:* An Account of Maritime Revenue and Contraband Traffic in England, etc. . . . to 1800, 2 vols. 1908.
BEER, G. L. *The Old Colonial System.*
BELLAMY, R. REYNELL (see Cremer, Capt. John).
BOURNE, H. R. FOX. *English Merchants.* Memoirs in Illustration of the Progress of British Commerce, 1866.
CHATTERTON, E. KEBLE. *Ships and Ways of Other Days.* London, 1913.
CHATTERTON, E. KEBLE. *The Mercantile Marine.* London, 1923.
CHILDERS, Col. S. (see Richardson, William.)
CLAPHAM, SIR JOHN H. *An Economic History of Modern Britain.* The early Railway Age. Cambridge, 1926.
COATES, W. H. *Good Old Days of Shipping.* 1900.
COLQUHOUN, PATRICK. *A Treatise on the Commerce and Police of the River Thames.* London, 1800.
COLQUHOUN, PATRICK. *A Treatise on the Wealth, Power, and Resources of the British Empire.* London, 1815.
CREMER, CAPTAIN JOHN. *Ramblin' Jack.* The Journals of Captain John Cremer. Edited by R. Reynell Bellamy. London, 1936.
DEFOE, DANIEL. *A Plan of the English Commerce.* Being a Compleat Prospect of the Trade of this Nation. 1728, reprinted Oxford, 1928.
DEWAR, CAPTAIN A. (see Uring, Captain Nathaniel.)
DOW, G. F. *Slave Ships and Slaving.* Marine Research Society. Salem, 1927.
EASTWICK, CAPTAIN R. W. *A Master Mariner.* Being the Life of Captain R. W. Eastwick. Edited by H. Compton. 1891.
EDEN, SIR F. *Address on the Maritime Rights of Great Britain.* 2nd edition. London, 1803.
FAYLE, C. ERNEST. *A Short History of the World's Shipping Industry.* London, 1932.
FAYLE, C. ERNEST (see Wright, Charles).
GARSTIN, CROSBIE (see Kelly, Samuel).
GOLDINGHAM, C. S. *Historical Sketch of Convoying at Sea.* 1918.
HALL, CAPTAIN BASIL. *Fragments of Voyages and Travels,* including Anecdotes of a Naval Life, 1931.
HANNAY, DAVID. *The Sea Trader, his Friends and Enemies.* London, 1912.
HISTORICAL MANUSCRIPTS COMMISSION. Vaux Collection, VI.
HURD, SIR A. *The Merchant Navy of the Past,* 1921.
JONES, R. J. CORNEWALL. *The British Merchant Service.* London, 1898.
KELLY, SAMUEL. *An Eighteenth Century Seaman.* Edited by Crosbie Garstin. London, 1925.
KIRKALDY, PROFESSOR A. W. *British Shipping, its History, Organisation and Importance.* London, 1914.
LINDSAY, W. S. *History of Merchant Shipping and Ancient Commerce.* 4 vols. 1874.

MACPHERSON, DAVID. *Annals of Commerce*, 4 vols. London, 1805.
MARTIN, FREDERICK. *The History of Lloyd's and of Marine Insurance in Great Britain.* 1876.
MARVIN, W. L. *The American Merchant Marine, its History and Romance, 1620 to 1902.* U.S.A., 1902.
McCULLOCH, J. *A Dictionary of Commerce and Commercial Navigation.* London, 1839.
MONTEFIORE. *A Commercial Dictionary ;* containing the present state of Mercantile Law, practice and custom. London, 1803.
MOREAU, CÉSAR. *Chronological Records of the British Royal and Commercial Navy.* London, 1827.
MORISON, S. E. *The Maritime History of Massachusetts, 1783-1860.*
MORTIMER, THOMAS. *Universal Commerce,* or the Commerce of all the Mercantile Cities and Towns of the World. London, 1818.
MORTIMER, THOMAS. *A General Dictionary of Commerce, Trade and Manufactures.* London, 1810.
RICHARDSON, WILLIAM. *A Mariner of England.* Edited by Col. S. Childers. London, 1908.
STANFIELD, J. F. (formerly a Mariner in the African Trade). *The Guinea Voyage* : a Poem ; to which are added Observations on the Voyage to the Coast of Africa. 1807.
STEPHEN, JAMES. *War in Disguise, or the Frauds of the Neutral Flags.* Published 1805. Reprinted 1917. Sir F. Piggott, editor.
SHEWAN, CAPTAIN ANDREW. *The Great Days of Sail.* London, 1927.
SMART, WILLIAM. *Economic Annals of the Nineteenth Century,* vol. I. 1910.
URING, NATHANIEL. *Voyages and Travels.* Edited by Captain A. Dewar, R.N. London, 1928.
WILLAN, T. S. *English Coasting Trade, 1600-1750.* 1938.
WILLIAMS, G. *History of the Liverpool Privateers,* with an Account of the Liverpool Slave Trade. 1897.
WORSLEY, COMMANDER FRANK, and GLYN GRIFFITH, CAPTAIN. *The Romance of Lloyd's.* 1932.
WRIGHT, CHARLES, and C. ERNEST FAYLE. *A History of Lloyd's.* London, 1928.

CHAPTER II

THE SEAPORTS

(I) GENERAL

FAY, C. R. *English Economic History,* mainly since 1700. Cambridge, 1940.
KIRKALDY, PROFESSOR A. W. *British Shipping, its History, Organization and Importance.* 1914.
LINDSAY, W. SHAW. *History of Merchant Shipping and Ancient Commerce.* 4 vols. London, 1874-76.
OWEN, DOUGLAS. *Ports and Docks, their History, Working and National Importance.* London, 1904.
PHILLIPS, J. *General History of Inland Navigation, Foreign and Domestic,* containing an Account of the Canals already executed in England with considerations on those projected. 1792. Reprinted 1803.
VAUGHAN, WILLIAM, F.R.S. Tracts on Docks and Commerce printed between the years 1793 and 1800, and now first collected. London, 1839.
WILLAN, T. S. *River Navigation in England.* 1936.

(II) THE PORT OF LONDON

COLQUHOUN, PATRICK. *A Treatise on the Commerce and Police of the River Thames.* London, 1800.
McCULLOCH, J. *A Dictionary of Commerce and Commercial Navigation,* 2 vols. London, 1835.
MORTIMER, THOMAS. *Universal Commerce,* or the Commerce of all the Mercantile Cities and Towns of the World. London, 1818.
PARKINSON, C. N. *Trade in the Eastern Seas, 1793-1813.* Cambridge, 1937.

REPORT FROM THE COMMITTEE appointed to enquire into the best mode of providing sufficient accommodation for the increased Trade and Shipping of the Port of London. Ordered to be printed, 13th May, 1796.

REPORT BY COMMITTEE OF CUSTOMS on the Several Plans for Providing Sufficient Accommodation for the Increased Trade of the Port of London. 1796.

REPORT. Port of London, 1800. Third Report (with Appendices) from Commissioners on the Improvement of the Port of London, 1800.

(III) THE PORT OF LIVERPOOL

BAINES, THOMAS. *History of the Commerce and Town of Liverpool.* Liverpool, 1852.
BROOKE, RICHARD. *Liverpool in the Last Quarter of the Eighteenth Century.* Liverpool, 1853.
BROWN, R. STEWART. *Liverpool Ships of the Eighteenth Century.* London, 1932.
GORE'S DIRECTORIES. *The Annals of Liverpool.* From 1818.
GRIEVE, A. MACKENZIE. *The Last Days of the Slave Trade.* London, 1941.
MUIR, J. RAMSAY. *A History of Liverpool.* Liverpool, 1907.
PICTON, SIR JAMES A. *Memorials of Liverpool.* 1875.
SMITHERS, HENRY. *Liverpool ; its Commerce, Institutions, etc.* 1825.
TOUZEAU, JAMES. *The Rise and Progress of Liverpool.* London, 1910.
WALLACE, J. *A General and Descriptive History of Liverpool.* Liverpool, 1795.
WILLIAMS, GOMER. *The Liverpool Privateers and the Liverpool Slave Trade.* London, 1897.

PERIODICALS :

Shipping Registers. London, 1790 and 1801.
Liverpool Trade Lists. Liverpool, 1801-4, and 1813-14.
Newspaper Files :

Liverpool Mercury, 1811-1815.
Williamson's Liverpool Advertiser and Mercantile Register, 1794-1815.
Gore's General Advertiser, 1788-1815.
The Gentleman's Magazine, 1780-1815.

(IV) THE PORT OF BRISTOL

I. SOURCES (*a*) UNPUBLISHED

BRISTOL MUSEUM AND ART GALLERY :
Powell, J. W. Damer. Ships Built in Bristol, 1793-1815.

SOCIETY OF MERCHANT VENTURERS, BRISTOL :
Book of Petitions
Books of Proceedings : Volume 12, 1789-97 ; volume 13, 1797-1807 ; volume 14, 1807-19
Papers Read at the Hall
West India New Society, 1782-93.

UNIVERSITY OF BRISTOL LIBRARY :
Pinney Family Business Ledgers, 1793-1815
Pinney Family Business Letter-books, 1793-1815

(*b*) PUBLISHED

Bristol Imports and Exports, 1801-1815. Printed for George Worall, Sub-Patentee, by Authority

(*c*) BOOKS AND PAMPHLETS

EDWARDS, B., *The History, Civil and Commercial, of the British Colonies in the West Indies,* 2 vols. London.
EVANS, R. J., *The Picture of Bristol.* Bristol, W. Sheppard, 1814.
GOUGH, R., *Camden, W., Britannia.* Translated from the edition published by the author in MDCVII. Enlarged by the latest discoveries. 2nd edition, 4 vols. London, J. Nichols & Son, 1806.

Lewis, E. B., *A Brief Memoir of Edward Broad Lewis of the City of Bristol*. Written by himself. London, John Bale Sons & Danielsson, Ltd., 1931.
Malcolm, J. P., *Excursions into Kent, Gloucestershire, Herefordshire, Monmouthshire and Somersetshire, made in the years* 1802, 1803 and 1805. London. Longman, Hurst, Rees and Orme, 1807.
Matthews, W., *The New History, Survey and Description of the City and Suburbs of Bristol, or Complete Guide*. Bristol, W. Matthews, 1794, 4th edition, J. Matthews, 1815.
Reed, J., *The New Bristol Directory for the Year* 1792. Bristol.
Shiercliff, E., *The Bristol and Hotwell Guide*. 2nd edition. Bristol. Bulgin and Rosser, 1793. 3rd edition, Bristol, J. Mills, 1805.

(*d*) Newspapers and Periodicals

Bonner and Middleton's Bristol Journal (files).
Felix Farley's Bristol Journal (files).
The Monthly Magazine, No. XLV, June 1st, 1799.

II.—Secondary

Hudleston, C. R., *The Bristol Cathedral Register*, 1669-1837. Bristol, St. Stephens Press, 1933.
Hunt, W., *Bristol*. London, Longmans, Green & Co., 1887.
Latimer, J., *Annals of Bristol in the Eighteenth and Nineteenth Centuries*, 3 vols. Bristol, J. W. Arrowsmith, 1887-1902.
— *The History of the Society of Merchant Venturers of the City of Bristol, with some Account of the Anterior Merchants' Guilds*. Bristol, J. W. Arrowsmith, 1903.
MacInnes, C. M., *A Gateway of Empire*. Bristol, J. W. Arrowsmith Ltd., 1939.
Powell, J. W. Damer, *Bristol Privateers and Ships of War*. Bristol, J. W. Arrowsmith Ltd., 1930.
Wells, C., *Short History of the Port of Bristol*. Bristol, J. W. Arrowsmith, 1909.

Chapters IV and V

SHIPS OF THE PERIOD, AND SEAMEN

Anon. *Observations on the present Construction of Ships, with an Account of the four-masted vessel* Transit. 1806.
Cupples, George. *The Greenhand*.
Cooke, E. W. *Fifty Plates of Shipping and Craft*, drawn and edited by E. W. Cooke. 1829.
Coates. *Good Old Days of Shipping*. 1900.
Fletcher, R. A. *In the Days of Tall Ships*. London, 1928.
Glascock. *The Naval Sketch Book*. London, 1826.
Gower, R. H. *Treatise on the Theory and Practice of Seamanship*, by an Officer in the Service of the East India Company. 1793.
Hannay, David. *Ships and Men*. Edinburgh, 1910.
Hannay, David. *The Sea Trader, His Friends and Enemies*. London, 1912.
Leslie, R. C. *Old Sea Wings, Ways and Words in the Days of Oak and Hemp*. 1800.
Lever, Darcy. *Young Sea Officer's Sheet Anchor*. or a key to the leading of Rigging, and to Practical Seamanship. 1808.
Lubbock, Basil. *The Blackwall Frigates*.
Manuscripts :
    East Indiamen's Logs and Journals. India Office.
    Whaling Journals. Hull Museum.
    Whaling Journals (in the author's possession).
    Collection of Ships' Plans (in the author's possession).
Mariner's Mirror. Journal of the Society for Nautical Research.
Marryat, Captain C. Novels.

MOORHOUSE, E. HALLAM. *Letters of the English Seamen.*
MORSE, H. B. *The Chronicles of the East India Company Trading to China*, 4 vols. Vol. III. Oxford, 1926.
NAVAL CHRONICLE, THE
NAVY RECORD SOCIETY'S PUBLICATIONS.
NICOL, J. *Life and Adventures.* Edited by John Howell. Edinburgh, 1822.
PERIODICALS. Extracts from Contemporary News Sheets, etc.
POWELL, J. W. DAMER. *Bristol Privateers and Ships of War.*
ROBINSON, COMMANDER C. N., R.N. *British Tar in Fact and Fiction.* London, 1909.
SCOTT, MICHAEL. *Tom Cringle's Log.*
SCOTT, MICHAEL. *Cruise of the Midge.*
STEEL, D. *The Ship-Master's Assistant and Owner's Manual.* 1792.
STEEL, D. *Seamanship both in Theory and Practice.*
STEEL, D. *Elements and Practice of Naval Architecture.*
STEEL, D. *Sailmaking, Mastmaking and Rigging.*
STEWART-BROWN, R. *Liverpool Ships in the Eighteenth Century.*
TIMBS, JOHN. *Book of Naval Anecdotes.*
UNITED SERVICE JOURNALS.
WHALL, W. B. *The Romance of Navigation.*

CHAPTER VI

HEALTH AND SICKNESS

BANCROFT, E. N. *An essay on the disease called Yellow Fever with observations concerning febrile contagion, Yellow Fever, Dysentery and the Plague.* London, 1811.
BARKER, ROBERT. *The Unfortunate Shipwright ; or Cruel Captain ;* being a faithful narrative of the unparalleled sufferings of Robert Barker, late Carpenter on board the *Thetis*, now of Bristol, in a voyage to the Coast of Guinea and Antigua. ? 1761.
BARON, J. *Life of Jenner*, 2 volumes. London, 1838.
BIRKET-SMITH, KAJ. *The Eskimos.* London, 1936.
BLANE, SIR GILBERT. *Observations on the Diseases of Seamen.* London, 1875.
Journal of the Royal Naval Medical Service, 1937 (H. D. Rolleston).
BROUGHTON, W. R. *A Voyage of Discovery to the North Pacific Ocean.* London, 1804.
BROWNING (G. A., R.N.). *The Convict Ship or England's Exiles.* 1847.
BURNETT, WILLIAM. *An account of the fever commonly called the bilious remittent.* London, 1814.
CLARK, THOMAS, M.D. *On Ipecacuanha Enema in Dysentery.* (*Medical and Physical Journal*, 1812, XXVIII, page 94). *Observations on the Nature and Cure of Fevers and of Diseases of the West and East Indies and of America . . . and general remarks on Diseases of the Army.* Edinburgh. 1801.
COCKBURN, LIEUT.-GENERAL G. *A Voyage to Cadiz and Gibraltar, up the Mediterranean to Sicily and Malta in* 1810-11. London, 1815.
COLLINS, DAVID. *An Account of the English Colony of New South Wales.* London, 1798.
COOK, CAPTAIN JAMES, F.R.S. *Voyages to the Pacific Ocean.* 1785.
CUMPSTON. *History of Small Pox in Australia.* 1788-1908. Service Publication No. 3. Quarantine Service. Commonwealth of Australia. 1914.
DARWIN, SIR F. S. *Travels in Spain and the East*, 1808-1810. Cambridge, 1927.
EPPS, JOHN. *Life of John Walker, M.D.* London, 1832.
FALCONBRIDGE, A. *An account of Richard Smith's MS. memoirs at Bristol Royal Infirmary.*
FANNING, E. *Voyages Round the World*, with selected sketches of Voyages to the South Seas, North and South Pacific Oceans, China, etc., 1792-1832. New York, 1833.
FERGUSSON, W. (1) *Medical and Physical Journal*, 1812, XXVIII.
(2) *Notes and Recollections of a Professional Life by the late William Fergusson, Esq., M.D.* Edited by his son, James Fergusson. London, 1846.
FIELDING, HENRY. *Voyage to Lisbon.*
FORREST, CAPTAIN T. *Voyage from Calcutta to the Mergui Archipelago*, 1792.

GILLESPIE, LEONARD, M.D. *Observations on the Diseases which prevailed on board a part of His Majesty's Squadron on the Leeward Island Station between November, 1794 and April, 1796.* London, 1800.

JAMES, REAR ADMIRAL BARTHOLOMEW, JOURNAL OF. *Spencer Papers*, vol. I. *Navy Records Society Publications*, vol. VI.

JANE, LETTERS TO (see Mozley).

JOHNSON, JAMES. *The Influence of Tropical Climates on European Constitutions.* 6th edition. 1841. London.

KRUSENSTERN, ADMIRAL ADAM JOHN VON. *Voyage Round the World*, 1803-06. Translated by R. B. Hoppner. London, 1813.

LANCASTER, SIR JAMES. *Hakluyt's Principal Voyages of the English Nation.* Everyman's Library.

LEWIS, MICHAEL. *England's Sea Officers.* London, 1939.

LIND, JAMES M. D. (1) *An Essay on the Most Effectual Means of Preserving the Health of Seamen in the Royal Navy.* London, 1757.
(2) *A Treatise on the Scurvy*, 3rd edition. London, 1772.

LISIANSKY, UREY. Captain in the Russian Navy. *A Voyage Round the World*, 1803-06, in the ship "Neva." 1814. (Continuation of Krusenstern.)

LUBBOCK, B. *The Blackwall Frigates.* Glasgow, 1922.

MacINNES, C. M. *England and Slavery.* Bristol, 1934.

MARCHAND, ETIENNE. *Voyage Round the World and to the North-West Coast of America*, 1801.

MINUTES of the Evidence taken before a Committee . . . appointed for the purpose of taking the examination of such witnesses as shall be produced on the part of the several petitioners . . . against the abolition of the Slave Trade.

MINUTES of the Evidence taken . . . before the Committee . . . to whom the Bill for providing certain temporary regulations respecting the transportation of the Natives of Africa in British Ships, to the West Indies and elsewhere, was committed. 1789.

MOZLEY, GERALDINE, edited by. *Letters to Jane from Jamaica*, 1788-1796. West India Committee, London. N.D. (? 1939).

NELSON, HORATIO VISCOUNT. *Letters and Despatches.* J. K. Laughton, London, 1886.

PARKINSON, C. N. *Trade in the Eastern Seas.* Cambridge, 1937.

PERON. *Voyage for Discovery of Southern Lands*—see Pinkerton.

PETTIGREW. *Life of Lettsom.*

PINKERTON, J. *Voyages and Travels*, 17 volumes. London, 1808-1814.
Peron—Volume XI, 1800. Thunberg, do., volume XVI.

PRINGLE, SIR JOHN, BART. *Six Discourses delivered when President of the Royal Society* (with life by A. Kippis). London, 1783.

REPORT to Admiral Christian on *Health Measures for the West Indies.* Signed by Johnston and Trotter (Spencer Papers, volume I). Navy Records Society Publications, vol. VI.

REPORT of the Lords of the Committee of Council submitting the evidence and information they have collected concerning the Present State of Trade to Africa and particularly the Trade in Slaves, etc., 1789.

ROSEN, GEORGE. *Occupational Diseases of English Seamen in the Seventeenth and Eighteenth Centuries.* (Bull. of the Inst. of the Hist. of Med.) Johns Hopkins University. 1939. vii. 751.

SAUGNIER AND DE BRISSON. *Voyages to the Coast of Africa*, 1792. London.

SCHOUTE, DR. D. *Occidental Therapeutics in the Netherlands East Indies during Three Centuries of Netherlands Settlement*, 1600-1900. Batavia, 1937.

SHILLIBEER, LIEUT. J. *A Narrative of the Briton's Voyage to Pitcairn's Island*, including an interesting sketch of the present state of the Brazils and of Spanish South America. Taunton, 1817.

SLAVE TRADE. See Falconbridge, Minutes of Evidence, Report of the Lords of the Committee, Barker, MacInnes, Saugnier and de Brisson.

SMYTH, JAMES CARMICHAEL. *An account of the experiment made at the desire of the Lords Commissioners of the Admiralty on board the Union Hospital Ship to determine the effect of the nitrous acid in destroying contagion and the safety with which it may be employed.* London, 1796.

THOMSON, FREDERICK. *An Essay on the Scurvy*, 1790.
THUNBERG, C. *Voyage to the Cape of Good Hope*, 1795. See Pinkerton.
TROTTER, T. *Medicina Nautica*. An Essay on the Diseases of Seamen, 3 volumes, 2nd edition, London, 1804.
    Also *Journal of the Royal Naval Medical Service*, 1919. H. D. Rolleston.
TSCHIFFELY, A. F. *This Way South*. London, 1940.
VOGEL, K. *Scurvy, 'The Plague of the Sea and the Spoyle of Mariners'* 1933.
VOGEL, K. *Sea Surgeons in the Days of Oak and Hemp.*
WALKER, JOHN. *Life of*, By John Epps. London. 1832.
WAITZ, DR. F.A.C. *Tropical Diseases*, Amsterdam, 1829.
WATSON, JOHN. *Some observations on the diseases that occurred on board the ship* Europa, *in the service of the Honourable East India Company during a voyage from England to and from Madras and Bengal by Mr. John Watson, late Surgeon of the said ship, and now surgeon at Wellingborough in Northamptonshire. (Medical Facts and Observations.* 1794. Vol. 5, page 20).
WILLIAMS, GOMER. *History of Liverpool privateers and the slave trade.* 1897.
WILSON, CAPT. J. *A Missionary Voyage to the Southern Pacific in* 1796-98, *in the ship* Duff. 1799.
WOODALL, JOHN. *The Surgeon's Mate.* Bourne. 1639.

CHAPTER VII

THE EAST INDIA TRADE

ADDISON, THOMAS (see Laughton, J. K.).
ADOLPHUS, JOHN. *The substance of the speech of John Adolphus Esq. before a Select Committee of the House of Commons, in summing up the case of the English shipbuilders, on their petition respecting ships built in India.* London, 1814, pp. 46.
ANON. *Papers respecting the trade between India and Europe. Printed by order of the Court of Directors.* London, 1802. pp. 190.
ANON. *Considerations upon the trade with India ; and the policy of continuing the Company's monopoly.* London, 1807. pp. 159.
ANON. *Hints for an answer to the Letter of the Chairman and Deputy Chairman of the East India Company to the Right Hon. Robert Dundas dated 13th January, 1809.* London, 1812. pp. 75.
ANON. *General thoughts contained in a letter on the subject of the renewal of the East India Company's Charter.* London, 1812. pp. 54.
ANON. *Free Trade ; or an Inquiry into the pretensions of the Directors of the East India Company to the exclusive trade of the Indian and China Seas.* London, 1812. pp. XI, 70.
ANON. *The Question as to the renewal of the East India Company's Monopoly examined.* Edinburgh, 1812. pp. 117.
ANON. *Remarks on the Charter of the East India Company.* Cambridge, 1813. pp. 60.
ANON. *The present system of our East India Government and Commerce considered ; in which are exposed the fallacy, the incompatibility and the injustice of a political and despotic power possessing a commercial situation also within the countries subject to its dominion.* London, 1813. pp. 68.
ANON. *Some facts relative to the China Trade ; shewing its importance to this country, and the inexpediency of its remaining exclusively in the hands of the East India Company.* Edinburgh, 1813. pp. 44.
ANON. *Free Trade with India. An Enquiry into the true state of the question at issue between His Majesty's Ministers, the Honorable East India Company, and the public at large.* By "Common Sense." London, 1813. pp. 23.
ANON. *Remarks on the Calumnies published in the Quarterly Review on the English Shipbuilders.* London, 1814. pp. 44.
ANON. *Memorial of the Committee of the East India Company's Maritime Service, presented to the Honorable the Court of Directors,* July 30th, 1834. London, 1834. pp. 23.
ANON. *The East India Company and the Maritime Service.* London, 1834. pp. 27.

ANON. *An Appeal to His Majesty's Government and the Honourable East India Company for justice to the claims of the Honourable East India Company's Maritime Service to compensation.* By an Officer of the Service. London, 1834. pp.84.

ANON. *A Short Account of the Prince of Wales's Island*, pp. 27.

ASIATIC JOURNAL AND MONTHLY REGISTER FOR BRITISH AND FOREIGN INDIA, THE: Vol. XVIII. London, 1835. pp. 316. Article entitled "Outward Bound" (p. 195).

AUBER, PETER. *An Analysis of the Constitution of the East India Company.* London, 1826. pp. LXXII, 804.

BARLOW, GLYN. *The Story of Madras.* Madras, 1921. pp. VI, 117, with 22 illustrations.

BERNARD, W. D. (see Hall, Commander W. H.).

BOSANQUET, AUGUSTUS H. *India Seventy Years Ago.* By the nephew of an East India Director. London, 1881. pp. VIII, 311, with frontispiece portrait.

BRADSHAW, JOHN. *Rulers of India.* Sir Thomas Munro and the British Settlement of the Madras Presidency. Oxford, 1894. pp. 233, with a map.

BURKE, EDMUND. *The Works of the Right Honourable Edmund Burke*, vol. II. London, 1855. pp. 538.

CAMPBELL, ARCHIBALD. *A Voyage Round the World, from 1806 to 1812.* Edinburgh, 1816. pp. 288, with a chart.

CAPPER, JAMES. *Observations on the Winds and Monsoons*; illustrated by a chart and accompanied with notes, geographical and meteorological. London, 1801. pp. XXVIII, 234.

CAREY, W. H. *The Good Old Days of Honourable John Company.* Simla, 1882. 3 vols. pp. 292, 288, XXXI and 166.

CHATTERTON, E. KEBLE. *Ships and Ways of Other Days.* London, 1913. pp. 292, with 130 illustrations.

CHATTERTON, E. KEBLE. *The Ship Under Sail.* London, 1926. pp. 224, with 36 illustrations.

CHATTERTON, E. KEBLE. *The Old East Indiamen.* 2nd edition. London, 1933. pp. 308, with 15 illustrations.

CLEVELAND, RICHARD J. *A Narrative of Voyages and Commercial Enterprises.* London, 1842. pp. 123.

COATES, W. H. *The Old "Country Trade" of the East Indies.* W. H. Coates, F.R.G.S., Commander, R.N.R. (retired). London, 1911. pp. IX, 205. Chart and 9 illustrations.

COBBETT, WILLIAM. *Mr. Cobbett's Remarks on our Indian Empire and Company of Trading Sovereigns.* (Reprinted from the Register of 1804 to 1822). London, 1857. pp. 23.

COMPTON, H. (see Eastwick, R. W.).

CORDINER, REV. JAMES. *A Voyage to India.* Aberdeen, 1820. pp. XI, 315, with a portrait frontispiece.

CORRIE, RT. REV. D. *Memoirs of the Right Rev. Daniel Corrie, LL.D.*, First Bishop of Madras. Compiled chiefly from his own letters and journals, by his brothers. London, 1847. pp. 640, with frontispiece.

COTTON, JOSEPH. *A Review of the Shipping System of the East India Company;* with suggestions for its improvement, etc. 1799. pp. 59.

CUNNINGHAM, W. *The Growth of English Industry and Commerce in Modern Times.* Cambridge, 1912. Vol. III (*Modern Times*, Part II). pp. 1039.

CUPPLES, GEORGE. *The Green Hand.* Adventures of a Naval Lieutenant. London, 1900. First published in 1849. pp. XI, 413.

DALRYMPLE, A. *A Fair State of the Case between the East India Company and the Owners of Ships now in their Service.* To which are added Considerations on Mr. Brough's Pamphlet concerning the East India Company's Shipping. London, 1786. pp. 54.

DARTON, F. J. HARVEY (see Sherwood, Mrs.).

DELANO, AMASA. *Narrative of Voyages and Travels in the Northern and Southern Hemispheres.* Boston, 1817. pp. 598, with three illustrations.

DEWAR, DOUGLAS. *In the Days of the Company.* Calcutta, 1920. pp. 210.

DEWAR, DOUGLAS. *Bygone Days in India.* London, 1922. pp. 287, with 18 illustrations.

DOUGLAS, JAMES. *Glimpses of Old Bombay and Western India*, with other papers. London, 1900. pp. X, 334.

DREWITT, F. DAWTREY. *Bombay in the Days of George IV : Memoirs of Sir Edward West.* London, 1907. Republished, 1935. pp. 342, 7 illustrations.

DULLES, FOSTER RHEA. *The Old China Trade.* Cambridge, U.S.A., 1930. pp. 228, with 12 illustrations.

DUNN, SAMUEL. *A New Directory for the East Indies. A work originally begun upon the plan of the Oriental Neptune augmented and improved by W. Herbert, W. Nicholson, now . . . further enlarged by Samuel Dunn.* London, 1780. 5th edition. pp. 554, with frontispiece.

EAMES, J. B. *The English in China ; being an account of the intercourse and relations between England and China from the year* 1600 *to the year* 1843. London, 1909. pp. 662. Two maps and 7 illustrations.

EAST INDIA COMPANY. *Proceedings relative to Ships tendered for the service of the United East India Company*:
  (1) January, 1780 to March, 1791. London, 1802. pp. 1,150.
  (2) April, 1791 to February, 1796. pp. 1,450.
  (3) February, 1796 to May, 1799. pp. 2,283.
  (4) September, 1800 to April, 1803. pp. 540.
      Appendix Vol. pp. 2,130.
  (5) April, 1803 to June, 1806. London, 1806. pp. 1,506.
  (6) July, 1806 to September, 1809. London, 1809. pp. 1,360.

EASTWICK, R. W. *A Master Mariner.* Being the life and adventures of Captain Robert William Eastwick. Edited by H. Compton. London, 1891. pp. 351 with six illustrations.

EDGELL, T. C. P. *English Trade and Policy in Borneo and the Adjacent Islands,* 1667-1786. Thesis, unpublished, in the Library of the University of London. Submitted, 1935. pp. 265, with a map.

EGERTON, HUGH EDWARD. *Sir Stamford Raffles : England in the Far East.* London, 1900. pp. 290. Frontispiece and two maps.

EDWARDES, S. M. *The Rise of Bombay. A retrospect.* Bombay, 1902. pp. 345. Plans and illustrations.

ELMORE, H. M. *The British Mariner's Directory and Guide to the Trade and Navigation of the Indian and China Seas.* London, 1802. pp. 342.

FAYLE, C. ERNEST. *A Short History of the World's Shipping Industry.* London, 1933. pp. 320, with eight illustrations.

FIOTT, J. *Three Addresses to the Proprietors of East India Stock, and the Publick, on the Subject of the Shipping Concerns of the Company.* Mr. J. Fiott, merchant, of London. London, 1795. pp. 322.

FLETCHER, R. A. *In the Days of Tall Ships.* London, 1928. pp. 348, with 30 illustrations.

FLINDERS, MATTHEW. *A Voyage to Terra Australis ;* undertaken for the purpose of completing the discovery of that vast country. By Matthew Flinders, Commander of the *Investigator.* 2 vols., with Atlas. London, 1814. pp. CCIV, 269 and 613. Numerous illustrations.

FORBES, JAMES. *Oriental Memoirs ;* a narrative of seventeen years' residence in India. 2nd edition. London, 1834. 2 vols. pp. XIX, 550 and VIII, 552. Frontispiece to each volume.

FORBES, R. B. *Remarks on China and the China Trade.* Boston, 1844. pp. 80.

FORREST, CAPT. THOMAS. *A Treatise on the Monsoons in East India.* Calcutta, 1782. pp. VII, 51.

FOSTER, SIR WILLIAM. *The East India House, its History and Associations.* London, 1924. pp. 241, with 37 illustrations.

FOSTER, SIR WILLIAM. *John Company.* London, 1926. pp. 276 with 24 illustrations.

GRAHAM, MARIA. *A Journal of a Residence in India.* Edinburgh, 1812. pp. 211, with 16 illustrations.

GRAND, G. F. *The Narrative of the Life of a Gentleman long resident in India.* First published, Cape of Good Hope, 1814. New edition, edited by W. K. Firminger, Calcutta, 1910. pp. XIX, 333, with 14 illustrations.

GRANT, CHARLES. *History of Mauritius.* London, 1801, pp. XXI, 571.

GRANDPRE, L. DE. *A Voyage in the Indian Ocean.*

GRANT, ROBERT. *The Expediency Maintained of continuing the System by which the Trade and Government of India are now regulated.* London, 1813. pp. XIX, 404.

GRIBBLE, CHARLES B. *A Brief Statement shewing the Equitable and Moral Claims of the Maritime Officers of the Honourable East India Company for Compensation.* London, 1834. pp. 24.

GROSE, MR. *A Voyage to the East Indies.* 2 vols. New edition. London, 1772. pp. 343, 478. Plans and illustrations.

HALL, CAPTAIN BASIL, R.N. *Narrative of a Voyage to Java, China, and the great Loo-Choo Island.* London, 1840. pp. 81 with two charts.

HALL, CAPTAIN BASIL, R.N. *Fragments of Voyages and Travels.* Second series. 2nd edition. London, 1840. pp. 160.

HALL, CAPTAIN BASIL, R.N. *Fragments of Voyages and Travels.* Third series. London, 1840. pp. 169, with four illustrations.

HALL, COMMANDER W. H. *Narrative of the Voyages and Services of the "Nemesis," from 1834 to 1840, and of the combined naval and military operations in China,* from notes of Commander W. H. Hall, R.N., with personal observations by W. D. Bernard, Esq. 2nd edition. London, 1844. pp. 488, with 15 charts, plans, diagrams and illustrations.

HAMILTON, WALTER. *East India Gazetteer.* London, 1815. pp. 862.

HANNAY, DAVID. *The Sea Trader, his Friends and Enemies.* London, 1912. pp. 388, with 22 illustrations.

HARDY, CHARLES. *Register of Ships Employed in the Service of the Honourable the United East India Company,* from the union of the two companies, in 1707, to the year 1760 . . . to which is added from the latter period to the present time. London, 1799. pp.280 with a chart.

HARDY, H. C. *A Register of Ships Employed in the Service of the Honourable the United East India Company from the Year 1760 to 1812.* Revised by H. C. Hardy. London, 1813. pp. 308, with indexes and appendices.

HARRISON, W. *The Substance of the Speech of William Harrison, Esq.* before the Select Committee of the House of Commons on East India-built Shipping, on Monday, April 18th, 1814. Sir Robert Peel in the chair. London, 1814. pp. 23.

HARRISON, W. *The Substance of the Reply of William Harrison, Esq.* before the Select Committee of the House of Commons on East India-built Shipping, on Tuesday, June 28th, 1814. London, 1814. pp. 56.

HENCHMAN, THOMAS. *Observations on the Reports of the Directors of the East India Company* respecting the Trade between India and Europe. 2nd edition. London, 1802. pp.461.

HERVEY, CAPTAIN ALBERT. *Ten Years in India ;* or the Life of a Young Officer. London, 1850. 3 vols. Vol. I, pp. XVI, 358.

HICKEY, WILLIAM. *Memoirs,* edited by Alfred Spencer. Vol. IV. (1790-1809). pp. XII, 512, with seven illustrations. London, 1925.

HOLZMAN, JAMES M. *The Nabobs in England:* a study of the returned Anglo-Indian, 1760-1785. New York, 1926. pp. 186, with four illustrations.

HORSBURGH, JAMES. *Directions for Sailing to and from the East Indies, China, New Holland, Cape of Good Hope, etc.* London, 1809-1811. 2 vols. pp. 397, 518.

HOSKINS, H. L. *British Routes to India.* New York, 1928. pp. 494, with 11 illustrations.

HOTHAM, R. *Instructions, etc., given by Owners of the good Ship called the "Royal Admiral" in the Service of the Honourable United Company of Merchants of England, trading to the East Indies.* 1778. Rd. Hotham to Captain Edward Berrow.

HUNTER, SIR W. W. (see Samuelson, James).

IRVING, B. A. *The Commerce of India:* being a view of the routes successively taken by the commerce between Europe and the East. London, 1858. pp. XII, 271.

JACKSON, JOHN. *Journey from India towards England in the year 1797 ;* by a route commonly called over-land . . . London, 1799. pp. 277, with a map and illustrations.

JAMES, SILAS. *Narrative of a Voyage to Arabia, India, etc.* Performed in the years 1781-1784. London, 1797. pp. 232, with a frontispiece.

JOHNSON, GEORGE W. *The Stranger in India ; or Three Years in Calcutta.* London, 1843. 2 vols. pp. VIII, 304 and VI, 294.

JOHNSON, J. *The Oriental Voyager ;* or descriptive sketches and cursory remarks on a voyage to India and China, in His Majesty's Ship *Caroline,* performed in the years 1803-6. London, 1807. pp. XVI, 388, with a map.

JOHNSON, J. *The Influence of Tropical Climates on European Constitutions.* London, 1827. 4th edition. pp. VIII, 680. First published in 1813.

KAYE, JOHN WILLIAM. *The Administration of the East India Company.* London, 1853. pp. VI, 712.

KAYE, JOHN WILLIAM. *The Life and Correspondence of Major-General Sir John Malcolm, G.C.B., late Envoy to Persia, and Governor of Bombay.* 2 vols. London, 1856. pp. XII, 538 and VI, 631. Frontispiece to each volume.

LAUDERDALE, EARL OF. *An Inquiry into the Practical Merits of the System for the Government of India, under the superintendence of the Board of Control.* Edinburgh, 1809. pp. 260, with a map.

LAUGHTON, J. K. *The Naval Miscellany,* Vol. I. N.R.S. Vol. XX, edited by J. K. Laughton. 1902. pp. 462, with eight illustrations and maps. P. 333. Extracts from the Journals of Thomas Addison, 1801-1830.

LAURIE, DAVID. *Hints regarding the East India Monopoly; respectfully submitted to the British Legislature.* Glasgow, 1813. pp. 66.

LEE, IDA (Mrs. Charles Bruce Marriott). *Commodore Sir John Hayes, his Voyage and Life* (1767-1831). London, 1912. pp. XVI, 340. 34 illustrations.

LESTER, W. *The Happy Era to One Hundred Millions of the Human Race; or the Merchant, Manufacturer, and Englishman's recognised Right to an unlimited Trade with India.* London, 1813. pp. 48.

LINDSAY, LORD. *Lives of the Lindsays.* Wigan, 1840. Vol. IV, pp. 295. *An Adventure in China* (p. 281), Hon. Hugh Lindsay.

LINDSAY, W. S. *History of Merchant Shipping and Ancient Commerce.* 4 vols. London, 1874. Vol. II, pp. 610. Plan and illustrations.

LOCKHART, J. C. *Blenden Hall.* London, 1930. pp. 232. Map and eight illustrations.

LONG, REV. J. *Peeps into Social Life in Calcutta a Century Ago.* Calcutta, 1868. pp. 25.

LORD, WALTER FREWEN. *Sir Thomas Maitland, the Mastery of the Mediterranean.* London, 1897. pp. 301, with portrait and two maps.

LOW, C. R. *History of the Indian Navy* (1613-1863). London, 1877. 2 vols. Vol. I, pp. XX, 541.

LUBBOCK, BASIL. *The Blackwall Frigates.* 2nd edition. Glasgow, 1924. pp. 332, 72 illustrations, with maps and appendices.

MACCAULY, THOMAS. *The Indian Trader's Complete Guide; being a correct account of coins, weights, measures, etc., etc., at the different Settlements of India and Asia.* Calcutta, 1816. pp. 116.

MACKINTOSH, RT. HON. SIR JAMES. *Memoirs,* edited by his son, Robert James Mackintosh. London, 1835. 2 vols. pp. VII, 527 and VII, 516. Frontispiece to each volume.

MACKONOCHIE, ALEXANDER. *Theory and Practice of Naval Architecture . . . Comparative State of Naval Architecture in Great Britain and India.* (Prospectus announced in 1803. The work, however, if ever published, appears to be unobtainable.)

MACPHERSON, DAVID. *Annals of Commerce.* London, 1805. 4 vols. Vol. IV, pp. 550, with appendices, gazeteer, etc.

MACPHERSON, DAVID. *The History of the European Commerce with India, to which is subjoined a review of the arguments for and against the trade with India and the management of it by a chartered Company.* London, 1812. pp. VI, 440, with a map.

MALCOLM, MAJOR-GENERAL SIR JOHN (see Kaye, J. W.).

MARRYAT, CAPTAIN, R.N., C.B. *Newton Forster; or, the Merchant Service.* London, 1838. pp. 383, with a frontispiece.

MASEFIELD, JOHN. *The Travels of Marco Polo, the Venetian,* with an introduction by John Masefield. London, 1907. pp. XVI, 461.

McCULLOCH, J. R. *A Dictionary, Practical, Theoretical, and Historical, of Commerce and Commercial Navigation.* New edition. London, 1854. First published, 1832. pp. 1,484, with numerous maps and plans.

McCULLOCH, J. R. (see Smith, Adam).

MEARES, JOHN. *Voyages Made in the Years 1788 and 1789 from China to the North-West Coast of America.* London, 1790. pp. 372, XCV, with appendices. Numerous illustrations and charts.

MILBURN, WILLIAM. *Oriental Commerce*. Containing a geographical description of the principal places in the East Indies, with their Produce, Manufactures and Trade. London, 1813. 2 vols. pp. CIII, 413 and 581. 12 maps and charts.

MILL, JAMES. *The History of British India*. (Continued by H. H. Wilson). London, 1840-1845. Vols. VI and VII, pp. 683, 608.

MINTO, COUNTESS OF. *Life and Letters of Gilbert Elliot, First Earl of Minto, from 1807 to 1814, while Governor-General of India*. Edited by the Countess of Minto. London, 1880. pp. 403, with a map.

M'KONOCHIE, A. (see Mackonochie).

M'LEOD, JOHN, M. D. *Voyage of His Majesty's Ship "Alceste" to China, Corea, and the Island of Lewchew, with an account of her shipwreck*. 3rd edition. London, 1819. pp. 339. Seven illustrations.

MONEY, WILLIAM TAYLOR. *Observations on the expediency of Shipbuilding at Bombay for the Service of His Majesty and of the East India Company*. London, 1811. pp. 73, with appendices.

MONTEFIORE, J. *A Commercial Dictionary* containing the present state of Mercantile Law, practice and custom. London, 1803.

MORRIS, HENRY. *The Life of Charles Grant, Sometime Member of Parliament for Inverness-shire and Director of the East India Company*. London, 1904. pp. XVIII, 404. Four illustrations.

MORSE, H. B. *The Chronicles of the East India Company Trading to China, 1633-1834*. 4 vols. Oxford, 1926. Vol. III, pp. 388. Six illustrations and a map.

MORTIMER, THOMAS. *A General Dictionary of Commerce, Trade, and Manufactures ;* exhibiting their present state in every part of the world. London, 1810.

NAVAL CHRONICLE. Vols. 1-39.

NAVY RECORDS SOCIETY (see Laughton, J. K. and Richmond, Sir H. W.).

NUGENT, MARIA, LADY. *A Journal from the Year 1811 till the Year 1815, including a Voyage to and Residence in India*. 2 vols. London, 1839. Vol. I, pp. XII, 428.

OWEN, S. J. *A Selection from the Despatches, Memoranda, and other papers relating to India, of Field-Marshal the Duke of Wellington, K.G.* Edited by S. J. Owen. Oxford, 1880. pp. CLV, 670, with seven maps and plans.

OWEN, S. J. *A Selection from the Despatches, Memoranda, and other papers relating to India of the Marquess Wellesley, K.G., during his Government of India*. Edited by S. J. Owen Oxford, 1877. pp. CXI, 813, with nine maps and plans.

PARKINSON, C. NORTHCOTE. *Trade in the Eastern Seas, 1793-1813*. Cambridge, 1937.

PARLIAMENTARY PAPERS. India Office. Vol. for 1808-1813.

PARSHAD, I. DURGA. *Some Aspects of Indian Foreign Trade*. London, 1932. pp. 238.

PERCIVAL, ROBERT. *An Account of the Island of Ceylon*. London, 1803. pp. 420. A map and two charts.

PERCIVAL, ROBERT. *An Account of the Cape of Good Hope*. London, 1804. pp. 339.

PHIPPS, JOHN. *A Guide to the Commerce of Bengal*, for the use of merchants, shipowners, commanders, officers, pursers and others resorting to the East Indies, containing a view of the shipping and external commerce of Bengal. Calcutta, 1823. pp. XVIII, 489.

PHIPPS, JOHN. *A Practical Treatise on the China and Eastern Trade ;* comprising the Commerce of Great Britain and India, particularly Bengal and Singapore, with China and the Eastern Islands. Calcutta, 1835. pp. V, 338. Appendices, LXVI.

POLO, MARCO. *The Travels of Marco Polo the Venetian*, with an Introduction by John Masefield. London, 1907. pp. XVI, 461.

POPHAM, SIR HOME. *A Description of Prince of Wales Island, in the Straits of Malacca :* with its real and probable advantages and sources to recommend it as a marine establishment. London, 1805. pp. 72.

PRIOR, JAMES. *A Visit to Madras ;* being a sketch of the local and characteristic peculiarities of that Presidency in the year 1811. London, 1821. pp. 35.

PRIOR, JAMES. *Voyage along the Eastern Coast of Africa to Mozambique, Johanna, and Quiloa ; to St. Helena, etc., in the Nisus Frigate*. London, 1819. pp. 114, with one illustration.

PRIOR, JAMES. *Voyage in the Indian Seas in the Nisus Frigate, 1810 and 1811*. London, 1820. pp. 114. A chart, two plans and one illustration.

QUARTERLY REVIEW :
> Vol. X. October, 1813. p. 18.
> Vol. XI. April, 1814. p. 215.

QUINCY, JOSIAH. *The Journals of Major Samuel Shaw*, the first American Consul at Canton. With a Life of the Author, by Josiah Quincy. Boston, 1847. pp. 360, portrait frontispiece.

RICHMOND, ADMIRAL SIR H. W. *Private Papers of George, second Earl Spencer, First Lord of the Admiralty*, 1794-1801. Edited for the Navy Record Society by Rear-Admiral H. W. Richmond. Vol. IV. 1924.

RICHMOND, ADMIRAL SIR H. W. *The Navy in India*, 1763-1783. London, 1931. pp. 430, with 16 diagrams and maps.

ROBERTS, EMMA. *The East India Voyager, or the Outward Bound.* London, 1848. pp. LXIII, 263.

ROBERTS, P. E. *India Under Wellesley.* London, 1929. pp. IX, 323. Frontispiece and four maps.

ROBINSON, F. P. *The Trade of the East India Company from 1709 to 1813.* Cambridge, 1912. pp. 186.

SAMUELSON, JAMES. *India, Past and Present, Historical, Social and Political.* London, 1890. pp. 390. 23 illustrations and a map. Bibliography by Sir W. W. Hunter.

SARGENT, REV. J. *The Life of the Rev. T. T. Thomason, M.A.*, late Chaplain to the Honourable East India Company. London, 1833. pp. XI, 344, with frontispiece.

SCOTT-WARING, MAJOR. *Observations on the Present State of the East India Company.* 4th edition. London, 1808. pp. LXXVI, 76.

SETON-KARR, W. S. *Selections from Calcutta Gazettes of the years 1798-1805*, showing the political and social condition of the English in India. Vol. III, Calcutta, 1868. pp. XVI, 586.

SHAW, MAJOR SAMUEL (see Quincy, Josiah).

SHERWOOD, MRS. *The Life and Times of Mrs. Sherwood* (1775-1851), from the Diaries of Captain and Mrs. Sherwood. Edited by F. J. Harvey Darton. London, 1910. pp. XIV, 519, with 11 illustrations.

SMITH, ADAM, LL.D. *An Inquiry into the Nature and Causes of the Wealth of Nations.* Edited by J. R. M'Culloch, Esq. Edinburgh, 1839. pp. 648.

SMYTH, H. WARINGTON. *Mast and Sail in Europe and Asia.* London, 1906. pp. 448, with numerous illustrations.

SMYTH, CAPTAIN W. H. *The Life and Services of Captain Philip Beaver*, late of His Majesty's Ship *Nisus.* London, 1829. pp. 339.

SPEAR, T. G. P. *The Nabobs, A Study of the Social Life of the English in Eighteenth Century India.* Oxford, 1932. pp. VII, 210.

SPEARS, J. R. *The Story of the American Merchant Marine.* New York, 1910. pp. 340, with 16 illustrations.

SPENCER, ALFRED (see Hickey, William).

STAPLETON, COMMANDER G. *The Blue Peter*, vol. 14, No. 151, October, 1934. Article on Minicoy.

STEEL, DAVID. *The Ship-Master's Assistant and Owner's Manual.* London, 1803. 10th edition, very considerably improved and enlarged. pp. 450 and 168 pp of appendices.

STEEL, DAVID. *Elements and Practice of Naval Architecture.* Illustrated with a series of 38 large draughts and numerous smaller engravings. London, 1805. 2 vols., with atlas of illustrations. Also another edition, 1822, revised by John Knowles. pp. 438, with appendices, plates, etc.

STEPHEN, J. *War in Disguise ; or the Frauds of the Neutral Flags.* London, 1805. pp. 315.

STEVENS, ROBERT. *The Complete Guide to the East India Trade, addressed to all Commanders, Officers, Factors, etc., in the Honourable East India Company's Service.* Robert Stevens, Merchant in Bombay. London, 1766. pp. 157.

SWETTENHAM, F. *British Malaya.* London, 1910. pp. XI, 354, with 50 illustrations.

THOMASON, REV. T. T. (see Sargent, Rev. J.).

TILBY, A. WYATT. *The English People Overseas.* Vol. II. *British India*, 1600-1828. 1911. pp. 286.

TWINING, THOMAS. *Travels in India a Hundred Years Ago ;* being notes and reminiscences by Thomas Twining. Edited by Rev. William H. C. Twining. London, 1893. pp. XII, 537, with portrait and maps.

VALENTIA, GEORGE, VISCOUNT. *Voyages and Travels to India, Ceylon, the Red Sea, etc., in the Years* 1802-1806. 4 vols. London, 1811. Vol. I, pp. 439.

WALLACE, JAMES. *A Voyage to India :* containing reflections on a voyage to Madras and Bengal, in 1821, in the ship *Lonach ;* instructions for the preservation of health in Indian climates ; and hints to surgeons and owners of private trading ships. London, 1824. pp. VI, 166.

WATHEN, JAMES. *Journal of a Voyage in* 1811 *and* 1812 *to Madras and China.* London, 1814. pp. XX, 246, with 24 illustrations.

WELLESLEY, MARQUESS OF (see Owen, S. J.).

WELLINGTON, DUKE OF (see Owen, S. J.).

WELLINGTON, DUKE OF. *Supplementary Despatches and Memoranda of Field-Marshal Arthur, Duke of Wellington, K.G., India,* 1797-1805. Edited by his son, the Duke of Wellington. 2 vols. London, 1858. Vol. 1, pp. 592, with a map.

WHALL, W. B. *The Romance of Navigation,* London, n.d. pp. 292, with 33 illustrations.

WILLIAMSON, CAPTAIN THOMAS. *The East India Vade-Mecum ;* or complete Guide to gentlemen intended for the Civil, Military, or Naval service of the Honourable East India Company. London, 1810. 2 vols. pp. XVI, 520, and VII, 506.

WILSON, H. H. (see Mill, James).

WISE, HENRY. *An Analysis of One Hundred Voyages to and from India, China, etc., performed by Ships in the Honourable East India Company's service.* Henry Wise, late Chief Officer of the Honourable Company's Ship *Edinburgh.* London, 1839. pp. 120 Frontispiece and three diagrams.

WISSETT, ROBERT. *A Compendium of East Indian Affairs, Political and Commercial,* collected and arranged for the use of the Court of Directors. Robert Wissett, Clerk to the Committee of Warehouses. 2 vols. London, 1802.

WYATT-TILBY (see Tilby, Wyatt).

CHAPTER VIII

THE WEST INDIAN TRADE

PRIMARY

PUBLIC RECORD OFFICE :
C.O. papers relating to each island, especially C.O.137 to C.O.142 Jamaica. The shipping lists, submitted by the naval officer, are invaluable. They are not complete.
F.O. papers relating to Spain, for 1808 to 1815.
Admiralty. In-letters from the Admirals on the West Indian stations, letters relating to convoy, and licences.
B.T. Board of Trade. Minutes and In-letters and Miscellaneous.
Customs. States of Navigation and Commerce to 1808, and Ledgers in Imports by Countries, Customs 17 and 4.

CUSTOMS HOUSE :
Plantation Papers, Jamaica, Trinidad and others, not complete, most of the early bundles were lost in the fire of 1814.

WEST INDIA COMMITTEE, 14 Trinity Square, E.C.3 (expected to move to the West End):
Minutes of the Meetings of the West India Merchants, 7 vols., 1769-1843.
Minutes of the Meetings of Planters and Merchants, 6 vols., 1785-1834.
Micellaneous Papers, including a merchant's account book.
Minutes of the Glasgow West India Association, 1802-1809.

WILKINSON AND GAVILLER, 34 Great Tower Street, E.C.3 :
Letter and Account Books of the firm of Lascelles & Maxwell from 1739.

BRISTOL, MERCHANTS' HALL. Minute Books of the Bristol West India Club, 1782-1857.

PARLIAMENTARY PAPERS, numerous, see Ragatz, L. J., *Check List of House of Commons Sessional Papers relating to the West Indies,* 1763-1834. Others are to be found under South America, Commercial Credit, etc., in the General Index.

RAGATZ, L. J. *Statistics for the Study of British Caribbean History,* 1927.

GUIDES

BELL, PARKER AND OTHERS. *Guide to British West Indian Archive Materials*, 1926.
CUNDALL, F. *Bibliographia Jamaicensis*, 1902.
CUNDALL, F. *Bibliography of the West Indies, exclusive of Jamaica*, 1909.
NEW YORK PUBLIC LIBRARY. *List of Works relating to the West Indies*, 1912.
RAGATZ, L. J. *Guide for the Study of British Caribbean History*, 1932.
Royal Empire Society Catalogue, West Indies.

SECONDARY

Contemporary, numerous, see Guides. The following is a short select list of the more
outstanding :
BOSANQUET, C. *Thoughts on the Value to Great Britain of Commerce in General and on the
Importance of the Colonial Trade in particular.*
BROUGHAM, H. *An Inquiry into the Colonial Policy of the European Powers*, 1803.
COLQUHOUN, F. *A Treatise on the Wealth, Power and Resources of the British Empire*, 1815.
CUNDALL, F. *Lady Nugent's Journal*, 1934.
DEPONS, F. *Voyage to South America*, 1807.
EDWARDS, B. *History of the West Indies*, 1810.
HUMBOLDT, A. DE. *Political Essay on the Kingdom of New Spain*, 1811.
GOWER, R. *Remarks Relative the Dangers of Convoys*, 1811.
Facts Relative to the Cotton Colonies, 1811.
On Throwing Open the Trade in Foreign Linens, 1816.
PINCKARD, G. *Notes on the West Indies*, 1806.
REEVES, J. *A History of the Law of Shipping and Navigation*, 1792.
SHEFFIELD, LORD. *Strictures on the Necessity of Inviolably Maintaining the Navigation and
Colonial System of Great Britain*, 1804.
STEPHEN, J. *War in Disguise*, 1805.
SOUTHEY, T. *Chronological History of the West Indies*, 1827.
WALTON, W. *Present State of the Spanish Colonies*, 1810.
WALTON, W. *An Expose of the Dissentions of Latin America*, 1814.
YOUNG, W. *The West India Commonplace Book*, 1807.

MODERN WORKS—SELECT LIST :

ALLEN, H. *British Commercial Policy, 1783-1793 ;* thesis in the Library of the University
of London.
BELL, H. C. *British Commercial Policy in the West Indies*, H. R., 1916.
FRASER, L. *History of Trinidad*, 1892.
HORSFALL, L. F. *The Free Port System in the British West Indies ;* thesis in the Library of
the University of London.
GOEBEL, D. B. *British Trade to the Spanish Colonies*, A. H. R., 1938.
JENKS, L. *Migration of British Capital*, 1927.
JONES, J. S. *Historical Study of Anglo-South American Trade, 1807-1825 ;* thesis in the
Library of the University of London.
LANGNAS, A. I. *The Relations Between Great Britain and the Spanish Colonies, 1808-1812 ;*
thesis in the Library of the University of London.
LAWSON, L. A. *The Relation of British Policy to the Declaration of the Monroe Doctrine*,
1922.
MANCHESTER, A. K. *British Pre-eminence in Brazil*, 1933.
MANNING, H. T. *British Colonial Government after the American Revolution*, 1933.
PENSON, L. M. *The Colonial Agents of the British West Indies*, 1924.
RAGATZ, L. J. *The Fall of the Planter Class in the British Caribbean*, 1927.
ROSE, J. H. *British West India Commerce as a Factor in the Napoleonic Wars*, in *Cambridge
Historical Journal*, 1929.

CHAPTER IX

THE AMERICAN TRADE

ALBION, R. G. *The Rise of New York Port*, 1815-1860. (New York : Scribner, 1939).
BUCK, N. S. *The Development of the Organization of Anglo-American Trade*, 1800-1850. (New Haven : Yale University Press, 1925.)
BURT, A. L. *The United States, Great Britain, and British North America from the Revolution to the Establishment of Peace after the War of* 1812. (New Haven : Yale University Press ; London : Oxford University Press, 1940). The best account of diplomatic relations between Great Britain and the United States.
GALPIN, W. F. *The Grain Trade of England during the Napoleonic Period.* (Ann Arbor : Michigan University Press, 1925.)
HANSEN, MARCUS LEE. *The Atlantic Migration*, 1607-1860. (Cambridge : Harvard University Press, 1940), Chapter III.
HEATON, HERBERT. *Yorkshire Cloth Traders in the United States*, 1770-1840, in *Thoresby Society Miscellany*, XXXVII, Part III, pp. 225-287. (Leeds : Thoresby Society, 1944).
HEATON, HERBERT. *Non-Importation*, 1806-1812, in *Journal of Economic History*, Vol. I, pp. 178-198. November, 1941.

(Manuscript and printed document sources not included)

CHAPTER X

THE NEWFOUNDLAND TRADE

BIRKENHEAD, LORD. *The Story of Newfoundland.* London, 1920.
CARSON, W., M.D. *Reasons for Colonising the Island of Newfoundland.* Greenock, 1813.
CHAFE, L. G. *Statistics of the Seal Fishery.* St. John's N.F.
CONDON, MICHAEL E. *The Fisheries and Resources of Newfoundland.* St. John's, 1925.
FAYLE, C. E. (see Wright, Charles).
GLASCOCK, W. *The Naval Sketch Book.* London, 1826.
HATTON, H. AND HOLLAND, H. H. *The King's Customs.* London, 1908.
INNIS, H. A. *The Cod Fisheries, the history of an international economy.* Yale University Press, 1940.
JAMES, WILLIAM. *The Naval History of Great Britain.* London, 1847.
JOB, JOHN. MS. Diary of John Job. Quoted by kind permission of T. B. Job, Esq.
NAVAL CHRONICLE, THE
NEWFOUNDLAND. *The Book of Newfoundland.* London, 1937.
PROWSE, D. W. *A History of Newfoundland.* London, 1895.
PERIODICALS :
  The Times, London, 1800-1815.
  Gore's Liverpool Advertiser. Liverpool, 1790-1815.
  Liverpool Mercury. Liverpool, 1813-1815.
  Evening Telegram, various dates. St. John's, N.F.
REGISTERS OF SHIPPING. Registers preserved at the Custom House, Liverpool, 1790-1815.
REPORTS OF ROYAL COMMISSION ON NEWFOUNDLAND.
SHIPPING REGISTERS. London, 1790-1815.
WRIGHT, CHARLES, AND C. E. FAYLE. *A History of Lloyd's.* London, 1928.
  See also Public Record Office, Colonial Papers.

CHAPTER XI

THE SLAVE TRADE

(*a*) UNPUBLISHED :

CENTRAL REFERENCE LIBRARY, BRISTOL
Jefferies Collection of MSS., newspapers and magazine extracts, public notices, etc., relating to the *History of Bristol.* Volume XIII.
SOCIETY OF MERCHANT VENTURERS, BRISTOL
Book of Petitions.
West India New Society, 1782-93.
UNIVERSITY OF BRISTOL LIBRARY
Pinney Family Business Letter-books, 1793-1815.

(*b*) PUBLISHED :

An Abstract of the Evidence delivered before a Select Committee of the House of Commons in the years 1790 and 1791 ; on the part of the Petitioners for the Abolition of the Slave Trade. London, James Phillips, 1791.
Annual Register, 1788 ff. Longmans, Green & Co. Ltd.
Cobbett's Parliamentary Debates, 1803-12.
Parliamentary Debates. Published under the superintendence of T. C. Hansard. 1812 ff.

(*c*) BOOKS :

BESSETT, DR. *A Defence of the Slave Trade on the Grounds of Humanity, Policy and Justice.* London, 1804.
CLARKSON, T. *An Essay on the Slavery and Commerce of the Human Species.* London.
— *History of the Rise, Progress and Accomplishment of the Abolition of the African Slave Trade by the British Parliament.* London, John Parker, 1839.
CRUNDALL, F. (Edited by). *Lady Nugent's Journal, 1801-15. Jamaica, One Hundred Years Ago.* London, A. & C. Black, 1907.
EDWARDS, B. *The History, Civil and Commercial, of the British Colonies in the West Indies.* 3 vols. 3rd edition. London, Stockdale, 1801.
MATTHEWS, W. *The New History, Survey and Description of the City and Suburbs of Bristol, or Complete Guide.* Bristol, W. Matthews, 1794. 4th edition, J. Matthews, 1813.
The Memoirs of the late Captain Hugh Crow of Liverpool. London, Longman, 1830.
PINCKARD, G. *Notes on the West Indies.* 2 vols., 2nd edition. London, 1816.
RENNY, R. *An History of Jamaica.* London. Printed for J. Cawthorn, 1807.
YOUNG, SIR W. *A Tour through the Several Islands of Barbadoes, St. Vincent, Antigua, Tobago and Grenada in the years 1791 and 1792.* London, Stockdale, 1801.
— *West India Commonplace Book.* London, Stockdale, 1807.

(*d*) NEWSPAPERS AND PERIODICALS :

Bonner and Middleton's Bristol Journal (files).
Felix Farley's Bristol Journal (files).
The Monthly Magazine, No. XLV, June 1st, 1799.

II. SECONDARY

BESANT, SIR W. *London in the Eighteenth Century.* London. A. S. C. Black, 1902.
BRAYLEY, E. B. *London and Middlesex.* 4 vols. London, Wilson, 1810-1816.
COUPLAND, R. *The British Anti-Slavery Movement.* London, Thornton Butterworth, Ltd., 1934.
— *Wilberforce.* Oxford, Clarendon Press, 1923.
HUNT, W. *Bristol.* London, Longmans, Green & Co., 1887.

LATIMER, J. *Annals of Bristol in the Eighteenth and Nineteenth Centuries.* 3 vols. Bristol, J. W. Arrowsmith, 1887-1902.

MacINNES, C. M. *A Gateway of Empire.* Bristol, J. W. Arrowsmith, Ltd., 1939.

—- *England and Slavery.* London, J. W. Arrowsmith, Ltd., 1934.

PICTON, SIR J. A. *City of Liverpool Municipal Archives and Records, from A.D.* 1700 *to the Passing of the Municipal Reform Act,* 1835. Liverpool. C. W. Walmesley, 1886.

WILLIAMS, G. *History of the Liverpool Privateers and Letters of Marque, together with an Account of the Liverpool Slave Trade.* London, W. Heinemann, 1897.

CHAPTER XII

THE POST OFFICE PACKETS

HEMMEON, J. C. *The History of the British Post Office.* Harvard Economic Studies, VII, Cambridge, U.S.A., 1912.

JACKSON, G. GIBBARD. *From Postboy to Air Mail.* London, N.D.

JOYCE, HERBERT, C.B. *History of the Post Office.* London, 1895.

KELLY, SAMUEL. *An Eighteenth Century Seaman.* Edited by Crosbie Garstin. London, 1925.

NORWAY, ARTHUR H. *History of the Post Office Packets.* London, 1895.

PARKINSON, C. NORTHCOTE. *Edward Pellew, Viscount Exmouth.* London, 1935.

NEWSPAPER FILES :

    The Times, 1793-1815.

    Williamson's Liverpool Advertiser, 1793-1815.

    Gore's General Advertiser, 1793-1815.

    Liverpool Mercury, 1811-1815.

Index

[For names of individual vessels, see under 'ships']

Able Seaman, examination to pass as a, 111

Abolition of Slavery, its expected results in the West Indies, 266

Abolitionist Movement, for ending the Slave Trade, 251

Acts of Trade, the terms of the, 178

Adams, Captain, the death of, 120

Admiralty, the, 15
  convoys arranged by, 19
  correspondence with West India Merchants, 161

African Trade, the, 77
  goods exported in the, 262

Agreement, Articles of, made compulsory, 35

Amelia Island, smuggling at, 226

American Chamber of Commerce at Liverpool, the, 213

American Colonies, revolt of the, 25

American frigates, danger of, 43

American Independence, War of, 19

American neutrality, the advantages of, 194

American prizes, the capture of, off Newfoundland, 239

American privateers, danger from, 43

American residents in Liverpool, 213

American ships, seizure of in 1797, 42
  U.S. legislation to protect, 203
  British use of, 18

American shipowners, success of, 84

American trade, 194

American trade statistics, first compilation of, 195

Anchors, description of, 93

Anderson, John, Surgeon and afterwards Master of Slaver, 274

Angerstein, John Julius, adviser of William Pitt, 39
  financial stability of, 42

Anglo-American Trade, 198
  details of the, 212

Angola, slaves procured at, 264

Anson, Admiral Lord, 8

Anspach, description of schooners by, 233

Antigua, decline of the sugar plantations in, 166
  importance of the naval base at, 184

Antiscorbutics, as used by Krusenstern, 125
  those used by the Dutch, 126

Antwerp, 17

Apprentices, protection of against impressment, 35

Apprenticeship, details of, 111

Arabia, trade between India and, 155

Arctic whaling, as school of seamanship, 112

Arctic Whalers compelled to carry a surgeon, 137

Arnold, James, evidence against Slave Trade given by, 274, 275, 276

Articles of Agreement, made compulsory, 35

Articles of apprenticeship, protection afforded by, 35

Assurances, Court of, Act for establishing a, footnote to p. 37

"Atlantic Graveyard", the, 12

Austen, Jane, 17

Avon, River, at Bristol, 66

Bahama Channel, route via the, 158

Bahamas, organisation of convoys bound for, 161

Bahamas, the, Free Port established in, 177
 ships sailing for the, 189

Balance of trade, favourable, desire for, 80

Ballast passage, avoidance of, 31

Baltic ports, seizure of ships in, 42

Baltic Trade, details of, 31
 risks of, 43
 ships in, 78
 freights and premiums in, 84
 interruption of, 84

Baltic Shipping Exchange, the, origin of the, 30

Baltimore, influence of the shipyards at,101
 ships arriving at, 205
 strictness of Customs at, 215

Bancroft, quotation from the works of, 133

Banks of Newfoundland, fishing on the, 77

Baptist Mills, Bristol, brass manufactory at, 65

Barbados, strategic value of, 157
 decline of the sugar plantations in, 166
 description of the harbour at, 184

Barbary States, trade with the, 77

Barber Surgeons of London, examination conducted by, 136, 137

Barcelona, vessel chartered for, 32

Barges, numbers of in the Port of London, 51

Baring, Sir Francis, 39

Barings of London, Bankers, 202

Barker, Robert, carpenter, ill-treatment of, 277

Barnards', Thames Shipbuilders, 143

Barnes, James, financial stability of, 42

Barquentine, comparative rarity of, 95

Barque-rig, comparative rarity of, 95

Barrel staves, the need for in the sugar trade, 168

Baxter, Brothers, of Dundee, Sail Manufacturers, 92

Bay de Verde, Newfoundland, landing of passengers at, 229

Beatty, Admiral of the Fleet the Earl, 10

Bell, Captain, presentation of sword to,284

Bengal Government, the surplus revenues of the, 141

Bengal Hurkura, advertisement in the, quoted, 148

Benjamin Lester & Co., shallops employed by, 233

Bennett, John, of Lloyd's, 44

Benson, E. F., 10

Bentham, General, discovery attributed to, 122

Berbice, English occupation of, 158

Berlin and Milan Decrees, 45

Bermuda Company, Agents at St. John's maintained by the, 232

Bight of Benin, the dangers of the, 261

Bill of Lading, provisions of a, 29

Billingsgate, 51

Birmingham, exports to America from, 29

Birmingham hardware, Spanish-American demand for, 176

Black Ball Line, foundation of the, 199

Blackwall, the Brunswick Dock situated at, 51
 proposed canal at, to connect with Wapping, 54
 shipbuilding at, 143, 150

Blackwall Frigates, the, 19, 90

Blane, Sir Gilbert, quotations from the medical works of, 122, 123, 124
 remarks by, on malarial infection, 133

Blanning, Nicholas, Shipbuilder at Redcliff, 67
 William, Shipbuilder of Bristol, 67

Blewfield Bay, assembly of convoys in, 191

Blockade runners, French, u elessness of, 18

Board of Trade and Plantations, intervention by the, 46

Boarding pike, use of the, 102

Bombay, reason for occupying, 142
 Country Trade at, 155, 156
 dockyard, ships built in, 89
 shipwrights, the work of, 89

Bonaparte, Jerome, capture made by, 248
Bonavista, seal fishery at, 232
Bonded Warehouses, the system of, 56
Bonny, slaves procured at, 264
Boston, arrival of ships at, 206
Bourbon sugar cane, the, 166
Brackenbury, Mr., inventor of signals for
   ships in distress, 46
Branker, P. W., presentation to, 252
Brazil, ships trading to, 16
   sighting of by East Indiamen, 152
   the opening of trade with, 217
Brent, S. & D., Thames Shipbuilders, 143
Brick-goëlette, French type of Brigantine,
   95
Bridgwater Fair, business at, 64
Bridport, and the Newfoundland Fisheries,
   232
Brig, vessels rigged as, 95
Bristol, comparative neglect of in text-
   books, 14
   freight market at, 29
   underwriting at, 40
   prosperity of, 49
   growth of, 50
   the port of, 64
   clearances and entries, 67
   West Indiaman built at, 180
   excellence of water at, 122
   ships for U.S.A. from, 204, 205
   its relative growth checked by the rise of
     Liverpool, 206
   and the Newfoundland Fisheries, 232
   the Slave Trade at, 255
   decline of local interest in the Slave
     Trade, 256
   interest in plantation slavery, 257
Bristol Infirmary, 137
Bristol Society of Merchant Venturers,
   petitions from the, 251, 256
Bristol Water, demand for, 65
British Copyright Law, not applied to
   Ireland, 211
British exports to U.S.A., the decline of, in
   1811, 222

British India, mortality among white
   population in, 142
British Isles, threat to the, 17
British North America, the trade with, 77
   importance of the route to, 84
   United States excluded from trade with,
     195
   Squadron stationed in, 237
British Plantation Registry, the, 34
British residents in U.S.A., 213
British ship, definition of, under the Navi-
   gation Acts, 33
British shipping industry, the, 48
British shipping, protection of, 34
   Russian seizure of, 42
   entries and clearances in 1792, 73
British West Indies, 157
   United States excluded from trade with,
     195
Broad Fourteens, patrol of, 12
Brodbelt, Mrs. Ann Gardner, extract from
   letter of, 132
Broke, Captain, R.N., of the *Shannon*, 246
Brown, Colin, Surgeon, observations by
   on the subject of convicts, 136
Brown, Thomas, Master of vessel in New-
   foundland Trade, 243
Brunswick Dock, the, at Blackwall, 51
   and Masthouse, 143
Bucklers Hard, 15
Bulley, Samuel, merchant of Teignmouth,
   247
Bulley & Job, merchants of Liverpool in
   Newfoundland Trade, 249
Bullion, export of from Peru, New Spain,
   and Brazil, 164
Burnett, Sir William, typhus epidemic
   described by, 134
Butter-rigged schooner, definition of a, 95

Cabin-space in East Indiaman, cost of, 150
Cables, dimensions and weight of, 93
Cadiz, cargo of wheat for, 32
Cairo, 17
Calcutta, Country Trade at, 155, 156

Callender, Sir Geoffrey, 9, 10

Cameroons, the, slaves procured at, 264

Canadian border, goods transported across the, 225

Canadian Fur Trade, competition for the, 26

Canadian Timber Trade, the, 84

Canal Age, the, 49

Canal projects, Bristol interest in, 64

Canal system of South Lancashire, a factor in Liverpool prosperity, 58

Canals, construction of, 49

Canning, George, repudiation of pact by, 219

Canning of food, the invention of, 131

Canvas, the manufacture of, 92

Cape of Good Hope, voyage via the, 18 usual approach to the, 152

Cape de Verde Islands, an Indiaman calls at the, 129

Cape Nicolas Mole, French naval station at, 187

Captains' Room, the, at Lloyd's, 30

Cargo, definition of, 28

Caribbean Sea, the, 157

Carronade, introduction of in merchant service, footnote, p. 83

Chamber of Shipping of the United Kingdom, the origin of the, 37

Channel, Privateers in the, 18

Channel Isles, trade with the, 41

Channel Islands, increase of traffic with, 86

Chapelle, Mr. H. I., quotation from works of, 95

Charter Party, provisions of, 29

Chartered Companies, supplanting of the, 26

Chatham, typhus epidemic at, 134

Chester, participation of in Slave Trade, 255

Childers, Colonel S., work edited by, footnote, p. 32

China, the East India Company's trade with, 14

China, length of voyage to, 74

China Clippers, the, 19

Cholera, the infective nature of, 121 misapprehension concerning, 127

Churchill, Rt. Hon. Winston S., Prime Minister, 11

Clark, Dr. Thomas, observation by on the subject of scurvy, 123, 124 table of diseases compiled by, 126 cure for dysentery suggested by, 129

Clark Russell, quotations from the works of, 95, 106

Clarkson, his horror on seeing the behaviour of seamen ashore, 260

Classification of shipping, the, 47

Claxton, William, impoverishment of, 257

Clothing worn in merchant service, description of the, 117, 118

Clyde Canal, and the Baltic Trade, the, 163

Coal, supply of, for London, 78

Coal Exchange, the, 39

Coastal Batteries, cover provided by, 18

Coasting Trade, the, 15, 79

Cochrane, Lord, advocate of flatter sails, 92

Codfish, export of, to the United Kingdom, Spain and Portugal, 231

Cod-Fishery, value of in 1814, 232

Coffee, importation of, 165 difficulty of marketing in England, 169

Coffee-Houses, collection and forwarding of letters from, 287

Coffee Room at Lloyd's, the resort of shipmasters, 30

College of Surgeons, Edinburgh, 136

Collier brigs, characteristics of the, 96

Colliers, numbers of frequenting London River, 51 average size of, 78

Colquhoun, Patrick, statistical evidence of, 36 treatise written by, footnote p. 52 his estimate of West Indian Trade, 182

Commerce and Navigation, United States Report on, 202

Commercial Coffee-House, rise of the, 26, 29

317

Commercial intelligence provided by Post Office Packets, 287

Committee of Lloyd's, efforts made by to amend Convoy Acts, 36 and footnote the, 38

Conception Bay, sealing craft from, 233

Condition of seamen's accommodation afloat, evidence concerning the, 119

Congress of the United States, declaration of War by the, 221

"Constant Traders", definition of, 32

Continent, European, privations of the, 18

Continental markets, attempt to force, 80

Continental System, effect of the, 43
the, 66
causes of the failure of, 81
results of the, 168
the, 216
its breakdown in Europe, 222
its extension to the U.S.A., 222

Contraband trade with the Spanish Settlements, 175

Convict ship, experiences aboard a, 115

Convoy, organization of a, 19
reduction in insurance premiums for ships sailing in, 43
breaking of, 45
complaints relating to, 45
delays caused by, 70
unimportance of delays occasioned by, 82
East India, system of organizing the, 152
Act of 1798, the, 83, 234 and 236
system for West India Trade, the, 188
assembly at Spithead of a, 189
discipline of a, 190
size of, 191
difficulty of providing adequate escort for, 192
duty, the payment of, 236

Cook, Captain James, R.N., early career of, 96, 121
error made by with regard to scurvy, 124

Cooke's etching of the Thetis, 94

Copenhagen, insurance at, 40

Copper sheathing, the extensive use of, 182

Corbett, Sir Julian, 9, 10

Cordova, Admiral, his capture of East and West Indiamen, 38

Cork, convoys assemble at, 70, 189
Newfoundland vessels at, 244

Corn Laws, effect of on the importation of wheat, 196
grain export limited by the, 173

Corn shipments, licence of by Napoleon, 81

Coromandel Coast, privateers off the, 18

Corporation of the City of London, docks built by the, 56

Cotton, Joseph, East India Director, 156

Cotton, attempts to cultivate in the West Indies, 171

Cotton industry, writings on the, 14

Country craft, Indian, characteristics of the, 90

Country Trade, of India, the, 74
details of the, 141, 155
with China, value of the, 155

Cowes, sailmaking at, 92

Craig, Sir James, 11

Creswell, Commander, R.N., calculation made by, 85

Crewkerne, sailmaking at, 92

Cripps, W. B. & Co., merchants of Liverpool, 249

Crooked Island Passage, the, 188

Cross-Trades, importance of the, 79

Crow, Hugh, Slaver Captain of Liverpool, 259

Cuba, privateers off, 18
Spanish settlement in, 157
French privateers off, 192

Cupples, George, quotation from, 89

Curaçao, English occupation of, 158

Curling & Co., Thames Shipbuilders, 143

Customs House, historical material of the, 14

Custom House, the, at London, 51

Cutter Rig, characteristics of the, 96

Dalzell, Archibald, Surgeon in the Slave Trade, 274

Dartmouth, and the Newfoundland Fisheries, 232

Newfoundland vessels sailing from, 243

Deal, embarkation of passengers at, 151

De Brisson, description of Slave Trade by, 273

Defoe, Daniel, the commercial failure of, footnote, p. 37

Dekker, Dutch Physician, the work of, 131

Delaware, the freezing of the, 210

Demerara, the British occupation of, 158

sugar exports from, 167

Deptford, East Indiamen moored at, 51

shipbuilding at, 143, 150

De Valera, Irish Premier, lecture by, 11

Devonshire, decline of the ports in, 50

its loss of the old connection with Newfoundland, 249

Dewar, Captain A., R.N., editorial work by, footnote, p. 28

Diamond Harbour, the limitations of, 144

Dibdin, Thomas, verses quoted from, 117

Dictatorship, struggles against, 17

Dock, old meaning of the word, footnote, p. 51

Docks at Liverpool, value of in 1800, 62

Dogger Bank, the, 10

Dominica, lack of sugar at, 166

Dover Packets, arming of the, 289

Droghers, West Indian craft used in sugar trade, 168

Dublin publishers, pirated editions by, 211

Dudman & Co., Thames Shipbuilders, 143

Dunkirk, reverse suffered at, 17

Dunscombe & Harvey, Agents at St. John's for Bermuda Co., 232

Dutch East India Company, medical service maintained by, 137

Dutch, the ousting of from the carrying trade, 32

Dutch antiscorbutics, 126

Duties payable on sugar, 174

Dyewoods, the trade in, 172

Dysentery, infective nature of, 121

the ravages of, 129

East Anglia, decline of the ports in, 50

East India Company, the Honourable, 26

the carrying of own risks by, 40

bonded warehouses used by, 57

ships employed by, 88

career offered in the ships of, 106

trading privileges allowed in, 108

medical services provided by, 136

monopoly of the, 141

East India Docks, the completion of the, 154

East India Dock Company, the, 155

East Indiamen, numbers of frequenting London River, 51

numbers of, footnote to p. 74

their exemption from convoy, 83

size of the, 88

trading privileges allowed to officers of, 108

surgeons carried aboard, 136

officers of the, 146

crews of the, 147

passengers carried by the, 149

East India Shipowners, formation of Dock Co. by, 57

East India Trade, value of cargoes in, 41

the nature of the, 76

the need for bullion in, 164

Eastland Company, decline of the, 27

Egypt, French attempt against, 17

Elphinstone, Captain, in Packet Service, 285

Emancipation of slaves in the West Indies, the effect of the, 193

Emancipation Act of 1833, compensation paid under the, 257

Embargo Act, enacted by United States Congress, 210

the passing of the, 216

failure of the, 217

Emigration from Ireland, 211

Enderby & Son, Messrs., Whaler owners, 94

Enteric Fever, the cause of, 121

Entrance and clearance formalities, the laws relating to, 34

Erith, 7

Erskine, British Ambassador to U.S.A.,218

Escort vessels, shortage of, 19

Esher, Lord, writings of, 10

Essequibo, British occupation of, 158

European trade, the, 79

European waters, control of, 17

Examination to pass as Able Seaman, 111

Exeter, and the Newfoundland Fisheries, 232

    participation of, in Slave Trade, 255

Exports to India, nature of the, 142

"Extra ships", definition of, 143

Falconbridge, Alexander, evidence against Slave Trade given by, 274

Falmouth Packets, mentioned, 184, 278

    arming of the, 281

    losses among the, 282

    tonnage of the, 288

Fanning, American fur trader, 137

Fayle, C. Ernest, the loss of, 19

Factory Acts, the, 14

Fayal, popularity of in 1809, 218

Ferguson, Mr., dysentery misunderstood by, 127

Fisher, Admiral Lord, 11

Fisheries, Newfoundland, how regarded by Government, 227

Fisheries, why not dealt with, 15

Fishing Admirals, justice in Newfoundland administered by the, 229

Fishguard, French landing at, alarm caused by, 64

Flax, for sailcloth, 92

Flax cultivation, details concerning, 210

Flaxseed imported by Ireland, 197

Floating Harbour, the, at Bristol, 71

Florida Channel, route via the, 187

Fogo, seal-fishing at, 232

Foreign Coasting Trade, the, 41, 72, 86

Foreign Ships Registry, the, 34

Foreign ships, employment of, 34

Foreign Trade of Great Britain, 72, 74

Foreign Trade, British ships engaged in the, 85

Fox, Charles James, in power, 254

France, finances of, 81

    trade policy of, 81

Fraudulent stranding, temptation to engage in, 36

Free Port Act of 1787, discussion of by Jamaica planters, 161

Free Port System, the, 175

Freeling, Francis, Secretary to the Post Office, 288

Freights, the earning of, 28

French Coasts, raids upon the, 17

French plantations, destruction of, in St. Domingue, 164

French planters, refugee, migration of to Jamaica, 170

French West Indian Colonies, the capture of the, 84

Frome River, the, footnote, p. 51

Fur ships, the, from Quebec, 78

Fur Trade, Canadian competition for the, 26

Furniture, mahogany used in the making of, 172

Galapagos Islands, Whale Fishery off the, 94

Gallatin, U.S. Secretary of the Treasury, trade report by, 202, 215

Gardner, James Anthony, quotation from, 132

Garstin, Crosbie, work edited by, footnote to p. 28

Gaulois, Newfoundland, factory at, 245

Gaultois, vessels built at, 233-4

George III, Jubilee of, 25

    remark by, on a Jamaica merchant, 159

George, Lloyd, British Premier, Memoirs of, 11

Georgia, cotton grown in, 172

General Shipowners' Society, the membership of the, 28

Gibraltar, passenger fare to, 285
Gillespie, quotation from the works of, 126
Girard, Stephen, Philadelphia merchant, 202
Gladstone, John, Shipowner, engages in Far Eastern Trade, 59
    West India interests of, 162
Glasgow, underwriting at, 40
    the port of, 49
    re-export trade of, 163
    share of Slave Trade, 255
Glascock, Captain William, quotation from the works of, 102
Gold Coast, slaves procured on the, 264
Gold, desire to deprive enemy country of, 80
Goods, English, European demand for, 85
Gower, Captain Richard, designer of the Transit, 98, 97
Grand Fleet, the, 11
Gravesend, embarkation at, 150
"Green Book", the (or Underwriters' Register), 47
Greenhand, the, work by George Cupples, 89
Greenland Dock, Rotherhithe, 51
Greenland Dock, acquired by Commercial Dock Co., 57
Greenlandman, Whaler, the, 94
Greenlandmen, resistance offered to press-gang by, 112
    character of the, 114
Greenock, imports and exports of, 207
Greenock, and the Newfoundland Fisheries, 232
    Newfoundland vessels sailing from, 243, 244
Greenspond, seal fishery at, 232
Gregory, George, longevity of, 114
Grenada, civil war in, 166
    Free Port established at, 177
"Gruff" goods, description of, 144
Guadeloupe, British occupation of, 158
    French privateers from, 192

Guinea Coast, trade with, 77
    imports from, 77
Guineaman, the crew carried by a, 261

Haiti, effects of the negro revolt in, 159
    French privateers from, 192
Halifax, Nova Scotia, shipment of goods via, 223
    trade via, in 1814, 225
Hamburg, insurance at, 40
Hamburg Company, or Merchant Adventurers, 27
Hamilton & Graham, merchants, of Liverpool, 248
Hammocks, use of by sailors, 118
Harbour Breton, Newfoundland, factory at, 245
Hardy's Register of Ships, 144
Harewood, Earl of, 162
Harvey & Co., of St. John's, Newfoundland, 232
Harwich, collision off, 96
    Packet vessels stationed at, 278, 281
    tonnage of the Packets at, 288
    arming of the, 289
Hawke, Admiral Sir Edward, 8
Hayward, Richard, Sail Manufacturer, 92
Headgear worn by sailors, 118
Hemp, rigging made of, 92
Hermaphrodite, American privateers rigged as, 95
Hibbert family, influence of the, 162
Hibbert, George & Co., merchants and shipowners, 179
High Seas Fleet, the, 10
Hillhouse, J. M., Son & Co., Bristol Shipbuilders, 67
Hills, Captain, evidence on Slave Trade given by, 276
Hobson, George, premium paid to, 43
Holyhead, Packet vessels stationed at, 278, 281
Honduras Bay, logwood imported from, 172
Hopes, of Amsterdam, Banking Firm, 202
Horseferry Tier, London River, 51

Hotham, Captain Henry, R.N., 100
Hotwell water, from Bristol, 66
Howell, John, of Edinburgh, 114
Howland Dock (or Greenland Dock), used by Whalers, 51
Hoy, definition of a, 97
Hoys, number of in Port of London, 51
Hudson Bay Company, the monopoly of the, 26
Hudson Bay Company's ships, exemption from convoy of the, 83
Hull, or Kingston-upon-Hull, under-writing at, 40
  mention of, 49
  growth of, 50
  as port for arctic whalers, 94
  ships sailing to U.S.A. from, 204, 205
  its relative growth checked by the rise of Liverpool, 206
  its minor role in American trade, 206, 207
Hull-design, defects in, 34
Huskisson, his reforms and trade treaties, 193
Hungroad, Bristol anchorage, 71
Hygiene, ignorance of, 118

Immigrant traffic, in U.S.A., the revival of the, 222
Indian country craft, the characteristics of the, 90
Indentures of apprenticeship, extract from the, 111
Indigo, British importation of, 172
Imperial Defence, College of, 19
Industrial Revolution, the effects of the, 25
Inner Passage, via Mozambique Channel, 153
Insurance, Marine, growth of, 37
Insurance of French ships, the, 81
Insurance of West India cargoes, 174
Insurance brokers, difficulties of the, 30
Insurance Offices, material in, 14
Insurance market, the marine, 30

Insurance premium, reduction in, after convoy made compulsory, 242
Ireland, the trade with, 15, 41
  insurance of voyages to, 43
  trade with Bristol of, 66
  trade with, 72, 74
  foreign trade of, 79
  importance of the trade with, 86
  exports of to the West Indies, 173
  linen industry of, 197
  its growth of population, exports, 207
  emigration from, 211
  exports of, 211
Irish Channel, raids by privateers upon the, 248
Irish immigrants in Newfoundland, 238
Irish linen industry, the, 197
Irish Packets, immunity of the, 289
Irish Sea, privateers in the, 18
Irish trade with the U.S.A., 207
Isle of Dogs, proposal for docks to be made at the, 54
  docks constructed at, 56

Jacobinism, the fear of, a deterrent to reform, 252
Jamaica, insurance of passage from, 43
  the capture of, 158
  prosperity of, 166
  production of coffee in, 170
  importance of Free Port trade at, 177
  passenger fare to, 285
Jamaica Coffee House, the, 30, 39
Jamaica rum, the supply of, 261
James, Rear-Admiral, remarks by, on sick-ness in the West Indies, 131
  his career in the merchant service, 180
"Jamie Green", or spritsail, 92
Jane's *Fighting Ships*, 8
Java, return of to the Dutch, 18
  Dutch medical problems at, 130
Jefferson, United States President, embargo enacted by, 210
  appointment of consul by, 214
  rejection of pact by, 216

Jellicoe, Admiral of the Fleet the Earl, 10
Jenner, control of smallpox due to, 121
Jerusalem Coffee House, resort of East India Merchants, 30, 39
Jesuits Bark, or quinine, the use of, 128
Job, John, extract from the diary of, and career of, 247, 248
Johnson, James, quotation from the works of, 127
Jutland, Battle of, 11

Kains & Co., of Shields, 115
Kamtschatcha, arrival of Russian ship at, 125
Kelly, Samuel, Shipmaster, the career of, 28, 32
Kempe firm, schooner fitted by, 233
Kerr, William, feats performed by, 112, 113
Kilve, cloth bought at, 64
Kingston, Jamaica, the strategic importance of, 158
entrepot trade of, 177
Kingston Gazette, advertisement in the, 270
Kingston-upon-Hull (see under "Hull")
King, Captain, R.N., shrewd observation by, 121
Kingroad, Bristol anchorage, 71
Krusenstern, Admiral in the Russian Navy, 125, 138

Lading, Bill of, 29
Lancashire and the cotton trade, 142
Lancashiremen, colony of, in New York City, 220
Lancaster, participation of in the Slave Trade, 255
Lancaster, Sir James, prevention of scurvy by, 123
Lannon, James, neglect by, and fine paid by, 228, 229
Lascars, employment of, 149
Lascelles family, interests of the, 162

Latrine accommodation, inadequacy of in the Navy, 122
La Rochelle, English prize taken into, 247
Laughton, Sir John, 9
Lawson, Captain Caesar, master of Slaver, 263
Leadenhall Street, East India House situated in, 142
Leeward Islands, raid on by Missiessy, 158
Leeward Islands Stations, the, 104
Legal Quays, the number and location of the, 51
Lemon juice, value of as an antiscorbutic, 124
Leslie, R. C., views of, quoted, 104
Lesser Antilles, the, 157
Lester, Benjamin, and the seal fishery, 244
Letters of Marque, taken out by Slaver, 263
Levant Company, subsidisation of the, 27
Levant Trade, losses in the, 42
Lewis, Mathew, voyage of, 183
Liability of owners, limitation of the, 46
Lice, typhus transmitted by, 121
Lifeboats, establishment of, 46
"Light Horsemen", river thieves, 52
Lighthouses, U.S., extinction of, 226
re-lighting of, 226
Lighters, numbers of in the Port of London, 51
Limehouse Reach, London River, 51
Lind, medical author, common disorders listed by, 123
Linen industry, the Irish, 197
Lisbon, vessel proceeds to, 32
Lisbon Convoy, the assembly of the, 99
Lisiansky (Captain in the Russian Navy), quotation from, 122
antiscorbutics used by, 125
Liverpool, neglect of in text-book history, 14
cargo for, from Bristol, 29
underwriting at, 40
Underwriters' Association formed at, 40
growth of, 49
success of the docks built at, 54

pioneer port in wet-dock construction, 58
docks at, value of the, 62
distress in, during American War, 62
examination of surgeons at, 137
importation of cotton at, 171
American consul at, 203
ships sailing to U.S.A. from, 204, 205
rising importance of, in U.S. trade, 205
as outlet for north central regions, 207
American residents at, 213
embargo-breakers arrive at, 218
exports to Newfoundland from, 231, 232
Newfoundland vessels sailing from, 243, 244
connection with Newfoundland, 248
petition from against abolition, 252
defence of the Slave Trade centred upon, 253
prosperity of, before 1807, 258
statistics of slavers sailing from, 258
organization of the Slave Trade at, 259
Lloyd, Edward, 44
Lloyd George, British Premier, 10, 11
Lloyd's Coffee House, Subscription Rooms and Underwriters' Association
Origin and rise to importance of, 15, 25, 30
Minute Book of, 36
importance of, 37
organization of, after 1774, 38
supremacy of, 43
Committee of, 44
Committee of, consulted by Admiralty, 45
Committee of, promotes the Act of 1803, 46
Agents of at British and foreign ports, 46
Admiralty correspondence with, 161
Register Books at, 150
Correspondence of, with Vice-Admiral Waldegrave, 235
protest by, against inadequate naval escort, 236

Lloyd's List, publication of, 44
losses shown in, 86
Lloyd's Register, 289
classification of ships in, 47
London Assurance Company, grant of charter to, in 1720, 30, 39
London, Port of, 50 et seq.
London Bridge, 51
London Docks, opening of the, 56
London, supply of coals for, 78
as port for South Sea Whaling, 94
Statute compelling ships sailing from to carry a surgeon, 137
West India interests in, 162
West India trade centred at, 162, 163
ships sailing to U.S.A. from, 204, 205
deterioration of her position in American trade, 205
exports to Newfoundland from, 231
and the Newfoundland Fisheries, 232
Long family, of Jamaica, the, 162
Long-distance trades, the, 31
Lubbock, Basil, the death of, 19
Lumpers, pilfering by, 52

Macadam, roadmaker, 64
Macao, visit paid to by Russian ship, 125
Mackintosh, Rt. Hon. Sir James, quotation from the works of, 155
Madeira, East Indiamen call at, 152
Madeira wine, commanders' privilege of importing, 109
Madison, James, President of the United States,
exporting interests of, 214
non-intercourse ended by, 218
non-intercourse re-established by, 219
Madras, unhealthiness of, 129
reason for occupying, 142
Mahan, Captain A. T., 9
Mahogany, importation of, 172
Mail services, the extent of the, 283
frequency of the, 287
Malabar teak, used for shipbuilding, 89

Malacca, Straits of, privateers in the, 18
passage via the, 153
Malaria, conveyed by mosquitoes, 121
Malt, essence of, its inutility as a pre-
ventive of scurvy, 124
Malta, strategic use of, 17
passenger fare to, 285
Man, Isle of, trade with the, 41
Managing Owner, function of the, 146,
151
Manchester, frequent mention of in text-
books, 14
Manifest Act, the, 35
Manning, Cardinal, ancestry of, 162
Marine casualties, high rate of, 35
Marine insurance market, the, 30, 37
Marine Insurance Committee of 1810, the,
39, 42
Maritime History, need for the study of,
12, 13, 14
Marryat, Captain F., works of quoted, 105,
106, 151
Martinique, prizes brought into, 126
English occupation of, 158
French privateers from, 192
Masts, importation of from Canada, 84
Matthews' New History of Bristol, foot-
note to p. 65
Mauritius, privateers based upon, 18
Maury, James, U.S. Consul at Liverpool,
214, 218
Measles, occasional severity of, 123
Mediterranean, abandonment of the, 17
Mediterranean Fleet, the, 17
Meeting of West India Planters and
Merchants, 161
Menzies, Dr., fumigation carried out by,
135
Mercantilist approval of West Indian
trade, 174
Mercantilist theory, British and French
belief in, 80
Merchant Adventurers, the Company of,
its survival at Hamburg, 27
Merchant Service, the, 106

Mersey Docks, results of the construction
of the, 50
Mersey, River, connected by canal with
the Trent, 49
Messina, 17
Mexican Coast, Whale Fishery off the, 94
Middle Passage, the, in Indian Ocean, 153
Middle Passage, in Slave Trade, treatment
of negroes during the, 252
details of the, 267
Midlands, canal outlets from the, 49
Milan Decrees, the, 45
Milbanke, Governor, Court-of-Law estab-
lished by, in Newfoundland, 229
Milford, Packet vessels stationed at, 278,
281
Ministry of All the Talents, attitude of to
the Slave Trade, 254
Minute Books at Lloyd's, the, 45
Molasses, by-product of sugar, 168
Montreal, North-West Company formed
at, 26
shipment of goods via, 223
Moore, General Sir John, the work of, 17
Mortality among white population in
India, 142
Mortality in Slave Trade, 275, 276
Mortier, Marshal, British property seized
by, 27
Mosquito, malaria conveyed by the, 121
Mozambique Channel, route via the, 153
Mudheavers, strike amongst, at Bristol, 70
Mudlarks, River thieves, 52
Muscovado, partly refined sugar, the
packing of, 168

"Nabobs", patronage of the, 150
Naples, 17
Napoleon, Emperor of the French, 18
corn-shipments to Britain licensed by, 81
conditional revocation of Berlin Decrees
by, 219
diplomatic success of, 221
Napoleonic Wars, the study of the, 16

Nassau, Free Port in the Bahamas, 177
Naval Chronicle, quotation from the, 103
Naval History, 16
Naval Historian, the fault of the, 16
Naval Sketch Book, the, 102
Naval Staff College, the, 10
Naval Stores, trade in with Baltic, from Liverpool, 59
Naval superiority, British, 18
Navigation Acts, the objects and results of the, 32, 33
  the enforcement of the, 34
  mentioned, 72, 78
Neale, John, merchant of Liverpool, 250
Negro slaves, the price paid for, 266
  the treatment of, on the Middle Passage, 268
  different value of those from different tribes, 264
"Nelly Ray", song entitled, 117
Nelson, Vice-Admiral the Lord, mentioned, 11, 16, 92
  his good opinion of Lloyd's, 44
  remark attributed to, 103
  quotation from letters of, 123
"Nelson touch", the, 10
Neutrals, invasion of West India trade by the, 71
Neutral ships, extensive employment of, 85
Nevis, the sugar production of, 166
New Archangel, Russian visit to, 125
New Brunswick, ships built in, 84
New Calabar, slaves procured at, 264
Newcastle-on-Tyne, mentioned, 15, 31, 49
  underwriting at, 40
  coal exported from, 78
New England shipowners, exclusion of from protected trades, 25
Newfoundland, Bristol imports from, 65
  fisheries at, 84
  activities of planters at, 227, 228
  restrictive influences felt by, 227
  useless population at, 228
  Commander-in-Chief at, 229
  justice at, administered by naval officers, 230

exports from, 231
shipbuilding at, 233, 234
convoys to and from, 234, 237
navigational risks of, 239
types of vessel employed in trade with, 242
New Holland, East Indiamen's approach to, 153
"New Lloyd's", 38
Newman's, shipbuilders, of Dartmouth, 233, 244
  privilege accorded to, 246
New South Wales, convict ship bound for, 115
New South Wales, mortality among convicts destined for, 136
New York, Anglo-American trade at, 203
  export of flaxseed from, 210
  ships arriving at, 204
Nicol, John, autobiography of, 114, 115
Night-blindness, mention of by Blane, 124
Night Plunderers, of London River, the, 52
Nile, Battle of the, 11
Non-importation Act passed by U.S. Congress in 1806, 210, 215
  repeal of the, 225
Nootka Sound dispute, the effects of the, 203
North Africa, imports from, 77
North American timber, the demand for, 84
Northfleet, shipbuilding at, 143, 150
North West Company, the formation of the, 26
Nova Scotia, ships built in, 84, 244
  smuggling via, 226
Nugent, Lady, and the smell of sugar, 181

Officers of an East Indiaman, the, 146
Old Calabar, slaves procured at, 264
"Old Falcon" Inn at Gravesend, 151
Orders in Council, the, as affecting the United States, 206
  the revocation of the, 221
Ostrige's purifying machine, a description of, 122

Packets, Post Office, the risks run by the, 19
  neglect of duty by captains of, 279
  freightage of goods in the, 279
  unprovoked attacks made by, 280
  reduction in armament of, 280
  fraudulent surrender of, 280
  reform of the, 281
  popularity of the, 282
  general usefulness of the, 283
  passengers carried in the, 285
  seamen employed in, 289
  guns mounted by the, 289
Parliamentary Committee on the Port of London, 1796, 52
Parliamentary Committee on the West Indian Islands, 167
Parsee shipwrights, the work of the, 155
Passengers carried in East Indiamen, 149
Passenger ships, compelled by statute to carry a surgeon, 137
Patriotic Fund, the establishment of the, 44 and footnote
Paul, the Russian Emperor, death of, 42
Pay of seamen, inadequacy of the, 36
Pellew, Admiral Sir Edward, his message to an Indiaman, 88
  mentioned, 135
Penang, reason for occupying, 142
Pennant, Richard, Lord Penrhyn, 162
Pennsylvania, flaxseed cultivated in, 210
Penrhyn, Lord, of Jamaica, 162
Percentage of ships lost, 1793-1801, 41
Perry's Shipbuilding Yard, and the Brunswick Dock, 51, 57, 98, 143
Persian Gulf, trade in the, 155
Pillage in London River, the system of, 52
Philadelphia, trade with, 29
  demand for goods at, 31
  arrival of ships at, 204, 205, 206
Picknell, Charles, the diary of, 115
Pilotage, the laws relating to, 35
Pilots, West Indian, the character of, 186
Pinckard, Dr., voyage to Barbados of, 180, 184
Pinney, John, Bristol Merchant, 64, 66, 70, 160
  his views on plantation slavery, 257

Pitcher's, Thames Shipbuilders, 143
Pitt, Rt. Hon. William, Prime Minister, mentioned, 10
  advised by John Julius Angerstein, 39
  member of Parliamentary Committee, 54
Plantation Register, the, 77
Plantation Trade, the, 78
  the importance of the, 165
Plunder of tackle and cargoes in London River, 36
Plymouth, participation of in the Slave Trade, 255
Polar voyages, frequency of, 133
Policy Committee of Lloyd's, the, 38
Pool of London, the crowd of shipping in the, 51
Poole, connection of with Newfoundland trade and fisheries, 232, 243-4
Porter, drink, recommended as a preventive of scurvy, 125
Port de Grave, Newfoundland, factory at, 245
Porto Rico, Spanish settlement in, 157
Port Royal, Jamaica, sickness on board the ships at, 132
  description of, 185
Portsmouth, assembly of convoys at, 151
Portugal, Commercial Treaty with, 16
  disposal of cargoes in, 77
  supplies for British troops in, 222
  importation of codfish by, 231, 232
Postage, rates of, in 1813, 286
Post-Masters General, the, 278, 279, 282
"Post Office Guns", description of the, 289
Post Office Packets, system of hiring, 32, 278 (see under "Packets")
Potash, export of from America, 196
  importance of, in bleaching, 211
Poyning's Act, the iniquities of, 11
Press Gang, fear of the, 70
  resisted by Greenlandmen, 112
  activity of the, 148
Preventive medicine, lack of, 121
Pringle, Sir John, an error propagated by, 124
  his views on dysentery, 127

Prisoners-of-war, epidemics among the, 135

Private Trade, of officers in East Indiamen, 147

Privateers, defence against, 144
overcrowding in, 118
lack of discipline in, 119
American, danger from, 43
American, activity of the, 237
British, commissioned at Liverpool, 59
French, danger from, 18
French, in the West Indies, 192

Protecting and Indemnity Societies, origin of, 40

Protheroe & Claxton, merchants, of Bristol, 257

Public Record Office, correspondence with Lloyd's preserved at, 45

Public Vendue, auction of imported goods at a, 212

Punts, numbers of in Port of London, 51

Pursers crabs, footwear known as, 118

Quakers, visit of, to Convict Ship, 116

Quarantine, laws relating to, 35

Quarterly Review, mentioned, 180

Quebec, value of cargo from, 41
fur ships from, 78
shipment of goods via, 223

Quinine, the value of, 128

Randall's, Thames Shipbuilding Yard, 143

Rangoon, shipbuilding at, 156

Ratsey, George Rogers, Sail Manufacturer, 92

Ratsey, Thomas W., Sail Manufacturer, 92

Ray, Nelly, song composed on the subject of, 117

Record transatlantic passage, a, 200

"Red Book", the (or Shipowners' Register), 47

Refugees from Ireland, embarkation of, 211

Register Book, the, of Shipping, 35, 47

Register of Ships, the, by Charles Hardy, 144

Registration Act of 1787, 34

Renny, quotation from the works of, 268

Reveley, Mr., proposals made by, for diverting Thames, 54

Revenue Officers, bribing of the, 52

Regularity of passage, instance quoted of, 200

Regulative Act, the, of 1788, 251

Rice Trade, the, 156

Richardson, William, discretion allowed to as shipmaster, 32

Richery, Admiral, captures made by in 1795, 42

Rigging, details of, 91

Rio de Janeiro, Portuguese Royal Family at, 217

River Police, London, establishment of in 1798, 36, 52

Roberts, Dr. John, the alleged cruelty of, 277

Rotherhithe, Greenland Dock situated at, 51
proposal to build docks at, 54
shipbuilding at, 143
West Indiamen built at, 180

Routine on board an East Indiaman, 153

Royal African Company, decline of the, 27
forts maintained by, 264

Royal College of Physicians, award made on the advice of, 135

Royal Commission, evidence given before a, 119

Royal Exchange Assurance Company, grant of a charter to the, 30, 39

Royal Exchange, Lloyd's established at, in 1793, 30

Royal Navy, the ascendancy of the, 17
manning of the, 35

Royal Society, Sir John Pringle's discourse to, 124

Rum, made from molasses in West Indies, 168
its use in the Royal Navy, 169

"Runners", ships armed to sail without escort, 19, 189

Russia, the invasion of, 17

Russia Company, and the Archangel trade, 27

Ryan & Sons, merchants, of Liverpool, 248

Sailing, order of, 19

St. Domingue, destruction of French plantations in, 164

St. Eustatius, British occupation of, 158

St. Helena, East Indiamen call at, 154

St. John's, Newfoundland, maintenance of supplies at, 227
risk of fire at, 229
vessels entering each year, 243

St. Katherine's Dock, opening of in 1828, 56

St. Kitts, British settlement in, 157

St. Lucia, excellence of the harbour at, 184

St. Malo, privateers based upon, 18

St. Petersburg, shipment of gold to, 41

St. Saviour's Dock, London River, 51

St. Thomas, British occupation of, 158

St. Vincent, civil war in, 166

St. Vincent, Admiral the Earl, 8, 99

Salmon Fisheries, the, of Newfoundland, 233

Salt, cargo of, 32

Salt, Cheshire, export of from Liverpool, 248

"Sam's next the Custom House", Coffee House, resort of shipbrokers, 30

San Domingo, Spanish settlement at, 157

San Domingo, effect of the negro atrocities at, 252

Sangaree, West Indian drink, composition of, 183

Sanitary Science, slow progress of, 121

Saugnier, description of Slave Trade by, 273

Savannah, cotton trade at, 206

Schanck, Captain, R.N., Agent for transports, 132

Schooners, Bermuda-built, suggested use for, 192

Schoute, Dr., 122

Scoresby, Captain William (senior), extract from log-books of, 133

Scoresby, Captain William (junior), description of Northern Whale Fishery by, 133

Scotland, 15

Scotsmen, colony of in New York City, 220

Scott, Sir Walter, quotation from the works of, 114

Scott, Michael, quotation from the works of, 186

"Scuffle-Hunters", River Thieves, 52

Scurvy, the incidence of at sea, 123-126

Scuttling, fraudulent, temptation to engage in, 36

Sea Island cotton, the cultivation of, 171

Seal-Fishery, the, of Newfoundland, 232

Seamen, shortage of in war-time, 34
welfare of, 35
poverty of after the war, 120

"Seekers", vessels not established, 179

Select Committee on Marine Insurance, the, 42

Selkirk, Alexander, the Life and Adventures of, 114

"Sentimental Journey", quotation from the, 125

Severn River, connected by canal with the Trent, 49
the navigation of the, 64

Sheathing, copper, the extensive use of, 182

Sheffield cutlery, Spanish-American demand for, 176

Sheffield, Lord, and the shipping interests, 195

Shiercliff's Bristol Guide, footnote to p. 65

Ship-rig, definition of, 90

Shipbuilding on Merseyside, 59

Ship-Letter Act, criticism and failure of the, 288

Ship-Letter Office, establishment of the, 287, 288

Ship-Letter system, the, 284

Shipowners, Clubs formed by, 40
  General Society of, 28
  Society, the, 46
  parsimony of, 35
  Register, Society of the, 47
Shippers, Committee of, 19
Shipping, classification of, 47
"Shipping Interest", the nature of the, 142
Ships, average tonnage of, 87
Ships, individual, named (H.C.S. = Hon.
  Company's Ship, East Indiaman)
Abercrombie Robinson, H.C.S., built in
  India, 89
Active, brig, in Newfoundland Trade, 246
Acorn, merchantman, Spanish capture of,
  238
Active, sealing schooner, 233
Admiral Watson, H.C.S., Sir R. Wigram's
  service aboard, 136
Adriana, merchantman in American trade,
  199
Agincourt, H.M. Ship, carrying flag of
  Vice-Admiral Waldegrave, 235
Alert, H.M. Sloop, the taking of the, 238,
  239
Alfred, merchant vessel in Newfoundland
  trade, the taking of the, 238
Allison, merchantman, in Newfoundland
  Trade, 246
Amelia and Eleanor, slave ship, action fought
  by the, 120
Anaconda, United States privateer, prize
  taken by the, 284
Arethusa, H.M. Ship, 100
Aspasia, American merchantman, 138
Avenger, H.M. Sloop, the foundering of
  the, 239
Belle Poule, of the French Navy, taken by
  H.M. Ship Experiment, 88
Berbice, Packet, of Teignmouth, the
  capture of the, 238
Betsey, merchantman, speedy voyages by,
  200
Blenheim, Hull whaler, resistance offered to
  press-gang by, 112
Bold, H.M. Brig, cruising with privateer,
  246

Bombay, H.C.S., built in India, 89
Boxer, H.M. Ship, on convoy duty, 238
Brooke, slaver, Dr. Trotter serves as
  surgeon in the, 274
Brotherly Love, collier, 96
Buckinghamshire, H.C.S., built in India, 89
Camilla, H.M. Ship, her losing touch with
  convoy, 237
Caroline, merchantman, capture and
  recapture of, 239
Catherine, merchantman in the Newfound-
  land Trade, 243
Centurion, H.M. Ship, last member of her
  crew, 114
Ceres, slaver, of Liverpool, 259
Charles Grant, H.C.S., built in India, 89
Charlotte, merchantman in Newfoundland
  Trade, 249
Chaser, South Sea whaler, recapture of the,
  113
Chesapeake, United States frigate, fired
  upon by British, 216
Cognac Packet, collier, 96
Commerce, Dartmouth brig, capture of the,
  238
Cornwallis, packet, her voyage to Malta,
  286
Crescent, H.M. Ship, on convoy duty, 238
David Scott, H.C.S., 88
Despatch, Dover packet, the surrender of
  the, 281
Diana, H.M. Ship, specie carried in, 40
Dove, brig, of Dartmouth, armament of,
  in Newfoundland Trade, 244
Dragon, H.M. Ship, recapture made by,
  238
Draper, merchantman, regular passages of,
  200
Duck, brig, in Newfoundland Trade, the
  capture of the, 246
Duke of Kent, merchantman, in Newfound-
  land Trade, the taking of, 238
Eagle, schooner, in Newfoundland Trade,
  244
Earl of Balcarres, H.C.S., built in India, 89
  her service as hulk, 90
Edgar, H.M. Ship, 132

Edward, barque, in Newfoundland Trade, 250

Electra, H.M. Sloop, on convoy duty, 238

Enterprize, slaver, of Liverpool, mention of, 263
successful voyage of the, 271

Essex, United States ship, prize taken by, 238
sloop taken by, 238-9

Europa, H.C.S., sickness aboard the, 128-9

Experiment, H.M. Ship, her capture of the *Belle Poule*, 88

Express, packet, action fought by the, 283-4

Factor, merchantman in American Trade, 201

Fanny, merchantman in American Trade, 291

Fanny, schooner in Newfoundland Trade, 228-9

Flora, merchantman in Newfoundland Trade, the capture of the, 247

Fly, H.M. Sloop, the foundering of the, 239

Forester, of Shields, the, 78

Fortune, slaver, of Liverpool, voyage of the, 271

Francis Freeling, Falmouth packet, successful action of the, 284

Freelove, collier, of Whitby, 96

Gazelle, la, French brig-schooner, 95

General Plumer, United States privateer, capture of the, 246

Goliath, H.M. Ship, 115

Great Harry, the, 7

Gustavus Adolphus, name assumed by U.S. vessel, 225

Harmony, Baltic trader, recapture of the, 113, 114

Harmony, merchantman, the capture of the, 238

Hazard, H.M. Sloop, on convoy duty, 238

Henri-Grace-a-Dieu, the, 7

Herefordshire, H.C.S., built in India, 89

Hilton, merchantman in Newfoundland Trade, the capture of, 248

Immortalite, H.M. Ship, 100

Indian, H.M. Sloop, capture made by the, 238

Java, coal hulk at Gibraltar, 90

Jesus Maria and Joseph, Spanish privateer, capture made by, 238

John, constant trader to Philadelphia, 29

John, ship, the freight of, 32

Kains, convict ship, 115

King David, West Indiaman, 70

King George, merchantman, the capture of the, 238

Lady Frances, packet, the guns mounted in the, 289

Lady Julian, convict ship, the, 115

La Gazelle, French brig-schooner, 95

Lapwing, H.M. Sloop, discomfiture of the, 237

Latona, H.M. Ship, on escort duty, 235

L'Invention, French four-masted privateer, 99

Lively, brig, regular transatlantic crossings made by the, 200

Live Oak, brig, Spanish capture of the, 238

Lord Sheffield, West Indiaman, the amenities of the, 180

Louisa, slaver, of Liverpool, profits made by the, 272

Manchester, packet, action fought by the, 285

Margery and Mary, schooner, the capture of the, 238

Maria, American merchantman, in fur trade, sickness aboard, 138

Maria, merchantman, in West India Trade, 180

Maria, brig, her resistance to the press-gang, 245

Marquis of Cornwallis, H.C.S., nickname given to the, 88

Mars, merchant brig in American Trade, 215

Mary, collier brig, 114

Mary, slaver, gallant action fought by the, 120

Mary, slaver, of Liverpool, 259

Melpomene, H.M. Ship, merchantman retaken by the, 238

Muros, H.M. Sloop, on convoy duty, 238

Nancy, merchantman, capture and recapture of the, 238

Nancy, merchantman in Newfoundland Trade, 245

Nautilus, packet brig, long service of the, 289

Neva, Russian exploration ship, 125

Nevis, West Indiaman, 70

Nightingale, packet brig, long service of the, 289

Nonsuch, H.M. Ship, 112

Nottingham, H.C.S., dimensions of the, 88
mention of the, 117

Olive, merchantman in American Trade, the, 215

Osprey, H.M. Sloop, in trials against the *Transit*, 99

Otway, slaver, cargo of the, 270

Pacific, merchantman, her record transatlantic crossing, 200

Parr, slaver, of Liverpool, the, 259

Penelope, brig in Newfoundland Trade, 249

Pigou, merchantman in American Trade, 199

Pilgrim, slaver, hygienic conditions aboard the, 270

Pique, H.M. Ship, the timber of, 89

Placentia, H.M. Ship, built in Newfoundland, 234

Plover, H.M. Ship, recapture made by the, 238

Pomone, H.M. Ship, American ships taken by the, 239

Portland, merchantman in Newfoundland Trade, 243

Portland, packet, action fought by the, 285

Powerful, H.M. Ship, ravages of yellow fever aboard the, 132-133

Prince de Neufchatel, American privateer, the, 95

Princess, H.M. Ship, guardship at Liverpool, the, 62

Princess Elizabeth, packet, the capture of the, 285

Raith, Hull whaler, recapture of the, 113

Redpole, packet brig, long service of the, 289

Robust, H.M. Ship, typhus outbreak in, 135

Roebuck, merchantman in American Trade, 199

Role, French privateer, capture made by the, 247

Rosamund, H.M. Ship, on convoy duty, 238

Royal Charlotte, H.C.S., large tonnage of the, 88

Royal George, H.C.S., crack ship of East India Fleet, 88

Royal George (II), H.C.S., destroyed by fire at Whampoa, 89

Royal Sovereign, merchantman in Newfoundland Trade, 243

St. Vincent, West Indiaman, 67

Sarah Kempe, sealing schooner, 233

Scaleby Castle, H.C.S., built in India, 89

Scout, H.M. Sloop, shipwreck of the, 239

Shannon, H.M. Ship, action with U.S. Frigate *Chesapeake*, 246

Simon Taylor, West Indiaman, 133

Sir John Sherbrooke, privateer, of Liverpool, capture made by, 246

Star, merchantman in Newfoundland Trade, the armament of the, 244

Temeraire, French privateer, capture of by Falmouth Packet, 285

Townshend, packet, the guns mounted by the, 289

Thames, H.M. Ship, recapture of slaver by, 269

Thetis, West Indiaman, 94

Thetis, Snow, slaver of Bristol, 277

Thomas, slaver of Liverpool, mutiny aboard the, 269

Transit, experimental ship, 97

Trepassey, H.M. Ship, built in Newfoundland, 234

Tweed, H.M. Sloop, the shipwreck of the, 239

Union, hospital ship, the, 135

Union, merchantman, capture of the, 238

Victory, H.M. Ship, size of the, 88
topsail of, 92

Virginie, H.M. Ship, recapture made by the, 238

Wanderer, H.M. Sloop, on convoy duty, 238

Will, slaver, of Liverpool, 259, 261

William, of Bristol, capture of the, 238

William Penn, merchantman in American Trade, 199
  regular arrival of in America, 200

Wolverine, H.M. Ship, loss of on convoy duty, 45, 236-7

York Town, United States privateer, capture made by the, 205

Ship's Husband, function of the, 146

Shipwrights, strike of, at Bristol, 70

Shorncliffe Camp, 17

Sicily, strategic use of, 17

Slade, John, of Poole, merchant, 244, 245

Slave Ships, compelled to carry a surgeon, 137

Slave Trade, as conducted at Liverpool, 58
  reaches its peak in 1798, 62
  character of the seamen in the, 119
  and the West Indies, the, 164
  movement for abolishing the, 251
  mortality in the, 276
  British exports for the, 262

Slave Traders, demand for compensation made by, 254

Slaves, effect of the emancipation of the, 193

Sleeping on deck, the arguments for, 127
  the occasions for avoiding, 128

Smith, Adam, Economist, 25

Smith, Dr. G., of New York, 137

Smuggling, reasons for omitting a chapter on, 15
  in London River, 36
  in America, 196
  tendency of packet vessels to engage in, 279

Smyrna Fleet, French capture of the, in 1693, 37

Smyrna, fruit trade at, 95

Smyth, James Carmichael, fumigation carried out by, 134, 135

Snow, vessels rigged as, 95

Soap, raw materials for, 197

Society of Shipowners, the formation of the, 37

Society of the Shipowners' Register, 47

Society of Underwriters, formation of, 47

Society of West India Merchants, the, 161

Soldiers, mortality of, aboard ship, 117
  boredom of, 149

South America, markets in, 18
  seizure of merchantmen bound for, 225

South American Trade, growth of the, 15, 46
  boom in, 220

South Sea Company, decline of the, 27
  Greenland Dock used by the, 51

Southseaman, Whaler, the, 94

South Wales, exports from, 206

Southern Italy, landing in, 17

Southern Whale Fishery, the, 51

Southwark, inhabitants of want dock at Rotherhithe, 54

South West-India Dock, taken over by West India Dock Company, 56

Spaarman, Dr., evidence on Slave Trade given by, 273

Spain, war with, 15

Spain, disposal of cargoes in, 77
  becomes ally of Great Britain, 84
  ports of closed to Newfoundland Trade, 84
  supplies for British troops in, 222
  importation of codfish by, 231, 232

Spaniards, obstinacy of, 16

Spanish possessions, nature of exports for the, 176

Spanish settlements, the contraband trade with the, 175

Spanish wool, Bristol importation of, 66

Special licences, the issue of, 81

Speed of merchantmen, instances quoted, 200

Spence, Graeme, Surveyor to the Admiralty, evidence of, 52

Spencer, Earl, First Lord of the Admiralty, 98

Spithead, assembly of convoys at, 189

Spritsail, importance of the, 91

"State of Navigation and Commerce", the, of 1808, 163

Staysails, use of the, 91

Steering or studded sails, 91

Stephen, James, works of, quoted, 167

Stevens, James, London Merchant, 161

Stevenson, Robert Louis, 9
Straw hats, worn by sailors in the tropics, 118
Strike of shipwrights at Bristol, 1794, 70
Studding or Stunsails, 91
Subscribers' Room, Lloyd's, exclusiveness of the, 30, 44
Subscribers to Lloyd's Coffee House, the, 38
Sufferance Wharfs, number of in London River, 51
Sugar Droghers, West Indian craft called, 168
Sugar, refineries for, at Bristol, 65
    importance of the supply of, 158
    improvement in the cultivation of, 166
    over-production of, 167
    evils of an exclusive cultivation of, 173
    duties payable upon, 174
Sunda, passage via the Straits of, 153
Sunderland, the port of, 31, 49
    coal supplied from, 78
Supercargo, duties of the, 31
Surgeons Company, examinations conducted by the, 136
Surgeons, in merchant ships, qualifications of, 137
    in slave ships, qualifications of, 255
    in slave trade, the duties of, 266
    description of the, in slave trade, 274
Surinam, Dutch preservation of lime-juice at, 126
    British occupation of, 158
Surrey Canal Company, 57
Surrey Commercial Dock Company, origins of the, 57
"Sworn Officers", position of the, 146
Sydenham Teast, shipyard of, 67

Tahitian sugar cane, the, 166
Taylor, Captain, the death of, in action, 285
Tea, British Trade in, the importance of, 142
    British preference for, 169
Teak, use of in shipbuilding, 89
    valuable qualities of, 156

Teignmouth and the Newfoundland Fisheries, 232, 243, 247
Thames, connected by canal with other rivers, 49
Timber ships, the number of frequenting London River, 51
Thackeray, W. M., quotation from the works of, 159
Thibault, French designer of L'Invention, 100
Thompson, Vice-Admiral G., drastic action by, 132
Thomson, Frederick, naval surgeon, quotation from the works of, 124
Thornton, Richard, wealth of, 39
    risk accepted by, 41
Timber, duty free importation of from America, 195, 197
Timber, importation of from British Colonies, 84
Timmins, Captain, 88
Tobacco, American, preferential treatment of, 195
    industry at Bristol, 65
Tobago, British occupation of, 158
Tonnage, shortage of, in time of war, 34
Tonnage measurement, 34, 94, 145
Tonningen, ship from, 41
Topsail, proportions of a, 91
Topsail schooners, 95
Torrington, Lord, 107
Tourville, Admiral, his capture of Smyrna ships in 1693, 37
Tower Dock, London, 51
Trade, British overseas, 15, 18
Trade, illicit, frequency of, 36
Trade Protection Act of 1803, the, 242
Trade routes, the, 11
Trade Statistics, American first compilation of, 195
Trade Treaties, Huskisson's, 193
Traitorous Correspondence Act of 1793, 80, 81
Treaty of Amiens, effects of in U.S.A., 212
Treaty of Ghent, receipt of in New York, 226
Trinidad, British occupation of, 158
    exports of Spanish colonies from, 177

Trinity House, approval of signals by, 46
  disapproval of Revely's plans by, 54
  approval of Newman's vessels, 234
Troops sent to India, system of transporting the, 149
Tropic, ceremony of crossing the, 184
Trotter, Thomas, M.D., Naval Surgeon,
  the character of, 132
  voyage made in slaver by, 274
Tuberculosis, not known to be contagious,
  121
Typhoid fever, the causes of, 121
Typhus, an outbreak of described, 134

Underwriters, instability of, 37
  losses of in 1780, 38
  number of in 1810, 39
  Society of formed in 1760, 47
  suppport given by to convoy system, 236
Uniform worn by officers of East Indiamen, 110
United States, markets in the, 18
  recognition of the, 25
  insurance in the, 40
  importance of market in, 76
  trade of secured by American shipowners, 84
  source of West Indian food supply, 174
  declaration of war by, in 1812, 221
Unseaworthiness, liability of owners resulting from, 46
Uring, Nathaniel, Shipmaster, the career of, 28

Van Dieman's Land, destiny of Nelly Ray,
  117
Venice, cargo for, 32
Ventilation, lack of, at sea, 122, 127
Vera Cruz, specie from, 40
Victualling Board, purchases of brandy made by the, 169
Victuals on board convict ship, details of,
  116
Victuals, decay of the, 122
Villeneuvre, Admiral, effect of his arrival in West Indies, 43

Virginia and Maryland Coffee House, 30
Virginia, Bristol imports from, 65
Volunteer Movement, the, 17

Wabshutt, Captain Robert, the alleged cruelty of, 277
Wadia, Parsee shipbuilders, 89
Wadstrom, evidence on Slave Trade given by, 273
Waldegrave, Vice-Admiral, letter from, concerning convoys, 235
Walpole, Sir Robert, and his Excise Bill,
  56
Wapping, proposal for a dock at, 54
  docks built at, 56
War Finance, how provided, 80
"War in Disguise", work quoted, 167
Warehousing Act of 1803, the, 59
Warren & Company, shipowners, of Teignmouth, 243
Washington, George, his giving up tobacco planting, 214
Waterford, emigrant vessel sails from, 228
  Newfoundland vessels call at, 244
Water, drinking, detrioration of, 122
  methods of purifying, 122
Watson, John, Surgeon, fever described by, 128
Wellington, Duke of, his views on keeping soldiers occupied at sea, footnote 149
Wells's, Thames Shipbuilders, 143
West Country merchants, interest of in cod-fishery, 227
West Country, exports to Newfoundland from, 231
West Indies, Bristol imports from the, 65
  Associations of merchants trading to, formed in Bristol, Liverpool and Glasgow, 160
  smuggling via the, 226
  Newfoundland fish exported to the, 231
  prosperity of dependent on slave labour,
  253
West India Dock Company, the, 46, 56,
  163

West Indiamen, value of the, 41
numbers of frequenting London River, 50
design of, 77
description of the, 94
average tonnage of the, 180
inadequate armament of, 181
the copper sheathing of, 182
the relative size of, 182
West India Merchants, the Committee of, 27
losses of through pilfering, 52
their interest in dock building, 54
in Parliament, 161
the Society of, 161
West India Planters, the Navigation Acts modified for, 33
the wealth of the, 159
West India Station, headgear usually worn on the, 118
West India Trade, resort of merchants interested in, 30
shortsighted policy of merchants in, 30
value of the, 163
Wexford, Newfoundland vessels call at, 244
Wilberforce, determination of, 252, 253
Windward Coast, the procuring of slaves on the, 264
Whalers, use of Greenland Dock by, 51
specialised construction of the, 76
activities of the, 94
Wheat, American export of, 196

Whitby, West Indiamen built at, 180
Whitcombe, T., painting by, 98
White Booth Roads, activities of press-gang in, 112
Whitehaven, port of, 49
West Indiamen built at, 180
and the Newfoundland Fisheries, 232
Whydah, slaves procured at, 264
Wigram, Sir Robert, early service as surgeon, 136
Wigram's, the firm of, 143
Willyam, Naval Chaplain, 131
Windward Passage, difficulty of the, 158
danger of the, 187
reason for preferring, 188
Wiveliscombe, cloth bought at, 64
Wolley, Captain Thomas, R.N., 100
Wright, Charles, work by, footnote to p. 30
Wyatt, Mr., proposals made by for dock construction, 56

Yellow fever, conveyed by mosquitoes, 121
how to be avoided, 133
Young, Sir William, calculations made by, 174
his views on convoy arrangements, 191
remarks of on Slave Trade, 270
Yorkshiremen, colony of in New York City, 220

For Product Safety Concerns and Information please contact our EU
representative GPSR@taylorandfrancis.com
Taylor & Francis Verlag GmbH, Kaufingerstraße 24, 80331 München, Germany